UNDERSTANDING
EXECUTIVE
COMPENSATION
& GOVERNANCE

A PRACTICAL GUIDE

FOURTH EDITION

Edited by
Irving S. Becker & Kurt Groeninger
Korn Ferry

WorldatWork.
Total Rewards Association

About WorldatWork®
The Total Rewards Association

WorldatWork is the leading nonprofit professional association in compensation and total rewards. We serve those who design and deliver total rewards programs to cultivate engaged, effective workforces that power thriving organizations. We accomplish this through education and certification; idea exchange; knowledge creation; information sharing; research; advocacy; and affiliation and networking. Founded in the United States in 1955, today WorldatWork serves total rewards professionals throughout the world working in organizations of all sizes and structures.

Certified Compensation Professional® (CCP®), Certified Benefits Professional® (CBP®), Global Remuneration Professional (GRP®), Certified Sales Compensation Professional (CSCP)® and Certified Executive Compensation Professional (CECP)® are registered trademarks of WorldatWork.

©2021 Korn Ferry

Soft-cover ISBN: 978-1-57963-395-0
E-book ISBN: 978-1-57963-396-7
Editor: Brittany Smith
Graphic Design: Kris Sotelo

WorldatWork
Total Rewards Association

www.worldatwork.org

Contents

Chapter 26: Initial Public Offerings 443

Understanding Equity Compensation Prior to an IPO
Preparing Compensation Programs for Public Company Life
Key Processes for a Newly Public Company
ESPPs and Setting Policies for 10b5–1 Plans
Points to Remember

Chapter 27: Bankruptcy, Retention and Other Special Situations 457

Bankruptcy
One-time Grants — Common Purposes
Private Equity Firms: Compensating the Executives of Portfolio Companies
Summary

Chapter 28: Executive Compensation in Tax-Exempt Organizations 473

Current Influences on Executive Compensation in the Tax-Exempt Sector
Good Governance Practice
SERPs and LTIs: Components of the Compensation Program and Design
Issues to Consider
Excise Taxes on Remuneration over $1M and on Certain Severance Payments
Considerations for Board Pay

Chapter 29: Compensation Litigation 493

Claims Alleging Excessive Executive and Director Compensation
Claims Specific to Public Companies
Claims Specific to Family Businesses
Claims Specific to Nonprofit Organizations
Executive Compensation in Wrongful Death Claims
Executive Compensation in Divorce
Executive Compensation in Bankruptcy
Wrapping Up

Chapter 30: International Compensation 507

PROLOGUE

This fourth edition of our book has been titled *Understanding Executive Compensation and Governance: A Practical Guide* to reflect our expanded scope on critical topics that boards of directors must address. Our book is a reference guide for compensation committees and other board members, HR professionals, corporate management and other decision makers. Its purpose is to furnish readers with easy access to a wide range of executive compensation and board governance topics by providing insight on current best practices, design techniques and trends.

Understanding Executive Compensation & Governance is a hands-on, practical guide that we hope helps in the evaluation and refinement of executive compensation programs and board governance. A major challenge confronting boards and executive compensation professionals today is establishing a consistent and transparent connection between pay and value added. This must be done in an environment in which regulators, shareholders and even lawmakers carefully scrutinize all aspects of executive compensation, benefits and perquisites — especially the relationship between pay and performance. In addition, boards need to both evaluate top executive talent and the board itself, while also managing succession for the CEO and board members in an orderly and thorough process.

We believe companies are well-positioned to respond to current challenges surrounding executive compensation. The requirements of the say-on-pay provisions under Dodd-Frank and enhanced compensation disclosure have improved transparency of the programs and facilitated competitive analysis, thus providing a clearer idea of how companies think and operate. Korn Ferry's work with The Aspen Institute has produced five Modern Principles for Sensible and Effective Executive Pay. These principles are designed to further advance boardroom dialogue and will be briefly discussed in a newly added Chapter 1. In addition, we have added a new chapter on emerging trends in performance management that covers the topic of adding environmental, social and governance (ESG) metrics to incentive plans. Finally, we have added a chapter on the evolving role of the compensation committee to highlight the expansion of responsibilities that we see in the marketplace.

These issues are only some of the topics we address in this new edition. The following chapters are a compilation of articles by Korn Ferry consultants from The Executive Edition series, supplemented by material written specifically for this volume. This book is not meant to be a technical reference, per se; in focusing on what works best, we have avoided presenting too much detail on tax, accounting and regulatory issues. This book is targeted mainly to a U.S. audience; nonetheless, with its focus on design, we believe it is a useful resource for non-U.S. companies operating in a pay-for-performance environment.

The chapters are grouped in five sections:

- "Part I: Executive Pay Design and Strategy" examines issues relating to overall executive compensation strategy and includes design issues relating to the basic components of pay — base salary, annual incentives, equity and non-equity long-term incentives — plus discussions of related topics, such as peer group selection, performance measurement, competitive benchmarking, stock ownership guidelines, executive benefits, equity retention and employment agreements.
- "Part II: Governance, Disclosure and Compensation Committee Initiatives" begins with a discussion of compensation committee governance followed by a chapter on the tools compensation

committees use in overseeing executive compensation. We next discuss the basic principles affecting current executive compensation disclosure, followed by a chapter on the requirement to address potential risk in executive compensation programs.

- "Part III: The CEO Life Cycle" starts with a summary explaining the three core topics of CEO evaluation, succession and special compensation. Because much of the preceding chapters address executive compensation matters that are especially pertinent to CEOs, we devote a chapter to the often-neglected area of CEO evaluation and feedback before turning to the critical area of planning for CEO succession. Too often these topics are examined in isolation when a more effective approach is to consider them together. Finally, we discuss two special topics relating to CEO pay — compensation strategies related to various CEO transitions and CEO compensation when preparing for an IPO.

- "Part IV: The Board Life Cycle" identifies three core components of board evaluation, succession and board pay, following a similar approach as was taken in Part III regarding CEOs. In today's governance climate, the duties and responsibilities of directors have expanded significantly; boards cannot fall behind in addressing the challenges and opportunities presented in a fast-changing business world.

- "Part V: Executive Compensation in Special Settings" addresses the compensation issues that arise in situations such as mergers and acquisitions, initial public offerings, bankruptcy, retention, CEO recruiting, tax-exempt organizations, private equity-owned portfolio companies, and executive and director litigation.

Finally, we end with a chapter on international compensation which addresses executive pay issues in the following countries: Australia, Canada, France, Germany, Japan, the Netherlands, and the United Kingdom.

I would like to thank WorldatWork for publishing this fourth edition of our book, and Korn Ferry for its ongoing support of our executive compensation business. I also want to thank our clients who furnished insights in working together on executive pay and board projects.

Special thanks to Kurt Groeninger, my co-editor. Kurt has worked closely with our team to make this book update a reality. His insights and efforts are greatly appreciated. I also wanted to acknowledge Bill Gerek, who helped edit the previous editions of the book. Bill retired at the end of 2019 and we miss his input and sound guidance. Most of all, I would like to thank the Korn Ferry Executive Pay & Governance team who have contributed their time, effort and intellectual capital to making this book possible.

— Irving (Irv) S. Becker
Vice Chairman —
Executive Pay & Governance

PART I

Executive Pay Design and Strategy

18

CHAPTER 1

Emerging Trends and Challenges in Executive Compensation

By Don Lowman

During the recent past, public interest in executive compensation around the world has intensified, shareholder advisory firms have adopted new approaches to evaluating executive pay, and many countries have adopted new disclosure rules intended to provide greater transparency to shareholders about how much executives are paid and how compensation committees make their decisions. Compensation committees, in turn, have become more self-reflective and are holding themselves to higher standards of independent governance and decision making.

The public disclosures on executive pay now provide considerable detail about how pay decisions are made, and insights into any discretion that is used. The results of formal shareholder votes on executive pay are displayed, and if there is sufficient negative sentiment, companies routinely consult with shareholders on preferred program modifications. It is now typical to see lists in company disclosures of things the company does (and does not do) that are positive from a corporate governance point of view. Companies are also now required to disclose pay ratios comparing CEO pay to that of the average worker. In short, most organizations have become very self-conscious about their executive pay decisions, and outside observers have more information to decide if company boards have properly exercised their fiduciary responsibility.

Despite the many reforms adopted to improve executive pay design and governance over the past decade or so, there is still widespread criticism of how senior executives are paid and a continuing perception that there is a different set of rules for executives that enables them to enjoy significant pay increases while the wages for average workers stagnate. These concerns will challenge boards for years to come.

This chapter:

- Discusses the growing disconnect between how much executives are rewarded relative to the broader workforce. This, in turn, is a key contributor to growing societal concerns about a widening "wealth gap."
- Evaluates the role of total shareholder return (TSR) in incentive programs. Although TSR is a valuable measure of performance, it has also distracted boards of directors and senior leadership teams from giving appropriate consideration to other important areas of performance that contribute to longer-term organizational health (e.g., non-financial drivers such as safety, sustainability, diversity and inclusion, employee engagement, leadership development, talent retention, etc.).
- Proposes that executive pay philosophies and strategies need updating. There is a disconnect between corporations' mission statements and the pay philosophies they describe in their public filings.

Executive Compensation and the Wealth Gap

CEOs and other senior executives are entrusted to lead increasingly dynamic organizations that are operating during a period of unprecedented disruption. Their roles have grown more complex and are subject to increasing risk as a diverse array of shareholders expect them to develop and execute strategies that will produce favorable long-term returns on their investments. Success requires an unusual and evolving combination of traits and attributes that are in short supply, and the demand for the individuals who possess them has never been higher. It is no surprise that the market for top

FIGURE 1-1

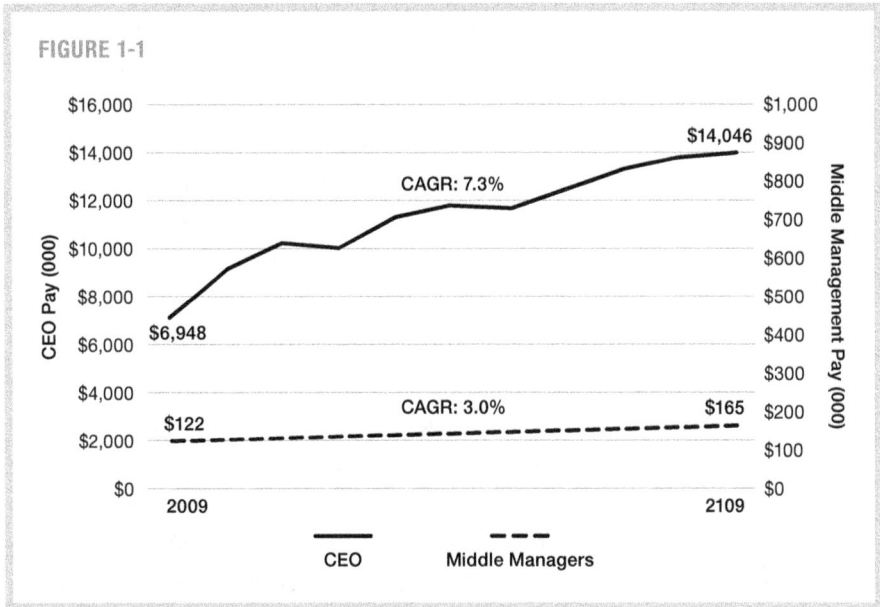

talent requires significant investment, and the price tag for CEOs moves ever higher.

Much has been written with respect to the high multiple of CEO pay versus that for the average-paid employee in organizations; public companies in the United States have been required to publish that information for the last several years and, while no one really knows quite what to make of the numbers, the increased transparency has sparked considerable commentary and debate. Regardless of one's view of what a reasonable pay multiple might be, there is no escaping the fact that, over the past ten years, the multiple has only increased. See Figure 1-1 comparing CEO pay in the Top 300 U.S. companies to that for middle managers.

This phenomenon materially contributes to a growing perception of an unacceptably high "wealth gap" and provides increased ammunition for critics that claim that the current executive pay model is broken and that the rules are written to favor executives at the expense of the average worker.

We can all acknowledge that senior executive roles have become increasingly challenging and complex. And while executive total pay may have increased at higher rates than the average employee, their base salaries have risen at roughly the same rate as those of the average worker. Executives have received outsized total pay increases primarily because the "at-risk" elements of annual and long-term incentives (the latter often denominated in company equity) have paid out well during a period of strong economic growth and a prolonged equity bull market. CEO pay has been generally well-aligned with shareholders' interests, in keeping with most companies' pay philosophies. This begs the question — is there really a problem here?

There is no easy answer. Compensation committees have been doing their jobs well based on the established rules of the game and using the tools in their legacy toolkits. But therein lies the problem. Company priorities have evolved over the past decade, and as company leaders have articulated support for an emerging set of values aligned with diversity, inclusiveness and corporate and social responsibility, their continued adherence to dated pay philosophies and decision making is producing outcomes that look out of alignment with their values, and certainly out of alignment with the rewards for everyone else in the enterprise.

The Role of TSR in Measuring Company Performance

Shareholder advisory firms have conditioned compensation committees to focus on TSR and external benchmarking as their main criteria in assessing organization performance and determining executive pay. This narrowed focus on TSR has not only helped drive outsized increases in executive pay in recent years — especially relative to the general employee population — but has also distracted boards of directors and senior leadership teams from giving appropriate consideration to other important areas of performance that contribute to longer-term organizational health (e.g., non-financial drivers such as safety, sustainability, diversity and inclusion, employee engagement, leadership development, talent retention, etc.). While organizations like the Business Roundtable in the United States have formally adopted the position that TSR is only one of many measures of success that companies should consider in evaluating performance, most executive pay programs remain firmly aligned with TSR as the center of their performance measurement universe.

There is no question of the importance of TSR to shareholders and the logic in including it as a measure of long-term executive performance. Indeed, long-term TSR is likely the most all-encompassing measure of company success in the eyes of shareholders, which makes it hard to argue with tying a significant portion of senior executive rewards to the goal of maximizing long-term returns.

But as a focus becomes a fixation, it can distract from other important areas and produce unintended outcomes — and that is where many companies find themselves today. The fixation on TSR (measured in shorter and shorter durations) may have unwittingly played a role in driving up CEO pay at a faster rate. Why? Because as say-on-pay results have become a referendum on TSR outcomes, many compensation committees have satisfied themselves that higher incentive awards are well-justified in light of strong TSR performance, leaving little room for evaluating broader organizational health. The reality is the say-on-pay process is too blunt an instrument to catch other than the most egregious pay increases or pay-TSR disconnects. While most compensation committee members continue to be frustrated by the influence of shareholder advisory firms, they have allowed the TSR model pushed by these firms to become the primary way to define pay for performance.

The time is right to build new incentive design models, or to adapt current ones. Three models that should be pressure tested are: private equity (increased rewards and penalties for performance changes); the UK model (in which pay increases are dampened except for dramatically outsized performance); or even health care, where community or societal impact is measured along with financials. Whatever models emerge they should be driven by more contemporary and differentiated pay strategies.

Outdated Executive Pay Philosophies and Strategies

An increasing number of organizations now describe their mission and vision in terms of a broader societal "purpose" — the larger role of the enterprise as a responsible global citizen and helping improve the world around us — and many organizations speak compellingly about how they prioritize various non-financial measures of success. But there is a visible and glaring disconnect between these updated mission statements and the outdated executive pay philosophies they describe in their public filings.

Many organizations have not taken a serious look at their executive compensation philosophies and strategies in several years, and this is not serving them well. It is not that the current statements are poorly written, confusing or unclear. But many organizations have adopted significant and fundamental shifts in business strategy and priorities without revisiting their pay philosophies and pay programs, and various areas of misalignment have arisen.

As an example, if a company has launched significant new initiatives around diversity, inclusion, ESG metrics, employee engagement or customer service (and some have done several of these simultaneously) but the executive pay strategy essentially says, "executive rewards are designed to be competitive with peers, to attract, retain and motivate superior talent, and to reward for improving shareholder value," there is an opportunity for improvement.

Many organizations have put off for too long rethinking and updating their executive pay philosophies and strategies. We have seen significant competitive disruption and changes in company business strategies and priorities due to a confluence of factors. These include increased global competition, technology advancements, new workforce strategies, increased focus on environmental responsibility, and fresh concerns about pay equity. With all of this change in strategic and operational focus, it is imperative that executive pay strategies catch up with current and emerging business realities.

What Needs to Change?

From a governance standpoint, it is timely for organizations and their compensation committees to examine their executive compensation philosophies, strategies and program designs. Recent trends are prompting precedent-setting pay actions. We believe the most important areas for focus include:

- Clarity and specificity of the principles underlying the design of the pay program
- Consistency of the messages articulated about organization purpose and values with those embedded in the executive pay philosophy and strategy
- Specific reference to how the philosophy and strategy of the executive pay program relates to the organization's overall rewards philosophy and strategy for the broad employee population
- Specification of the criteria that will be considered when determining executive total compensation, including the relative importance of TSR in that process.

We believe that if compensation committees approach this exercise with the determination to be bold, unbound by conventional wisdom, and committed to developing philosophies that are clear and contemporary, many positive changes will result. The outcome will be programs that are tangibly aligned with today's and tomorrow's priorities (including rewards explicitly tied to important ESG metrics), less concerned with emulating the pay practices of a set of "peers," consciously balanced to distribute company profits to fairly reward all of the people who teamed to produce them, and, yes, even expected to enhance long-term total shareholder return.

Conclusion

As of the writing of this book, we are in the midst of an unprecedented period of change in the world. The world is engulfed in the COVID-19 pandemic, accompanied by the financial crisis it has spawned. Organizations have been forced to respond and adapt to the reality of COVID-19 (with pay cuts, staff cuts and substantial near-term executive pay modifications), and that has brought the concerns about executive compensation described above into even sharper focus.

COVID-19 is only one of many factors and forces combining to place increased pressure on leaders to step up and lead in new ways.

Rewards decisions must be made in different and unfamiliar contexts. The decisions we make now and in the next few years will be critically important. They will make statements, intended or otherwise, about what we stand for and what we value. The best advice is to be deliberate and clear about what you value, and then make bold decisions that are clearly consistent and well aligned with those values.

CHAPTER 2

Compensation Strategy

By Irv Becker and Craig Rowley

C reating an effective executive compensation strategy is a complex process — more so than ever before. On one hand, the strategy must incorporate and reflect important internal issues unique to the company: short- and long-term business objectives, internal pay equity/positioning, industry market competitiveness, accounting costs for the company, administrative processes and perceived value by executives. On the other hand, the strategy must be formulated to withstand external scrutiny from shareholders, regulators, institutional investors, proxy advisers and the press, all of whom increasingly demand information not just on generic guiding principles, but on details of the rationale of specific program design elements as well.

Thus, a compensation strategy must consider many factors and elements if it is to fulfill its purpose of supporting organizational goals, reflecting actual business performance, paying competitively and rewarding executives for value provided. These objectives are valid regardless of the organization's size, industry or developmental stage.

A compensation strategy must be reviewed and revised as the company grows and matures. The need to update the strategy can come from inside the company, such as when a new business strategy is implemented, an acquisition takes effect or new talent must be recruited. The need for revision also can arise from outside the company through changes in compensation trends, tax and accounting rules, the performance of the overall economy and stock market, or increased demand for executive talent in the marketplace. Whatever its specifics, a compensation strategy must have senior executive and outside director buy-in and be accepted and understood by all parties.

This chapter:

- Relates compensation strategy to business strategy and discusses approaches for evaluating the current program, developing performance metrics and maximizing the effectiveness of various long-term incentive vehicles.

- Recommends that organizations look beyond simple pay multiples and consider factors such as job size and complexity in analyzing internal pay equity. The importance of incorporating internal and external pay equity considerations is stressed.

Providing a Strategic Guide for the Compensation Committee

The articulation of a formal executive compensation philosophy has taken on critical importance at public companies in the current environment of enhanced disclosure and shareholder say-on-pay voting. The need for compensation committees to clearly explain the rationale underlying the design of various pay components of the executive compensation program has grown due to heightened scrutiny by the business media, proxy advisory groups, U.S. Congress, regulators (especially the IRS and the SEC), and institutional shareholders, among others.

An organization's executive compensation philosophy must encompass much more than the unhelpful and overused phrases that "we target the market median" or "we pay for performance to attract, retain and motivate talent." The compensation philosophy should offer specific guidance for the compensation committee's numerous decisions concerning executive pay and be used to evaluate the effectiveness of the compensation program by identifying any potential shortcomings in existing plans. The compensation committee should view the philosophy as a tool to influence management's performance and reaffirm the business strategy, not simply as a perfunctory task to "check the box" on corporate governance compliance.

Surfacing Issues in Compensation Design

In addition to furnishing important information to outside parties, the actual exercise of developing a robust executive compensation philosophy offers the compensation committee an opportunity to learn whether its members are on the same page in the design of appropriate compensation programs. The process needs to consider members' views on target pay levels, mix of pay elements, the comparator peer group or relevant survey data (i.e., the market for talent), the value of various executive jobs, performance metrics and targets, and other pay design issues.

The development of a compensation philosophy also can provide needed insight on whether the senior executive team and the compensation committee view the pay program's strengths and areas for improvement in the same manner. Ideally, management needs to own the design of compensation programs, which are tools to implement the company's business strategy. In addition, due to management's tremendous personal stake (some may call this "enlightened self-interest") in the compensation arrangements, the compensation committee may discover that any proposed changes actually provoke a long-overdue dialogue with management on various design issues that have been on autopilot for some time. The compensation committee may use this interaction to signal to management the committee's ultimate stewardship of the executive compensation program, along with the importance of needed input from the management team.

Addressing Business Strategy

When compensation committee members and senior management work together as a design team to develop a comprehensive compensation philosophy, it is critical to start with the organization's business strategy. For example, each participant could be asked to explain, in up to three sentences, the annual and long-term strategies for creating shareholder value. These might include initiatives such as acquisition of competitors or complementary businesses, creation or acquisition of new service lines or products, increased market share, an emphasis on international growth, divestitures of underperforming assets, privatization, positioning for a sale or rapid organic growth.

Defining the meaning of "high performance" should be explored by the team of compensation committee members and senior management. Each person could outline what superior business and operational performance at the company should look like. These descriptions should include financial (e.g., earnings growth) and nonfinancial (e.g., customer satisfaction) metrics. Superior performance also can include qualitative measures, such as the creation of a succession plan or talent management program. The desired outcome is, in a subsequent step, to be able to define clear goals (threshold, target and maximum, where appropriate) for the variable pay plans that promote the agreed-upon business strategy.

Evaluating Current Executive Pay Programs

As noted, the development of a compensation philosophy should involve a candid exchange among the team members concerning the core strengths and possible weaknesses of the current executive compensation program. Ascertaining the program's strengths guards against detrimental changes, while a consensus on opportunities for improvement may surface needed modifications that can promote talent retention and improve financial performance.

To avoid addressing the elements of total direct compensation (TDC) — base salary as well as short- and long-term incentive opportunities — in a haphazard or piecemeal fashion, the team members should agree upon an overall TDC competitive market position for executives for planned, budgeted or targeted company financial performance.

In other words, by salary grade or officer title, a competitive market position (e.g., 60th percentile) should be established for a typical competent executive when the organization performs at pre-established annual target levels that are expected (i.e., 50 to 60 percent achievable). This competitive position creates an overall framework by which the mix of the three elements of TDC can be "sized."

The approach can be viewed as establishing the size of the TDC "pie," which can then be sliced into three pieces that form TDC.

Once this is accomplished for planned performance, the mix of pay elements can be addressed by answering the following questions:

- What is the desired base salary competitive position in the talent market?
- For variable compensation, what percent should be focused on short-term financial results, assuming target financial performance of the organization? What percent should be focused on long-term financial results?
- What percent of LTIs should be cash versus equity and performance based versus nonperformance based?

Performance Metrics

Once the TDC competitive position and mix of pay elements are established, the process can turn to the performance metrics of the variable pay program (which measures are discussed in more detail in Chapter 8). The dialogue should start with the development of a list of financial and/or operational metrics that drive company success and positively impact share price. Examples to consider could be earnings or revenue growth, expense control and profit margin. Next, macro financial performance indicators that outside analysts use to compare the organization to its competitors could be developed. Examples include return on capital, earnings per share and return on assets. Identifying these drivers may help establish both short- and long-term incentive plan performance metrics.

Agreement also should be reached concerning the minimum annual level of return on a shareholder's investment that warrants a financial payout to executives. This threshold return could be expressed as earnings growth or share price appreciation, and it should guide the development of performance plan goal setting that results in cash payouts and/or vesting of equity awards.

Finally, the method of evaluating financial and operational performance metrics should be established, which could include absolute internal financial targets, performance relative to industry peers, or performance relative to an index (e.g., S&P 500). Measuring performance relative to peers can motivate "best-in-class" performance during weak economic seasons; measuring performance relative to realistic internal goals promotes participants' engagement by focusing their attention on specific outcomes that they believe they can influence.

Long-Term Incentives

The compensation philosophy also should address the use of long-term incentive (LTI) vehicles (e.g., stock options, performance shares, time-vested restricted stock). Therefore, a conversation around the proper role(s) of LTIs in executive compensation programs can help with the compensation committee's selection of the appropriate instruments. Examples of the role of LTIs and potential vehicles are shown in Table 2-1.

TABLE 2-1 Examples of the Role of Long-Term Incentives and Potential Vehicles

Desired Role of LTI	Potential LTI Vehicle
Retain executive talent	Time-vested restricted stock
Encourage capital accumulation in rising market	Stock options
Encourage capital accumulation in flat or depressed market	Time-vested restricted stock
Drive company performance	Performance shares/units
Promote stock price appreciation	Stock options
Provide tax efficiency for the executive	Restricted stock units
Promote actual ownership	Time-vested restricted stock

Other Compensation Strategy Questions

Numerous other questions and procedures could be addressed by compensation committees and management that might affect the executive compensation philosophy and its effectiveness:

- What multiple of base salary should executives hold in stock?
- How can the philosophy be communicated so that all parties understand it and have buy-in toward the compensation program?
- To what degree should individual behavior and performance factor into base salary increases and the size of incentive awards each fiscal year?

- To what degree should public disclosure affect the design of the executive compensation program and levels of compensation?
- To what degree should the company be involved in the planning and funding of executive retirement?
- How should decisions concerning which benefits/perquisites to offer be made (e.g., employee feedback, best practices, peer-group prevalence, general industry prevalence)?
- How might the compensation philosophy affect shareholders' say-on-pay voting?

A compensation committee needs to take seriously its vital role in establishing a comprehensive philosophy that guides all aspects of executive compensation. The more that senior management can be engaged in this process, the more likely the total compensation program will increase perceived value to those executives, thereby increasing the likelihood of retaining talented executives and motivating them to performance that increases the organization's value.

Additionally, the compensation philosophy should be reviewed regularly to confirm that it aligns with current business strategy and responds to changing organizational and economic conditions, and that it continues to effectively aid executive pay decisions.

Building Internal Equity

Compensation committees increasingly are asking questions about what internal equity is and how to implement it as part of a well-designed executive compensation process and program.

The concept of internal equity is not new. However, the discussion of internal equity — which focuses on pay relationships between executives — has become carelessly oversimplified in many cases. Focusing only on pay relationships between executive roles without understanding how those roles differ can yield information that is not only meaningless, but potentially debilitating to the health of an executive compensation program.

Debates and discussions on internal equity typically define the term narrowly as the pay relationships between different positions at different levels in a single organization. This approach looks to understand whether executives in that organization are paid appropriately relative to each other rather than relative to the external market. However, the concept of internal equity also should examine pay differences as a function of organization structure, job size and incumbent performance. While some may consider internal equity to mean the relationship of the pay of the CEO to the next level of executive reporting to the CEO, that focus may be overly simplistic.

A Useful but Often Misunderstood Concept

The landscape for executive compensation has changed — and is changing. Shareholders and compensation committees have become proactive in challenging the externally focused, peer-group driven approach to benchmarking executive pay. Many have complained that an over-reliance on external market data from a peer group or survey has led to a "ratcheting" effect, where the same group of comparator organizations benchmark against each other's pay levels, to find that what was a 75th percentile market positioning one year is a 50th percentile positioning just two years later.

Market comparisons encourage the lower-paying companies to accelerate their pay increases to meet the market. The result has been an ever-escalating executive pay structure that compensates on a mindset that an organization's executives need to be paid at least at the market median rather than on the actual demands of the role or its performance.

As a result, the need for a true internal equity-based approach — one that helps compensation committees understand the market but is driven by internal fairness — has never been more apparent.

The Problem with Multiples

In managing the concept of internal equity, companies have been encouraged by some commentators to use "pay multiples" in which one position is targeted at roughly "x" times another position. For example, this concept is promoted by the suggestion that the CEO should be paid at a level that is no more than two times that of key executives reporting to the CEO. In building on this questionable approach, some companies use pay multiples to manage the internal equity among executives. This ensures that an employer's pay relationships are linked to each other rather than to the external market (which may lead to a greater, or in some cases smaller, multiple). While the internal fairness of executive pay is very important, a simplistic approach that does not consider other relevant factors is misguided.

The problem with a multiples approach is that top organization structures are not the same across a peer group and, as a result, not all executive roles at a given organizational level are equal in value. Some organizations have a narrow span of control, and possibly a COO is the top position reporting to the CEO. Another organization may operate as a holding company, with group heads reporting to the CEO. Still others may have a more integrated structure, with either vertical or horizontal integration of businesses.

In short, not all organizations — and, therefore, not all executive roles — are structured similarly. As such, a pay multiple that is appropriate for one employer may be entirely meaningless for another due to differences in structure. Even less useful are comparisons of CEO compensation to that of a company's median employee under Item 402(u) of Regulation S-K (as required by the Dodd-Frank Act). Differences among companies, their operations and their workforces make disclosures of such "CEO pay ratio" little more than blunt tools aimed at limiting CEO pay without regard to these differences in organizations, executive roles or, most notably, performance.

Further, an individual executive's pay is a function of how the incumbent secured the job, as well as his/her sustained performance and potential. A CEO recruited from the outside by a company in a turnaround situation likely will be paid more than a newly appointed CEO in a more stable organization who is promoted from within.

Consider two separate companies with "group head" positions accountable for $2 billion in revenue in a parent company with $5 billion in total revenue. In most surveys, both the CEO and the group head positions would be valued as the "same-sized" job in comparing the two organizations. Look at the facts in Table 2-2 more closely.

Using traditional market data, the CEOs of both companies would be priced as each heading a $5 billion international company. Both group heads would be priced the same as well, relative to group

TABLE 2-2 Company Example Assumptions

Dimensions/Company	A	B
Parent Company:		
Revenue	$5 billion	$5 billion
Countries (with assets)	40	5
Employees	12,000	5,000
Value added	High	Low
Complexity	High	Low
Group Head		
Revenue	$2 billion	$2 billion
Countries (with assets)	30	3
Employees	5,000	1,500
Value added	High	Low
Complexity	High	Low

Company A

The chairman of the board is the former CEO. The CEO was "homegrown" and came out of the group-head position a year ago. Currently, the incumbent is paid low relative to market references. The company has 12,000 employees in 40 countries, and key staff functions are decentralized. The relatively new group head (one of three) reports to the CEO, was a candidate for the CEO position and was managing a smaller group prior to the decision to fill the CEO position with the current incumbent. The group head is paid slightly above market for this position. The group head is accountable for five separate high value-added, high gross-margin industrial product businesses that are characterized by proprietary technologies and consultative relationships with customers. The group has 5,000 employees in 30 countries around the world. North America represents 40 percent, Europe 40 percent and Asia-Pacific 20 percent of assets, employees and revenue generation.

Company B

The CEO recently was recruited from the outside and given the chairman of the board responsibility, as well. Pay to recruit the best candidate is above market references. The company has experienced performance issues and the new CEO has a mandate to turn performance around. The company sells into 10 countries, with assets in five of these. All business operations are based in the Americas, and there are 5,000 employees. Key staff functions are highly centralized. The group head reports to the CEO. The incumbent was promoted up from the head of manufacturing position, and the former incumbent was given an early retirement package. The new incumbent is paid below market references. The group-head position (one of three) has responsibility for two commodity products manufactured in a single plant location. Raw material accounts for 75 percent of product value, and gross margins are relatively low. The group employs 1,500 employees in the United States, Canada and Mexico. It manufactures in the United States and exports 15 percent of its production to Canada and Mexico, where distribution centers and sales offices are located.

heads managing $2 billion in revenue. Using an approach based on job content, the first company's CEO position likely would have a higher market value than the second but, using traditional market pricing, both would have the same market value. The same is true for the group head position — the market value of the job in Company A would be higher than in Company B using a job content-based approach that recognizes complexity as well as size. As discussed here and amplified in Table 2-3, a job-content approach to defining job size would result in a difference in both job size as well as market value for these positions.

TABLE 2-3 Job-Content Approach to Defining Job Size

Survey Level/Company	A	B
1	CEO	
2		CEO/COB
3		
4	Group head	
5		
6		Group head

Incumbent pay would be driven by the situation and by incumbent background as well. In Company A, the ratio of the CEO's pay to that of the group head would be expected to be much smaller than in Company B. It would not make sense to say that the multiple should be two times in both companies. Further, the multiple would narrow in both companies if a COO position was established.

A More Balanced Approach

The answer is to look not only at job titles and the size of the organization, but also at the jobs themselves: How big and complex are they? What do they actually do? The key is to understand the size of each role. In addition, incumbent experience, performance and prior compensation history should be considered. "Job sizing" allows a more informed snapshot into the internal equity of pay practices. Simply put, it focuses on the design of each job and essentially looks to rank (or score) jobs based on their content and complexity. Chapter 4 includes a discussion of common work-valuing processes and explains how they can be used in making decisions on executive compensation.

External Benchmarking Still Matters

Taking an internal equity approach absolutely does not mean that a company should avoid incorporating external benchmarking into the process. However, the market should be viewed as a point of reference, not a mandate on precisely how a position should be paid. Before making a decision on pay, external market data should be balanced against the internal perspective.

Balancing internal equity with external benchmarking can be done in a variety of ways. In its simplest form, compensation committees can consider internal equity alongside external market competitiveness, balancing the need to pay executives at a certain level of competitiveness with the need to pay executives appropriately relative to other roles and incumbent factors. Pay levels for executives should be a function of:

- Organization structure
- Size and complexity of the job
- Incumbent experience and demonstrated performance
- Potential (will current pay keep other interested employers at bay?)
- Succession (can pay for increased responsibility be managed effectively?)
- Internal equity (will pay be viewed as fair, all factors considered?)

Managing All Factors

However it is done, integrating internal equity into the compensation benchmarking process will move compensation governance going forward, as it adds another important dimension to looking at executive pay.

That said, there is a danger in examining internal equity in a vacuum. Using only a blind application of a pay-multiple approach can lead to recruitment and retention issues for some executives, and overpayment for others. Neither of these outcomes should be acceptable to shareholders.

For these reasons, it is clear that both the relative size of an organization's executive jobs and the "going rate" matter. Using internal equity in pay decisions forces a company to account for how its executive roles are unique. Compensation committees that consider internal equity alongside external competitiveness are able to create an executive compensation program that balances fairness and competitiveness with what jobs actually do, and that helps ensure that compensation decisions are not at the mercy of the market, but make sense — all factors considered.

Implications

On the surface, defining a competitive pay level seems easy. Companies have embraced a free-market approach by paying their executives similar to other executives in a representative group of peer organizations. The size of the company — typically defined by revenue — is the most common approach to recognize company and job differences when determining a competitive compensation level.

However, relying solely on a market-based approach could provide a false sense of security. Although size is an important consideration, it does not adequately address the value that the job is adding to an organization. For example, even in organizations of similar size, not all CFO positions are created equally. Factors such as importance of international markets, type of ownership and capital structure greatly influence job complexity — hence the value that these jobs add to the organization. Some CFOs have accountability for other functions, such as information technology, administration, and strategic planning; others do not. These additional variables should be considered when determining an appropriate pay level, much the same as companies use a host of financial measures to evaluate investment alternatives.

Final Thoughts

Building a compensation strategy requires consideration of multiple factors. But it is also a process, one that requires monitoring and revision as circumstances change. As such, compensation committee members should dedicate time each year to reconsider its business strategy and amend or ratify the compensation strategy as the situation dictates.

CHAPTER 3

Peer Groups and Alternative Approaches to Benchmarking

By Cory Morrow and Casey Martinez

Increased disclosure requirements, shareholder activism and media attention have reinforced a market-based approach for executive compensation analysis and design. Given the high level of scrutiny associated with executive compensation, devising an appropriate peer group is an important activity for the compensation committee. Directors are faced with publicly disclosing peer group companies, explaining the selection criteria used in developing the peer group and defending the peer group's appropriateness for benchmarking compensation, performance analysis and pay program design.

In this environment, the development and use of compensation peer groups are critical tools for assessing the competitiveness and appropriateness of the various elements of a company's compensation programs. Utilizing properly constructed peer groups can provide a valuable perspective on issues such as compensation levels, performance benchmarks, pay elements, as well as short- and long-term incentive plan design. In some cases, the peer group may also be used in a relative total shareholder return (rTSR)-based long-term incentive design. Each company needs an objective and systematic approach to constructing a peer group that best fits its unique organizational characteristics, one that goes beyond simply targeting executive pay levels and allows the committee to assess compensation in relation to the value delivered to the company and shareholders.

This chapter:

- Introduces the sources from which companies can benchmark executive pay and describes factors used in the peer selection process. It also outlines an approach that results in a more comprehensive picture of competitor practices by supplementing proxy peer analysis with functional job information from a larger database of employers.

- Provides an overview of other peer groups that are utilized in addition to a company's primary proxy peer group, including general industry peer groups, rTSR peer groups and peer groups used by shareholder advisory firms.

- Discusses the need for a dual analysis that not only may target compensation at a percentile of market, but also uses business performance analysis to rank executives' annual and TDC against the company's performance relative to competitors.

- Addresses the use of external performance comparisons in setting and validating performance measures across various time periods and, ultimately, how peer group analysis and market data can be used in setting executive compensation.

Proxy and Survey Comparison Groups

Companies generally have two alternatives for benchmarking executive pay: published survey data from third-party providers and company-selected proxy peer groups.

Survey databases are an excellent source for broad, robust data for almost any type of executive position. General market or all-industry databases provide the broadest scope of data for compensation comparisons. These databases are particularly appropriate for corporate and staff roles in which industry expertise is not necessarily required and executives can move fairly easily between industries. General market data may also be appropriate for organizations in niche industries or with few direct competitors of similar size. Alternatively, many surveys are available for specific industries. This allows benchmarking to markets that are more similar to the subject organization and still provides robust compensation data.

In terms of matching executives to a database, the most precise approach is to use job size/grading that allows for considerations such as company revenue size, industry, degree of internationality and governance structure. This methodology can be the best way of capturing the scale and complexity of a business while still using a wide set of comparators; however, the downside is a loss of transparency because data are summarized and presented in aggregate (i.e., there is no individual detail on each company's executives). Whether this level of sophistication is necessary depends on the organization's circumstances. In our experience, such an approach is the most appropriate for:

- Comparing roles where job title matching alone can be extremely imprecise, particularly in today's complex matrix structures in which roles with the same title often have very different responsibilities
- Injecting some rigor in the process of assessing the appropriate effect of an organization change to pay levels
- Organizations that are at the top or bottom of a comparator group where the data may represent outliers.

Best Practices in Proxy Peer Group Selection

SEC disclosure requirements (see Chapter 17) as well as increased activism by shareholder groups are leading compensation committees to take a closer look at the process for determining executive pay. One area receiving significant attention is the selection of an appropriate peer group for executive pay comparisons.

For benchmarking of named executive officers (i.e., CEO, CFO, and the three other highest paid executives), developing a custom peer group of other publicly traded companies can be a solid source of competitive data. Not only is this a way to obtain compensation values, but it also can provide details on incentive program design, benefit and perquisite offerings and other executive policies, such as severance and change-in-control agreements.

Comparator peer groups are used by compensation committees to inform executive compensation decisions, including the establishment of target levels for executive pay and the design of short- and long-term incentive compensation programs. A peer group used for compensation benchmarking should be constructed:

- Specifically for the individual company. Because each organization has unique characteristics, the comparator group must be custom-built for that particular entity.
- Based on a set of sound design principles and criteria. Beginning the peer group design with a set of principles helps ensure that the process is sustainable and objective. It also avoids a course that many shareholder activists suspect is too often followed — starting with the answer and working backward.

The most effective peer groups typically include 12 to 20 companies that represent the company's market for talent (where it looks to recruit executives and which organizations poach its talent). Fewer than 12 companies may not provide statistically significant results and can be skewed by outliers; having more than 20 companies introduces the likelihood that the group has gone beyond true and relevant "peers." In developing a compensation peer group, the focus should be on design principles that drive the success of the individual company and reflect the market for executive talent. Selection criteria for developing a peer group commonly include:

- **Organizational size**. Size is measured by revenue for most industries, but asset-based for a handful of others (particularly financial institutions). A general rule suggests peer companies should be between 0.5 times and two times the size of the subject organization. Although some companies look at market capitalization, use caution when considering this measure. Market capitalization typically is not the preferred measure of scale because it:
  - Can be volatile, which should have a limited effect on pay.
  - Is aligned to (expected) profitability rather than scale. Therefore, it can understate comparisons for companies in low-margin sectors and arguably inflate salary and annual incentive benchmarks for speculative enterprises.
- **Industry**. Use of industry classifications, such as Global Industry Classification Standard (GICS) codes, can help identify companies either narrowly in common sub-industries or more broadly in

industry groups or sectors. The broader classifications may be more appropriate for companies that operate multiple lines of business, or simply when there is an insufficient number of companies in the narrower classifications.

- **Business model/complexity.** Organizations may choose to screen companies or refine the groups by only selecting companies with similar business models. For example, a company that develops, produces and markets its product may choose to exclude companies in the same industry that only provide a related service but do not actually develop and produce a product.
- **Global versus domestic operations.** Companies that operate on a global basis with executives who have accountability for global results may exclude (or limit the number of) domestic-only companies and vice versa.
- **Regulatory environment.** For many companies (e.g., utilities), regulatory complexities play a significant role in executive responsibilities; in those situations, constructing a peer group with companies that have similar complexities would be appropriate.
- **Founder-headed or -controlled businesses.** These types of executives often have compensation arrangements that differ from typical market practices and, therefore, it may be inappropriate to include these companies in a peer group (unless the subject company is a founder-led or -controlled business, in which case it may actively seek to include these types of organizations).

Peer groups should be reviewed annually to ensure they remain relevant and continue to meet the aforementioned criteria. Companies often need to be removed due to mergers, acquisitions, going private, bankruptcy, regulatory changes and other developments.

Of course, these standards need to be adapted to the particular organization. For example, in some industries, the number of companies that truly could be considered peers is quite small. An independent U.S. corporation's most direct competitors may be relatively small divisions of much larger U.S. employers (or foreign-owned companies) that do not file proxy statements, or privately owned companies for which pay information is difficult to obtain. In this case, a design principle that requires selecting the corporation's closest business competitors would result in few peers with publicly disclosed information. In other instances, a company may compete for talent with much larger organizations, and it may be appropriate to include a limited number of such companies in the peer group. An alternative approach is to denominate the larger company as a peer but exclude its pay levels from any summary statistics (e.g., they can be shown separately). (See "Suggested Attributes of a Peer Group" below.) By following these practices, a compensation committee will be able to develop a peer group of companies that provides valuable and representative data on market compensation practices.

Other Peer Groups

General Industry Peer Groups

In addition to using their industry-specific peer group, companies sometimes develop a general industry peer group for purposes of benchmarking executive compensation and company performance. This provides a supplemental reference on market pay practices for executive roles as well as non-employee director compensation. These peer groups generally contain a larger sample of companies vs. the industry-specific peer group.

Reasons for developing a general industry peer group may include:

- The company competes in a variety of industries.
- The company is the largest (or one of the largest) in its industry, making the development of an industry-specific peer group of sufficient size and revenue range difficult.
- The company recruits for talent outside of its primary industry; this may be particularly true for functional roles (e.g., HR, Finance, Legal, etc.).
- There may be insufficient title matches for certain positions in the industry-specific peer group (e.g., General Counsel, CHRO, CIO).
- Enables benchmarking of company performance relative to a broader set of competitors for business and talent.

In developing a general industry peer group, many companies begin with a nationally recognized list, such as the Fortune 50. Then, the company will pare down the list to an appropriate comparator

Suggested Attributes of a Peer Group

The development of an appropriate peer group involves a consideration of various factors, but should include at least the following four attributes:

Be Current

Markets are dynamic. As a result, a corporation that was an appropriate peer last year may have changed its focus, modified its line(s) of business, been acquired, experienced a dramatic change in performance or even gone out of business. For these and other reasons, a company may no longer truly be a peer. Similarly, the company itself may have changed, either by organically growing faster than its peers or through acquisition, divestiture, or by entering/exiting various markets. Accordingly, it requires effort to evaluate the companies included in the comparator group on an annual basis. In addition, it is essential to understand the peer companies being utilized by institutional shareholders to assess a company's pay-performance relationship. Where these data points are available, it is worth taking the effort to compare these peer groups to the one approved by the compensation committee.

Be Composed of a Representative Number of Companies

A base number of organizations is key for the validity of the summary statistical compensation data. Companies with a few direct competitors often focus on too narrow a group of potential organizations and may face difficulties establishing a valid peer group. Consequently, for purposes of compensation benchmarking, it may be necessary to loosen the rigidity of the selection process to create a sample size that is sufficiently robust to provide meaningful data from a statistical viewpoint.

Be Reasonable in Relationship to Peer Companies

More specifically, an appropriate peer should be reasonably related to the companies used in the performance graphic in the corporation's annual report, particularly to the industry line-of-business index. Because a large portion of executive pay is variable and often linked to corporate performance, best practices suggest that there should be commonality among the companies used to determine whether compensation is appropriate and those used to illustrate corporate performance.

For example, there may be a disconnect if the company's compensation peer group consists of companies in the Dow Jones Industrial Average Index — all household-name, large-capitalization corporations — while the company's performance graph contains relatively unknown, small capitalization companies. Also, shareholder interest groups compare key aspects of a company's program to business peers, especially when looking at share allocations.

Be Performance Based

Frequently, comparisons are made on the basis of organizational size, not performance. The most useful size metric generally is company revenue. While there is a strong correlation (especially with base salary) between revenue size and pay (within the same industry), other variables may need to be considered.

group by either scoping within an appropriate revenue range and/or removing certain industries which may have an altogether different market for talent. (For example, a large industrial company may decide to start with the Fortune list, but then remove sectors with drastically different pay models, such as banking and financial services).

Considering Peer Groups Used by Shareholder Advisory Firms

Shareholder advisory firms often develop their own peer groups for purposes of benchmarking CEO pay and company performance. These peer groups are used to evaluate the relationship between CEO pay and performance as well as pay practices. As such, these peer groups can inform the advisory firm's recommendation on "say-on-pay" and director elections.

It is important to understand proxy advisory firm methodologies and why their peer groups may differ from the company's formal peer group(s). Generally, these firms use a formulaic approach to develop peer groups, which considers the industry classification in which the company resides, as well as market cap and revenue size. They typically use the Global Industry Classification Standards ("GICS") to determine other companies within the industry, and generally use companies within the range of 0.4x to 2.5x revenues. In addition, they may consider the peer groups of other companies (known as a "peers-of-peers" analysis).

However, there are some exceptions to their formulaic approach. For example, if there is an insufficient number of companies within the industry and revenue range, an advisory firm may look to a broader industry segment and/or expand the market-cap range.

It is important to note that these firms will consider the peer group selected and disclosed by the company in making their determination of appropriate peers. Therefore, a public company's disclosure of its peer group is an important factor in influencing how its executive pay will be evaluated.

Relative Total Shareholder Return Peer Groups

Beyond pay benchmarking, companies must establish peer groups for purposes of measuring relative performance in long-term incentive plans. An increasing trend in performance-based long-term incentive plans has been the use of rTSR as an independent measure or modifier to payouts calculated using financial goals. In order to implement rTSR, a company must first establish a rTSR peer group.

Potential choices for a rTSR peer group include:

- The same peer group used to benchmark executive and non-employee director compensation
- A recognized third-party index, such as the S&P 500 or Russell 3,000
- A pre-established industry index (e.g., S&P maintains several indices that comprise certain industry sectors)
- A custom developed rTSR peer group — this comparator group is typically broader in scope than the pay benchmarking peer group, including a wider revenue range and a more expansive selection of companies

In implementing a rTSR peer group, consideration should be given to how to handle changes in the peer group composition over time (e.g., in the case of bankruptcies, mergers & acquisitions, etc.) The company and/or board should establish rules upfront, which helps prevent any uncertainty when determining ultimate payouts under the plan.

Using Comparator Peer Groups in Shareholders' Best Interests

A compensation committee should use the peer group to compare compensation levels (how much) and design (forms of pay delivery). The "how much" analysis should be informed by title-match benchmarking (e.g., CEO, CFO) and compensation rank where sufficient title matching is not possible (e.g., second-highest paid officer). The levels should be viewed not only by total dollar amount, but also by the mix of fixed, variable and equity pay at the peer companies. Given that a large percentage of executive pay is not in the form of guaranteed compensation, it is useful to examine a company's compensation structure in comparison to that of its peers. This may include a review of target incentive award opportunities, types of equity used and performance metrics selected.

The decision about the type of awards can be informed by current peer group and market practices, but primarily should be driven by assessing which award vehicles most closely align executive pay with the organization's strategic goals. In nearly all cases, an organization's pay should be informed by the market, but also tailored to its own unique circumstances.

Comparing Performance of Peer Group Companies

While peer groups are used to assist with the establishment of top executive pay levels, they should also be used to compare the company's performance with that of its peer group. This comparison allows the compensation committee to determine the degree of alignment of executive pay with actual business performance relative to the comparator peer group. Analyzing this pay for performance also serves the best interests of the company's shareholders. Results provide insight into the relationship between executive pay levels and company performance as well as whether pay is commensurate with the performance level achieved (i.e., where a company provides executive pay above median, does it consistently exceed peer group median performance?).

In evaluating the degree of alignment between company performance and executive pay, compensation committees should look for directional, as opposed to precise, relationships. It is unrealistic to expect a company that performs at the peer group's 40th percentile to have its executive compensation pegged precisely at the 40th percentile. However, if this company properly aligns its pay programs with performance considerations, shareholders should reasonably expect executives' compensation to be directionally equivalent to that of company performance and fall between the 25th and 50th percentiles of the peer group, particularly over the long run.

As shown in Figure 3-1, area B displays a pay-for-performance directional relationship; areas A and C do not. Concerns with the shaded areas include:

- In area A, executive compensation may be viewed as an excessive expenditure of the shareholders' assets because compensation rank is significantly higher than performance rank. In this case, the compensation committee may consider one or more of the following:

    – Freezing or slowing the growth of base salaries

    – Modifying the relationship between performance and payout

    – Revisiting the payout opportunities

    – Raising the performance metric targets

    – Changing the performance metrics

    – Modifying relative performance metrics that compare the company's performance against a peer group

    – Delving deeper into the cause of the apparent pay-for-performance disconnect.

- In area C, there may be a risk of losing talented executives because performance rank significantly exceeds compensation rank. In this situation, retention concerns may cause the compensation committee to raise salaries, increase payout opportunities or review the performance metric targets.

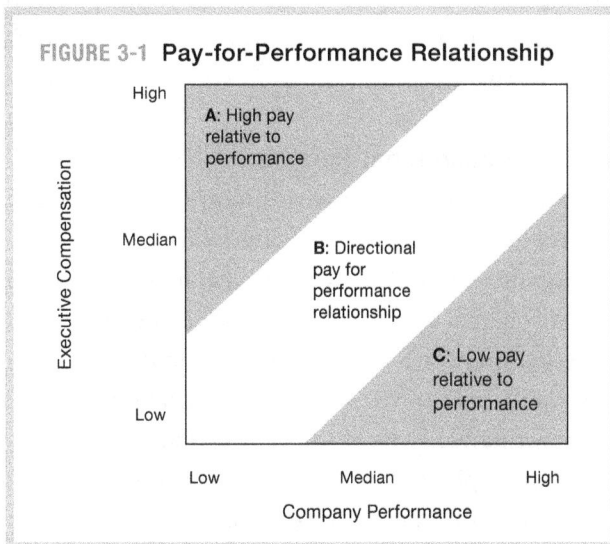

FIGURE 3-1 Pay-for-Performance Relationship

Peer Group Financial Performance Comparisons

A robust pay-for-performance analysis does not involve merely a comparison of a company's absolute business performance to its internal, committee-approved performance targets (absolute performance goals). This type of analysis should focus on a company's performance relative to its peer group's performance. It is possible for a company to repeatedly achieve or exceed its internal financial and nonfinancial goals, resulting in incentive awards paying out at or above target levels, but still fall behind the performance of its peer companies.

Another benefit of a performance comparison is that the compensation committee is able to validate the goals it establishes for its executive variable pay programs. The analysis can reveal whether the internal performance goals warrant the corresponding payouts when compared to the peer group's aggregate historical performance.

For example, an examination might reveal that the one-year earnings growth goal established by the compensation committee for target performance corresponds to the historical 25th percentile earnings growth of a comparator peer group. Such a discovery might prompt the compensation committee to increase the annual incentive plan's earnings growth target, lower the payout opportunities, or further explore the rationale behind how and why the performance objectives were set.

Performance Measurement Periods

Performance for the selected metrics might be evaluated for both one- and three-year (possibly up to five-year) performance periods for each company. Then, for example, each company's CEO cash compensation and total direct compensation can be ranked and plotted against its corresponding composite performance ranking. Figure 3-2 shows an example of CEO cash compensation versus one-year company performance, with a ranking of the best performers. As shown, Company Alpha has the best composite one-year performance ranking as well as the highest CEO cash compensation. However, Company Charlie, with the third-highest performance ranking, is next to last in cash compensation. Absent other retention, organizational and personal factors, Company Charlie may be at risk of losing its CEO to another company unless changes are made to the CEO's cash compensation or long-term incentive award program.

Although no analysis of executive pay relative to company performance will be all encompassing, the approach suggested can show whether a directional relationship exists between pay and performance. Given the increased corporate governance requirements and outside scrutiny of executive compensation, it is crucial that compensation committees make efforts to assure investors that they truly are overseeing an executive compensation program that aligns pay and performance.

FIGURE 3-2 CEO Cash Compensation vs. One-Year Company Performance

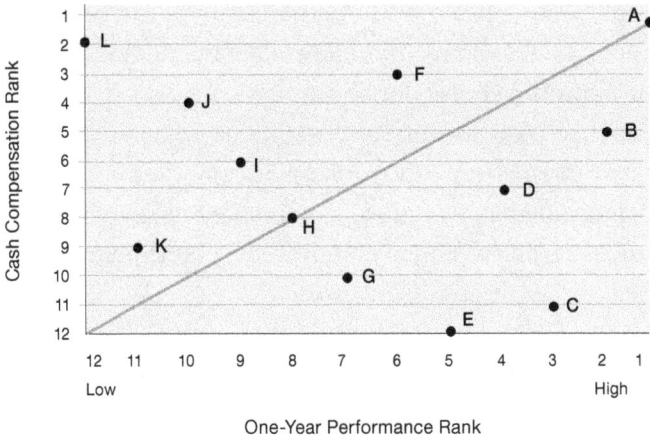

Company Name	Performance Rank
Alpha	A
Bravo	B
Charlie	C
Delta	D
Echo	E
Foxtrot	F
Golf	G
Hotel	H
India	I
Juliet	J
Kilo	K
Lima	L

Use of Peer Groups in Setting Compensation

Once a peer group is established and data have been collected, the work is not done. Compensation committees have a responsibility to apply their judgment in evaluating peer group data. For example, after selecting the suitable peer companies based on the aforementioned criteria, an organization may find that its revenue is at the 30th percentile of the group. If this organization has a philosophy of paying at the median of its market, is it appropriate to target the median of its peer group? Similarly, if a company has been performing poorly, it may be inappropriate to select only high-performing peer companies and target the median of that group. Consideration needs to be given to these factors so that the compensation philosophy works in alignment with the peer group.

Market data will always have a role to play in setting executive pay. How else can the compensation committee be assured that pay is sufficient to attract and retain its key talent but not excessive? In any case, the approach chosen for benchmarking needs to be thoughtful and deliberate. This means selecting the right comparators, taking the context into account and looking at competitiveness in various performance scenarios. Ultimately, a compensation committee needs to rely on its business judgment while using benchmark data as one input, but not as an absolute answer.

Making the Business Case for CEO Pay

Peer group benchmarking has its place in deciding how and how much to pay a top executive, but it is only part of the decision-making process. To really make the most of the opportunities presented by CEO pay determinations, we suggest boards (and their compensation committees) take a broader view — and make the business case for CEO pay.

Building the Business Case

To start building the business case for executive reward, the board needs to ask questions like:

- What do we want to achieve as a business?
- How will our CEO pay design support that?
- How will we measure the return on our investment?

It sounds simple but doing this is actually a fairly involved exercise — and one that is worth the time and effort. In addition to creating a context for a CEO's pay that makes sense to both the organization and outsiders, building a business case can help the board close the gap between the CEO and the day-to-day realities of the organization and make the board better equipped to address any challenges around "fairness."

Why There Is More to Life Than Just Benchmarking

Historically, the consensus has been that pay levels are the key to attracting, retaining and motivating the right chief executive. As a result, companies saw the data gleaned from peer group benchmarking as enough to justify decisions around pay. Many still do.

To get to "the" number, organizations would work out the size of the individual's job, benchmark it against similar organizations in the market, and find their target level (typically the median). And, historically, this basic approach has worked well enough.

But changes in the economy as well as added pressure from shareholders have affected the way we think about executive compensation, to expose the shortcomings of the traditional benchmarking process and put pressure on organizations to find new and better ways to reward their top people.

Traditional peer group benchmarking is commonly criticized for two main reasons:

1. The ratchet effect. CEOs are a relatively small and static pool. As such, there are not many points of comparison. And as everyone in that pool seeks to be competitive, companies rarely want to pay below the 50th percentile — which drives pay levels up.
2. Getting in a muddle over the median. If you are car shopping, you do not buy a car just because it costs an average price for that make and model — you buy it because you think you are getting the best quality car at the right price, all factors considered. It should be the same with setting and designing CEO pay. The median (or above) should not dictate what an organization pays — it is one data point of several factors to consider when making pay decisions. Too many organizations still see it as the "magic number," and it simply is not.

Also, CEOs do not tend to leave for other CEO roles. So, while peer group benchmarking is a helpful reference, it is not enough on its own to justify pay levels. The board must look at factors specific to the organization, its business and culture, and the person in the job (or the one the board is hoping to hire). For examples, see, "Building the Business Case for CEO Pay: Questions to Ask."

FIGURE 3-3 **Building the Business Case for CEO Pay: Questions to Ask**

The strategic case	What is it we want to achieve as a business? Is this person going to take our organization where it needs to go next? How will the way we propose to pay support our strategy?
The economic case	How much can we afford to pay? Does that mean we need to promote internally or can we hire externally? Who are our competitors for people and for business, and what do they pay? How will we measure our return on investment?
The personal case	Why is this the right person for the task? Are they going to be the right fit? How do their competencies match the task at hand? What do they think about the issue of pay, and will that affect their behavior — positively or negatively?
The political case	What is the desired message? What will the reaction be to this appointment among investors, other stakeholders and the general public? Could it affect our share price? How will this person deal with our stakeholders?

Fairness Is in the Eyes of the Beholder

The perception of fairness is understandably a factor in evaluating CEO pay, and the discussion has gone beyond the boardroom and entered the mainstream. This means that the number of people who have an opinion on how fair (or not) a CEO's pay is has grown exponentially. Boards need to take these views seriously when making decisions around pay.

A "moral compass of fairness" can illustrate these many perspectives. It starts with the classic benchmarking question: what is the size and scope of the job compared to peer organizations?

But then boards need to consider:

- What that person has done to deserve that pay
- What the shareholders think is fair, based on the outside world as they see it
- What individual board members think (e.g., "that's a lot more than I got when I was a CEO")
- How it appears to the rest of the organization: is it more of a pay gulf than a pay gap?

From there, the debate extends to the general public, which, thanks to increased disclosure, can now act as judge and jury. As potential customers, clients and shareholders, it matters what they think.

Finally, and at the heart of the issue, the CEO's view of his/her pay package requires consideration. While magnitude is important, the structure and design of the package can send very clear signals to the CEO about the company's expectations and how success will be measured.

The company should consider several factors, including the following:

- Fairness at the top
- Pay differentials between CEO and direct reports
- The impact of shareholders
- What is the pay philosophy and culture?
- Is there a successor standing in the wings?

Fairness at the Top

With the spotlight still on CEO pay, many organizations have started to talk about establishing "internal equity" (the perception that the organization pays people according to the relative size and difficulty of the job they do). But few are doing something about it. Internal equity is not the ratio between CEO pay and that of the "median" employee. That ratio might be interesting to the media, but it is typically meaningless to the business, because it does not, on the most basic level, take the structure, size and uniqueness of the CEO's job (or organization) into account.

Pay Differentials Between CEO and Direct Reports

Looking at the internal equity between the chief executive and his/ her direct reports, then evaluating the relative size and complexity of those roles, brings an important perspective to the CEO pay debate. It also makes sure that the people at the layer below feel appropriately rewarded for the work they do. At this next level, the market data tends to be a truer reflection of the market for talent, partly because the pool of people to compare against is much larger. And because those people are more likely to leave to become CEOs at other companies, benchmarking becomes a more useful (and justifiable) exercise than at the CEO level. By benchmarking pay for these jobs and comparing their size and complexity with the CEO's role, we can build internal equity considerations into a recommendation for how much the company pays the CEO compared to the layer below.

Sometimes, a large pay gap between the CEO and other executives reflects the fact that responsibility for delivering the business strategy sits solely on that person's head. However, this may also be a red flag to investors, who question what would happen to the company if the CEO got hit by the proverbial bus.

The Impact of Stakeholders

Organizations have many stakeholders, and as the moral compass of fairness shows, they may all have different ideas about what constitutes appropriate pay for your CEO. Is it privately held, publicly traded, government controlled, or some other type of organization? Each ownership model may lead to a different kind of reward structure because different owners have different aims and different ways of rewarding a CEO who achieves them. A chief executive brought into a family-owned business, for example, probably will not be a big shareholder because it is not in the family's interest to relinquish control. But a publicly traded company that wants to encourage a long-term view may require its CEO to build up a large number of shares to drive that view, and to reflect shareholders' interests. The chief executive of a failing company, where the government has become a majority shareholder, might need to give up his or her annual bonus as a public display of belt-tightening.

Is There a Successor Standing in the Wings?

A substantial majority of CEO jobs go to insiders. This has a big impact on pay, not just for the person who is eventually promoted into the post, but for the person in the role now. For example, if a company has three solid options for a successor, it does not need to pay its current CEO as much as if a replacement is hard to find. And when the time comes to appoint a successor, the internal candidate will not become twice as valuable overnight. But the board will need to adjust the executive's compensation package to reflect what it wants the new CEO to achieve, and the risk to which that exposes both them and the organization. While investors may balk at the inevitable premium needed to pay for an external candidate, they equally may need reassurance that a company "lifer" has the broad experience and understanding of the wider market needed for the business to thrive. In both scenarios, adjusting the design of the CEO's incentives, and the balance of base/variable pay in the package, can soothe shareholder concerns.

Pulling It All Together

Once the internal and external benchmarking is done and other factors are considered, the board just needs to come up with a number, right? Not quite. The board must now set both the levels and the structure of the package. And this can take many different shapes; there is no need to constrain the board's thinking to what is considered "normal."

Consider this example: Company A wants a chief executive who can keep the business stable for five years. So, it says to its new CEO, we'll pay you $1 million a year for five years, guaranteed — but in five years you will not have a job. So, after three years, we will start looking for someone to replace you, and we expect your last year to be all about handing over the reins.

Meanwhile, Company B wants to grow rapidly. In five years, it aims to be snapping at the heels of the market-leaders in its industry. So, it hires a CEO on a fixed annual salary of only $1, on the understanding that if that person takes the business to new heights, he or she will receive a huge bonus.

Both packages have their merits, but for the one chosen to succeed, the CEO needs to perceive what is offered as being of equal value to a package with a different structure elsewhere. Getting to a package that both the CEO and the board or compensation committee can agree upon might involve time and trade-offs, but it is worth the investment to make sure the CEO is not only happy, but understands what needs to happen in order for the incentives to pay out. Otherwise, he/she might perceive the package as being worth less than it is.

Final Cautions

It is clear that both the relative size of an organization's executive jobs and the "going rate" matter. Using internal equity in pay decisions forces a company to account for how its executive roles are unique and allows it to create an executive compensation program that balances fairness and competitiveness with what jobs actually do. So rather than being at the mercy of the market, its pay decisions make sense, all factors considered.

Boards need to be wary of exaggerating the importance of the individual in its calculations. The impact of an overpaid CEO on morale in an organization is potentially much greater than the impact on that person's pride of being paid below the median. Transferring too much power to the CEO puts the business in a vulnerable position, too. When designing a CEO pay package, a board must remember that at the end of the day, the organization should be stronger than the individual. If the CEO is stronger, the company is on dangerous ground — what happens if and when he/she leaves?

CHAPTER 4

Valuing Work and Establishing Base Salary

By Tom McMullen and Bill Reigel

As its name implies, base salary is the foundation for the other components of an executive compensation program. Every paycheck is a reminder of the link between the executive's efforts over the last pay period and how the organization perceives the value of those efforts.

Many organizations today determine base salary levels (and other elements of compensation) by benchmarking their job functions or titles to external compensation surveys. However, these types of survey matches often provide limited value in determining how much a job is really worth to a specific organization as strategies, structures and scale differ. The data provide information on what is paid in the market for comparable positions but do not reflect incumbent experience and performance or the value of the role within the organization.

This chapter:

- Reviews key concepts and terms in valuing executive jobs.
- Provides you with an understanding of common work-valuing processes in use today, and how they support executive compensation and talent management decisions.
- Discusses the importance of the base salary component in the total compensation equation. It defines the purpose of salary and its use as the starting point in determining the value of annual and

long-term incentive awards as well as benefits programs, such as pension, long-term disability and paid time off.

- Explains how executive pay can be affected by many factors, including company size and scope, industry, geography, brand, supply/demand, executive negotiations, incumbent track record, and other factors.

Examining Markets and Jobs

First, a few basic definitions. "Market" is typically defined as economic activity where buyers and sellers are driven by the principles of supply and demand. "Job evaluation" is about determining how much the job (or role) is worth to the organization. "Market pricing" is about determining how much others in the labor market pay for the capability required to accomplish the objectives in a defined job or role. "Valuing work" is the combination of these internal and external factors. The market for talent often is not clearly defined and certainly is not managed within a precise range.

Market pricing may have a surface appearance of being precise and defensible, but market data is typically a sample based on matching titles and basic functions without consideration for other relevant factors.

For example, consider the two group head positions described in Table 2-2 of Chapter 2. Both are accountable for $2 billion in revenues and in most surveys would be matched to the same job and result in the same benchmark compensation levels. However, as observed in Chapter 2, the two positions are clearly not worth the same in the market. The group head position at Company A has a much larger size job and should be compensated greater than the group head described for Company B, holding all other variables constant. A job evaluation process enables a company to decode its organizational structure and incorporate all elements of job design to ensure it is making the most accurate job content matches to the market. Job evaluation-based market pricing would produce substantially different values for the above two positions, while market pricing without job evaluation would not. Job evaluation adds precision to market pricing.

The Role of Job Evaluation

Robust job evaluation methodologies can help sort out the value of jobs to the organization and directly link this to a market price. Job evaluation makes market pricing easier and more precise as it enables pricing of all executive jobs (even unique jobs), not just a subset of jobs, available in compensation surveys. Job evaluations can be priced relative to specific jobs, functions, geographies, industries and organization size.

Many of the world's largest and most admired organizations use job evaluation to facilitate executive compensation decisions. Job evaluation works regardless of the organization or compensation structure. It provides a company with better defensibility and rationale to support market pricing processes as well as flexibility with managed control. Further, the process of job evaluation helps to clearly define job content in terms of the capability required, position accountabilities and performance standards of the role.

The process of defining the price range of a job — its base salary range as well as short- and long-term incentive opportunities — combines the value of the job to the organization with the price of the job in the market. Once the value range is established, the actual price paid incorporates other factors, such as incumbent skills and performance. In its most basic form, job evaluation is a system for determining the size of a job relative to other jobs in the organization. Beyond that, it is used to derive a market value for jobs of similar size. Rather than simply benchmarking to a "job match," compensation data can be derived for a particular point value or range of point values.

Korn Ferry's job evaluation methodology was initially developed by Edward N. Hay in the early 1950s and was previously known as the Hay job evaluation methodology. It has been refined over the years to align with evolving management processes. It is comprised of three main factors: (1) know-how, (2) problem solving, and (3) accountability.

The three main factors can be represented by a simple model:

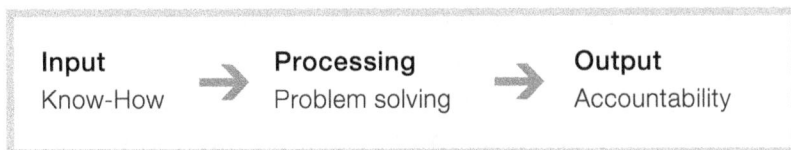

Input		Processing		Output
Know-How	→	Problem solving	→	Accountability

For any given job, there is a relationship among the three factors. The Output, or end results expected of the job (the accountability), demands a certain level of Input (know-how) and Processing of this know-how (problem solving) to enable delivery. The criteria used are common and universal compensable factors and have been proven to be compliant with government regulations around the world.

In determining the value of executive jobs through the process of job evaluation, the following factors should be considered:

- **Industry** — the nature of the industry sector(s), unique industry challenges, breadth of functional portfolio and the degree of regulation have an impact on job complexity.
- **Revenues** — good predictor of job size within an industry and one of the key factors utilized in determining the level of executive accountability, but value added (revenues minus purchases) should also be considered.
- **Assets** — often utilized to determine executive accountability in financial services or insurance companies but also relevant for industrial companies.
- **Market capitalization and/or enterprise value** — sometimes considered, but only for named executives in the proxy. Use of these values typically reflect performance and are therefore used as judgment checks on revenue-driven comparator organizations rather than the primary metric.
- **Employee headcount** — an important measure, but it can be misleading. An organization should be careful to use full-time equivalents; also location and reliance on technology and outsourced labor can skew comparisons. In addition, an organization with many hourly employees may be less complex and challenging to manage than an organization with fewer professional and technical employees working on complex and/or technical issues/products.
- **Governance** — clearly has impact on the top job (e.g., CEO vs. CEO/Chairman or the dual board structure existing in some countries as well as Co-CEOs). Publicly held organizations often have more inherent complexity than privately held organizations.
- **Geographic scope of company** — adds complexity, and thus job size (e.g., solely domestic operations vs. international operations

vs. a broad global footprint) given diversity in socio-economic groups, cultures, regulatory environments, etc.

- **Organization strategy/structure and span of control** — affects the relative value of positions below the CEO (i.e., NEOs).

Once these factors are utilized to develop job evaluations and resulting grades for the CEO and other executives, more precise market data can be collected that better reflects specific job accountabilities (vs. using only external market pricing). In addition, job evaluation has applications for managing executive talent beyond determining competitive compensation levels. This includes:

- Succession planning (job evaluation can be linked to competencies and behaviors, executives can be assessed vs. what is required for their role and the next role)
- Linking executives to the organization strategy by describing their specific accountabilities and the nature of how they affect the accountabilities (e.g., developing a clear plan for implementing the strategy)
- Defining the impact of acquisitions, joint ventures, matrix organizational structures (e.g., the executives in an acquired company may not be compensated to the same degree as a stand-alone company).

Compensation Benchmarking with Public Disclosures

Compensation committees are certainly familiar with the process of compensation benchmarking from proxy statements, which starts with developing a peer group (as discussed in Chapter 3). Compensation data so obtained are then summarized by job match or pay rank. The approach has become a standard analysis typically performed on an annual basis to benchmark the competitiveness of executive pay. Proxy data provides the compensation committee with a great deal of information, as more detail is disclosed in proxy statements than ever before.

While proxy analysis is a great tool for benchmarking pay and has a level of transparency that market pay surveys do not, it falls short in several areas:

- Revenues alone do not adequately estimate compensation levels. Typical R-squared values (i.e., measures of strength of correlation) for regressions of pay relative to revenue are 0.3 to 0.5, whereas R-squared values for pay on job evaluation scores are in the range of 0.6 to 0.8 (note: R-squared value of 0 indicates no relationship, R-squared value of 1.0 indicates a perfect relationship).

- Typically, only CEO and CFO positions can be directly matched in a proxy-based compensation benchmarking analysis. When identical roles do not exist in the peer group companies, executives are matched by their internal pay rank among the other named executive officers (NEOs). While this provides data on other similarly ranked executives, it fails to consider complexity or responsibilities of the job.

- The approach fails to establish specific market rates for "combined" or "hybrid" roles (e.g., CFO is also the chief information officer or accountable for a business unit). Further, a CFO role may differ depending on acquisition focus, need for more creative financing for growth, or degree of international business. Proxy data does not provide sufficient insight on the internal organization structure and succession planning effects on pay.

- Job titles also do not reflect the business strategy of the organization and how this impacts job size (e.g., low-cost, high-technology or high-customer focus).

- Many organizations develop a compensation philosophy whereby they target a given competitive market percentile versus the proxy peer group — often the market median. Paying at the median of the market is not always a sound strategy as other factors such as organization value-add, pay mix or performance are not considered. When assessing pay, it is important to have a strong performance connection. Market values are merely a point of reference and should not be deemed a mandate of a pay positioning strategy.

One thing is clear: Pay data and resulting decisions should be based on more than either simply matching your job titles to the market or using internal job evaluations without reference to the external market. We suggest a combination of internal value and external market pay as the key elements to determine the value of the executive role. An organization should know both; one approach without the other will yield an incomplete answer.

Base Salary: The Foundation of Total Compensation

Base salary is the least complex form of compensation, yet some would argue it is the most important when viewing pay relative to the broader workforce. For top executives, base salary typically is not the highest value of all compensation elements, but it can have a significant bearing on the actual value of other pay components, which are often based off of base salary. Salary as a percentage of total compensation is even as low as 10 percent or below for CEOs of large capitalization companies.

In addition to driving the value of other forms of compensation, salary is an important part of the attract-and-retain equation. It is not considered as strong in its ability to provide motivation to an executive; arguably, compensation is most motivational when it is at risk. Psychologists generally have maintained that salary is more of a hygienic factor rather than a motivational one. That is, base salary either satisfies or dissatisfies, but does not motivate or change behavior. For lower-level jobs, salary is much more important to meet basic needs (e.g., security, ability to provide basic needs for self and family). While these needs may be lessened for executives due to higher pay levels, security cannot be ignored as a psychological factor for executives. At executive job levels, salary is often a way for executives to "keep score" relative to the perceived job worth when compared to others within and outside the organization.

With the current focus on executive pay, base salary may be viewed negatively by shareholders and other interest groups if it appears too high from some perspectives. Increasingly, public companies emphasize performance-based compensation to appease proxy advisors.

Relation to Market

As discussed previously, determining an executive's base salary typically is a function of the market and the value of the position, and person in it, to the organization. Most organizations measure the market for executives based on some combination of the nature of the job, organization size (revenues), industry sector and job size (job evaluation).

Employers often claim that they establish the market reference or midpoint of a salary range on the basis of market median of the relevant peer group. The vast majority of companies state that their pay philosophy is at market median; yet, as measured in compensation surveys, actual pay varies significantly from the median — especially at executive levels. The salary range (often at +/- 20 to 30 percent) around market reference produces a pay spectrum from about the 10th percentile to the 90th percentile of market for most executive positions. The actual pay variation around market reference is based on incumbent experience, performance, job tenure as well as incumbent negotiation power.

Many companies maintain that base salary is largely paid for incumbent factors, including how one performs the job, and not just on achieved results. As such, competencies and behaviors are significant factors in determining the appropriate salary increase and resulting new salary.

Managing Salary

Given the importance of base salary as referenced above, it would seem that salary should be managed more effectively and with greater differentiation than is typically done. Some employers overly rely on market salary movements and adjust executive base salaries fairly consistently. These same employers often do not manage salaries to reflect the performance and value of the person and position to the organization. A more effective approach involves managing the market as a reference point rather than as a driver for how much an executive should earn in base salary. In addition, the actual base salary within the salary range should reflect demonstrated performance over time as opposed to pay for tenure within the company. Over the past decade, we have generally seen base salary increases for executives match, in percentage terms, what other employee groups receive. In challenging economic cycles such as the 2009-10 recession and the 2020 pandemic, we have seen executive populations receive smaller salary increases — and often salary cuts in hard hit sectors — versus other employee groups.

Managing salary is important because it is the foundation for other compensation programs and represents one of the largest fixed costs in managing an enterprise. At a market reference of $300,000, the typical market range from P10 to P90 is +/-$60,000 to $90,000. (See Table 4-1.) However, an incumbent paid at the maximum versus the minimum would find a total direct compensation difference of $360,000, assuming target short- and long-term incentives as a consistent percentage of base salary. This does not include the value difference in benefits (e.g., income replacement and retirement).

TABLE 4-1 Impact of Salary on Total Direct Compensation

Salary	STI %	STI $	TCC*	LTI %	LTI $	TDC**
$210	50%	$105	$315	50%	$105	$420
$300	50%	$150	$450	50%	$150	$600
$390	50%	$195	$585	50%	$195	$780

TCC* = total cash compensation (salary plus annual incentive pay)
TDC** = total direct compensation (TCC plus long-term incentive pay)

When organizations search for talent from the outside, potential recruits often focus on increasing their base salary. But employers should exercise care not to place too much emphasis on salary. Doing so may distort internal pay relationships. For example, consider two executives in the same position — a long-tenured employee is paid $210,000 and a newly hired individual is paid $390,000. This pay relationship will generate quite different TDC costs over time. The difference over 10 years is roughly $4.9 million in TDC, assuming a four percent annual increase. Not small change. Instead of paying more salary and affecting internal equity, signing bonuses and restricted stock can be helpful in both attracting and retaining top talent.

Tenure and experience in a role may also help determine where an executive's base pay falls along a salary range. Employees in the lower half of the salary range (1st to 50th percentile) are continuing to grow and develop in their capabilities related to the job. The top half of the range (50th to 100th percentile) should represent above-market pay for sustained, high performers or newly hired executives who bring unique and proven skills and experiences to the job (for example, someone hired from a competitor who has been highly successful in a similar role).

The middle half of the range (25th to 75th percentile) represents market pay for solidly performing executives who are competent in the core aspects of their role. Note that there can often be an obsession with attaining the midpoint of the salary range. Sometimes "market data" may imply a level of perceived precision in measuring the market that does not actually exist (a reported midpoint of $345,352 for example). While the development of a compensation structure is based on a significant amount of data and analysis, there is quite a bit of art and smoothing to the process as well. Organizations often use the "compa-ratio" statistic (an executive's base salary divided by the midpoint of the salary range) to determine where one's pay falls within the range. Over time, companies would like to have a positive correlation between performance and position in the salary range (i.e., top performers paid above market, solid performers paid around the market, marginal performers below market). In reality, employees are paid throughout the salary range and their pay at any point in time may or may not reflect their current level of performance.

Another core concept in executive base pay management is allocating salary increases relative to performance. First, organizations need to ensure that performance assessments translate into differentiated rewards. Many organizations spend an agonizing amount of effort to ensure that managers comply with some sort of a distribution curve of performance ratings. But what value is this if the highest performer still receives only marginally more rewards — whether in merit pay, incentive pay or options — than the average performer? These performance ratings are a means to an end. And the end game is higher compensation for the highest performance, not just a perfect performance distribution curve. Both pay and performance need to be differentiated to be meaningful.

Other Elements of Managing Base Pay

There are several other practices when making individual executive base salary decisions. These include the following:

- **New Hires**: Senior leaders are faced with a wide range of candidates (both internally and externally) whose qualifications are at the minimum required for satisfactory performance to those who bring unique skills and experiences and can hit the ground running. Typically, most organizations strive to hire employees below the market target (midpoint) for the job. This helps limit risk and preserve internal equity (fairness) in the organization while giving newly hired executives the opportunity to earn healthier merit increases as they develop in the role. However, sometimes it is necessary to bring in an executive at a higher salary than the market target and often higher than internal executives in similarly sized roles. Decisions like that are usually driven by market demands, a need for the business or by the exceptional qualifications of the executive. Also, it is typically more expensive to replace executives from the outside than to fill jobs internally, as a high performer in another company often demands a significant premium in pay to justify the risk in switching employers. Moreover, due to a changing regulatory environment in many U.S. states, most organizations cannot rely on the past compensation history to set the compensation of an executive. This puts more emphasis on robust job evaluation and market pricing processes as well as consistent principles on establishing executive base salary offers.

- **Promotions**: A promotion is traditionally viewed as a move from one executive role to another of greater authority, impact, complexity, scope and income. As such, a "promotional increase" should be larger than a normal merit increase or annual cost of living increase. If promotions are implemented at the same time as the annual merit increase, many companies take into account dollars allocated for the employee's annual increases in the promotional increase amount. Most executive promotions involve job changes that are significant and typically are more than one grade apart or have a clear difference in market value; a promotional increase in the 7 to 15 percent range is appropriate in most situations and in some cases greater than 15 percent if the new role requires a significant stretch for the executive.

- **Demotions**: A demotion is usually based on performance or business circumstances (job elimination, restructuring, etc.). Sometimes it is initiated by the employee (due to work-life issues). Many organizations are uncomfortable reducing an employee's salary in certain situations — especially in demotions due to business circumstances. While this may be understandable, it is critical that the organization has a set of principles around this and keep clear records because a future jobholder should be properly placed in a salary range geared to the job, not relative to the previous jobholder's salary.

- **Lateral Transfers**: A lateral transfer is a move to a new role in the organization that is similar in scope and complexity to one's current role. Ordinarily, lateral moves result in the transfer of an executive to a new job within the same pay grade (or band) with a similar market target. These moves may be employee driven (for example, a personal desire to learn a new area of the business) or company driven due to a re-organization, the need for executive development or because a current executive has skills for which the company has critical needs. A lateral move is an opportunity for an employee to try something new, face new challenges and add breadth to their work experience. While a lateral move may not automatically result in a pay increase — especially if it is driven by the employee's request — moving executives around for development and bench building is an investment in the organization's future. If the value of the development experience is obvious, then base pay increases may also be part of the offer.

- **Developmental Moves**: Developmental moves may be lateral or downward to new roles designed to expand the executive's capabilities while increasing their value to the organization. Developmental moves help executives prepare for larger roles in the company. These moves are crucial to increasing employees' skills and knowledge by enabling them to take on different challenges and learn new skills. Typically, executives receiving developmental moves are on a "fast track" and consistently rated as high performers. Most developmental moves do not require pay adjustments. However, based on the executive's potential, level of personal risk being taken, and the expectation of adding significant value in the short term, an executive could be eligible for an increase.

- **Hot Skills/Geographic Pay Differentials**: Sometimes, established guidelines just will not work for a job. When pay guidelines are established for a headquarters in Chattanooga, for example, but an executive needs to live and work in Manhattan, the organization is faced with a geographic premium issue. This also can happen when the organization is faced with a "hot skills" issue, such as a "seller's market" for information security executives with specific know-how. In these cases, many organizations simply add a figure — a "differential" — to the data they are using to determine salaries. Some organizations accommodate the special need by creating a distinct, time-bound "contract supplement."

- **Pay for Potential**: Sometimes it is necessary to protect against loss of mission-critical, high-potential talent by paying a premium relative to market. Most employers limit personal pay grades or levels to those with the highest performance and potential and use premium pay as a way to protect against regrettable turnover of key talent. Typically, such personal pay decisions are limited to a small percentage of the executive population – e.g., 10 percent or less.

- **Pay equity adjustments**: Given a shifting regulatory environment as well as socio-economic concerns, many organizations now assess if there are statistically significant differences in compensation paid to executives across gender and ethnicity groups. Formal pay equity analyses have become very common in organizations over the past decade and most are driven by the compensation committee of the board. In these types of analyses, organizations typically utilize a multi-variate regression analysis to analyze compensation relative to the key influencers of pay. These variables often include job evaluation, function, location, tenure and performance. The analysis will isolate the effect of gender and ethnicity on pay differences that cannot be explained by other variables that impact pay. Statistically significant differences in pay between these groups often result in pay remediation to the most negatively impacted pay outliers in the group. In addition to "being the right thing to do," organizations realize the employer brand opportunities that come along with these initiatives.

Final Considerations

While many executives are unaware of all the perquisites, benefits and intangibles their companies offer, nearly everyone knows their own base salary. Every paycheck is a reminder to executives of the link between work and reward — and an opportunity for leaders to reinforce key messages about their organizations' values, strategies and decisions.

CHAPTER 5

Annual Incentive Pay

By Brian Dresch and Brian Reidy

Annual incentives categorically fall under the general heading of variable compensation and the specific definition of short-term incentives. Defining characteristics of these programs are compensation tied to business outcomes, measured relative to an agreed performance standard, and earned during a 12-month period. People often use "annual incentive" and "bonus" interchangeably when, in fact, they are two different things. An incentive focuses on motivating and rewarding desired behaviors and results based on planned metrics and defined results, while a bonus tends to be after the fact and discretionary.

Annual incentives have been used in the U.S. business community for over 100 years. Originally, these programs were profit-sharing vehicles to reward non-owner managers. In the 1960's, these plans morphed to reinforce achievement of corporate budgets and during the 1990's companies began utilizing various value-based measures to reward participants. Today, according to recent WorldatWork research, virtually all public and privately held companies in the U.S. and most non-U.S. firms utilize annual incentive plans (AIPs) in not only their executive compensation schemes, but broader employee-base schemes as well.

As these plans have become ubiquitous and more complicated, competing interests and tension between senior executives and boards have developed around AIP design, including metric selection and target setting criteria. Executives seek to establish goals that are readily achievable while board members favor aspirational goals to motivate exceptional performance.

Additionally, with increased disclosure requirements and shareholders having the opportunity to vote on executive pay, compensation committees and organizations must formulate incentive plans that can withstand scrutiny from a wide range of stakeholders. For instance, proxy advisory firms are looking for a direct linkage between an organization's business strategy and its annual incentive plan measures. This growing demand for correlation requires compensation committees to review annual incentive plan designs for applicability each year.

Ideally, an annual incentive plan provides strong motivation for executives to achieve strategic objectives, increase shareholder value, and remain with the organization. Best practices include:

- **Do what is right for the business strategy**: annual incentives should be designed to align and reinforce the business strategy.
- **Select appropriate performance metrics and target levels**: chosen metrics should clearly advance the business strategy and performance standards should be sufficiently rigorous and reasonable when compared to peer organizations.
- **Pay for performance**: when an organization outperforms versus its budget/forecast and its peers, the annual incentive plan should generate substantial payout; the plan should generate little or no payout when it underperforms.
- **Aim for a normal distribution**: a well-constructed annual incentive plan will result in maximum payouts 20 percent of the time, missing threshold payments 20 percent of the time and achieving target 50-60 percent of the time.
- **Strive for clarity and transparency**: compensation committees must be able to articulate how the plan aligns with business strategy, shareholder interests and participant needs.

Getting annual incentive plan design right is more challenging than ever. By focusing on the company's business strategy, key metrics and the overall business context for the company, management and compensation committees are well positioned to design plans and calibrate goals that satisfy various stakeholders.

This chapter:

- Discusses design considerations such as plan purpose and objectives, eligibility, funding, calculating awards and payout alternatives.
- The role of management and the board in annual incentive plan oversight.
- Addresses considerations and issues that arise in an economic downturn using the case study of market practices during the COVID-19 global pandemic.

The Design of Annual Incentives

Design is the foundation of an effective annual incentive plan. Well-designed AIPs align with the company's business strategy and drive behaviors and decisions that improve corporate performance. Specifically, AIPs that work:

- Communicate and reinforce critical corporate objectives (both financial and non-financial)
- Align executive interests with those of stakeholders
- Allow executives to share in the success of the organization
- Reduce the company's fixed cost exposure in difficult financial years
- Encourage desired behaviors
- Provide competitive total compensation opportunities
- Create a sense of common purpose and teamwork
- Diminish entitlement mentality and ensure pay is linked to performance
- Attract and retain key employees
- Create greater differentiation in pay levels

Eight key questions should guide development of an annual incentive plan:

- What is the plan's purpose?
- Who will participate?
- What objectives, measures and standards align with the business strategy?
- What is a reasonable opportunity level?

- What is the payout range?
- How is an award payment calculated?
- How is the plan funded?

Plan Purpose

Well-run companies, from the board of directors to participating executives, understand and communicate exactly what the purpose of their annual incentive plan is — including linkage to business strategy and the role each individual participant plays in the achievement of plan metrics.

When implementing a new plan, reviewing an existing AIP, or modifying an ineffective plan, being able to articulate precisely what the plan is intended to achieve is critical to successful outcomes.

Plan Participation

Determining which executives should be eligible to participate in an annual incentive plan is a fundamental design issue.

Whether reviewing the current participation levels of an existing plan or recommending a totally new incentive program, a critical success factor for the plan will often begin with who is — and is not — eligible to participate.

A good place to start is a review of typical practices among similar types of companies. For example, according to past research from WorldatWork covering publicly traded companies, just shy of 100 percent of companies had an AIP covering their officers/executives and exempt salaried employees.

In addition to practices of peer organizations, Table 5-1 highlights some things to consider when determining eligibility.

Variations in Plan Design

Annual incentive plans vary across all industries and geographies. This section outlines some of the more common characteristics and combinations used in AIP design.

Performance standards play a key role in the design of variable compensation plans. Before a company determines performance measures, it is essential to determine the intended goals and

TABLE 5-1

Cost	What is the incremental cost of including additional employees? Is it cost prohibitive to include a broader population?
Multiple Plans	If a position is not eligible for a specific incentive plan, are they eligible for other programs?
Impact	What is the line of sight for a potential participant? Can this role sufficiently influence the performance measure(s)?
Internal Equity	Does eligibility vary for similar jobs in the organization? Is there a good reason that it does?
Precedent	Is it contrary to precedent to limit eligibility? What are the potential implications? Do the cost savings outweigh any potential employee communications/relations challenges?
Timing	When does eligibility begin? Specific considerations include new hires, promotions, transfers, full-time/part-time status, etc.
Performance Ratings	Is there a minimum acceptable performance rating for participation in the annual incentive plan?

outcomes of accomplishments (objectives) and how the results will be measured (standards).

Performance standards can be organized into six different categories, as demonstrated in Table 5-2.

Once performance standards are established, organizational metrics can be discussed. When selecting the performance measures to use, a company first should examine the business strategy and determine how it intends to achieve the business results.

There is no shortage of performance measures and in fact finding the appropriate balance among corporate, business unit and individual metrics is an ongoing challenge for most organizations.

There is a broad spectrum of potential AIP financial measures. One way to consider metrics is on the type of performance they assess: growth, return, or value based. See Table 5-3 for examples.

Most companies rely on three to five key performance measures, often combining strategic, financial and individual performance assessment measures.

TABLE 5-2

Budgeted Performance	■ AIP payouts are based on actual performance relative to budgeted performance. ■ The company's annual budgeting process defines the performance standard. ■ One fundamental question committees continually wrestle with is does budget = target? ■ Examples: Revenue versus budget, net income versus budget.
Capital/Value-Based Standard	■ AIP payouts are based on a rate of return required by investors in a company given the riskiness of the investment (cost of capital); the company must provide an expected return that compensates investors adequately for the risk they are assuming. ■ Examples: EVA, MVA, CFROIC
Long-Term Strategic Objectives	■ AIP payouts are based on achievement of the company's business plan; standards can be quantitative or qualitative. ■ Once determined, the standards are fixed over a pre-defined term. ■ Examples: Growth, ESG, completing a successful merger.
Strategic Milestones	■ A performance measure which, when attained, immediately triggers an incentive award payment. ■ Typically linked to strategic initiatives. ■ Examples: New product launch, ESG, profit milestone, etc.
Timeless Standard	■ AIP payouts are based on a return measure that remains consistent from year to year. ■ Examples: ROE, ROI, ROA
Year Over Year Growth	■ Performance target based on improvement over prior year's results. ■ Examples: EPS growth, net income growth

Considering Adjustments for Incentive Plan Calculation Purposes

An increasingly common practice is to use adjusted profit metrics (e.g., adjusted operating income, adjusted EBITDA) as metrics in annual incentive plans. Adjusted profit metrics are more ideal than GAAP items for AIP calculation because it can help normalize profit metrics by removing anomalies so that the results are not distorted by irregular gains or losses. This tends to more accurately reflect the performance of the company and provide for better year-over-year comparisons. Some common examples include: One-time gains or losses, changes in accounting or tax laws, litigation expenses, M&A,

TABLE 5-3

	Accounting-Based Measures	Economic-Based Measures
Growth	■ Revenue ■ Net Income ■ Assets	■ EBITDA ■ Operating Cash Flow ■ Free Cash Flow
Return	■ Return on Sales ■ Return on Equity ■ Return on Assets ■ Return on Net Assets	■ Return on Invested Capital ■ Return on Gross Assets ■ Return on Gross Net Assets
Value Based	■ Highlights value creation of each business unit ■ Useful when business units are in different stages of maturity ■ Useful when investors or finance require cost-of-capital as part of design	■ Economic Value Added (EVA) ■ Cash Flow Return on Investment (CFROI) ■ Residual income spread ■ Market value added (MVA)

goodwill impairments and foreign exchange. Recommendations are typically made to the compensation committee by management based on past practice and perceived appropriate treatment.

Once standards and specific metrics have been identified, a final step involves a series of calibration exercises which consider multiple stakeholder perspectives and should be used to develop realistic targets and ranges.

Individual Payout Opportunity

Annual incentive plans generally express individual award opportunities as a percent of base salary. The actual incentive payout received in any given year typically varies around a specified target percent.

A company can determine appropriate incentive targets through benchmarking and peer group analysis. Key considerations in setting target levels include:

■ Is the AIP target structure aligned with our corporate rewards philosophy?
■ Is the annual incentive opportunity competitive given:
  - Role (e.g., CEO, CFO, COO, CHRO, etc.)?
  - Common approaches used by peers?

TABLE 5-4

Management Level	Example: Incentive Target as Percent of Base Salary
Chief Executive Officer	100%
Second to Fifth Highest Paid	75%
Executive	50%
Manager	25%

- Who we compete with for the recruitment and retention of talent, business and capital?
- Does the individual payout opportunity create sufficient incentive to drive business outcomes?
- Does the AIP target structure adequately address internal equity considerations and equal pay considerations?

Measurement Level

The level at which an AIP measures (e.g., corporate, business unit, individual) and rewards performance can have a significant effect on its overall effectiveness. A company must determine at what level performance should be measured, as well as how it will differ by employee/group. For example, should support staff be held accountable for overall corporate performance? Or should the CEO's performance be measured against individual goals?

The company's unique strategy, operating structure and stage of maturity should have significant influence in the measurement levels chosen. To determine the appropriate balance, an organization should consider:

- Business unit profiles, growth prospects, stage of maturity
- Amount of interaction and interdependency between business units and corporate
- Degree to which an executive can control key performance measures at various levels
- Corporate culture

TABLE 5-5 Setting Performance Targets

External	Investor expectations help determine what level of financial, customer and operational performance is required to achieve a cost of capital return for investors and therefore increase shareholder value	Investor Expectations	Final Performance Standards
	Analyst expectations are useful in providing Wall Street's perspective of operating performance in the short term	Analyst Expectations	
	Peer analysis provides an external competitive perspective on the appropriate levels of performance	Peer Group Analysis	
Internal	Probability analysis is intended to provide a realistic assessment of achievement at various levels of performance for each metric, ensuring the AIP design balances value creation and achievability	Probability Analysis	
	Management expectations reflect the company's knowledge of future plans and budgets	Management Expectations	

Once the proper levels of measurement are defined, the next step is identifying the appropriate weighting. A company must decide how measures at each level should be combined to determine a final award payment and the degree of influence that discrete measures have on the overall payout.

There are multiple approaches but some of the more common approaches include: additive, multiplicative and matrixed.

Additive: In this weighting model, award payments are calculated separately for each performance measure. The result of each discrete calculation is added together to determine the final individual incentive payout. In this model, measures are independent of each other and those with greater importance to the organization carry a greater "weight" or proportion of the outcome than those with less critical importance.

This weighting model is useful when a company is interested in reinforcing a series of metrics without regard to other measurements. Because the measures are independent of each other, achievement under one category of measure does not negatively impact the other categories.

This model is also useful for complex organizations with multiple lines of business where the company has an interest in developing a framework for metrics that can be adapted as appropriate for each line of business.

Performance categories can be deployed consistently across the organization (e.g., growth + return), but actual metrics can be tailored to meet the unique needs of an individual business unit. This model also allows for modifications based on the organization level of employees covered by the plan.

Additive example:

TABLE 5-6

Measure	Weighting (% of Target Award)	Actual Performance	Weighting (% of Target Award)
A	40%	80%	80% x 40% = 32.0%
B	20%	120%	120% x 20% = 24.0%
C	30%	100%	100% x 30% = 30.0%
D	10%	100%	100% x 10% = 10.0%
	100% of Target		96.0% of Target

Multiplicative and Matrixed Approaches: In both of these weighting models, award payments are mathematically linked to reward for suitable performance against multiple measures simultaneously. The effect is a "trade-off" between measures, with the intent of creating a balanced approach to running the business.

In the multiplicative model, the payment amount from one measure is adjusted based on the performance of another measure.

In the matrixed model, a measure is used for the "X" axis and another is used for the "Y" axis. The actual payment amount is found by pinpointing the intersection representing the performance level against each measure.

These weighting models are useful when a company is interested in reinforcing equilibrium in business decision making (e.g., profit + growth) and when prioritization of decisions can have a very positive or negative impact on business results. Because the measures are dependent, achievement requires executives to consider the broad impact of decisions.

Multiplicative Example:

TABLE 5-7

1	2	3
Measure A	**Measure B Multiplier**	**Final Award**
Performance: 120% of objective	**Performance:** 110% of objective	**120% x 120% = 144%**
Payout: 120% of target award		

Measure B % of Goal	Measure B Multiplier
120+	170%
110%	120%
100%	80%
<80%	50%

Matrixed example:

TABLE 5-8

		Measure A Performance (% of Target				
		80%	90%	100%	110%	120%
Measure B Performance (% of Target	80%	80%	88%	95%	103%	110%
	90%	83%	90%	98%	105%	113%
	100%	85%	93%	100%	108%	115%
	110%	88%	95%	103%	110%	118%
	120%	90%	98%	105%	113%	120%

Payout Range

It is common practice to set a range of performance targets relative to the company's business plan for the current year (e.g., target achievement equals 100 percent of plan). The payout range therefore describes the range of performance outcomes for which incremental increases in performance will result in incremental increases in awards. The payout range helps provide guidance to a series of questions such as:

- What do plan participants earn if performance is above or below target?
- Should participants have more opportunity for incremental results above target performance levels? Should they receive proportionately less for results below?
- At what performance level should they begin to earn an incentive award?
- At what level (if any) should their award be limited (or capped)?

Because these decisions can have significant impact on actual incentive payments, the payout range, and operating guidelines around it, significantly influence executive behavior. Therefore, besides the performance target, the two most critical components of any payout range are:

- Threshold: the level of performance below which no incentive award is provided.
- Maximum: the level of performance above which no additional incremental awards are earned.

The payout range can be symmetrical or asymmetrical. A symmetrical range allows the threshold for payment at the same percentage below the target as the maximum is above it, whereas an asymmetrical payout range typically provides more upside potential to plan participants.

An asymmetrical payout range reflects a philosophy to reward proportionately more for performance that is above target and less for performance that falls below objectives. A critical consideration in determining appropriate leverage is the relative positioning of performance targets to industry norms.

FIGURE 5-9 **Symmetrical and Asymmetrical Payout Ranges**

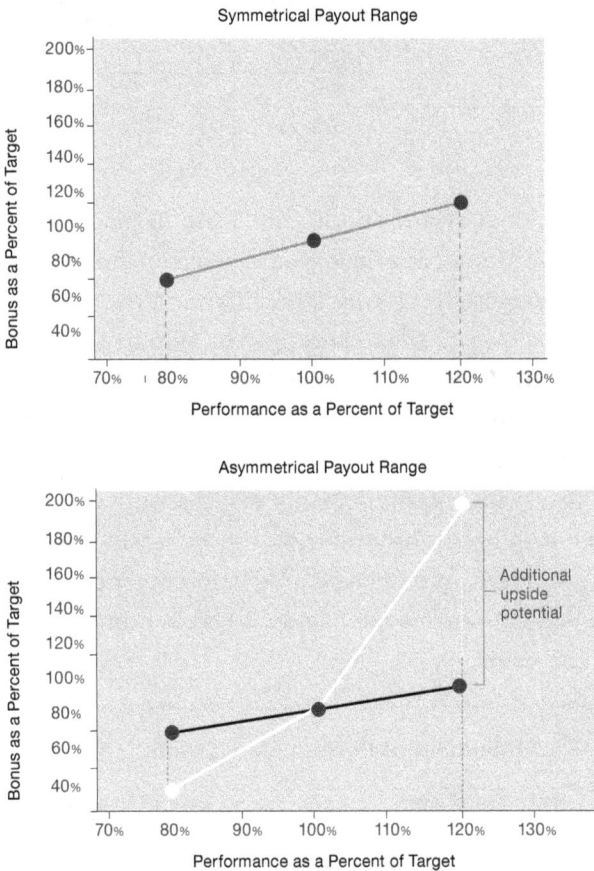

Symmetrical Payout Range

Asymmetrical Payout Range

If the performance targets are industry leading, the AIP could reflect higher-than-average opportunity with modest downside leverage and high upside leverage. Conversely, if the performance targets are within industry norms, high leverage may be appropriate on both sides of target.

For example, in the asymmetrical payout range shown in Figure 5-9, the company pays according to the following schedule.

At this point in the design process, plan standards have been established, participants have been identified, specific metrics have been

TABLE 5-10

	Performance as a % of Target	Bonus Payout as a % of Target
Threshold	80%	50%
Target	100%	100%
Maximum	120%	200%

chosen, individual award opportunities are in place, measurement levels are agreed upon, and the payout calculation formula is finalized.

Diligence suggests revisiting the calibration exercises completed during the performance standard process step to confirm that with all variables now identified, the plan has a realistic chance of success.

Participants must believe at the onset of the performance period that the goals have a reasonable likelihood of being achieved. If the goals are too stringent, participants will discount them and ignore the targets. If the goals are too easy, the plan will not drive stretch performance. From an employee motivation perspective, Table 5-11 lays out a general rule for the likelihood of attainment when setting performance goals.

TABLE 5-11 Attainment of Performance Levels

Performance Level	Odds of Attainment
Threshold	8 out of 10
Target	5-6 out of 10
Maximum (Stretch)	2 out of 10

Plan Funding

The way an organization funds its AIP plays an important role in achieving a fair balance between the interests of shareholders and plan participants. Funding for annual incentive plans is cash based and focuses on pools of money. There are two common approaches used to determine overall annual incentive plan funding:

- Sum of targets: the aggregate dollar amount of awards to be paid under the plan is determined by adding the target awards of all participants. Companies usually then modify the pool resulting from the aggregate targets based on a formal schedule relating to performance.

- Financial results-based sharing formula: a fund (or "pool") is established using a percentage of a financial measure (e.g., three percent of net income) or a percentage of a financial measure that exceeds a hurdle rate (e.g., five percent of net income in excess of an eight percent return on equity).

Both funding mechanisms have challenges. The sum of targets approach does not guarantee that incremental business performance will be adequate to cover the cost of the entire sum of target incentive payments. In theory, this means the company does not have the "ability to pay" these incentives. Conversely, the financial results-based formula is rigid with incentive payments made solely on financial performance. To address these challenges, many companies opt to use a combination of both approaches — top down (i.e., % of net income) and bottom-up (i.e., sum of targets).

For companies establishing a maximum pool, the most common method to express this is as a multiple or percentage of the target pool. It is not uncommon for a company to set an overall limit on the amount it will pay out in any one year. This limit sometimes is called a "stakeholder protection clause" because it protects stakeholders against possible windfall payments under the plan due to unforeseen events.

The Role of Management and the Board in Annual Incentive Plan Oversight

Over the past decades, a series of scandals created public and political perception that undue risk taking, in part driven by annual incentive schemes, was central to several economic downturns, including the 2008 financial crisis. This perception fueled an extensive legislative and regulatory focus on risk management and risk prevention. As a result, the SEC adopted disclosure rules requiring discussion in proxy statements of the board of directors' role in overseeing the relationship between a company's overall compensation policies and risk of scandalous behavior. Risk management and compensation have also received heightened focus from shareholder advisors, such as ISS.

Given these developments, oversight of annual incentive plans should be a priority for all compensation committees. While the compensation committee should not be involved in day-to-day management related to AIPs, directors should satisfy themselves that management has designed and implemented processes that (1) evaluate the nature of the risks inherent in compensation programs, (2) are consistent with the company's corporate strategy, (3) ensure proper governance and controls, and (4) foster a culture of risk-adjusted decision making throughout the organization.

Businesses necessarily incur risk in the pursuit of profits, and excessive risk aversion can be harmful to essential corporate goals. Periodic reviews by the compensation committee of annual incentive plans should attempt to ensure that the level of inherent risk is not excessive and is consistent with the corporation's articulated strategy.

A Note about IRC section 162(m)

The Tax Cuts and Jobs Act of 2017 (TCJA) upended public company compensation structures nationwide. Prior to the TCJA, Section 162(m) of the Internal Revenue Code of 1986, as amended, generally provided for a $1 million annual deduction limit for compensation paid to certain executives. This limit contained a carve-out that exempted performance-based compensation if it was paid under an arrangement that complied with strict rules regarding performance goals and plan governance. In an attempt to curb excess executive compensation, the TCJA amended Section 162(m) to eliminate the performance-based pay exemption. In addition, the TCJA expanded the deduction limit to include the CEO, CFO and the three most highly compensated officers (excluding the CEO and CFO). In 2021, the American Rescue Plan Act (ARPA) also increased the number of employees subject to the deduction limit. Beginning in 2027, Section 162(m) will expand to the five highest compensated employees beyond those specified by the TCJA. Given these two pieces of legislation, Section 162(m) will generally apply to the CEO, CFO and eight other highly compensated employees.

Dealing with Economic Turmoil

Case study: COVID-19 Global Pandemic

While there were echoes of the financial collapse of 2008, the economic pain from the COVID-19 pandemic was far wider and deeper. Fissures formed in entire industry sectors and millions of employees were terminated or furloughed. And yet the biggest casualties of the crisis were the hundreds of thousands of people who lost their lives, and the hundreds of thousands more who were hospitalized.

Given this social and economic backdrop, corporations around the world acted in unprecedented ways. They found ways to create new virtual work arrangements for large segments of their workforce. They kept employee well-being at the top of their priority list. They found new ways to stay connected to and interact with their customers.

Many CEOs and senior executives in the companies hardest hit by the COVID-19 crisis announced significant pay reductions of their own. Cutting pay for executives is a visible and potentially necessary step in stabilizing some companies as they manage through a crisis. It sends a positive message to both employees and shareholders, and could enhance, or at least limit the tarnishing of, the company's reputation. While some outside observers heralded these actions, others opined that they were too few and too limited.

Just as CEOs and other senior leaders must carefully weigh their decisions and approaches to implement pay cuts for the broad employee population, compensation committees must do the same with executive pay. Executive pay involves many more variables, and the approach and consequences (intended or otherwise) of possible changes must be carefully evaluated.

Four leadership behaviors and guideposts can help compensation committees in determining the best course of action during unprecedented social and economic turmoil:

Be Calm

There may be pressure for quick action. However, the business impact in these types of crises evolve daily. Stay strategic and above the frantic pace. Try to tune out wild speculation about a protracted depression or a snapback recovery, and deal with available facts. Do not make a rush to judgment.

Be Decisive

When the time comes for a decision, make it and move on. Companies do not have the luxury of discussing change over multiple quarters. The magnitude of the financial impact on their business does not allow it. That said, sometimes the best decision after studying the situation is to decide to act later.

Be Fair

Historically, executive pay actions have been disconnected from those for the broader workforce, both in quantum and decision rules. During the COVID-19 crisis, many companies sought to "flip the equation," to demonstrate that personal economic pain would be shared, and that CEOs and senior executives are subject to the first and most significant reductions in pay.

Most executive pay philosophy statements are silent on the issue of "fairness." Committees should consider including a clause addressing how the committee will assess and assure the fairness of various elements of the executive pay program and the decisions it will need to make each year and over time. How fairness is defined will depend on each company's business purpose. However, fairness suggests that CEOs and other top executives take the largest percentage reductions and for the longest duration, especially if job cuts are anticipated. Identify executive salary actions and communicate them clearly and broadly, preferably ahead of any broader pay or staffing actions.

Be Guided by Principles

Beyond fairness, companies that have adopted and abide by well-defined compensation strategies and that use systematic approaches to handling crises, exceptions, or discretionary decisions, are the ones that will generally make the best decisions in the long-term interests of the company and its many constituents and stakeholders.

Prioritize the Impact on Total Rewards

Prioritize the actions to take during a time of crisis. Adjustments will first involve base salary and any executive perquisites. These are the easy and obvious places to start and will generate cash savings the quickest.

Next in line is the annual incentive plan, where payments are usually and mostly denominated in cash, and then the long-term incentive and stock-based programs (which, by their nature, are measured over more than a year and should be the last area for change). And as any executive pay reductions are contemplated, the compensation committee should also assess adjustments to compensation for members of the board.

Determine if there is a need or perceived benefit to modifying the short-term incentive plan. Factors to consider are where the plan is in the performance cycle, how significantly the performance metrics are likely to be affected by the business downturn, what portion of target bonus is likely to be available to pay under various performance scenarios, and what the company's needs for cash are likely to be.

Depending on your answers to these questions, there are a variety of possible outcomes. If business impact has so far been light, you may decide to wait a quarter before deciding to make any changes. Other companies may decide to adopt a "stub plan" for the second half of the year when recovery is anticipated and develop metrics, goals, and pro-rated awards accordingly. Those facing significant business disruption may scrap their original plans and either commit to determining partial awards on a discretionary basis at year end, or scrap bonuses for the year in question altogether.

Companies deciding not to scrap their short-term incentive plan should consider building a framework for determining awards on a discretionary basis using two levers. First, making adjustments to the full-year metrics and second, applying overriding discretion to the formula-based payouts, taking into account a holistic view of company performance.

Also, some companies that benefited from the crises will need to consider adjusting or limiting outsized executive cash incentive awards resulting from spikes in revenue and profit generated. Just as some companies exercised positive discretion in adjusting awards for the negative impact of COVID-19, those that were positively affected by the health crisis considered negative discretion to dampen any unexpected windfalls from the positive impact on their business.

Consider the likely reactions of institutional investors and those who advise them. Also, given the nature of this type of crisis, consider reactions on "Main Street" and of the broader employee population. Well-informed and principled compensation committees, supported as needed by capable advisors, are in the best position to render decisions that are in the long-term best interests of the company and its stakeholders.

Assess the implications for the kinds of leaders you will need moving forward, and then determine the elements of the new rewards philosophy that aligns with the roles you will need them to play.

The compensation committee should commit to monitoring developments during this time and revisiting decisions made to evaluate if they continue to make sense and the need for any mid-course corrections. Economic turmoil creates a dynamic situation and requires continuous attention.

Compensation committees should plan to convene more often than in a "typical" year (at least quarterly during the current crisis) to review a scan of market developments and test current plans and processes.

Conclusion

The annual incentive says much about a company's business purpose. It can tell the world what the company wants to achieve and what it values. And, as such, careful deliberation is required to set eligibility, pay levels, metrics, the appropriate goal setting, and so on. In doing so, the committee must remember that the annual incentive is a means to an end. Incentives are a tool used to incentivize employees in building value for stakeholders.

CHAPTER 6

Public Company Long-Term Incentive Compensation: An Equity-Based Focus

By Tony Wu and Bryan Kligman

For senior executives at public companies, equity-based awards are usually the largest component of the pay package, often exceeding base salary and annual incentives by several multiples. Owing to the multi-year vesting periods and the potential for significant rewards, long-term incentives (LTIs) are a powerful and highly visible tool in retaining top executive talent. In addition, equity-based compensation is the principal agent in aligning company leadership with shareholders and reinforcing pay for performance.

In the 1980s through the early 2000s, stock options dominated LTI plans. More recently, changes in accounting, governance reforms, market downturns, shareholder scrutiny and concerns about high dilution levels have combined to alter both the design and use of LTIs. More than any other factor, however, the required expensing of stock options under accounting rules adopted in 2004 prompted significant strategic changes in LTI practices.

In addition to accounting rule changes, updated proxy requirements for compensation disclosure began drawing attention to practices and plans that previously might have been known only to a handful of company insiders and board members. Further, disclosure requirements demanded that companies explain why certain plan elements were used in addition to what existed. Thus, it became incumbent upon executives and compensation committees to rethink and re-evaluate their equity plans based on their specific business needs and strategies, all while taking into consideration how their shareholders were likely to view their plans.

Companies have broadened their approaches and applied a more strategic lens to LTIs and now often use a portfolio approach to making LTI grants by spreading more value over a combination of vehicles. The biggest gains have been seen in performance share unit awards (PSUs) that combine both share price increase and other key companywide performance to determine incentive value.

Many issues have to be addressed in designing LTI programs: the potential value of company shares, management's perception of share value, the optimum number of shares authorized for use, the effect of run rates and stock overhang, to name only a few. In this environment, setting performance goals has taken on a heightened importance in LTI design. Many companies are challenged just setting annual goals, let alone having to project multiple-year targets. Determining accurate performance measures that trigger appropriate plan payouts is, of course, crucial to the success of these plans, and often the most difficult. This chapter's objective is to provide practical insights on how companies can transition to a more balanced, strategic approach to LTIs.

This chapter:

- Examines how LTIs fit into an overall pay strategy and what compensation committees and senior management must do to address the share dilution and pay-for-performance issues relating to LTIs.
- Discusses the design flexibility available to companies seeking to include performance conditions in full-value stock awards. Considerations such as leverage, performance measures, goal setting, performance periods and eligibility for performance-vested plans also are addressed.
- Reviews the key accounting issues relating to LTIs, focusing on performance shares.
- Recommends that companies reconsider stock options in their LTI mix
- Suggests evaluation of stock options for efficiency and perceived value from both shareholder and executive perspectives.

Strategic Considerations for Long-Term Incentive Plans

Direct compensation in its many forms — base salary, annual bonuses and LTIs — is the single greatest expense for most companies in the United States. Accordingly, employee rewards represent a significant component of the financial strategy and decision process for any successful business.

Because the compensation system is such a large part of an organization's overall financial structure, it is strategic almost by definition. Nowhere is the strategic nature of the compensation program more evident than in the design of executive LTI programs. Specifically, an LTI program is:

- Likely the key element in a company's ability to attract and retain top executive talent — those individuals who develop and implement strategic business plans.
- Costly and creates significant multi-year liabilities, creating long-term commitments for the company.
- Highly visible; no board of directors or compensation committee wants to be in the position of defending compensation practices leading to excessive pay that have been reported at some well-known and respected organizations.

With the increases in proxy-related disclosure requirements, shareholders of public companies gained more and better information with which to evaluate a company's LTI program. As these shareholders began paying more attention to these disclosures, and as they were given more power with which to affect a company's compensation decision making, LTI practices began changing. Gone are the days in which companies would simply disclose that their program designs were a function of market practices and competitiveness; the SEC and shareholders began demanding that companies demonstrate the link between their programs and their strategy. Proxy advisers have also played their part in shaping LTI design as winning over shareholder support continues to be important to companies in the say-on-pay era.

Understanding Constraints in Granting Long-Term Incentives

LTI issues go beyond pure compensation design. They introduce issues relating to accounting, tax and use of a company's share pool — each of which provides some constraints. LTI awards entail real expense and potential dilution of shareholder value, adding levels of complexity when compared to other elements of the executive pay package.

These constraints are critical for all companies to understand as they look to balance their HR objectives with the cold, hard facts of their LTIs' effect on financials and share availability.

Key questions in this process include:

- How many shares are available for the company to grant?
- When will the available pool of shares be depleted?
- What is the company's current stock overhang relative to peer and shareholder benchmarks?
- What will be the expense impact of each type of share granted? How well does that expense correlate to perceived value on the part of recipients?
- What are the tax implications — to the recipient as well as the company — of the different LTI vehicles being considered?

Knowing the Hot Buttons

The landscape for LTI compensation changes annually, and every company needs to know what market trends suggest and what shareholders watch. As the largest part of an executive's compensation package, LTIs tend to attract significant shareholder attention on issues that relate to dilution of their share value and the pay-for-performance orientation of the company's program.

Some of the key questions companies need to ask regularly go right to the heart of these hot buttons:

- What is the right level of shares for the company to use annually (i.e., run rate)?
- Do additional equity grants provide additional motivation or retention value to an executive who already has a significant stake in the business?

- Do executives own enough shares to demonstrate adequate alignment with shareholders? Are the company's share ownership and retention guidelines/requirements set at the right levels?
- How long is "long term"? Should changes be considered that better align the vesting of these incentives with the time horizon for the company's business challenges?
- How much (if any) of the company's LTI mix should be performance vested vs. service vested?
- What should happen to unvested shares upon termination? Should they vest immediately, continue to vest, or not vest at all?
- What should happen to unvested shares upon a change in control? Should they vest immediately or continue to vest?
- To what extent does the LTI design "check the box" from a proxy adviser perspective?

While none of these questions necessarily have a single right answer for every company, many shareholders will have strong opinions on them. No compensation committee should ever be surprised by shareholders' reaction to its company's LTI program, which puts pressure on the compensation team to ensure that each and every one of these issues is given adequate attention and planning.

Performance Shares and Performance-Based Restricted Stock

Regulatory and corporate governance developments, combined with the refinement of a key design feature, have breathed new life into the use of PSUs in LTI programs. Full-value stock award plans like restricted stock — long-favored by recipients but often loathed by skeptical investors — have shown an increase in use since the stock option expensing rules changes. Today, however, the inclusion of performance criteria is an essential feature in these plans to meet shareholder demands for good governance and paying for performance.

Service-Based, Full-Value Plans (Restricted Stock and Restricted Stock Units)

Executives who receive traditional service-based, full-value awards are generally granted as either restricted stock (RS) or restricted stock unit (RSU) awards.

- **RS**: Award of actual shares with current ownership rights and subject to vesting (based on time and/or performance). Actual shares are issued at the grant date (with a restrictive legend on any certificate) but typically held by the company or in escrow until vesting. RS cannot be transferred until vested. Recipients are generally treated similarly to actual shareholders as both dividend and voting rights typically accompany such vehicle.

- **RSU**: Award of units (a bookkeeping account) representing a contractual right (but no current ownership rights) to receive payment (generally in shares but may be made in cash) at some point after vesting. No shares are issued until the time of actual payout/delivery (assuming equity "settlement"). RSUs cannot be transferred until they are converted into actual shares. Since the award of an RSU is essentially a contractual promise to pay at some time in the future with no shares actually issued upon grant, they do not have dividend or voting rights, although companies may provide "dividend equivalents" to mirror the availability of dividends on RS.

These awards entitle executives to actual shares or the right to shares of company stock, usually without cost, once prescribed terms and conditions are satisfied. In conventional practice, terms and conditions were limited to time-based vesting. Stay on the job for, say, four years, and the unit or stock becomes yours, either ratably over time (graded vesting) or all at once (cliff vesting) at the end of the restriction period.

All in all, this tends to be a good deal for the executive. The downside is limited (restricted stock/units do not go underwater), and the cost cannot be beat (by contrast, an executive must pay the exercise price for a stock option). Once restrictions lapse, the executive may sell shares or use cash (often from bonuses) to pay the resulting tax (at the time of vesting in the case of RS and actual payout/delivery in the case of RSUs). However, from the viewpoint of wary investors, this often is deemed too good of a deal; they tend to want to see more executive skin in the game and performance hurdles that are more robust than merely staying employed.

In concert with the increased use of full-value awards over the last decade (starting with the adoption of accounting changes under FAS 123R, now Accounting Standards Codification (ASC) Topic 718), RSUs have replaced RS as the favored type of full-value equity award for employers. The rationale for this trend can be found in one word — flexibility. From both design and administration perspectives, RSUs offer more flexibility than RS.

Adding Performance Conditions to Full-Value Awards

Recently, the use of PSUs has surged for a combination of reasons. First, aforementioned changes in the accounting rules eliminated a compelling advantage in favor of stock options by requiring companies to recognize a charge to earnings on fixed option grants issued at fair market value. This heavily debated action evened the playing field for other compensatory equity-based programs with stock options from an accounting perspective.

Additionally, with shareholders becoming more involved in all matters relating to executive pay, companies became more focused on the levels of dilution that resulted when the majority of LTIs were granted through stock options. Using PSUs or RSUs helps conserve shares because companies obtain more mileage from the full value of a restricted share than from the fair value of a stock option, which always will be worth less than the underlying price of the stock.

Most notably, PSUs are designed in part to respond to the perceived lack of pay-for-performance orientation from which service-vested vehicles suffer. PSUs provide a more direct link to performance than stock options or other service-based LTI vehicles by using two different levers to align pay and performance: the accomplishment of key goals (typically financial, operational or shareholder driven) that determine how many shares are earned, combined with the value of those shares earned at the end of the cycle.

PSUs are now viewed favorably by external constituencies, particularly when used as the dominant vehicle in an LTI program. At many of the largest U.S. public companies, CEOs and other C-suite executives often receive more than half of their TDC in the form of LTIs. In this pay mix, PSUs increasingly comprise at least 50 percent of the overall LTI value.

Designing Performance Share Plans

One key benefit of a PSU is the considerable design flexibility offered. However, before a PSU can be rolled out, numerous design features have to be thought through (including details). Given the significant organizational, employee and shareholder implications associated with PSUs, companies need to get it right when designing, implementing and communicating these programs. There is no one-size-fits-all approach to PSU design; rather it should support and promote each organization's unique business strategy and compensation philosophy while aligning with the interests of key stakeholders.

Leverage

PSUs usually have a degree of leverage, which refers to the relationship between performance and payout levels. Typically, these plans operate similarly to annual incentive programs in that there are scaled payouts available for performance that is both below and above target goals.

Many PSU programs contain the following three levels of performance and corresponding common payout levels (i.e., the performance/payout calibration):

- **Threshold**. A floor that represents the minimum level of performance that must be achieved before PSUs can be earned. For an absolute financial performance measures, threshold performance is generally in the range of 80 to 90 percent of target. For a relative performance measure (e.g., relative TSR), threshold performance is generally set around the 25th-35th percentile versus the applicable comparator group. In each of these cases, the threshold payout level is generally 25 to 50 percent of target.

- **Target**. The expected or planned (budgeted) level of PSU performance achievement and payout. For an absolute financial performance measure, 100 percent of plan/budget typically equals a 100 percent payout. For a relative performance measure, target is often set at the 50th percentile (median) versus the applicable comparator group, equating to a 100 percent payout. More recently, some companies are setting relative target performance standards at a higher bar (i.e., 60th percentile) in response to proxy advisers criticizing target payout for median level performance.

- **Maximum**. The total PSU opportunity that may be earned for superior performance, sometimes referred to as a cap. For an absolute financial performance measure, maximum performance is generally in the range of 110 to 120 percent of target. For a relative TSR performance measure, maximum performance is generally set around the 75th percentile (or higher) versus the applicable comparator group. In each of these cases, the maximum payout level is often 150 to 200 percent of target. In an effort to provide "fairness" and better align with shareholders, PSUs using relative TSR may include a limit on payout at target levels when an organization's TSR is negative over the performance period, but relative performance would have resulted in above-target/maximum payouts.

A common leverage curve provides something on the order of 50 percent of target shares for achievement of threshold performance, and 150 or 200 percent of target shares for achievement of stretch performance. (See Figure 6-1 on page 104.)

In both examples, shares are earned at a faster pace for incremental performance above target levels than they are below target levels. Achieving the right leverage relationship should be a function of a company's overall pay philosophy, business strategy and performance orientation. For example, a more leveraged curve may be appropriate for entrepreneurial organizations where executives are expected to take on more risk in an effort to drive the success of the business. In these situations, executives would be more generously rewarded for outstanding performance, but held more accountable for below-target

TABLE 6-1 Examples of Varying Performance Share Plan Leverages

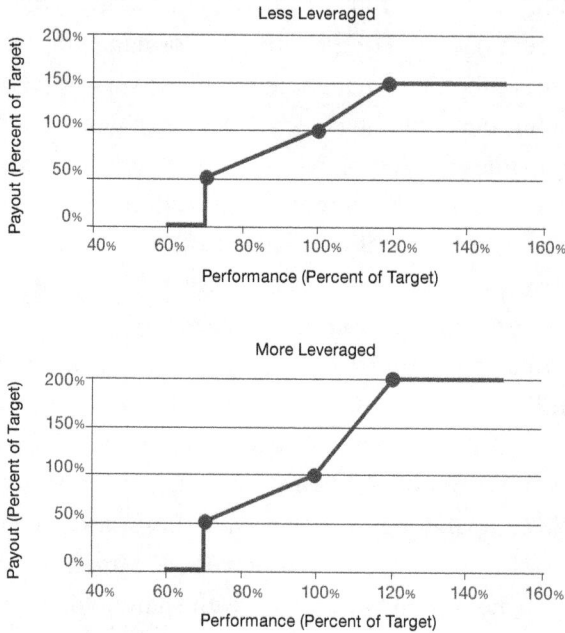

Less Leveraged

Payout (Percent of Target)

Performance (Percent of Target)

More Leveraged

Payout (Percent of Target)

Performance (Percent of Target)

performance. A flatter leverage curve, on the other hand, might be appropriate for a company with a less leveraged business strategy.

Performance Measures

A primary challenge with using performance shares is the difficulty in setting reasonably difficult yet achievable goals for an extended time. To fix goals, companies often rely on the forecasting abilities of their finance and strategic planning teams to develop realistic projections. However, while many companies use objectives that are absolute in nature, goals also can be relative.

Absolute goals are typically financial in nature but, increasingly, companies are adopting more strategic measurements that capture needed longer-term business transformations (e.g., sales or market share growth in a key product category). Relative goals are typically financial or stock price based and look to compare the company's performance against a peer group or broader index (e.g., the company's total shareholder return or top-line growth versus its peer group). Many companies use both absolute and relative measures to balance the benefits and drawbacks of each approach.

While there is a debate about the use of objective and subjective measures in annual incentive plans, most long-term plans make use of only objective measures that are easily measurable. The accounting rules penalize equity-based awards that are not based on the objective performance criteria, requiring such grants to be treated with liability accounting instead of the preferred equity accounting treatment.

Goal Setting

Many companies have difficulty determining whether the respective goal levels being proposed are reasonable; if goals are not properly set, the degree of pay and performance alignment may be skewed too far up or down. Easy goals may result in overpayment for under-performance, while stretch goals may result in under-payment or non-payment for performance that should warrant some payout.

When setting goal levels, several key parameters that drive the process and outcomes should be considered: a company's strategic plan, external performance expectations from shareholders and the market, internal performance expectations from participants (i.e., do the goals have a reasonable likelihood of being achieved?) and the odds of attaining different outcomes. As a general rule of thumb, threshold performance levels should be achieved about 80% of the time, target performance levels should be achieved about 50-60% of the time, and maximum performance levels should be achieved about 20%. Examining historical levels of short- and/or long-term performance achievements may help provide some insight on the degree of difficulty of past goal-setting practices. For example, if actual performance achievements are frequently skewed toward maximum or threshold performance levels over the last five performance cycles, then some recalibration may be warranted.

Eligibility

Performance share plans typically have been limited to senior executives as they represent the key players in driving the success of the business and may cascade one to three levels down depending upon various factors such as the company's size, structure, business/compensation strategy and compensation philosophy. For example, a company with $500 million in revenue and a flat organizational structure may limit PSU eligibility to C-suite executives only; in comparison, a company with $20 billion in revenue and a multi-layer structure may provide PSU to all employees at the vice president level and above. Employees below the vice president level may not always grasp the performance share design concept as it relates to their own positions. The less a participant understands about the award and the less ability to influence the outcomes, the less value that he/she ascribes to the award.

Performance Period

Most plans tend to include a three-year performance period, which is a function of the maximum length of time in which many companies are comfortable forecasting performance, as well as what is considered to be a market-standard vesting period. However, there are plans in the marketplace that are designed from one to five years. Such plans should maintain some alignment with the time horizon of the company's strategic challenges.

Accounting Considerations

A company's financial statements often affect the types of incentive compensation provided to executives. Accordingly, key accounting considerations may influence awards of performance shares.

ASC Topic 718 requires that all equity-based compensation granted to employees be accounted for at fair value, measured at grant date. Stock-based awards, including stock options and full-value share plans — whether time or performance vested — are classified as equity awards (as opposed to liability awards), assuming payments are settled solely in company stock. Dividends or dividend equivalents (if any) paid during the vesting or performance period are not recognized as additional compensation cost unless the underlying awards are subsequently forfeited and the dividends are not repaid.

However, accounting implications vary depending on the type of measures selected, probability of achievement and leverage.

Performance Conditions

For awards that may vary on the basis of performance conditions (as opposed to market conditions), accruals are recognized over the amortization period and are intended to reflect the probable payout outcome. At the end of each reporting period, the company has to assess the likely performance outcome. Expense recognition then tracks payout amounts based on this estimated performance outcome until the next period when this process is repeated.

If the probable performance outcome changes during the subsequent reporting period, expense accruals need to be adjusted to track new estimated corresponding payouts. Because the number of shares that can be earned likely will differ from target levels, the tracking of awards can cause volatility in compensation expense, as predictions for the likely outcome of shares earned will vary by reporting period. Expense accruals will fluctuate over the course of the performance period depending on whether probable performance outcomes go up or down. (See Figure 6-2.) One advantage of linking PSU to a performance condition is the reversal of the expenses if the performance condition is not met. Examples of performance conditions include revenue, earnings, cash flow or return-based efficiency measures (e.g., return on equity).

TABLE 6-2 **Expense Accruals and Performance Award Outcomes**

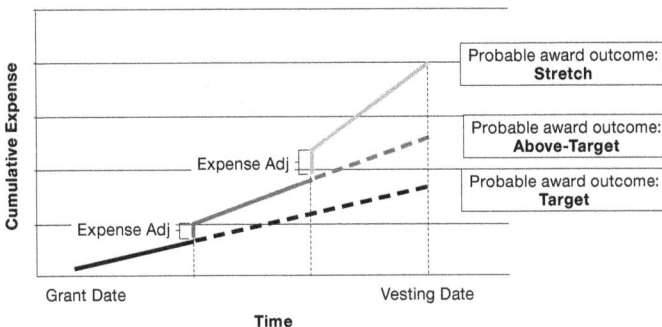

Market Conditions

For performance awards that may vary on the basis of market conditions (in which the stock price is a factor in triggering the award's vesting), the grant-date fair value is determined based on a Monte Carlo valuation model, simulating all possible outcomes over the term of the award. The resulting output is a single value incorporating the economic effect of the market condition over time. Expense is fixed at grant date and amortized over the performance period. (See Figure 6-3.) The expense is irreversible if the market condition is not met. Examples of market conditions include stock price and total shareholder return.

Other Considerations

Other design implications for a PSU are:

- **Share usage**. Performance shares are full-value awards and often are counted as more than one share toward the equity pool (i.e., shares available for award issuance) for the share usage and ISS' calculations. Depending on the plan's leverage curve, companies typically reserve their shares at stretch payout levels up front to ensure that the number of shares required is available at the time of payout. If the actual number of shares paid out is less than reserved, the excess number of shares reserved is available for future grants. Burn rate is closely monitored by many institutional shareholders so companies should be mindful of its share usage relative to market-standard levels.

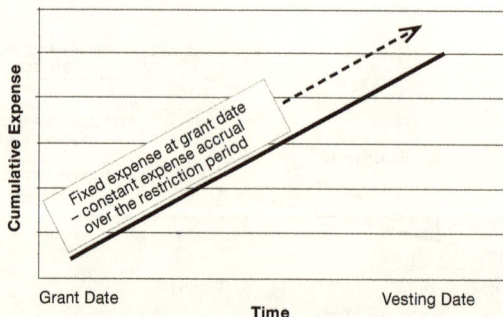

TABLE 6-3 **Fixed Expense Accrual**

- **Number of tranches**. The number of award tranches also has an effect on the ultimate design. Assuming a three-year performance period, a company may issue one award tranche at grant that spans the entire performance period, or three award tranches, one tranche at the beginning of each year of the performance cycle. One award tranche simplifies the accounting requirements, as this award is considered to only have one grant-date fair value. The latter, multi-award tranche design requires the company to determine a grant-date fair value for each award tranche. This not only adds to the accounting complexity, but the administrative complexity as well (e.g., tracking of performance for each award tranche).

- **Grant process**. LTI awards typically are granted annually. With such an approach, multiple awards overlap, therefore creating "glue" in the position. Executives are less willing to leave three award cycles on the table if another opportunity presents itself. However, with three award cycles come three sets of overlapping performance measures. A commitment generally must be made to the nature of metrics selected, as vastly different overlapping metrics may dilute the performance message. Executives may be confused as to which goals they should place their attention and focus.

Growing Use of Performance Shares

Performance shares continue to play a prominent role in an executive's total compensation package as pay for performance, corporate accountability and shareholder value creation have increasingly become focal points in today's executive compensation environment. Performance shares clearly have an advantage over time-vested equity vehicles. Design flexibility, a direct link to performance, favorable accounting treatment and the perceptions of shareholders have made performance shares a favored long-term incentive compensation delivery vehicle in the boardroom. However, a properly designed plan requires careful thought, rigorous modeling and refinement, as even the slightest design decision may have lasting program implications. While the complexities may seem overwhelming, PSUs are increasingly viewed as the best answer in balancing executive pay, shareholder interests and financial performance.

Stock Options' Place in the LTI Portfolio

In recent years we have seen a greater shift toward performance shares and away from stock options. In addition to the perceived value concerns and accounting implications of options falling "underwater" discussed above, influential proxy advisors like ISS do not view options issued at fair market value as "performance-based" vehicles. Meanwhile, performance shares are typically seen by boards as more flexible, less dilutive, more performance-oriented and ISS-friendly than stock options.

As a result of this trend, public companies and their executives have ended up with a somewhat standard compensation package: base salary, annual cash bonus and an annual equity-based grant that is typically split between time- and performance-vesting stock, both of which have three-year vesting periods. Options typically have a three- to four-year vesting period and a ten-year term, so executives typically hold them beyond three years before exercising to allow time for the stock price to appreciate. As companies continue to shift away from options in favor of full-value shares, the potential "tenure" of the LTI portfolio has therefore grown shorter and shorter.

One potential solution to the "shortening" of the LTI time horizon is for companies to take a portfolio approach of granting multiple vehicles, including stock options as well as time- and performance-vesting shares. Constructing an LTI package consisting of all these vehicles has many advantages, as each component award can address somewhat different LTI goals. Performance-based restricted stock yield strategy alignment over the performance measurement period and address the objectives of corporate pay-for-performance goals and shareholder alignment. Time-vesting restricted stock can aid retention while also providing shareholder alignment. Stock options offer a long-term outlook, strong alignment with stock price growth and the ability for the executive to time the income tax event.

Stock Option Efficiency and Perceived Value

There are several factors to consider before adding stock options to a long-term incentive program. Stock option efficiency (from both a shareholder and an employee perspective) as well as perceptions of value are among major topics to evaluate.

Stock options have low share-usage efficiency relative to other equity vehicles. To deliver the same expected equity value to employees, a company has to grant significantly more stock options than full-value restricted shares, which have built-in value at grant.

Since the introduction of stock option expensing, companies must consider the expense efficiency of stock options. In this process, two critical questions are being asked about their LTI plans:

- What is the stock option value actually realized by employee per dollar of expense? While stock options have the potential to deliver significant value to option holders, they may have zero realizable value unless they are in the money when exercisable. In companies where share price performance is poor, companies will incur expense for a vehicle that delivers no value to employees.

- What is the gap between the perceived value of stock options and the expense taken by the company? The binomial and Black-Scholes stock option valuation models provide an expected value of stock options. In theory, stock option recipients should value these options at the same levels produced by the valuation models. In reality, however, an employee's perception of the stock option value is typically much less than the expense value, creating a potentially significant inefficiency.

Perceived Value

For certain employees at some companies, the perceived value of stock options can be less than 50 percent of the option valuation. This means that, for every dollar of stock option value granted, the recipient credits the company with delivering less than 50 cents of value. Simply put, the employee would believe that a cash payment of 50 cents or less would be a fair exchange for a stock option grant.

The degree to which this discount exists involves a number of factors, including:

- The company's recent share price history. For companies with strong share price history where stock options have vested in the money, the perceived value of stock options is likely to be much higher than in companies with stagnant price history.

- Salary level and personal wealth situation. Highly paid employees such as executives tend to value stock options higher than lower-paid employees. In large part, this perception may be due to the fact that lower-paid employees generally have nearer-term cash needs and are more inclined to focus on the potential that a grant may yield little or no gain.
- Personal risk profile. Employees who are risk averse will place less value on vehicles that have the potential to finish underwater.

Examples of Perceived Value

Company A: Changing the LTI Mix to Increase Perceived Value

Company A is considering a move from stock options to time-vested restricted stock and wants to increase the perceived value of the LTI grant while maintaining the same current expense. The company grants an employee $90,000 worth of LTI value through 30,000 stock options, with a $9 current share price and a $3 option valuation.

However, the company's recent share price performance has been modest. Some previous grants are currently underwater, and an internal survey finds that most employees value the stock options significantly less than the expense value

would suggest, discounting the expense value by approximately 33 percent (for a value of $2 per stock option). As a result, the employee values the $90,000 grant at approximately $60,000.

In switching to time-vested restricted stock, the expense value of each restricted share will be $9, or three times each stock option, utilizing 10,000 shares to create an LTI grant with the same $90,000 expense. A survey by the company determines that employees tend to give roughly a 12 percent "haircut" to restricted shares (or $8 per option), for a perceived value of $80,000.

Company A	Value Granted	Share Price	Expense Valuation	Perceived Value	Number of Shares Needed	Expense Taken	Perceived Value
Stock Options	$90,000	$9	$3	$2	30,000	$90,000	$60,000
Restricted Stock	$90,000	$9	$9	$8	10,000	$90,000	$80,000

For Company A, this switch from options to restricted shares results in an increase in the perceived value of the grant by $20,000, while maintaining the same expense.

As companies begin looking at alternatives to stock options, it is imperative that they consider perceived value at different levels of their own organizations. Understanding how employees value these vehicles can provide significant opportunity to create LTI packages that increase perceived value, reduce share usage, limit expense and/or provide greater expense efficiency. (See "Examples of Perceived Value.")

Company B: Changing the LTI Mix to Reduce Expense

Company B is similar in all ways to Company A, but rather than looking to create the same expense, the company wants to re-create the same perceived value.

At Company A, time-vested restricted shares were substituted for stock options based on the expense relationship of $9 to $3, or a 3:1 ratio. However, when we look at the perceived value of the two vehicles — $8 for restricted shares and $2 for stock options — we see that these actually relate in a 4:1 ratio. Using the 4:1 ratio translates into a conversion of only 7,500 time-vested restricted shares, down from 10,000 at Company A.

Company B	# of Shares Granted	Share Price	Expense Valuation per Share	Perceived Value	Expense Taken	Perceived Value
Stock Options	30,000	$9	$3	$2	$90,000	$60,000
Restricted Stock	7,500	$9	$9	$8	$67,500	$60,000

Here, Company B has created the same perceived value, while reducing the expense of the LTI program by $22,500.

Share Conversion Ratios

As in Company A in "Examples of Perceived Value," many employers have long used a standard 3:1 stock option to time-vested restricted share conversion ratio based on the approximate expense relationship. For companies where the perceived value of stock options is relatively high, this ratio can re-create the perceived value.

However, in companies where the perceived value is significantly lower than the expense relationship — like Companies A and B — there is an opportunity to either increase perceived value or reduce expense. As illustrated, Company A was able to increase the perceived value of the grants with a 3:1 conversion, while Company B was able to reduce the expense of the grants with a 4:1 conversion.

Final Considerations

Each company has different needs, business objectives, employee mixes and shareholders. Compensation committees need to look at various considerations involving expense, share usage, retention concerns, perceived value, company performance and performance leverage to determine the right course for their organization. The one-size-fits-all approach is rarely a viable one.

As a starting point, however, companies need to understand how various vehicles support the execution of their business strategy, the extent to which employees value the different LTI vehicles being presented to them, and their alignment with shareholder value creation. By considering this information and assessing the degree of emphasis needed to be placed on each factor, companies and their boards will be best able to achieve the optimal portfolio.

CHAPTER 7

Long-Term Incentive Compensation in Private Companies and Business Units

By Daniel Moynihan and Theo Sharp

The competition for talent between publicly traded businesses and privately held businesses has never been fiercer. How you compensate key employees is an important factor in successfully attracting, retaining and motivating them for the long term. As such, long-term incentive (LTI) pay is a critical component of most executive compensation packages. LTIs can help recruit and retain high-performing executives, encourage specific executive behaviors and align executive financial interests with those of shareholders. In addition, LTIs can focus executives on what is best for the organization well into the future and, if well-designed, promote superior corporate performance that directly benefits shareholders. Employers are seeking methods of compensating executives that are based on sustained, long-term performance. And, there is increasing need to focus beyond the short term, and align private company executives with long-term value creation in the business.

While there are some differences, the basic objectives for LTI programs hold true for both public and private companies. Public companies have considerable flexibility in designing LTI programs through stock options, restricted stock, performance shares, phantom plans and other forms of equity compensation, as well as cash programs. Private companies often must compete with public companies for talent and want executives to make decisions as if they have the same economic interests as the owners. Ongoing equity grants, however, are not usually effective, or, in many cases, desired in private companies. In these businesses, equity generally is illiquid and subject to numerous restrictions that cause executives to substantially discount the value they place on any such awards. Also, founder-owners (or their families) are seldom willing to dilute their ownership stakes. This often leads these businesses down the road of some alternative to equity, and the creation of a cash-based LTI plan for their executives.

The following pages focus on approaches to non-equity LTIs specifically designed for private companies and the business units within public companies where compensation strategy dictates that LTIs focus on business unit rather than corporate performance.

This chapter:

- Explains why a performance unit plan is a viable LTI for a private company and what financial and nonfinancial performance measures may be used in the plan design. We illustrate how performance unit plans work through two examples — a single performance factor example and a matrix example.
- Describes a value creation plan, an easy-to-administer and easy-to-understand LTI vehicle in which participants share in an incentive pool that varies up or down based on company or business unit "economic profit." Using an example, an explanation is provided about how a measure of profit is defined and how the incentive pool is determined and awarded.
- Provides an overview of how phantom equity is used in private companies, as well as within the business units of publicly traded businesses.

The Performance Unit Plan Alternative

Performance unit plans (PUPs) often make good sense for private companies. They are one of the available performance plans that link cash payments to the operating performance of the company during a multi-year performance period. Unlike annual bonuses, PUPs tie financial rewards to the company's long-term performance while avoiding prolonged financial obligations.

Under a typical PUP, participants receive a fixed number of performance units, each with a target value. Each grant of performance units relates to a performance period that typically stretches over a three- to five-year horizon. The final value of the units at the end of the cycle correlates with the achievement of pre-established performance objectives. Depending on the company's objectives, performance periods may run sequentially (end to end) or may overlap. Research shows that overlapping plans are more commonly used, but the end-to-end style has its place as well.

Performance Measurement

A PUP relies upon carefully selected performance measures to evaluate executives' contributions. Performance measures must be well understood, and performance expectations must be well communicated if a program is to be effective. A properly designed PUP focuses executives on achieving desired results and promoting actions consistent with the business strategy. Ideally, these measurements will be different from those in the annual plan, and will be directly tied to the strategic plan and vision for the business.

Financial and Nonfinancial Performance Measures

Nonfinancial measures can be quantitative (e.g., market share, product mix, productivity, cost position) or qualitative (e.g., customer satisfaction, quality, service level, process excellence).

Financial measures are more traditional and typically found on company accounting statements. They typically are income-based (e.g., net income, operating income, earnings per share, revenue) or return-based (e.g., return on equity, return on assets, return on capital).

The overriding role of financial performance is to link behavior with value creation. As this link becomes more straightforward and transparent, the measures generally become more effective. The selection of financial measures often requires a balance between accuracy and complexity. The financial measures that most accurately reflect the value of the company tend to be the ones that are the most complex.

What and How to Measure

The performance measurement involves two decisions: what to measure and how to measure. Performance measures identify what to measure, and performance goals determine how to measure by establishing target levels of performance. Goals can be established using internal or external benchmarks. While internal benchmarks (or absolute goal-setting method) have been the most common approach, external standards (or relative goal-setting method) are becoming more prevalent.

At the end of the performance period, actual performance against objectives is evaluated. Based on this evaluation, the performance unit value is determined. Each unit has a target value if the plan's target performance is achieved for the period. The actual performance unit value varies depending upon the long-term performance during the period. It is common in most plans to have a threshold performance level so that the performance unit has no value if the threshold level is not achieved. A performance range is set, which determines the payout at threshold, target and maximum levels. The unit value for threshold performance typically is 50 percent of target value. Likewise, a maximum performance level is established correlating to a maximum unit value, which commonly is set at 150 to 200 percent of the target value.

Single Performance Factor Example

In the single performance factor approach, only one measure is used to determine the incentive payout. While perhaps the simplest structure (because it uses only one measure), it does not diversify an executive's incentive opportunity. (See Figure 7-1.)

In this example, the awards are generated in a range of zero to 150 percent the target award based upon sales growth performance versus goal. Under other designs, multiple factors may be considered with the total payout opportunity representing the sum of performance on all measures.

FIGURE 7-1 Single Performance Factor Example

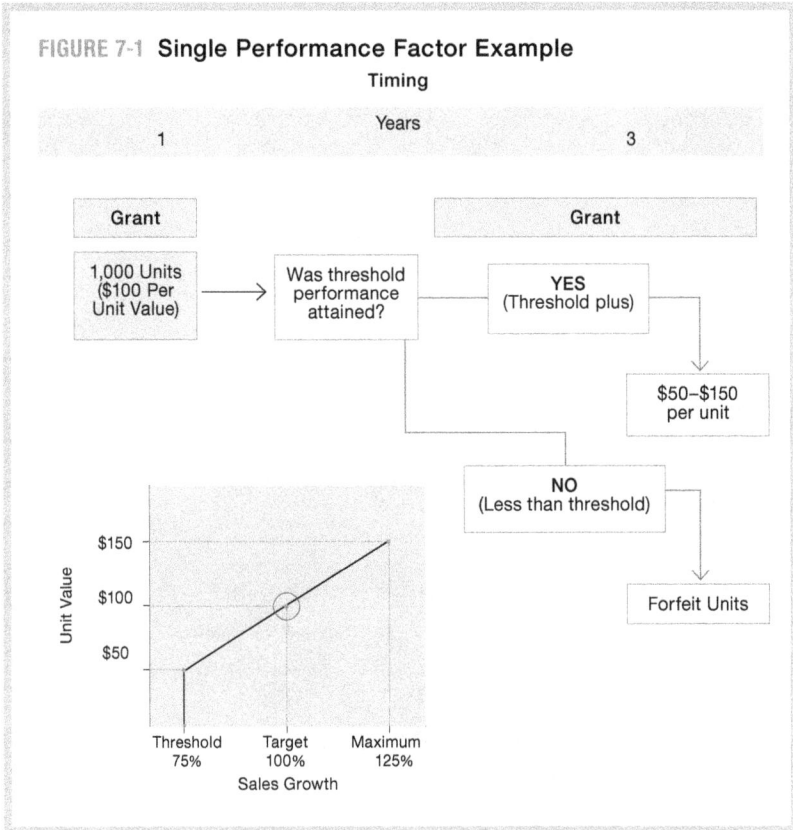

Matrix Example

In a matrix approach, two measures are used to determine the incentive payout. This method is more complex than the single factor, and an advantage is that the combination of the two measures can be weighted differently at varying performance levels to reflect strategic priorities. (See Figure 7-2.)

Looking at a matrix of performance measures, if a company was below target in sales but above target in earnings before interest and taxes (EBIT) margin, the plan still can pay out at 100 percent of target (See "Advantages and Disadvantages of PUPs").

Overall, a PUP can be easy to administer and explain, and it provides an alternative to a stock-based program in which such an equity award is not practical or desirable.

FIGURE 7-2 Matrix Using Sales and EBIT Margin

EBIT Margin Performance	0% Payout ↕	95% $0.950 billion	97.5% $0.975 billion	100% $1 billion
110% / 11%		$104.5 MM / 100%	$107.25 MM / 125%	$110 MM / 150%
105% / 10.5%		$99.75 MM / 75%	102.38 MM / 100%	$105 MM / 125%
100% / 10%		$95 MM / 50%	$97.5 MM / 75%	$100 MM / 100%
95% / 9.5%		$90.25 MM / 37.5%	$92.63 MM / 50%	$95 MM / 75%
90% / 9%		$85.5 MM / 25%	$87.75 MM / 37.5%	$90 MM / 50%

← 0% Payout

Sales Performance

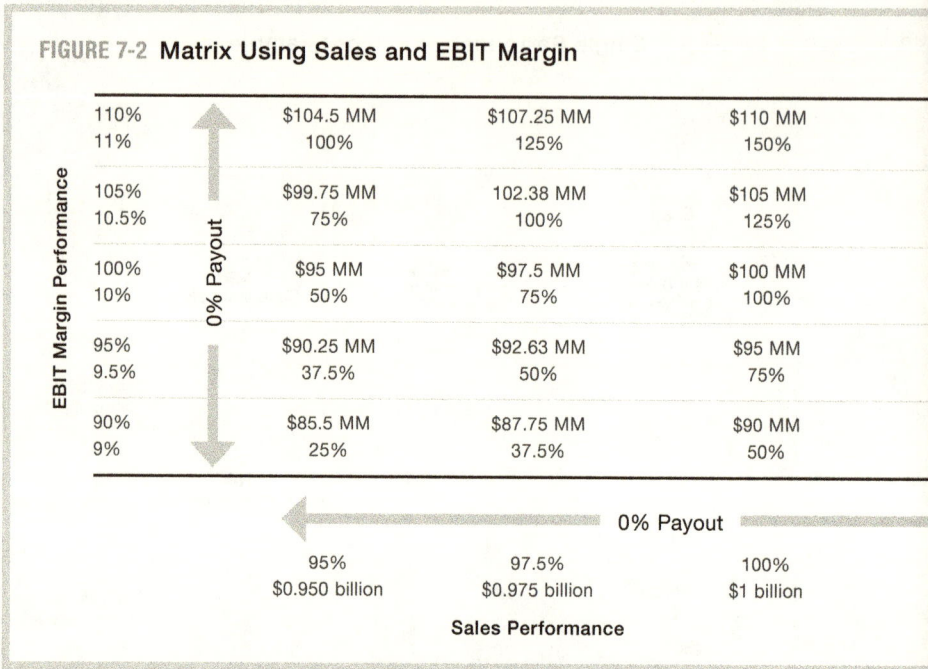

The Value Creation Plan Approach

In many cases, a viable alternative to stock-based LTI awards can be found through the use of a value creation plan (VCP) that shares a portion of earnings above a pre-established threshold with executives. A VCP can be understandable for participants and relatively simple to administer based on measurable returns at the business-unit level or consolidated level (for private companies).

In essence, each VCP participant has an ownership interest in an LTI pool that grows or shrinks based upon the private company or business unit's performance relative to the annual expected return on investment in the entity. A VCP eliminates the need to settle upon a method to value company stock (for private companies), set multi-year performance goals or establish peer group or index benchmarks.

Designing the Program

To establish a VCP, both a measure of profit and return must be defined and understood by all participants. Examples of profit measures include EBIT, net operating profit after taxes (NOPAT) and bottom-line net income. Examples of return measures include return on equity and return on invested capital (debt and equity). The threshold return must be periodically adjusted as the cost of investment funds and/or debt-to-equity ratio change. Further, as the private company's or business unit's capital

$112.75 MM	$115.5 MM	EBIT $
175%	200%	Payout as a percent of target
$107.63 MM	$110.25 MM	EBIT $
150%	175%	Payout as a percent of target
$102.5 MM	$105 MM	EBIT $
125%	150%	Payout as a percent of target
$97.38 MM	$99.75 MM	EBIT $
100%	125%	Payout as a percent of target
$92.25 MM	$94.5 MM	EBIT $
75%	100%	Payout as a percent of target

102.5%	105%
$1.025 billion	$1.050 billion

base grows, so too would the required profit to meet the expected threshold return to investors.

Sharing Ratio

When a VCP is created, a sharing ratio needs to be established whereby a portion of the private company or business unit's annual economic profit is contributed to an LTI pool. The sharing ratio is based upon market target awards and determined at the start of the plan and held constant for a defined period. If an economic loss occurs (i.e., earnings below the expected threshold return), then the sharing ratio's proportion is deducted from the incentive pool. The annual contribution (or deduction) is then allocated among the plan participants' account balances using a predetermined formula.

This two-step exercise occurs annually over the life of the plan. To mitigate risk for the participants, a floor could be placed upon deductions from the incentive pool; a corresponding limit could be placed on annual contributions to the pool to limit the company's liability. Special provisions would be crafted regarding a potential sale of the company/business unit or if the private company completes an initial public offering.

Example

For an example of how a VCP could work, consider the co-founders of a debt-free private company who want to establish an LTI plan for their senior executive team but are unwilling to dilute their ownership in the company. The co-founders decide to set up a VCP that rewards executives for NOPAT above a threshold return on the co-founders' equity in the company.

In this example, the sharing percentage of NOPAT that exceeds the company's cost of capital would be added to the incentive plan pool annually and allocated to the individual participants' accounts according to formula. To the extent that NOPAT is lower than the cost of capital, the incentive pool would be reduced using the sharing percentage. (See Table 7-3.)

Vesting for each year's contribution to the LTI pool typically would be over three to five years, and distribution of a portion (e.g., one half) of the vested amount could be provided for at that time. The remaining portion of the vested balance could be required to remain in the pool until a fixed date in the event of a below-threshold performance year (which would cause the pool to shrink). Distribution could even be in the form of parent-company stock for participants

---

ADVANTAGES AND DISADVANTAGES OF PUPS

Advantages:

- Risk/reward balance can be precisely engineered.
- No shares are required.
- Design can result in low or zero payments during sub-par performance cycles.
- Charge to earnings is capped because there is a maximum payout.
- Can be used to reinforce mid-term performance objectives.
- Relatively easy to communicate.

Disadvantages:

- Difficult to set long-term performance goals.
- Subject to liability accounting treatment.

FIGURE 7-3 Illustration of a Value Creation Plan

A	Calculate NOPAT at end of year	$5,000,000
B	Calculate owners' equity	$40,000,000
C	Factor in cost of capital ...	X 10%
D	... to get to threshold return	$4,000,000
E	Subtract threshold return from NOPAT to get economic value creation	$1,000,000
F	Apply the sharing ratio ...	X 15%
G	... to get contribution to incentive pool	$150,000
H	Allocate contribution among plan participants (as shown below)	

$$\frac{\text{Individual's target}}{\text{Sum of participants' target}} \quad X \quad \text{Contribution to pool}$$

who are employees of a business unit of a publicly traded company. The design would need to consider the potential application of the tax rules governing nonqualified deferred compensation plans under IRC section 409A. If section 409A applies to the specific design, its deferral requirements would need to be satisfied to avoid taxation and penalties when there is no longer a substantial risk of forfeiture (e.g., on vesting).

VCP rewards investors before rewarding executives by motivating the executive team to focus on attaining an earnings level above the cost of the investors' capital. For executives in business units, a VCP provides a performance metric directly connected to their business unit's financial performance, which they can influence more directly than the parent company's overall stock price. A VCP can be easy to administer and explain, and it provides executives an alternative to company stock where such an award is not always practical or desirable.

Phantom Stock

A tool that has languished in obscurity at public companies, phantom stock recently has shown signs of emerging there while continuing its more common usage at privately held firms. In the appropriate situation, phantom stock can provide valuable attributes of equity and help with motivation, focus and retention.

The basic concept of a phantom stock program involves a company's agreement or promise to pay the recipient of an award an amount equal to the value of a certain number (or percentage) of shares of the company's stock. Commonly structured through the award of units, a phantom stock program enables a company to make an award that tracks the economic benefits of stock ownership without using actual shares. Because phantom stock is a contractual right and not an interest in property, the tax event for the executive and the employer occurs at the payment in settlement of a properly designed phantom stock arrangement. Normal taxation, and not capital gains, is one of the downsides of these types of plans.

Phantom stock plans are shadows that mimic their real equity counterparts; phantom stock and shadow stock are terms that often are used interchangeably. Although shares of real stock can be traded at will, phantom shares or units take on value only when key contingencies or vesting conditions are met. A phantom stock plan typically does not require investment or confer ownership, so its recipient does not have voting rights. It is essentially an upside opportunity, as participants' investments typically are limited to their services; they stand to gain from any upside growth of the company. Some companies will provide the underlying value of the award, as well, but this is a minority practice.

Valuation

In making awards under a phantom stock plan, there is a determination of the value of a phantom share or unit in connection with awards to one or more participants. Valuations also will be needed for periodic reporting to participants (and to actual shareholders and the SEC if used by a public company) as well as for determinations of amounts payable at the time of settlement.

Phantom stock programs can be simply designed. However, they should be created to meet the company's specific needs and objectives in protecting the unique knowledge and skill base that is represented by those key employees selected for awards. The two types that are most prevalent are:

■ The appreciation-only plan (much like a stock appreciation right)
■ The full-value plan, where the award includes the underlying value of the unit (like a restricted stock unit).

Generally, a phantom stock plan or agreement spells out how the program operates and how payments are determined, along with other various details, often including:

■ Eligibility criteria
■ Vesting schedule
■ Valuation method or formula
■ Performance measurement
■ Settlement and payout events
■ Handling of various termination events, including:
  – Retirement
  – Death
  – Disability
  – Dismissal (involuntary)
  – Resignation (voluntary)
■ Restrictive covenants
■ Form of payment
■ Provisions for the sales of the company
■ Any funding vehicle

Design and Accounting

Accounting is a key challenge of phantom stock. Historically, phantom plans have been viewed as undesirable from an accounting perspective because of the resulting liability accounting treatment. This creates volatility on the company's income statement, which is something that concerns most financial officers. Generally, for accounting purposes, phantom shares must be treated as an expense over the required service period, and the company does not receive its income tax deduction until the benefits are paid out. This timing is similar to other equity awards but can prove to be not as advantageous in periods when the value of the award increases. With liability accounting, the accounting expense and corresponding tax deduction are the same. When real equity is used, the company may get a tax advantage, as the expense can be locked in at grant while the tax deduction can grow as the value of the equity grows.

In addition, coming up with cash to cover phantom payouts can be tricky. Phantom stock plan gains (in appreciation-only programs) or current fair value (in full-value programs) must be paid by the company versus the public markets which is the case when using publicly traded equity. Finally, phantom stock programs typically are subject to the complex rules applicable to nonqualified deferred compensation under IRC section 409A, so care must be taken in their design.

Why Use Phantom Stock for LTI Awards?

Phantom stock can help in getting an executive team to think and act like equity partners. It creates a sense of ownership in the success of the business because having phantom stock means the participants have "skin in the game." The concept of being an equity partner by having phantom stock can create the same feeling of connection as the more traditional equity tools (e.g., stock options, restricted stock). In addition to its incentive components, a phantom stock program involves deferred compensation and can act like golden handcuffs in retaining key executives. Phantom stock most often is used by privately held companies, but (as previously noted) some publicly traded organizations are using phantom stock or similar cash-based LTIs at the business unit level, as well.

Phantom stock plans can be especially useful in providing the economic benefits of equity without diluting shareholders. Because recipients of phantom units lack voting rights, a company can issue these units or shares without altering the governance of the company or worrying about dilution issues. Phantom stock does not directly dilute the value of real outstanding shares. Phantom stock awards do, however, have a significant effect on cash flow at payout. This is why some plans have a conversion feature and may pay out in actual stock.

Another advantage to a company is the ability to design an award so that an executive receives no benefit unless vesting conditions are met and, under the appreciation-only model, the company's value has increased. The fair market value of the stock is commonly used by public companies, while private companies have various approaches. For example, while a professional valuation may be preferred but viewed as too costly, many companies then turn to book value. Other approaches include a formula using revenue, EBITDA, net income, or a combination of relevant measures; a formula can also help with consistency of the valuation over time.

There are many reasons a company would consider a phantom stock arrangement:

- A public company may find that it has insufficient authorized shares to award the desired number of awards that require actual stock.
- A company's leadership may have considered other plans but found their rules too restrictive or implementation costs too high.
- The owner(s) may desire to maintain actual and effectual control, while still sharing the economic value of the company.
- There may be ownership restrictions for certain types of entities (i.e., sole proprietorship, partnership, limited liability company), such as the S-corporation 100-shareholder rule.
- The objective is to provide equity-type incentives to a restricted group of individuals.
- A corporate division that can measure its enterprise value and wants its employees to have a share in that value even though there is no real stock available.
- A desire to focus on an event or contingency (e.g., sale, merger, IPO).

Typically, a phantom plan can provide a more flexible alternative that is not subject to the same restrictions as most equity ownership plans. For many, the simple desire to use an equity-like vehicle without giving up true ownership may be reason enough to implement. In considering a phantom stock program, the advantages and disadvantages in Table 7-4 should be evaluated.

Who Is Using Phantom Stock?

Phantom stock is not only a private-company phenomenon. Research of proxy filings suggests some well-known, publicly traded companies that are using this tool to attract, retain and motivate select groups of employees, typically at the business unit level.

Phantom stock is a traditional LTI vehicle rather than a fad. While trends come and go, cash-based LTI plans do have a place in the executive compensation portfolio. While these plans generally are simple and provide flexibility to the company, they also can raise various issues that must be considered carefully. In the appropriate situation, a phantom stock plan can keep the company spirit alive in the executive suite.

TABLE 7-4 **Pros and Cons of Phantom Stock**

Advantages:

- Allows employees to share in the growth of the company's value without being shareholders
- No equity dilution, as no actual shares are awarded
- Powerful retention tool when combined with vesting
- Board/compensation committee has flexibility to design plans based on their own discretion

- Can be tied to overall company or business unit results
- No employee investment required
- Can provide for dividend equivalents
- Design can permit phantom stock to be converted into actual equity
- No income tax until proceeds are converted to cash or real stock
- Potential tax deferral of employee compensation
- Retirement benefit opportunity.

Disadvantages:

- If paid in cash, can be a financial drain on the company's cash flow
- At a private company, may require outside valuation on an annual basis
- Company needs to communicate financial results to participants

- Payments to employee are taxed as ordinary income
- May affect the overall value of the business in a transaction
- IRC section 409A rules add complexity and difficulty in achieving objectives.

CHAPTER 8

Performance Measurement for Incentive Pay Plans

Theo Sharp and Christopher Ewing

The importance of pay for performance as a principle of executive compensation philosophy can hardly be understated. Entire books and hundreds of articles and conference presentations have been devoted to showing the techniques and strategies needed to align executive pay with company performance. As has been often the case in the past, the focus on executive pay — especially the dollar amounts reported in the news — has distracted attention from performance, which should be the focal point of any pay-for-performance discussion.

There is no unified, standard way to address the performance side of the equation, and various metrics are in use. The use of multiple performance measures — financial, operational, strategic, non-financial and individual — is appropriate when performance is measured on a holistic basis and viewed through multiple lenses.

One of the biggest challenges within both short- and long-term incentive design is determining the most effective performance measures and measurement approach given each company's unique set of facts and circumstances. Once a metrically sound framework is in place, the goal-setting process can be a relatively unambiguous process for some companies, while others may struggle to set "meaningful" goals in context of the current state of the business, competitive landscape, performance measure(s) being utilized, and shareholder and senior management expectations.

This chapter:

- Discusses performance measurement approaches and considerations for incentive plans.
- Addresses the conditions under which an effective performance/payout calibration takes place and the identification of threshold, target and maximum performance levels used for goal-setting purposes.
- Explains in more detail the techniques used in incorporating TSR in LTI plan design. Taking a "high-definition" approach in choosing and implementing a TSR comparator group is recommended — one that entails testing, weighting and ranking the comparator group companies. In addition, examples of when not to use TSR are reviewed.

Performance Measurement Approaches and Considerations for Incentive Plans

From a performance measurement perspective, companies measure goals on either an absolute or relative basis:

- **Absolute (internal approach)**. Performance goals are measured vs. internal plan (budget/target). An internal approach requires a strong planning process and is difficult in industries in which external events can have a dramatic effect on results. Performance goals usually are effective when there is rigor around the goal-setting process and goals are based on the company's strategic, financial and operating objectives. This technique can be enhanced if shareholder expectations are incorporated in the process.
- **Relative (external approach)**. Performance goals are measured vs. an external comparator group. A relative or external approach measures the company against a comparator group of companies that are affected by similar macroeconomic factors, compete in the same market and/or have similar products. This method eliminates the need to set internal company performance goals because it focuses on how the company performs against its comparator group. It also mitigates the risk of setting the goals too high or too low. Depending upon the company and performance goals being

utilized, a comparator group may consist of a compensation peer group, custom performance peer group or broad market index.

Relative performance measurement is seldom used within STI plans and typically reserved for performance-based LTI programs. The choice of performance measures is also a key consideration in establishing absolute vs. relative performance measurement. Absolute performance measurement is typically utilized when long-term performance measures are based on profitability (e.g., EPS, EBITDA, etc.), revenue/sales, cash flow (free, operating, etc.) and/or capital-efficiency (e.g., ROE, ROIC, etc.). Relative performance measurement is typically employed when long-term performance measures are based on TSR or stock price (relative TSR is discussed in additional detail below). However, we are seeing an increasing interest in companies looking at adding relative financial metrics (e.g., EPS Growth, Revenue Growth, ROIC, etc.).

A potential drawback to a relative approach is that selecting a comparator group may be difficult for some companies. It may be particularly challenging for firms with a unique business model or in a consolidating industry. Also, the relative approach sometimes can result in unintended payouts. Even if a company outperformed the majority of its comparator group companies, it is possible that its absolute performance was poor and created "negative value" for shareholders. This situation can be addressed in the following ways:

- The compensation committee may apply negative discretion in determining the incentive payouts. Therefore, the compensation committee would have the ability to pay reduced or no incentives if the company did not create any shareholder value.
- In addition to the relative performance measurement versus the comparator group, an absolute threshold (or "circuit breaker") can be established under which no incentives are paid if the threshold performance level is not achieved (i.e., if the company does not reach an $X level of EBITDA, reduced or no incentives are paid, depending on the terms). In cases in which the circuit breaker is tripped, all incentive payments become discretionary.

132

TABLE 8-1 Common Metrics and Their Purpose

Measure	What it tells us	Why is it popular?	What are the drawbacks?
Revenue	■ How much money received ■ Can be measured company wide, by unit or product	■ Proxy for strength of brand, market share, global reach, etc. ■ Simplicity ■ Ability to zero in on one product/area	■ Not all revenue is created equally ■ Does not reflect capital or cost
Operating income/earnings before interest & taxes (EBIT)	■ How much money made from operating activities	■ Removes much of the "noise" from non-core or non-business activities	■ Can tell a very different story than net profitability ■ Does not reflect usage of capital
Operating cash flow	■ How much cash was generated from operating activities	■ Considered "pure" – no noise from non-core or non-business activities ■ Reflects earnings quality ■ Cash allows companies to invest, pay down debt, buy back shares	■ Can tell a very different story than net profitability ■ Does not reflect usage of capital
Free cash flow	■ How much operating cash flow was generated after removing cash outflows to support operations and maintain capital assets	■ Same as the above but may better reflect cash flow available for distribution to debtholders and shareholders after the financing of projects to maintain or expand assets	■ Can tell a very different story than net profitability ■ Does not reflect usage of capital
Return on equity	■ How many dollars of profit a company generates with each dollar of shareholders' equity ■ A measure of capital efficiency/productivity	■ Key comparison metric ■ Reflects profitability in context of the company's usage of equity capital	■ Does not reflect total capital (equity only, not debt)
Return on invested capital	■ How many dollars of profit a company generates with each dollar of capital (debt or equity) invested ■ A measure of capital efficiency/productivity	■ Key comparison metric ■ Reflects profitability in context of the company's usage of equity capital ■ When return on capital is greater than the cost of that capital, the company is creating value	■ Not all revenue is created equally ■ Accounting-based measure that can be manipulated

TABLE 8-1 **Common Metrics and Their Purpose** (continued)

Measure	What it tells us	Why is it popular?	What are the drawbacks?
Earnings per share (EPS)	■ How much money made on a per-share basis	■ The metric for the quarterly earnings release, making it a key investor metric correlated with stock price	■ Can be "gamed" (e.g., share buybacks) ■ "Just another way of looking at earnings"
Total share-holder return (more common in performance-based LTI)	■ How much money a shareholder made on their original invest-ment in the company	■ The most direct measure of share-holder performance ■ Key comparison metric ■ Theoretically reflects value creation	■ Earnings + outlook do not always trans-late to stock price performance ■ "I can't control stock price"

In the case of relative TSR, a cap may be placed on the payout — regardless of relative performance versus the comparator group — in the event that the company's absolute TSR is negative over the performance period (current trend is to set the cap at target).

In selecting a performance measurement approach, companies should consider several factors:

■ Management process. How much rigor and structure is in the process? How much information is available to management regarding shareholder and analyst expectations and peer company metrics?

■ Strategic priorities. What are the company's business objectives and ability to forecast performance based on the company's life cycle and maturity?

■ Company performance. How volatile is the company's performance on an absolute basis and relative to peers historically?

Setting goals for incentive plans is a subjective process that requires much discussion and consideration. The board of directors and management should be able to provide sound rationale for the goals and approach selected. See Table 8-1 for common metrics and their purpose.

Performance and Payout Calibration for Incentive Plans

With the increased scrutiny on executive compensation and greater transparency due to enhanced disclosure requirements, having a pay-for-performance compensation philosophy is practically a must. Companies not only need to show a relationship between executive pay and business performance, but also must demonstrate that they pay the appropriate level for commensurate performance. The pay-for-performance calibration/relationship should create and reinforce shareholder alignment.

A main challenge in designing an incentive plan (when based on absolute performance) is being able to forecast company performance and set goals at the right level, especially for periods longer than one year. Executives are motivated, and the likelihood of desired performance increases under incentive plans when the following conditions are met:

- Executives have a line of sight in which they understand the performance goals and view them as realistic and achievable.
- There is a clear link between performance and pay.
- Executives view the pay associated with the incentive plan as meaningful (i.e., large enough to justify the effort required to achieve the performance goals).

If performance goals are not appropriately set, there can be negative consequences. If performance objectives are set too high, executives will not be motivated, knowing there is little likelihood of achieving the targets. At the other extreme, if executives consistently and easily achieve performance targets, they are being sent the wrong message that superior performance is not required to receive a meaningful incentive payout.

As noted in discussions of incentive programs in preceding chapters, STI plans and performance-based LTI programs typically have pre-established performance levels:

- Threshold. A floor that represents the minimum level of performance that must be achieved before an incentive can be earned.

- Target. The expected and/or planned (budgeted) level of achievement or a realistic goal that is achievable and meaningful.
- Maximum. The total incentive opportunity that may be earned for superior performance, sometimes referred to as a cap.

The level of performance relative to target that should correlate with threshold and maximum payout levels can be difficult to calibrate. A simplified approach would be to set the threshold performance level at 80 or 90 percent of target performance and set the maximum performance level at 110 or 120 percent of target performance.

Calibrating threshold and maximum goals appropriately can depend greatly on the performance measure. One way to test the reasonableness of the goal-setting process is to estimate the probabilities of achieving the performance levels and compare them to standard achievement frequencies (as discussed in Chapter 6 in the section titled "Performance Shares and Performance-based Restricted Stock").

Say on Pay? What About Performance?

A pay-for-performance debate has long dominated the corporate governance agenda. While great progress has been made in enhancing transparency and aligning the interests of management and shareholders, there has been surprisingly little consensus on what constitutes best practices in performance management. Boards and investors must hold management accountable for achieving performance objectives that are comprehensive, actionable and value creating.

For compensation professionals, aligning executive pay with performance is the great work in progress of our time. The plot is well understood — align management with investor objectives by rewarding executives for their enterprise's performance and voilà ... all stakeholders are satisfied.

So why does the drama continue to escalate? Because the mainstream focus to date has been on the pay side of the equation.

While significant and important progress has been achieved, the critical problem of effectively assessing performance remains largely unaddressed. Unless and until this changes, the plot will continue, intensifying during worsening economic times.

Defining Performance

Pay-for-performance depends entirely on the definition of performance. While executive pay is an easy target, it is a distracting sideshow to the management imperative of assessing and improving corporate performance. So why has progress been so elusive? The two primary reasons — comparability and complexity — are well-known:

- First, establishing standards for industries or enterprises that have different economic dynamics can be contentious at best. The question "Who had a better year, the World Series champion or the Super Bowl winner?" illustrates the point.
- Second, "corporate performance" math is difficult to measure and not necessarily supported by historical accounting measures. Much like a horse race, corporate performance is best thought of as a firm's position at any given point in time relative to its long-term objectives. While the past is certainly prologue, current expectations define performance, not vice versa. It is a world in which "What have you done for me lately?" is trumped by "What can I expect from you tomorrow?"

Measuring Performance

Relative TSR is a common feature in long-term incentive programs for a variety of reasons, including:

- Preference by large, influential institutional shareholders and other key stakeholders;
- Prevalence as a performance measure within large public company long-term incentive plans; and
- De facto definition of "performance" for the pay-versus-performance disclosure requirements established under the Dodd-Frank Wall Street Reform and Consumer Protection Act of 2010.

For some companies, there are very good reasons to use relative TSR as a performance measure for LTI plans. For example, in mature businesses that are cyclical and/or significantly affected by external factors, relative TSR can be an excellent way to assess the achievements of management in the prevailing market, economic and regulatory context. Conversely, relative TSR is of limited validity and application for the following types of organizations:

- Companies targeting substantial growth;
- Firms in a turnaround situation;
- Companies that are not competing with others for customers or investors to any meaningful extent; and
- "Grow or die" companies.

For these types of organizations, absolute performance is what matters most. If relative performance is to be used at all, it might be used as a multiplier or modifier to the short- or long-term incentive award rather than as a primary measure.

Incorporating Relative TSR in Performance-Based LTI Plans

When incorporating a relative TSR measure into a performance-based LTI plan, not all companies take a high-definition view in selecting and implementing a TSR comparator group, despite the fact that the choice of comparator group can have a big effect on both performance and payout outcomes. Similarly, high-definition thinking may allow an organization to reduce the level of random "noise" in the comparator group, which may in turn make the use of relative TSR more appealing to executives who often are suspicious of its use as a performance measure.

Historically, the common approach with relative TSR plans was to base the comparator group on the most obvious alternative investments for a shareholder. This reflected the origins of relative TSR in the relative performance-driven bonus plans operated for mutual fund managers themselves. In the early days, this often meant simply using the S&P 500 or some other very broad comparator group. However, hindsight and experience have exposed this as low-definition thinking. Such broad comparator groups include a high degree of randomness due to the very different degrees of volatility and cyclical exposure faced by different sectors and businesses. In addition, when looking at the stock market in high definition, we see that the U.S. shareholder base has become more diverse in the past 10 to 20 years and the alternative investments are not always obvious.

With this richness and diversity in both the shareholder base and the nature of potential alternative investments, it becomes necessary to think about relative TSR in a different way. In essence, this means considering which businesses face broadly similar economic, market, regulatory and operational challenges. This generally includes direct business competitors and/or businesses with a similar profile in terms of complexity, structure, products, sectors and locations. Size also can be a factor, but wider size variations can be accepted for TSR than would be appropriate when selecting a peer group for compensation benchmarking purposes.

Of course, not all businesses have competitors that look like them or face the same challenges. For example, in some highly consolidated sectors there may only be a handful of competing firms, and some of these may not be listed on a stock market. In these circumstances, assuming that TSR remains a valid metric, it becomes necessary to choose on the basis of factors such as:

- **Correlation**: How well does the historical TSR of different sectors correlate to our company/sector?
- **Volatility (beta)**: How does the historical share price volatility for different sectors compare to our company/sector?

Having developed a potential comparator group, it is important to model and test this group. This means tracking TSR for the potential comparators over several overlapping historical performance periods and computing what the plan would have paid in these scenarios. This modeling allows the following key questions to be addressed:

- Do the performance outcomes fit with what we believe about the historical performance of our business?
- In a small group, are any comparators miscorrelated? Why? Does the miscorrelation invalidate the outcomes? Is this likely to recur?
- In a larger group, are many sectors miscorrelated to us and our main competitors?
- In a global group, are any countries miscorrelated?

Ideally, this exercise answers whether the proposed comparator group is suitable and/or highlights any necessary modifications. It is possible that the modeling will produce a set of notional historical payments that seem to be driven by random factors rather than the performance of the business. In this event, either the proposed comparator group needs to be significantly revised or the use of relative TSR as a measure needs to be rethought.

Some companies may have a small number of highly relevant comparators and a larger number of companies with whom they have some similarity. In this case, the aim is to make sure the comparator group is large enough to be robust without it being dominated by the less relevant comparators. The answer here could be to weight the companies in the comparator group such that the most relevant companies have a larger effect on the result.

When assessing performance against a comparator group, there typically are three approaches:

- **Simple percentile ranking**. This is the simplest, most common approach and would be the low-definition default choice. However, under this approach incentive payments are sensitive to the level of clustering of comparator companies. Therefore, incremental improvements to TSR may have a very large or very small effect on plan vesting/payouts.

- **Percentage outperformance**. An example of this approach provides for full vesting/payout where TSR is at median plus 10 percent per annum, with linear interpolation used between median and this level. This approach avoids material differences in incentive awards arising from small differences in performance. However, this approach does require a percentage outperformance target to be set for full vesting/payout.

- **Smoothed ranking**. This is a compromise option between the two approaches described above. For example, TSR at median- and upper-quartile companies is calculated with vesting/payout between these points calculated by linear interpolation. Again, this avoids material differences for incentive awards arising from small differences in performance.

Simple percentile ranking works best for very large comparator groups. Otherwise, the other methods are preferable. If the comparator group is very small, the percentage outperformance approach generally works best.

Any high-definition approach requires active consideration of the following issues:

- **Start and end dates within the performance period**. Depending upon a company's objectives and intent, TSR is generally measured over one of the following periods: calendar year, fiscal year or grant date to vesting date.
- **Share price averaging period.** Generally, the authors recommend an averaging period of at least one month (typically 30 to 90 days) at both the beginning and end of the performance period as a "spot price" approach is not aligned with the desired intent of the program.
- **Treatment of companies leaving the comparator group**. This typically depends upon the comparator group being used to measure relative performance and reason for exit (acquired, taken private, bankruptcy, etc.).
- **Termination provisions**. It is important to define the provisions around relative TSR performance, vesting and payout in the event of various termination scenarios (CIC, by the company "without cause," by the executive for "good reason," etc.). These provisions should be addressed up front and are generally memorialized in the individual LTI award agreement, LTI plan document or employment agreement.

Conclusion

Picking the most effective metrics for incentive programs is among the more challenging decisions for compensation committees. Boards and committees are required to balance several factors, including strategic priorities, desired pay outcomes, and external performance expectations. Success in this regard requires an annual calibration of incentive plans. Boards should also remember that executive pay is an outcome of this process, it is not the goal. Incentivizing and measuring corporate performance should be the focus for boards.

CHAPTER 9

Emerging Trends in Performance Measurement

By Irv Becker and Kurt Groeninger

T he last chapter discussed the nuts and bolts of performance measurement in incentive programs. However, understanding these mechanics is only part of a fuller picture. Compensation committees must remember that their decisions have a broader audience than just the executive teams. Other stakeholders, such as employees and institutional shareholders, review these pay plans for fairness, reasonableness, and an overall alignment with company performance.

These internal and external audiences can create a bit of tension. Managers may seek to establish goals that are readily achievable while boards and shareholders generally seek meaningful objectives to push the corporation forward. Proxy advisors have only strained the situation in recent years given their intense focus on program rigor and mechanics.

Given the various parties and perspectives, compensation committees must craft incentive plans that can withstand a wide range of scrutiny. Plans that do not hold up to examination may stymie an organization's potential success and create questions about the board's governance abilities.

The involvement of shareholders and proxy advisory firms in executive pay has forced committee members to rethink their own priorities in designing pay programs. Instead of focusing solely on what may be best for the company, committees are essentially forced to include the viewpoint of external stakeholders. This has created a balancing act for many boards, with sometimes ineffective results.

It goes without saying that a compensation committee's first duty is to the organization. Although there are multiple forces pulling on compensation decisions, committees must prioritize the business and advance the internal strategy.

The overall goal is to create a compensation plan that provides a strong incentive for managers to achieve financial objectives, increase shareholder value, and remain with the company.

This chapter:

- Addresses some techniques to improve the goal setting associated with executive incentive programs.
- Discusses the use of Environmental, Social & Governance (ESG) metrics in incentive programs.
- Explains Economic Value Added (EVA) and how it plays into ISS's pay-for-performance analysis.

Getting Performance Measurement Right

Certain trends have emerged to achieve an appropriate balance between incentivizing executives and pleasing stakeholders.

Incentivize Strategic Milestones

Following the introduction of say on pay, there was a shift towards annual incentive programs that either entirely or heavily relied upon financial metrics. This approach was favored by proxy advisors and shareholders alike given the quantitative nature of these programs. However, the pendulum appears to be swinging in the other direction.

Simply focusing on financial metrics may not be sufficient in incentivizing executives and providing them with a clear line of sight to corporate achievement. Compensation committees should also consider what actions may advance corporate strategy.

An incentive program may require the incorporation of non-financial metrics related to achievement of certain business objectives, such as completion of a factory, closing of an acquisition, or moving to a new stage in a drug trial. These objectives may be distinct or "housed" and weighed in a broader category of strategic priorities. For example, 70 percent of the cash incentive may be based on revenue while the remaining 30 percent is part of a "Strategic Objectives" component.

These objectives may be assessed on a binary basis (achieved versus not achieved) but are more commonly evaluated with recognition of partial completion (i.e., full achievement, partial achievement, or not achieved).

In general, the use of non-financial or strategic goals accounts for 10 to 30 percent of an incentive program. Allotting more than 30 percent will typically raise concern with shareholders and proxy advisors.

Disclosure is an increasingly important issue with strategic goals. While disclosure, in certain cases, may create some competitive harm, it is important to be as specific as possible when describing the objectives. The goal is to demonstrate that each strategic metric is objective in nature and that the board has little qualitative input on deciding achievement.

Focus on Goal Rigor

There is a common misperception that proxy advisors prefer the use of certain metrics. In fact, proxy advisors take no position on which metrics are used as long as the company provides justification for their use. Some institutional shareholders, on the other hand, have preferences and make known what metrics a particular company should consider. Although these two external groups take different positions on metric selection, they agree that the related goals should be "rigorous."

Goal rigor can be difficult to nail down. Internal and external groups may have different ideas as to what a challenging goal may look like. It is entirely possible that a company's budget and financial expectation is lower than the previous year, and a performance goal is set accordingly. While this goal may reflect the real world, many external parties would agree that the lowered goals should not lead to the same level of pay. In these cases, some shareholders believe that potential cash bonuses should be reduced commensurate with the lowered goals.

Shareholders are concerned with goal rigor to varying degrees. Some groups care to the extent that bonus payouts look reasonable in light of recent share price performance. Other shareholders aggressively review goals set by management and the board. Proxy advisors apply various tests to determine rigor. For example, if a performance target increases above actual performance in a prior year, the goal will be considered rigorous. Additionally, if a company provides the maximum cash payment for three consecutive years, the goals set by the board may not be viewed as sufficiently challenging. These tests are not particularly sophisticated, but advisors are unable to perform more complex analyses given the multitude of programs evaluated each year.

Select Appropriate Peers for the Benchmarking Group

When using relative metrics, consideration should be given to the comparison group. In some cases, companies often pick an index, such as the S&P 500 or other industry index, to compare performance. While this approach has certain advantages, it may not be right in all circumstances.

In many cases, picking a more tailored group of companies may be appropriate. Comparison groups should include organizations that serve similar markets, have comparable strategies, and are at a similar place in the business cycle. A turnaround situation will require a level of performance different from that expected from a fast-growing, entrepreneurial organization.

If a company uses one peer group for benchmarking pay and a different peer group for benchmarking performance, it should be able articulate a good reason for this practice. Without such rationalizing, proxy advisors and shareholders alike may conclude that the compensation committee cherry picked peers to manipulate program payouts.

Aim for a Normal Distribution

As noted above, programs should be rigorous enough so as not to continually generate maximum payouts under the incentive programs.

A well-constructed compensation plan generally results in maximum payouts about 20 percent of the time. On the other end of the spectrum, a committee should expect the executives to miss threshold levels only 20 percent of the time. Target awards should be achieved approximately 50-60 percent of the time.

Obviously, this distribution of payouts is only revealed after years of running the same plan. In reality, committees often make changes to metrics, weightings, and performance expectations over the course of time. Given all of these moving parts, reviewing historical payouts is not always an apples-to-apples comparison. However, this review process should still be undertaken periodically to inform committee members how incentive programs are paying out over time. Even programs providing target awards year after year may signal that the goals are not sufficiently challenging for the executive team. Armed with information about historical and expected payouts, via a normal distribution, the compensation committee should be able to calibrate its performance goals appropriately.

Clarity and Transparency Should Be a Priority

With executive compensation under more scrutiny than ever before, it is critical that compensation committees are able to articulate how their pay packages align with shareholder interests and meet the needs of the executive team and the board of directors. With this goal in mind, CD&A disclosures should clearly articulate the metrics as well as the threshold, target and maximum performance levels required to earn a payout. The disclosures should also include a clear description of any adjustments made when using non-GAAP metrics. This allows shareholders to probe more deeply into the committee's discretionary actions and judge appropriateness.

Beyond these disclosure practices, clarity and transparency demands simple approaches to compensation programs. Overly complex programs, or those with dozens of metrics, do not aid executives or shareholders. Rather, these types of programs reduce line of sight for program participants. Uncomplicated incentive programs, with two to three metrics, generally meet company needs while also allowing shareholders a better understanding of the board's strategic priorities.

Avoid Conformity

Each company is unique with differing priorities and strategies. Given this, it is unreasonable to assume that any company can pick up the compensation program from a competitor or peer and be successful. Although competitors may have similar external factors, the internal dynamics often differ greatly. These distinct corporate features should inform the compensation committee's decisions. For example, if a corporation places great value on worker or environmental safety, these factors can be included in the incentive program. This also extends to financial metrics given different corporate business plans.

When making compensation decisions, the committee members should be informed of the practices and metrics of companies in the peer group. Members should take these features into consideration but not be limited by them. The committee must tailor its program to achieve goals established by its business strategy and compensation philosophy. In doing so, the committee members should select performance metrics and goals that make sense for the company and industry, taking into account the unique purpose and characteristics of the organization.

Reconsider Relative Metrics

Performance-based equity comes with a host of design challenges. For many companies using performance awards, the financial goals used to determine how many shares will ultimately vest are often "absolute" (i.e., the company sets the goals based on their budget or another internal benchmark, typically over a three-year cumulative period). Setting a multi-year financial goal with any level of precision is extremely difficult for most firms, particularly in cyclical industries or times of economic uncertainty.

Given the challenges inherent with absolute financial goals, many companies had moved to relative total shareholder return (TSR) metrics. Relative TSR plans are fairly simple to design (i.e., no need to forecast or set multi-year goals) and they are typically perceived to be defensible to both institutional shareholders and proxy advisors.

However, companies are now recognizing the limitations of a TSR-based program and turning to relative financial metrics, such as revenue growth, earnings growth or return metrics. One reason for this trend is the growing recognition that while TSR provides strong shareholder alignment, executives often feel that they cannot control the outcome given all the different factors impacting share price. Programs with relative financial metrics can provide greater clarity and certainty to executives while still securing proxy advisor and shareholder support.

ESG: The New Frontier in Performance Measurement

Corporations' role in society is changing. As demonstrated in the Business Roundtable's Statement on the Purpose of a Corporation (2019), the modern standard for corporate responsibility is partially about improving society. For example, the Business Roundtable now commits to supporting the communities in which the corporations operate, including respecting the people in those communities while also protecting the environment by embracing sustainable practices.

Many corporate boards have responded to this change. In turn, the use of metrics tied to environmental or social improvements have taken hold in many incentive programs. These so-called ESG metrics (environmental, social and governance) are quickly growing in use and are a main discussion topic in compensation committees.

ESG metrics come in all shapes and sizes (see Figure 9-1) and there is no common standard for measurement. The ESG categories include worker safety, employee satisfaction, employee turnover, diversity and inclusion, and other environmental goals, to name a few.

ESG metrics are growing in popularity, but corporate boards may have difficulty deciding on the ESG metrics most useful to corporate strategy and business purpose. This partial list is compiled from company CD&As. Note that many are vaguely defined.

The ESG metrics are often housed in overarching strategic goals or an assessment of individual performance. It is also common practice

FIGURE 9-1 ESG Examples

ESG Category	Examples
Diversity and inclusion	■ Increasing the number of women and/or ethnic minorities in senior roles. ■ Enhance system and capabilities for recruiting diverse talent. ■ Create and launch diversity and social responsbility programs.
Talent development and succession	■ Implement a talent development and succession plan. ■ Continue team member trainings, including executive-ready programs. ■ Develop and manage talent consistent with company values.
Safety and health	■ Reduce the total recordable incident rate. ■ Reduce loss time rate. ■ Complete targeted health, safety and environment improvements.
Environmental sustainability	■ Meet specific environmental standards set by global governance bodies. ■ Continue development of the company's sustainability efforts. ■ Execution of recycling initiatives. ■ Improve sustainability of company operations.
Employee engagement or retention	■ Improve employee engagement. ■ Strengthen corporate culture.
Ethics and compliance	■ Meet global ethics and compliance objectives. ■ Reduction in consumer complaints.

to evaluate ESG achievement on a qualitative basis. This is generally the case when the metric is included in an individual assessment.

In these cases, it is common for the disclosures to generally highlight the factors considered by the committee when determining individual performance but there is little to no explanation or specificity. For example, some CD&As indicate that "diversity and inclusion" will be used to gauge individual performance, but it is unclear how this personnel goal will be evaluated. This lack of clarity is expected to change in the future given the attention these metrics are gathering.

Getting to Know EVA

Economic Value Added, or EVA, has gained attention in recent years. This interest was largely due to its inclusion in ISS's pay-for-performance screening methodology. However, the metric is not particularly new, and several public companies use it successfully in their incentive programs. Given this, compensation committees should familiarize themselves with the metric and its use by proxy advisors.

EVA may be seldomly used in the boardroom and unfamiliar to some. As a refresher, EVA is a financial metric intended to calculate the value a company generated from its cost of operations and its investors' capital.

EVA is calculated as:

Net Operating Profit After Taxes (NOPAT)
– (Invested Capital x Weighted Average Cost of Capital (WACC))

It is important to note that this EVA calculation does not uniformly apply to all companies and industries. Like many other non-GAAP measurements, there may be several underlying assumptions and adjustments made to the calculation. As such, reviewing EVA numbers from the banking and mining industries, for example, may not be an apples-to-apples comparison.

Although the calculation has its complexities, its output can be most meaningful when viewed at a basic level: is it positive or negative? A positive EVA demonstrates that the company is profitable and generating a return on its investors' capital. On the other hand, a negative EVA suggests the company is not efficiently managing its operations and/or invested capital.

Beyond this simplistic approach, the actual EVA number is more revealing when viewed over a multi-year period, such as three or five years. A growing EVA is a positive sign that the company is growing value for investors. On the other hand, a declining EVA, even if positive, should trigger a deeper review of company operations and cash flow.

EVA and the Pay-for-Performance Analysis

Institutional Shareholder Services formally incorporated EVA into its quantitative pay-for-performance screen in 2020. The ISS screen is divided into four components: Relative Degree of Alignment,

Multiple of Median, Absolute Pay-TSR Alignment, and the Financial Performance Assessment. The Financial Performance Assessment (FPA) is the only measure that includes EVA.

The FPA evaluates a company's EVA in four different ways. Each of the four EVA metrics that follow are compared to those of the company's peer group. ISS relies on the following four metrics:

- **EVA Margin** is calculated as EVA divided by sales. A three-year average is used.
- **EVA Spread** is calculated as EVA divided by capital. A three-year average is used.
- **EVA Momentum (Sales)** is the three-year trend growth rate of EVA, scaled to Sales.
- **EVA Momentum (Capital)** is the three-year trend growth rate of EVA, scaled to Capital.

The FPA only acts as a modifier to the three initial quantitative tests. When a company is under ISS review, the FPA will come into play if one of the other three screens (Relative Degree of Alignment, Multiple of Median, or Absolute Pay-TSR Alignment) straddles the line between a low and medium concern. If this happens, the four EVA measures will be evaluated, along with CEO pay, and compared to those of the peer group. If the relative rankings of EVA performance and pay are not sufficiently aligned (i.e., EVA performance lags behind peers but CEO pay is relatively high), the model will increase the concern level to a medium. Alternatively, if EVA performance and pay are well aligned, the concern level will fall to low.

The use of EVA in the pay-for-performance screen should not cause any knee-jerk reactions from boards. Unlike the rush to adopt TSR following ISS's introduction of the pay-for-performance screen, EVA should only be considered if it is aligned to the company's business strategy. Given the limited impact EVA has on the pay-for-performance screen, there is no compelling reason to modify existing programs.

EVA is a valuable metric and may be beneficial when shown alongside the other, more common financials. While understanding EVA is important, the most critical thing to know is the metric's role in the ISS pay-for-performance screen.

Putting It All Together

Getting executive pay right is more challenging than ever before. By focusing on the organization's business strategy, key financial metrics, and the overall business context for the company, compensation committees will be well positioned to design plans and calibrate goals that satisfy shareholders, the board and the senior executive team.

CHAPTER 10

Executive Retirement Benefits and Deferred Compensation

By Melissa Rasman and Ron Seifert

Deferred compensation arrangements can help employers attract and retain key executives by furnishing benefits beyond the basic elements of base salary, annual incentive and long-term incentive structures typical of executive compensation packages. They are found in various forms in many organizations and are most common in large, publicly traded companies.

Broadly defined, a deferred compensation arrangement consists of an individual agreement or a plan that provides for payment of compensation to one or more employees for current services in a future year. The term "deferred compensation" encompasses both tax-qualified and nonqualified arrangements. Nonqualified programs generally are used for executive deferred compensation arrangements due to the limits on contributions and benefits under qualified plans, but can also support employee retention while providing wealth accumulation options for participants.

Employers typically use two basic categories of nonqualified deferred compensation plans: non-elective plans (commonly referred to as supplemental executive retirement plans [SERPs]) and elective deferral plans. The key difference is that employers fund non-elective plans, whereas employees contribute their own earnings to elective plans. Some employers offer plans that provide both non-elective and elective deferred compensation.

This chapter:

- Discusses the strategic objectives of a SERP program and the technical considerations that affect SERP design.
- Explains why the costs of a SERP are a crucial consideration and the five basic principles that underlie executive pensions. There also is a discussion of the rationale behind SERPs, including the role that executives themselves play in a SERP's design.
- Reviews the purpose and objectives of an elective deferred compensation program and the applicable tax and accounting rules that govern these plans. Key features and disadvantages of these plans also are discussed.

SERP Design and Organization Strategy

Supplemental executive retirement plans, as the name suggests, are designed to supplement a company's existing qualified retirement plans. Although executives generally are covered by the same qualified retirement plans as the rest of the employee population, tax-qualified retirement benefits are subject to limits on:

- Compensation taken into account for plan purposes.
- Benefit levels that can be provided (in the case of defined benefit plans).
- The amounts that can be contributed to a participant's account for a given year (in the case of defined contribution plans).

Due to these restrictions, the overall benefit levels provided under qualified plans are lower for the executive population relative to their compensation level than for the general employee population. To make executives whole for the effects of these limits, employers commonly establish SERPs. Further, organizations often design a SERP to provide a higher level of retirement income (relative to an executive's compensation) than is provided under their tax-qualified plans. These richer SERPs usually are designed to attract and retain executives. Perhaps the most popular income replacement ratio is 60 percent of compensation, which for many highly paid employees, would be impossible to achieve through tax-qualified retirement plans.

A SERP must be unfunded (generally meaning that any assets attributable to the SERP benefits must remain subject to the claims of the employer's creditors), and coverage must be limited to a select group of management and other highly compensated employees. Otherwise, legal mandates under the Employee Retirement Income Security Act of 1974 (ERISA) would make a SERP unworkable. Generally, SERP benefits are taxable to the executive (and deductible by the employer) when paid, subject to two key exceptions:

- Employees of tax-exempt employers subject to IRC section 457(f) are taxed when their benefits are no longer subject to a substantial forfeiture risk (i.e., when the benefits become vested).

- Executives of any type of employer may be taxed as vested benefits accrue if provided under a plan or arrangement that fails to meet the legal constraints on timing of benefit deferral elections, distributions and funding under IRC section 409A (which are discussed in the third section of this chapter).

Design flexibility has been critical to the popularity of SERPs. A SERP can be used to:

- Attract mid-career hires. Help supplement benefits to executives who are hired later in their careers; this can be an important recruitment tool for high-performing executives.

- Assist in succession planning. Offer an executive early retirement to facilitate necessary succession planning.

- Attach golden handcuffs. Retain an executive who may consider leaving for either retirement or a competitor.

- Provide competitive benefits. Close the gap between the existing qualified plans and what the market offers.

- Reward executive performance. Better align the interests of executives and shareholders.

A SERP's value to an executive and its strategic impact can be affected by certain critical factors, as discussed in "Key Value Parameters."

Key Value Parameters

Replacement Ratio
The target percentage of an executive's pay that the SERP is designed to pay annually during retirement. It is designed to help an executive maintain his/her accustomed standard of living in retirement. As previously noted, the most popular replacement ratio is 60 percent of an executive's total cash, with most organizations utilizing SERP objectives in the 50 to 70 percent range.

Definition of Pay
The pay definition is critical to understanding a SERP's true value. A 60 percent replacement ratio can look very different depending on whether it is pegged to salary versus total cash (salary plus annual incentive) or total direct compensation (total cash plus LTI).

Most organizations use total cash in their definition of compensation for SERP purposes. About one-quarter of organizations define compensation as base salary only, while a small number include long-term incentives. Arguably, using LTIs in defining pay is inappropriate. An LTI is intended as capital accumulation for the long-term, and it should not be replaced in a program that is designed to re-create a comparable post-retirement standard of living.

Average Pay Period
SERP values can be substantially affected by the final-pay averaging period. In companies where pay leverage and the resulting year-to-year differences are low, choosing a highest period will have little effect. But in companies with highly leveraged pay packages, such a plan could result in a significant windfall for executives. The most common choices are the highest consecutive three- and five-year periods.

Definition of Service
In this context, service refers to the minimum amount of time an executive must work with the company to earn a full retirement benefit. Retiring with less than the plan's service minimum usually requires pro-rating the targeted replacement ratio.

For companies that have a tradition of long-tenured executives, the service period may make little difference to executives. But for the increasing number of companies that recruit top executives from competitors later in their careers, the service period may be a critical determinant in the recruiting package. The typical minimum service period is 15 or 20 years. However, special provisions are sometimes crafted to recruit key executives closer to retirement.

Vesting
The vesting schedule also can have a significant effect on a SERP's value. The most prevalent practices are based on an executive's tenure with the company, with roughly

Examples of Customized Design Alternatives
Different situations may call for different designs. In examining three familiar scenarios, common design considerations are noted. First, consider the mid-career hire. Assume that a struggling company is dramatically changing its market strategy and the current executive

one-half of the SERPs using a cliff-vesting schedule that provides 100 percent vesting after a specified period of years of service (e.g., three, five, ten years), and the remaining organizations using either graded vesting, 100 percent immediate vesting or vesting at a particular age.

Retirement Age

Allowing executives to receive full benefits at an earlier age is becoming more popular. Consistently, the prevalent retirement age has been 65, but there continues to be notable prevalence for unreduced early retirement at ages 60 or 62.

Careful consideration should be given to any lowering of an unreduced retirement age. While there may be strategic reasons to facilitate an executive's early retirement, such changes can substantially increase the SERP's cost. In addition, company stakeholders may not benefit if the early retirees are vital to the company and no adequate succession plan is in place.

Actuarial Assumptions

The actuarial assumptions used to convert an annual target benefit to a lump sum can create significant differences in the present value. In practice, the selection of these assumptions — which include the assumed interest and mortality rates — can be both subjective and negotiable, but they should be considered "reasonable" from an actuarial perspective and be agreed to in advance.

Balancing Design Considerations

Each component of a SERP can be used more effectively to achieve desired results when companies do a better job of ensuring that their SERP design is driven by organizational strategy.

Organizations must ask critical questions regarding both strategy and the current makeup of the executive team. For example:

> How important is retention of the current executives in helping the organization meet its strategic objectives?

> Has the succession plan provided a strong enough executive pool with the right skills and competencies to lead the company where it needs to go?

> Does the organization need to recruit a new executive from a competitor to better enable that strategy?

> Is the current retirement package competitive enough to prevent executives from being poached by a competitor?

Generally, it is beneficial to have one program design that can serve most of the executive population. However, in many cases, the need to retain or attract particular top executives may necessitate a customized plan design.

team has little such experience. The company hopes to attract an executive from a competitor that has had success with a similar strategy. The design considerations here will be around making the SERP's upside attractive while also building in performance leverage.

Second, consider the golden handcuffs situation in which a company wants to retain its successful CEO by motivating the executive to retire later rather than earlier. Here, design considerations are around giving the executive more opportunity to obtain a larger SERP payout by staying past age 65.

Then there is the typical rising executive who is being promoted from a senior manager to a top executive. While the company's strong preference would be not to lose such an executive's talents, the board may believe that, given the company's strong succession plan, a replacement can be found if needed. Design considerations focus on increasing leverage to influence performance, with the understanding that consistently poorer performance could result in low payouts.

Each of these situations may call for a different approach to SERP design. (See Table 10-1.) In each case, the mix should be tailored to the organization's particular needs and objectives.

Executive Pensions/SERPs: An Approach Based on Core Principles

With enhanced disclosure of executive pensions, especially large (and arguably abusive) arrangements for top executives have attracted the attention of shareholders, proxy advisers and the press. Relevant questions to consider are:

TABLE 10-1 Alternative Approaches to SERP Design

	Replacement Ratio	Pay Definition	Pay Period
Mid-Career Hire	40%	**Total direct** (total cash + LTI)	3-year period average
Golden Handcuffs	60%	**Total cash** (base + bonus)	Highest 3-year period average
Rising Executive	50%	**Total cash** (base + bonus)	3-year period average
Typical Case	60%	**Total cash** (base + bonus)	3-year period average

- Are the programs reasonable and appropriate?
- Is the true potential cost reasonably determinable?
- How were they designed and approved in the first place?

Why the Cost of Executive Pensions Is Important

Executive pensions can be quite expensive, often constituting a significant portion of the value of an executive's total compensation. Historically, many executive pension arrangements were not fully and clearly disclosed to shareholders, although this was significantly improved by the enhanced disclosure rules issued by the SEC starting in 2006. However, even now the costs may not be well understood.

The most highly leveraged executive pension is the defined benefit SERP. Defined benefits (DB) plans are backloaded, with the funding cost increasing substantially as pay increases, particularly as the executive gets closer to retirement age.

For example, assume a long-serving executive covered by a 60-percent-of-final-salary defined benefit SERP is appointed CEO two years before retirement. Further assume that this resulted in his base salary increasing from $1 million to $1.5 million. While his projected annual pension benefit increased from $600,000 to $900,000, the single lump-sum cost increased to approximately $3 million. Even spread over his two remaining years, this would cost roughly $1.5 million per year, or 100 percent of his annual salary per year. This is before any bonus is even included in the pension formula. It would not be surprising to find that no board or compensation committee member was aware of this leverage and that the salary decision was made without even considering the resulting pension cost.

Minimum Service	Vesting Requirements	Retirement Age
10 years	5-year graded	60
15 years	10-year cliff	70
20 years	15-year graded	65
15 – 20 years	15-year graded	65

Although a fairly extreme example (but based on a real case), this situation illustrates just how important pension issues can be.

One-year value transfers of 50 percent to 150 percent of base salary to executives through executive pensions are common. The closer to retirement age this occurs, the more this hidden cost is leveraged. If incentive plans appear unlikely to pay out, final salary pension plans can provide a strong motivation for an executive to negotiate a salary increase.

Core Principles

Employers should reflect on certain core principles as guidelines for appropriate practice in developing executive pension programs:

- **Core Principle 1**: The provision for an executive pension is part of the rewards package the executive receives for work carried out for the organization and, as such, should be treated as part of the total compensation package, not as a separate entitlement.
- **Core Principle 2**: Realistic cost estimates of any pension proposals should be disclosed to compensation committees or other decision makers. In the case of DB plans, the cost estimates should reflect the value being transferred to the executive as well as the leveraging and phasing of that transfer — not simply the current cost charge or contribution. Salary comparisons, internal or external, and salary adjustments should consider the added effect due to significant differences in pension costs.
- **Core Principle 3**: Aside from any pension provision required by law or under a tax-qualified retirement plan available to all employees, the executive should determine the extent, if any, of the total compensation package that is apportioned to a pension.
- **Core Principle 4**: The provision of executive pensions generally should be made on a defined contribution (DC) basis (rather than on a DB basis). This DC pension (e.g., a percentage of base salary) then should be a component of the total compensation package each year. The particular amount of that component each year can be actuarially determined to produce target benefits each year of retirement, just like a DB SERP. Under a DC approach, deferred

compensation is shown as an account balance that recognizes the cost attributable to each year of employment.

- **Core Principle 5**: In accordance with enhanced executive compensation disclosure rules, the cost of executive pensions must be more fully described. In particular, DB plans often contain potentially costly ancillary benefits and special features in addition to the basic target replacement ratio. Examples are subsidized (unreduced) early retirement provisions, the inclusion of LTI awards in the definition of compensation, granting additional years of service for short-term executives, providing unrestricted joint and survivor benefits, as well as numerous other features.

Rationale

Providing a sound overall compensation package for a top executive was the focus in developing these core principles.

- Senior executives are, relative to most employees, highly paid. They have more opportunity during their working lifetimes to acquire significant assets or wealth to support that lifestyle in retirement.
- In addition, senior executives have more flexibility to determine and apportion the income level to spend currently versus save for retirement. Because this apportionment can vary substantially from person to person, it is more appropriate to allow the executive to make this decision rather than the employer. It is less appropriate for the employer to take on the financial risks associated with providing a high level of guaranteed benefits or to determine the extent to which executives should defer consumption.
- Executives should have the opportunity (and responsibility) for choosing the level of retirement income or target replacement ratio that they need and re-apportioning their total pay accordingly. In this process, executives can use an equivalent DC schedule that will produce this target. In other words, executive pensions should be considered more of an elective deferred compensation plan, although structured as employer-funded SERPs.
- Most executives are intelligent, responsible individuals who are relied upon by their employers to make sound decisions on complex

issues in their work. They often have responsibilities regarding asset values far in excess of their own pension assets. It is therefore appropriate that they take responsibility for determining the portion of their compensation packages allocated to retirement benefits.

Which Pay Components Should Be Used in Determining Pensions?

Variable pay has become a standard portion of executive compensation packages, and the level of retirement income generally is considered relative to pay. However, retirement income is not expected to be as volatile as pay can be from year to year. Accordingly, some judgment should be applied in targeting an executive's fixed retirement income to a variable rate of compensation while in active employment.

It can be appropriate to include annual bonuses in the definition of pay for purposes of determining pension contributions or benefits. Annual bonuses can be considered as part of the standard of living developed for an executive over the years. However, LTIs represent special awards that are intended to be capital accumulation devices in and of themselves (as is a SERP). Therefore, the inclusion of LTI in the definition of annual pay for pension purposes is redundant and inappropriate.

In some circumstances, the inclusion of annual bonuses in the pension formula is purely cosmetic. For example, an annual pension of 60 percent of base salary at retirement is the same as a pension of 50 percent of total cash compensation for an employee with a 20 percent bonus. A company may believe that one approach appears less controversial than the other even though they both produce the same benefit.

Removing Executive Distractions

A common argument is that DB plans enable an executive to ignore his/her personal financial security concerns and focus on the company's business, as opposed to the distractions associated with the variations in a DC structure.

If the employer wants to take such a paternalistic approach, this can be addressed by providing a basic level of DB protection. Beyond such a minimum, the second core principle would be applied.

Elective Deferred Compensation Arrangements

Nonqualified deferred compensation (NQDC) plans that are funded by executives through elective deferral arrangements also can help employers attract and retain key executives by furnishing benefits beyond the basic executive compensation package.

A nonqualified plan is not required to meet the coverage, vesting, funding or fiduciary responsibility rules of ERISA. Most of ERISA's reporting and disclosure requirements and the tax-qualification requirements applicable to qualified retirement plans under the IRC also are inapplicable. However, a nonqualified arrangement does not receive the favorable tax treatment accorded a qualified retirement plan.

Because nonqualified plans are exempt from the most restrictive provisions of ERISA and the IRC, they can be designed to cover selected executives. In fact, these plans generally cannot be made available to rank-and-file employees.

Elective deferred compensation plans enable an executive to defer payment of a portion of his/her compensation to a future date. Under a properly designed plan, executives of for-profit businesses can defer tax on compensation until they receive it without risking forfeiture if they voluntarily terminate employment; executives of tax-exempt organizations do not have this option due to special tax rules applicable to tax-exempt employers. Therefore, elective plans are a more valuable benefit in the for-profit sector.

Purpose

Elective NQDC plans are similar to section 401(k) plans in that a covered employee may elect to set aside a portion of his/her compensation for payment in the future. Such plans have several advantages:

- **Deferrals of compensation in excess of the statutory limitations on qualified plans**. Nonqualified plans can make up for regulatory limits on pre-tax contributions to tax-qualified plans, such as section 401(k) plans, and can recognize pay that may not be taken into account under a qualified plan. Because nonqualified plans allow executives to defer compensation above the statutory limitations, they can be used to supplement retirement benefits under a company's qualified retirement plans and provide for other future financial commitments.

- **Reduction of executive's current income taxes**. Current taxable income is reduced by the amount of compensation that is deferred. However, compensation will be taxed at ordinary income tax rates that are in effect when distributions are received. If the executive is in a lower income tax bracket when distributions are made (compared to the applicable rate when compensation is deferred), there may be additional income tax savings. On the other hand, if the applicable tax rate is higher, the executive could pay more in taxes than if the compensation had not been deferred.

- **Tax-deferred accumulation**. Income tax is not paid on earnings credited to a deferred compensation account until distributions are received (or vested, in the case of a tax-exempt employer's plan), allowing the deferrals and earnings to compound on a pre-tax basis.

- **Recruitment and retention of key employees**. An employer can use these plans as a recruitment incentive and retention tool. Many executives seek arrangements to supplement the company's retirement plans. In addition, these executives may be more likely to continue employment to avoid triggering a taxable distribution upon termination or, if vesting is deferred, forfeiting all or a portion of the benefit accrued.

- **Coverage and design flexibility**. Because there are no coverage, eligibility or nondiscrimination requirements applicable to nonqualified plans, an employer can provide these benefits to a select group of executives or highly compensated employees; coverage of other employees generally would subject the plan to the reach of ERISA. Because there are fewer formal requirements applicable to NQDC plans than to qualified plans, nonqualified programs can be simpler to establish and maintain. In particular, nonqualified plans have no funding requirements. However, employers must be careful to take into account the tax law restrictions that do exist. For example, running afoul of the rules of IRC section 409A can result in substantial tax penalties to an executive. In addition, beginning in 2018, a tax-exempt employer that pays more than $1 million in taxable pay in a given year to one of its five most highly paid executives (subject to certain exceptions) is subject to a 21 percent excise tax on the excess amount; this includes amounts that vest under a NQDC plan under IRC Section 457(f) in that year.

Taxation and Accounting

General rules on how NQDC is taxed and how it is treated under the accounting rules are summarized in Table 10-2. Under a taxable employer's deferred compensation arrangement that satisfies applicable tax law standards, neither the compensation nor the earnings on the deferrals is taxable to the individual until received. When the employee recognizes taxable income and incurs tax liability, the company receives a tax deduction in the same amount. In most cases, the company will have recorded an expense on its books at the time the compensation was earned, even though the tax deduction might not apply for many years.

TABLE 10-2 **How NQDC Is Taxed and Treated Under Accounting Rules**

	Company Accounting	Company Taxation	Individual Taxation
Compensation Earned	Charge to earnings	No tax deduction	FICA tax
Compensation Received	No charge to earnings	Tax deduction	Ordinary income tax

Applicable Tax Laws

Although NQDC plans have fewer restrictions than qualified plans, specific rules must be followed to accomplish the deferral of an employee's taxable compensation.

- **Constructive receipt**. If an executive can obtain funds at any time upon request or has control over them, the amounts are currently taxable under the long-standing doctrine of constructive receipt, regardless of whether the executive actually obtains the money. To avoid constructive receipt, a deferred compensation agreement must be entered into before the deferred income is earned or available; the arrangement also must substantially restrict the executive's ability to access the funds until a predetermined time or event (at which time it will become taxable). These requirements were formalized as part of IRC section 409A.

Section 409A and Elective Deferred Compensation Plans

Initial Deferral Elections

In general, elective participant deferrals are irrevocable and must be made before the start of the calendar year in which the related services commence. The election must identify the amount to be deferred, the length of period of deferral and the form of payment. For performance-based compensation relating to services performed during a period of at least 12 months, a participant's initial deferral election may be made at any time before the six-month period prior to the end of the performance period — if it meets certain criteria. For example, participants in a bonus plan that has a calendar-year performance period could make deferral elections regarding such bonuses anytime on or before June 30 of the calendar year in which the amounts are earned.

Changes to Deferral Elections

A subsequent participant election to delay a payment or change the form of payment must not take effect for at least 12 months and must further defer the payments for at least five years. If the payment is scheduled to be made on a fixed date, the subsequent deferral election may not be made sooner than 12 months prior to the date the amount is scheduled to be paid. In general, these restrictions also apply to changes to distribution provisions initiated by the employer.

Distributions

Payments of deferred compensation may only be made at a specified time or under a fixed schedule that is objectively determinable, or upon certain specified events — separation from service, death, disability, change in the ownership or effective control of the company or unforeseeable emergency, in each case as defined by the IRC and tax regulations.

■ **Section 409A**. IRC section 409A imposes a series of requirements on NQDC arrangements. The rules govern when deferral elections may be made, when deferrals may be modified, when deferred amounts may be distributed, and how they may be funded. Unless an exception applies, a nonqualified arrangement must meet these requirements in form and in operation. Section 409A accelerates income taxation and imposes a 20 percent tax penalty, as well as interest payments, on a covered executive if a plan is noncompliant. See "Section 409A and Elective Deferred Compensation Plans" for more information about specific rules that can apply.

To avoid current taxation of deferred amounts under the economic benefit and constructive receipt doctrines, nonqualified plan benefits must be unfunded and subject to the claims of general creditors. In

Acceleration of Payments

Deferred compensation payments generally may not be made before the permissible payment date or event specified in the plan. This anti-acceleration rule effectively bars distribution of benefits upon plan termination, except under certain limited circumstances.

Six-Month Delay to Specified Employees

Payments to a specified employee of a public company triggered by a separation from service must be delayed at least six months following the separation, except in the event of disability or death of the specified employee. For purposes of this provision, "specified employee" generally includes "key employees" of public companies as defined in the "top-heavy" rules governing benefits provided under tax-qualified retirement plans.

Restrictions on Setting Aside Funds

Section 409A limits the ability of an employer to informally set aside assets to pay deferred compensation benefits.

Economic Benefit

Under the economic benefit doctrine, income realized in any form by an executive is taxable upon grant if:

> It has tangible, quantifiable value that the executive has in effect received, and
> There is no substantial risk of forfeiture.
> The economic benefit doctrine was formalized in IRC section 83, governing when transfers of "property" are taxed.

the case of the company's insolvency or bankruptcy, the executive's right to receive payments may be no greater than that of any other general unsecured creditor. Although nonqualified plan benefits must be unfunded, they typically are informally funded with money set aside in trust accounts to cover the plans' liabilities while maintaining exemption from most ERISA requirements. These funds remain assets of the company and are within the reach of creditors in the event of insolvency or bankruptcy.

Informal funding can increase participant security but falls short of true funding. Two common informal funding devices are:

- Rabbi trust. An employer-established grantor trust into which the employer determines how much money or other assets are placed for the provision of benefits. These assets must remain subject to the company's creditors.
- Corporate-owned life insurance (COLI). Death proceeds or loans are used to recover benefit payments provided by the plan. COLI involves an employer's investment in cash-value life insurance policies that insure the lives of selected executives. The company pays the premiums, retains ownership and receives tax-free proceeds when the participant dies.

If assets are transferred outside of the United States or restrictions are triggered by an employer's poor financial health, section 409A accelerates income taxation and imposes penalties on executives covered by informal DC funding arrangements.

Section 409A also penalizes certain officers and top-paid employees of any public company that maintains a tax-qualified DB plan if the employer sets aside assets to pay deferred compensation in specific circumstances: while in bankruptcy, within six months of terminating an underfunded plan or while the plan is less than 80 percent funded under "at risk" funding rules.

Plan Design

In designing an elective deferred compensation plan, decisions on certain key features are needed:

- **Eligible deferral sources**. Which elements of compensation are allowed to be deferred? Base salary, annual incentive, cash-based LTI and/or RSU?
- **Deferral period**. What is the period for deferring compensation? Will payments be triggered at termination, retirement, death, disability, change in control or on a specified date? When will payment be made after the relevant trigger?
- **Form of payout**. What are the permissible forms of payment? Lump sum or installments? If the trigger is an employee's termination, the form of payment must be the same for each year's deferral.
- **Investment options**. Deferral accounts are usually credited with a return that can be fixed, based on a variable rate or floating rate (e.g., prime rate, U.S. Treasury bill rate), or tied to a hypothetical investment alternative (e.g., mutual fund).

These design decisions are also important for nonelective deferred compensation plans (e.g., SERPs).

Potential Disadvantages

Despite their many advantages, NQDC plans also have drawbacks. When evaluating such plans, consider the following disadvantages:

- **Current tax deduction unavailable to employer**. An employer cannot claim a current deduction for any NQDC amounts until the employee receives the amount as income.
- **Unfunded plan**. Deferred amounts under an NQDC plan are merely an employer's promise to pay the employee in the future. Because these amounts must remain subject to the claims of the employer's creditors in the event of insolvency, a company's obligation to pay may become an empty promise if it becomes insolvent.
- **Restricted access to money**. In general, participants do not have access to deferrals until the selected payment date or event.
- **Possible higher tax rate**. The applicable tax rate when payments are received may be greater than when funds are deferred, reducing the overall return on the deferrals.

- **Risk of tax penalty for section 409A violation**. If the employer fails to comply with the operational and written documentation requirements of section 409A, the executive will owe ordinary income tax earlier than expected, plus a substantial tax penalty.
- **Securities law registration**. An employee's interest in an elective deferred compensation arrangement is considered a security, subject to registration under federal securities and state blue-sky laws, unless an applicable exemption applies. Most deferred compensation plans are exempt from federal securities registration but may need to be registered in certain states where employees reside.

An executive's opportunity to defer compensation can be an effective recruitment and retention tool, so employers should consider making available nonqualified plans that are tailored to their particular circumstances. Executives usually appreciate being able to defer compensation in excess of the statutory limits. Before proceeding, an employer should understand the financial implications of the postponed tax deduction for the deferred compensation. An employer also must ensure that its nonqualified arrangements comply with the requirements of IRC section 409A and are designed to be tax effective for eligible executives.

Conclusion

Retirement benefits and deferred compensation arrangements are valuable components of an executive compensation program. However, the costs and administrative burden with these programs can be substantial. As such, the board should carefully consider the strategic advantages and drawbacks before entering into these arrangements.

CHAPTER 11

Executive Nonretirement Benefits and Perquisites

By Laura Balser and Stephanie Ma

Although not as prevalent as in the past, special executive health and welfare benefits and perquisites can be important adjuncts to executive pay packages. Perquisites of various kinds are found in most U.S. companies and are very prevalent outside of the United States. Whether offered in cash or in kind, perquisites cover a broad range of services and benefits. The most common perquisites include life insurance, disability insurance, executive physical exam, financial planning, tax preparation, company car or allowance, and personal use of corporate aircraft. Most perquisites have declined in prevalence over the last decade as shareholders and institutional investors questioned the reasonableness and costs as well as the attraction and retention impact of perquisites. More importantly, in its major overhaul of the executive compensation disclosure rules in 2006, the SEC lowered the financial threshold for aggregate perquisite disclosure for named executives and directors to $10,000, thus giving a much clearer picture of the extent of perquisite use in publicly held companies.

Tax law requirements can result in some or all of the perks' value being taxed as income to the executive. Health and welfare plans also may trigger additional taxes to executives. Nonetheless, they represent value to executives and, like perquisites, should be reviewed periodically to ensure that they use company funds efficiently and align with executive compensation and corporate strategies. Health and welfare benefits and perquisites that clearly benefit both the company and the executive without engendering unacceptable criticism, such as those affecting the health and safety of the employee, likely will continue to be offered, while others will be reduced or eliminated.

This chapter:

- Analyzes perquisites in large U.S. companies, with a discussion of which perquisites are the most costly to the company, which are likely to be discontinued and which may survive.
- Discusses the trends in executive health and welfare benefits, including the various kinds of executive life insurance, short- and long-term disability benefits, and health care benefits.

Executive Perquisites

Executive perquisites (perks) had been scrutinized for many years, so it was no surprise that the SEC targeted them in its 2006 reworking of the executive pay disclosure rules.

Companies now must break out perks that have an aggregate value in excess of $10,000, while the prior rules only required disclosure of perks that were worth more than $50,000 or 10 percent of cash compensation. Because most companies limited their perquisite disclosures to what was required, pre-2007 proxy statements did not furnish a true indication of the prevalence of various perks.

Most research found that the majority of companies now are disclosing all perks, even if they total less than $10,000 in value for complete transparency. Of course, some organizations follow the reporting requirements precisely and do not disclose the smaller perks.

Prevalence of Perks

Almost all large public companies provide at least one perk to their executives. The most common perks are financial planning, tax preparation services and an executive physical exam. Other notable perks are executive life insurance, executive disability insurance, company car or allowance, and providing company aircraft to the CEO for personal use.

Why Focus on Perks?

In dollar terms, perks are a very small slice of the pay pie. Then why have perks drawn such criticism from investors and corporate watchdogs over the years? In an effort to garner public attention, the media tends to focus on outliers — instances from corporate America that are at an extreme (i.e., the largest or smallest amounts). While these examples typically are not representative of the entire sample, they can make interesting news and great headlines. (See "The Outliers.")

Companies Discontinuing or Eliminating Perks

With investors gaining a better look at executive perquisites in post-2006 disclosures, many corporate boards re-examined the perks furnished to the company's executives. As part of the process, some employers discontinued selected (or even all) perks. In fact, since 2006 most companies have reported the discontinuance of at least one perk. The perks most frequently eliminated have been income tax gross-ups, country club membership dues and company cars. Companies in recent years have reported perks that, for the most part, related to the overall health and well-being of the recipient executives. Typically, companies have not cut back on most security-related perks for the CEO, such as personal use of the corporate aircraft, home security or a security driver. These security-related perks became very common after the terrorist acts of Sept. 11, 2001. Many companies specifically disclose that these perks are primarily for security purposes.

Will Perks Continue Declining?

Because the safety of senior executives is critical, companies appear likely to retain perquisites that enhance executives' safety. Similarly, because it is in the interests of both companies and their senior executives to manage the health of such executives, physical exams have continued to survive.

On the other hand, companies probably will continue curbing various club memberships (e.g., country clubs, health clubs, airplane

The Outliers

Where companies reported a substantial amount of CEO perk value, we reviewed the text to look for outliers. Aside from the use of corporate aircraft, the largest perk values were for the cost of home security, supplemental life insurance, a company car, personal and spouse travel, club dues and financial counseling. The smallest perk values, all under $5,000, were for the cost of a physical examination, health club membership, personal entertainment, airline club membership and gifts.

Personal Aircraft Usage

Personal use of the corporate aircraft, when provided to senior executives, typically is the most costly executive perk. The value of executive perks appears in the "All Other Compensation" (AOC) column in the proxy's Summary Compensation Table, along with the value of discount stock purchases, company contributions to defined contribution plans and company payment of insurance premiums. The median value of a CEO's personal use of the corporate aircraft recently has exceeded 50 percent of the AOC total value.

Companies also are continuing to put limits on how much plane usage the CEO and sometimes the other executives can use per year or by month. The limits are typically stated as a defined dollar amount or as a specific number of hours per year. While less common, we have also seen the limits stated as a number of trips per year.

Unusual Perks

We also examined proxy statements for descriptions of unusual perks, but it appears that larger companies have deliberately discontinued using perks that tend to stand out. There are still perks that involve the use of corporate facilities (e.g., company barbershop, boats, hunting and fishing clubs, company helicopter) and those that involve organizations providing company products or product discounts (e.g., tire program, theme park use, merchandise discount program).

clubs), free sporting and entertainment event tickets, and any tax gross-ups, as they are finding insufficient benefit to justify the criticism received from groups such as proxy advisers and the media.

In the 1980s and 1990s, cafeteria perks or perks allowances appeared on the verge of becoming popular but are rare today. The approach involves granting an executive an annual dollar amount that the executive then allocates among a select group or menu of executive perks. Most companies resorted to eliminating allowances and replaced them with a one-time salary increase. Of course, critics are quick to point out that this approach may have had an adverse cost effect for the company as base pay increases also raise the costs of items based on salary, such as annual bonuses, target LTI amounts, life insurance and retirement benefits.

Executive Health and Welfare Benefits

Executive benefits and perk programs are designed to attract and retain key employees and frequently are designed specifically for certain executives. While retirement benefits have received much attention, the focus here is on the nonretirement benefits components, often referred to as health and welfare programs. This terminology groups together the benefits received for certain specific life events: death, disability, illness, injury and paid time off, each addressing common health and welfare needs.

Executive health and welfare benefits are not particularly scrutinized because they usually follow the "same for all employees" approach that is found at a majority of organizations today. Supplemental benefits are found in less than a third of U.S. employers, with the prevalence rising as the size of the organization increases. Typically offered to a select group of employees, these benefits are usually add-ons or supplemental to existing plans available to all employees.

Clearly, cost is not an issue here, as most of these benefits are provided at little or no cost to the executive and represent minor incremental cost to the employer. However, the real value of any extra benefits may not be appreciated because the covered executives, like most employees, only focus on these benefits when they actually are needed.

Death Benefits

Executive term-life insurance comes in many forms and designs, with each serving a variety of purposes. The typical life benefit provides coverage based on a percentage of salary above that provided to all other employees. This benefit may be implemented because the basic coverage levels have caps or upper limits that preclude the executive from coverage of a full multiple of salary. For example, a basic plan may offer two times salary with a maximum of $400,000. This would clearly create a shortfall in intended benefits for anyone making more than $200,000 a year in salary. Thus, organizations may create a separate insurance class for the executives with higher limits or purchase individual coverage for the additional amounts. In either case, because it only is intended to make up for lost benefits, the full cost usually is paid by the firm.

While many other forms of life insurance are available to executives, all involve more permanent and expensive coverage instead of the typical term insurance.

Key-person life is an individual policy owned totally by the employer and is provided by only a very small percentage of employers. The most common reason for the coverage is to protect the employer against the sudden loss of a key executive. The organization pays the full cost of the policy and receives the full proceeds, which can be used for expenses until it can find a replacement. Other purposes include paying off debts, distributing money to investors, paying severance to employees and closing the business down in an orderly manner.

Disability Benefits

Short-term salary continuance and/or accumulation-of-days programs like PTO provide further coverage for executives. In salary continuation programs, this often takes the form of a 100-percent-of-pay benefit for the entire short-term disability period or an additional number of days (generally about a week) in a PTO bank.

Special long-term programs are provided by about one-third of organizations, with the majority of the cost covered by the employer. Where employers provide these extra benefits, the larger organizations lead the way. In addition, more than two-thirds of the health care industry provides these additional disability benefits, perhaps because of their health mission.

The design of these plans is intended to increase the level of coverage through various approaches, including:

- Shorter waiting periods for commencement of benefits
- Higher monthly maximum benefits

- Higher percentage of salary benefits (typically up to 70 percent of base pay)
- The definition of disability based on only the executive's current occupation
- Easing the maximums or expanding definitions all increase the value of this benefit if and when an executive incurs a disability.

One key item executives need to remember is that whatever portion of the premiums are paid by the employer, that same portion of the benefit, if received, also is taxable income.

Health Care Benefits

Due to the scope of health care coverage commonly provided by U.S. employers for all employees and the tax-free nature of these benefits, few special executive health care benefits are offered. In fact, the Patient Protection and Affordable Care Act in 2010 (ACA) included a provision prohibiting offering insured medical plans that discriminate in favor of a particular population like executives, but grandfathered insured health plans already in place if not modified after the date the ACA was enacted. As a result of seeking advice on complying with the new ACA provision, many employers learned that their executives should have been taxed in the health benefits they received under their discriminatory self-insured health plans. Since then, many organizations have closed their executive medical plans to new entrants or eliminated the programs altogether.

An annual physical examination was previously another key executive benefit, as companies and executives each understood the importance of maintaining a healthy executive team. However, as health care reform took effect, all employees have annual physicals covered at 100 percent under preventive-care mandates. Thus, except for situations in which the executive can obtain these physicals at high-end clinics, this no longer is seen as an executive perquisite.

Finally, very few organizations offer a formal medical expense reimbursement plan; the scarcity likely reflects the high cost of the premiums. To avoid tax implications, these plans must be fully insured and provide for reimbursement of medical expenses incurred by the executives and their dependents in excess of the amounts covered by the underlying basic plans. Most core plans are designed to cover catastrophic costs, so these reimbursement plans really provide coverage for the first-dollar type co-payments and deductibles in the base plans up to the annual out-of-pocket maximums.

CHAPTER 12

Stock Ownership Guidelines and Share Holding Requirements

By Cory Morrow and Casey Martinez

Shareholders, the business media and institutional investors all favor the notion that executives and outside directors should hold significant ownership positions in the companies they manage or oversee. To achieve that goal, publicly traded companies often provide a significant portion of an executive's compensation in company stock. Most public companies in the United States have adopted stock ownership guidelines which require select executives to acquire and maintain minimum ownership levels. These guidelines are intended to align the interests of executives with those of a company's long-term shareholders, helping ensure that company executives operate their companies in ways that benefit those same long-term shareholders.

Executives and outside directors (collectively "participants") receive stock awards that recognize their contributions to the company. By requiring that a significant portion of a participant's wealth be tied to company shares, stock ownership guidelines and share retention policies help to ensure that participants have a strong incentive to maximize shareholder value over time. These policies also serve to mitigate potential risk-taking behavior which may provide short-term benefits at the expense of long-term shareholder value.

This chapter:

- Describes stock ownership guidelines, stock retention policies and how they are used by public companies in the United States.

■ Outlines key questions and considerations for companies implementing stock ownership guidelines.

While there are multiple approaches to implementation and measurement of ownership guidelines, the primary objective is always to ensure that executives and directors maintain meaningful ownership positions in the companies they manage.

Defining Terms

Before getting started, it is important to clarify the differences between stock ownership guidelines and stock retention policies.

■ **Stock Ownership Guidelines**: A stock ownership guideline is a policy that establishes expected stock ownership levels for participants in various roles in the company.
■ **Stock Retention Policies**: A stock retention policy is a requirement that participants retain all or a portion of any vested company stock received as compensation from the company.

Although stock ownership guidelines and stock retention policies are often implemented together, it is necessary to recognize them as separate policies with different implications for participants.

Use of Share Ownership Guidelines

The majority of U.S. public companies use some form of share ownership guidelines for executives and outside directors. Implementing these guidelines publicly demonstrates a board's desire for executives to share in the same rewards and risks as long-term shareholders.

For executives, ownership guidelines typically only apply to the CEO, direct reports to the CEO, other executive officers of the company and other key executives. Guidelines are typically expressed as a multiple of base salary, with greater requirements for higher-level roles within an organization. For example, a CEO may be required to hold five to seven times their base salary, while other key executives may have to hold 50 percent to three times base salary.

Participants are typically given a reasonable time period (often referred to as the "accumulation period") — typically five years — to obtain company shares and meet the pre-established ownership levels. Once the required levels are reached, participants are expected to maintain those levels throughout their employment with the company. For purposes of determining compliance with the guideline, company stock that the participant owns outright (whether directly, by immediate family members or indirectly through a trust), vested shares in employee benefits plans, and unvested restricted shares (which vest solely on the passage of time) are typically included. Stock options are generally excluded from the ownership calculation, although some companies include the intrinsic value of vested but unexercised options (calculated as the number of vested but unexercised options multiplied by the difference between the current stock price and the weighted average option exercise price).

Guidelines are similar for outside directors. Most commonly, share ownership guidelines are expressed as a multiple of a director's annual board cash retainer. Unlike executives where the multiple corresponds to the executive's position, all outside directors are typically subject to the same multiple. Similarly, directors are provided with an accumulation period — typically five years — to obtain company shares and meet the required levels. Given the typical practice of providing the majority of a director's compensation in stock, directors are often able to achieve the ownership guidelines by holding the shares delivered to them through these grants.

Stock Retention Policies

In recent years, many companies have explored other approaches in lieu of, or in conjunction with, share ownership guidelines. A stock retention policy is one example of a policy that can increase share ownership levels and strengthen the alignment of interests between executives, outside directors and shareholders.

The key feature of a retention policy allows a participant to realize value and build share ownership while permitting diversification. Retention policies may be used as a stand-alone alternative to stock ownership guidelines, or as is most common today, in combination with share ownership guidelines.

When a participant exercises stock options, vests in a time-vested restricted stock award or receives an earn-out of performance shares, the participant is required to hold a specified percentage of the shares, net of tax withholding, for a designated period of time. The participant may sell the remaining net shares.

The holding requirements generally range from 50 to 75 percent of the net shares. A typical holding period is three to five years, although some companies may require executives and directors to hold the specified net shares until termination of employment or termination from the board.

With each exercise, lapse of vesting restrictions or earn-out, the participant builds his/her share ownership position while having the opportunity to diversify personal assets.

Some organizations have adopted retention policies requiring executives and outside directors to keep a significant portion of their stock awards until retirement and, in some instances, into retirement. The focus of these retention policies is to strongly link executive equity-based compensation — often the primary component of their pay packages — to long-term performance.

There are several types of retention policies, including:
- Retention ratios
- Retention policies used in conjunction with stock ownership guidelines
- Long-term vesting

Retention Ratios

The retention ratio is the most common design, requiring that an individual retain a fixed percentage (typically 50 to 75 percent) of the after-tax portion of earned equity awards until the executive leaves the company. Although less common, the holding period also can be extended for a period of time into retirement (i.e., hold through retirement).

The key is that the retention ratio applies to earned equity awards. When an executive or outside director receives shares of company stock (e.g., a stock option is exercised or a restricted stock vests), a portion of the net shares must be retained for the duration of the executive's career or director's tenure. The net shares are those that remain after the payment of taxes and, in the case of stock options, the exercise price. Because the equity awards have been earned, the executive or director is not in danger of losing the awards if he/she leaves the company.

Retention policies in conjunction with stock ownership guidelines

When used in conjunction with stock ownership guidelines, retention policies require participants to hold equity awards only until the traditional ownership guidelines have been met. For example, a company may require its executive officers and directors to hold 100 percent of their equity awards (net of taxes and exercise price) until stock ownership guidelines are satisfied. After achieving the guidelines, recipients may be required to hold a portion of the net shares for one year. This is intended to support the timely accumulation of stock toward the ownership guideline.

For example, a company may require executive officers or directors to retain at least 50 percent of common stock and equity awards (less allowances for the payment of any option exercise price and taxes) made to them while they are employed by the organization or serving on its board. Under this approach, a portion of an individual's net worth is tied to the company's share price. Proponents argue that this approach motivates executives to focus on long-term share price appreciation.

Long-term Vesting

Under the long-term vesting approach, a portion of an executive's equity grant does not vest until retirement. One consequence is that a participant cannot sell a portion of the equity grant until retirement, even if the executive is permitted to exercise vested stock options.

This is a notable difference between the retention ratio and long-term vesting approach. Under the retention ratio design, the ratio only applies to earned equity awards and, if a participant leaves before retirement, he/she is not in danger of losing the awards. Under the long-term vesting approach, the awards may be forfeited if the executive leaves before retirement age. This feature likely explains why the long-term vesting approach is far less prevalent than the retention ratio design.

Implementation Considerations

There are many practical decisions companies face when implementing ownership guidelines. This section addresses a number of the key questions companies face when considering share ownership guidelines, including:

- Who should be subject to the guidelines?
- How should companies denominate share ownership guidelines?
- How should companies determine the value of stock held by participants?
- What values and/or multiples should we use for affected participants?
- What shares/awards should be included in the calculation?
- Should a retention policy be implemented?
- How long should participants be given to achieve ownership guidelines?
- When and how often should guideline attainment of impacted participants be reviewed?
- How should companies treat non-compliance?

Who should be subject to stock ownership guidelines?

In nearly all cases, companies with ownership guidelines will include all executive officers (as defined by the U.S. Securities Exchange Act of 1934; "Section 16 Officers") and members of the board of directors. However, companies' selection of the employee populations subject to ownership guidelines varies significantly.

Companies may elect to include all employees at the Vice President level and above, the Senior Vice President level and above, or limit guidelines to those executives who have significant policy making or income statement responsibilities. There is no single right answer that will work for all companies. However, few companies extend ownership guidelines below the Vice President level.

How should companies denominate share ownership guidelines?

The most common approach for setting ownership guidelines is the use of a multiple of annual base salary for impacted executives. However, companies may also elect to set a fixed share, or fixed value guideline threshold. The type of guideline typically aligns with a company's approach to granting equity compensation. If a company uses a percent of a participant's salary to determine the size of an equity award, it may set ownership guidelines as a multiple of salary. However, if a company grants a fixed number of shares to participants, it will often use a fixed number of shares in its stock ownership guideline. Similarly, if a company grants a fixed value to participants of a certain level, the company may set its ownership guidelines in terms of fixed values.

How should companies determine the value of stock held by participants?

Determining the value of the shares subject to the ownership guidelines is a key decision which can impact participants' ability to achieve their guideline in a reasonable amount of time. Using a single trading day price may be the simplest approach but it subjects participants to the volatility of the company's stock price. A growing number of companies elect to use an average price, typically the average of close prices over a number of trading days (5-day, 20-day and 60-day averages are common).

If a company uses an average number of trading days to determine value, it should determine if there are any time-specific events that may affect close prices. For example, if a company uses a 20-day average, and the 20-day period encompasses the date of its earnings release, it should evaluate whether or not the average price is a true reflection of the stock price, or if the price is materially different after the earnings release than before. In this case, it may be more appropriate to use a shorter averaging period.

What multiples and/or values should we use for affected participants?

Ownership guidelines are typically higher for the most senior (and most highly compensated) executives. Guidelines for CEOs typically range from five times salary to seven times salary but can be as high as 10 times salary. The target multiple or value gradually decreases from the top executive down through the lowest levels subject to the guidelines.

What shares/awards should be included in the calculation?

One of the most significant questions when implementing ownership guidelines is which shares to include in the calculation. In all cases common shares owned outright by participants are included in the calculation. Many companies will also include shares that are held in a retirement account, such as a 401(k), to the extent they can be identified, and those purchases through employee stock purchase programs (ESPP). Companies typically also include unvested restricted stock and restricted stock units (RSUs), assuming they are not subject to performance criteria.

Some companies will also include the intrinsic value of unexercised vested (and in some cases unvested) stock options in the calculation (intrinsic value being the current stock price minus the exercise price times the number of options).

Typical Share Ownership Guidelines (US Public Companies)

CEO	5x to 7x base salary
Direct Reports to the CEO	3x to 4x base salary
Other Key Executives	0.5x to 3x base salary
Board Directors	3x to 5x annual cash retainer

Companies will typically exclude performance-vesting equity awards from the calculation as it may be difficult to determine the number of shares that will ultimately vest based on performance criteria.

A small number of companies have elected to discount the value of unvested (or unexercised) equity awards to account for the fact that in many cases, a portion of the award will be withheld to satisfy the participant's tax obligations when they vest (or are exercised). In those cases, companies will discount a portion of the value of the award by as much as 50 percent to account for the tax withholding.

Should companies adopt retention policies?

Retention policies require executives to hold all or a portion of vested shares. Retention policies may restrict executives from selling shares prior to meeting their guidelines and may also require executives to hold shares once they have met their guidelines (even into retirement).

A number of companies restrict a participant's ability to sell shares of company stock until they have met their ownership guideline level. Most companies that have retention requirements allow the sale (or exercise) of at least a portion of vested awards, often as much as 50 percent of vested equity. However, some companies will not allow the sale of any shares until the executive has achieved their ownership guideline level.

Shares Commonly Included/Excluded from Stock Ownership Guideline Achievement

Included	Excluded
■ Shares owned outright (by participant and immediate family members)	■ Unvested stock options
■ Shares held in benefits plans (such as 401(k) plans or other non-qualified deferred compensation plans)	■ Vested and unexercised stock options (companies do occasionally elect to include the intrinsic value of vested stock options in the ownership calculation)
■ Shares held by a trust to benefit the participant or immediate family members	■ Unvested stock appreciation rights
■ Unvested restricted stock (or restricted stock units – "RSU")	■ Unvested performance-based equity awards
■ Shares purchased through employee stock purchase program ("ESPP")	

Another consideration is to allow lower-level participants to sell shares while restricting higher-level executives. Companies will often restrict executive officers (who are subject to securities filing requirements) from selling any shares until they have met ownership guidelines, while permitting non-officers to sell a portion of their shares prior to meeting their guidelines. Further, some companies will restrict officers from selling a portion of their shares (as much as 50%) even after they have met their guidelines.

How long should participants be given to achieve ownership guidelines?

Most companies set an accumulation period by which they expect participants to have achieved their guideline ownership level. This should provide executives enough time to accumulate the share ownership level required through their annual equity awards, without purchasing shares on the open market. In practice, accumulation periods are typically five years. However, there may be extenuating circumstances under which companies provide additional time to achieve guideline compliance (e.g., sudden market price declines).

When and how often should guideline attainment of impacted participants be reviewed?

Companies typically review ownership guidelines on an annual basis. Guideline compliance is typically reviewed annually by the compensation committee. Committees typically receive a list of participants subject to stock ownership guidelines, their current required ownership levels, their current ownership levels and any mitigating considerations for individual non-compliance. During this annual review, committees may consider any actions to address participant non-compliance.

Companies with stock retention policies may allow participants to request re-evaluation of guideline compliance between annual guideline reviews if the individual has purchased shares on the open market or if the stock price has materially changed since the most recent review. This practice allows participants to realize the value of their equity compensation when guideline compliance is achieved outside of the annual review process.

A small minority of companies evaluate guideline compliance on a real-time basis. This allows participants to realize the value of their awards when their ownership level exceeds their guidelines. However, this practice also subjects participants to the volatility of the market. A participant who placed a sell order on Monday, when their ownership exceeded their guideline, may fall below the guideline by Wednesday, when the trade is executed in the market.

Many companies have adopted a "once met, always met" standard to mitigate the impact of market volatility on guideline compliance. Under this practice, once a participant has achieved his or her guideline ownership level, future declines in share price will not impact the participant's compliance, as long as the participant retains the number of shares required to initially meet the guideline. However, when executives are promoted into new roles (even if their guideline multiple is unchanged) or receive material increases in their base salary, companies will typically require the executive to meet a recalculated ownership level (based on their new salary and, if applicable, a new multiple).

How should companies treat non-compliance?

Few companies publicly disclose their policies for dealing with guideline non-compliance. In most cases, the board of directors will retain discretion on potential actions to address participant non-compliance. In some cases, penalties may include deferring cash incentive payments into restricted stock (or RSUs), enhanced holding requirements, or the prohibition of any sales of company stock until guideline compliance is achieved.

Conclusion

Market practices for stock ownership guidelines and retention policies continue to evolve as companies reevaluate their appropriateness and key design features. Regardless, they are likely to remain an important feature of public company compensation programs in the United States.

CHAPTER 13

Executive Employment Contracts and Post-Employment Arrangements

By Bill Gerek and Kurt Groeninger

L ike all other aspects of executive pay, employment contracts and post-retirement arrangements have garnered considerable attention from shareholders, proxy advisory groups and the press. They are concerned about policies that potentially result in windfalls to executives and excessive accounting and tax charges to the company. Moreover, through say-on-pay voting, shareholders can now voice their opinions on executive pay at public companies and can use this forum to press companies to revisit their policies and justify their actions. The ultimate question for a company is what makes sense given its particular corporate culture, business objectives and likelihood of a restructuring or a key executive retiring in the near future. Eligibility, costs and the specific purposes of any compensation arrangements need to be carefully weighed; what other companies do should not be the primary consideration.

This chapter:

- Outlines the reasons for having employment contracts, describes their pros and cons, and discusses the key provisions and issues companies should address in designing and refining their use of executive agreements.

- Discusses CIC design features such as eligibility, definition of change in control, single- and double-trigger payouts, benefits continuation, equity acceleration, and structuring cash payments.

- Describes how to handle unvested equity under various kinds of termination events and the accounting and tax issues that must be addressed.
- Analyzes the criticism and widespread abandonment of excise tax gross-ups, and compensation committee considerations in complying with the proxy vote on golden parachutes under say on pay.
- Suggests possible rationales for post-retirement consulting arrangements, including how payments might be structured and the abuses that often are found in such agreements.

Executive Employment Agreements: Why, When and What

Questions around whether an employer should have an employment agreement with one or more of its top executives, along with the associated practices, often are prompted by negotiations with a potential top executive hire or a reconsideration of existing arrangements with the current executives. The heightened focus on good corporate governance in recent years has caused many companies and compensation committees to re-examine the rationale for, and terms and conditions of, executive contracts. In determining whether and when to use contracts for executives, it is critical to examine an organization's specific facts and circumstances and to understand why employment agreements have been used or are under consideration. It generally is helpful to review the basic approaches for executive contracts and then consider the pros and cons of these agreements.

Approaches

The use of employment agreements for executives can vary considerably among companies, often depending on the organization's culture, views and compensation philosophy. There are four basic approaches:

- **No contracts**. Some employers do not use contracts at all, instead relying on company-wide policies or more limited agreements to address specific issues such as severance, change in control, confidentiality and noncompetition.

- **Only for top-team "new hires."** Other companies limit employ-ment agreements to new-hire situations, especially those in which a sought-after executive is reluctant to join a new and largely unfamiliar organization without the protections of a contract. A related question is if and when the entire contract or certain executive protections should "sunset."

- **Use for top executive team**. Many organizations extend employ-ment agreements to some or all of the top executive team. Certain organizations may have a contract with only their CEOs, while others may enter into written agreements with a dozen or so executives.

- **Broad use among executives**. A few companies use employment agreements to document their employment relationships with all executives above a certain level (e.g., vice president).

Rationale for Contracts

An executive contract sets out the key terms and conditions of the employment relationship. While contracts typically address salary, annual incentives, LTIs (often equity-based), benefits and perquisites, there is little need for a formal contract if the objective simply is to memorialize these items. Generally, the most important reasons for an employment agreement are to:

- Specify and make clear what an executive will receive upon various events resulting in a termination of employment (e.g., death, disability, retirement, resignation, resignation for good reason, dismissal and dismissal for cause).

- Address the impact of a change in control on the employer.

- Impose reasonable post-employment restrictions upon an executive (e.g., restrictive covenants addressing matters such as confidentiality and nondisclosure, non-competition, non-solicitation of employees and/or customers, and non-disparagement).

- Specify how and where disputes are to be resolved (e.g., through arbitration in a stated locale under identified rules versus through court litigation in a stated locale applying the law of an identi-fied state).

If properly drafted, employment contracts can help secure the future services of key employees critical to the organization's success. These agreements establish the respective rights, duties, obligations and responsibilities of the parties at a harmonious time; from this perspective they can be likened to premarital agreements.

Arguments Against Employment Agreements

While both the employer and the executive can be well-served by documenting the employment relationship through a contract, another view is that such agreements are either unnecessary or unduly favor executives. Arguments sometimes advanced against executive employment agreements include:

- **Pay for failure**. The heightened focus on executive compensation has highlighted instances in which an executive dismissed for poor performance was entitled to large severance pay based on the terms of an employment agreement. This view maintains that any payments would have been more reasonable if no contract had been in place and the executive had to negotiate a severance package in connection with his/her termination.

- **Performance equals security**. Some maintain that the protection provided by an employment contract is unnecessary for a top executive who is doing a good job and that an executive should not have this protection if he/she is not performing well. However, turnover levels among CEOs and other senior executives (a shorter job "life expectancy") have caused many executives to believe contractual protection is necessary for at least a limited term — especially for new outside hires.

Key Provisions and Usage

Severance and CIC protections usually are the most critical provisions for executives, while employers seek the benefits of restrictive covenants and clawback provisions. Both parties receive certainty (assuming the agreement is well drafted) of the terms that will apply in identified circumstances (especially various termination events). From an employer's perspective, a contract may discourage a competitor from recruiting an executive in jurisdictions that provide for tort damages for interference with the relationship of an executive under contract. An agreement may enable an employer to determine which state law will apply where there are contacts in multiple jurisdictions and, if desired, mandate arbitration of disputes regarding employment matters. Rather than simply limit the use of executive contracts, an objective should be to improve the contents of executive agreements. A consensus is developing regarding best practices that should be considered for employment agreements. (See "Checklist for Considering a New Contract or Evaluating an Existing Contract.")

Considerations in Change-in-Control Design

It has become critical for companies to examine their CIC programs in light of corporate governance considerations, special rules affecting nonqualified deferred compensation, and broad executive pay disclosure requirements. As part of their compensation disclosures, companies are required to identify and quantify all potential compensation payments for named executive officers (NEOs) in connection with any termination of employment, including a change in control.

One result has been increased attention to and scrutiny of CIC provisions. Compensation committees must understand the rationale around CIC plans to be able to defend and justify the plans to shareholder activists as well as for strategic business reasons.

Purpose

Before evaluating CIC provisions, it is necessary to understand their objectives. The main premise behind such arrangements is to protect shareholder interests by mitigating potential distractions to key executives regarding their future employment with the company in the event of a change in control.

However, critics of CIC arrangements question whether such payments are necessary because many executives already have accumulated significant wealth from the company, especially individuals with long tenure. The counterargument is that severance is needed to protect the executive from losing his/her job due to an event that

---

Checklist for Considering a New Contract or Evaluating an Existing Contract

- ❑ **"Evergreen" renewal.** Evergreen provisions typically call for automatic extension of renewal unless a specified advance notice is given. Procedures should be implemented to review agreements before any such extension becomes effective. In any case, an employer's advance notice not to extend the contract term or renew the agreement should not trigger severance pay.

- ❑ **Critical definitions.** The definitions of "change in control," "cause," and "good reason" should be particularly scrutinized. In reaction to some widely publicized severance payments to executives who were dismissed or resigned after poor corporate performance, companies may seek to expand cause definitions and constrict good reason events.

- ❑ **Calculating pay.** Where any payments are based on pay, a determination is needed on what amounts should be included. Some companies consider only base salary, while many others use salary plus annual incentive; very few include LTIs, especially because that is viewed as a poor pay practice that can produce excessive payouts. Also, the term "annual incentive" can be variously defined, so the method of its calculation should be specified.

- ❑ **Potential cost of retirement benefits or enhancements.** Shareholder groups may object to provisions that provide "deemed service credit" to increase an executive's retirement package (often coordinated with SERP benefits). Where that approach may be needed to recruit a midcareer executive to make up for benefits foregone at a former employer, the cost should be calculated and understood, with the rationale clearly documented and discussed in an effort to counter potential opposition, especially by proxy advisory firms.

- ❑ **Severance pay.** Any severance payments should be conditioned on the executive's agreement to reasonable restrictive covenants. Depending on what is permitted (and enforceable) under the laws of the relevant jurisdiction(s), covenants relating to non-competition, non-solicitation (of customers/clients and employees), nondisclosure of confidential information, and non-disparagement of the employer should be considered.

---

is outside the executive's influence. A severance program would be designed to bridge the executive financially for a reasonable period while he/she seeks another job. At times when the market for talent is particularly competitive, companies also use CIC arrangements to recruit executive candidates. A candidate who is considering multiple job offers will consider the potential payments in evaluating and comparing the total packages.

Design

In reviewing a company's CIC plans, there are several design features to consider:

- ■ **Eligibility.** While often available to a broader group than are employment contracts, most companies limit CIC programs or policies to the upper tiers of executive ranks (particularly focusing

❑ **Overall cost analysis.** The potential costs for all payments directly or indirectly affected by an executive's contract should be determined on a worst-case (most costly) basis. These costs should be reviewed periodically to make sure the compensation committee understands how changes in base salary, for instance, may affect these payments (e.g., where a target bonus is a multiple of base salary).

❑ **Vesting on a change in control.** Accelerated vesting may be appropriate when there is a non-cause dismissal of the executive following a change in control or the executive would have no continuing equity interest in a merged entity. In other cases, it may be appropriate to continue the vesting or provide for discretion in the board to accelerate vesting as appropriate under the circumstances, although there is mounting criticism of the latter approach.

❑ **Trigger event.** Any CIC severance benefits should require a "double trigger" for payment rather than simply the CIC event ("single trigger"). Thus, there would need to be a change in control and an involuntary termination of the executive within the change period (commonly one to two years after the change).

❑ **Section 409A.** The potential application of IRC section 409A (regarding nonqualified deferred compensation arrangements) should be considered when determining payment provisions. Because there are various exceptions and alternative approaches for compliance, section 409A can affect design and not merely legal language.

❑ **Responsibility for drafting.** The employer should have the contract drafted by its advisers, not by someone representing the executive's interests. The drafting process should be within control of the board. Also, a general counsel should not be put in the position of negotiating contract terms with an executive to whom he/she may report.

on the CEO and his/her direct reports). Some companies include another level of senior management or even a third tier.

▪ **Definition of change in control.** The following are the most common triggers used for defining a change in control:

- Acquisition of voting stock (generally ranging from 20 to 50 percent)
- Merger, consolidation or reorganization
- Change of board composition
- Sale of substantially all of the company's assets
- Liquidation or dissolution of the company.

Most companies use some or all of these triggers in their definitions of change in control, the terms of which may appear in agreements, policies and plans. The tax regulations under IRC section 409A also contain guidance on the thresholds for certain events that may need to be considered.

- ▪ **Triggers.** Payouts upon a change in control generally are triggered under three basic scenarios:
    - – **Single Trigger**. Only a change in control need occur.
    - – **Double Trigger**. Both a change in control and an involuntary termination (other than for cause) or a constructive termination (i.e., a resignation for good reason) must occur within a certain period (generally one to two years after the change in control). Some programs also are triggered when a change in control is after a dismissal if the event was the result of negotiations underway during a stated period (e.g., six months) prior to the executive's termination.
    - – **Modified Single Trigger**. A double trigger is in effect, except the executive may voluntarily terminate employment during a specific period of time and still receive a severance payout.

Until recently there often was a distinction between the trigger for cash severance under CIC arrangements and the trigger for acceleration of vesting under equity plans. While the long-time majority practice has been a double-trigger approach for cash severance, single triggers prevailed for equity incentives to provide accelerated vesting. However, expanded disclosure rules and criticism from proxy advisers (among others) caused companies to reconsider such equity single triggers. In just a few years, there was a rapid decline in single triggers for new equity awards as compensation committees acted to limit practices that could not be easily justified (after all, critics claimed that an executive should not need accelerated vesting and payout if he/she is still employed). (For more on accelerated vesting of equity, see "Equity Vesting Acceleration upon a Change in Control" later in this chapter.) Modified single triggers have also come under attack because they permit executives to resign after a certain period following a CIC event and receive payment even if he/she had not been actually or constructively terminated. Best practices and good governance now call for double triggers for new equity awards as well as for cash severance payouts.

- **Cash severance.** Most arrangements provide for cash severance expressed as a multiple of pay that is paid in a lump sum. Now that separation amounts payable in installments are potentially subject to the deferred compensation rules of IRC section 409A, installment payments have become much less common. There may be two or three tiers of multiples that correspond to levels within the organization. Among larger companies, three times pay has been the prevalent multiple for the CEO, while smaller companies usually provide two to three times pay. Organizations commonly provide one full multiple less in cash severance to the next level or tier below the CEO.

  Cash severance usually is determined as the relevant multiple of either base salary or base salary plus annual incentive (usually 1x to 3x). There are also variations on how annual bonus is defined, including:

  - **Target**. Target incentive for the year of change in control.
  - **Average**. Average incentive paid during a prior number of years.
  - **Highest**. Highest incentive paid during a prior number of years.

  Target is the most frequently used annual bonus definition, followed by some form of average incentive.
- **Benefits continuation.** Most companies also provide continuation of health and welfare benefits upon termination in the event of a change in control. The period of continuation usually is coordinated with the period represented by the cash severance multiple. In designing these arrangements, care must be taken to avoid unanticipated income tax consequences to the executive, including consideration of IRC section 409A.
- **Equity acceleration.** For equity plans, companies typically provide CIC protection in the form of accelerated vesting of equity awards. As previously noted, the once-typical approach of a single trigger for equity acceleration has been questioned, and a double trigger has surpassed it for new awards and agreements. A double trigger

prevents an executive from cashing out his/her equity before normal vesting if the individual remains employed.

■ **Excise tax treatment.** IRC section 4999 imposes an excise tax on a "disqualified individual" if parachute payments made in connection with a CIC exceed the safe-harbor limit, which is three times the individual's "base amount" (the average of the individual's total taxable compensation paid by the corporation for the five years preceding the year of the change in control). However, the excise tax amount is equal to 20 percent of all parachute payments in excess of one times the base amount. IRC section 280G provides that such "excess parachute payments" are nondeductible to the employer. Companies address this excise-tax issue in various ways:

- **Gross-up.** The company pays the executive's excise and related income taxes to keep the executive "whole" so that the individual receives the same after-tax amount as he/she would without the imposition of the excise tax.

- **Modified gross-up.** The company provides a gross-up only if the payments exceed the safe harbor by a certain percentage or amount (e.g., 10 percent or $100,000). If not, payments are cut back to the safe-harbor limit to avoid any excise tax.

- **Cut-back.** The company cuts back all payments to the safe-harbor limit to avoid the excise tax. The company cuts back parachute payments to the safe-harbor limit only if doing so would result in a higher after-tax amount for the executive.

- **Do nothing.** The company requires executives to pay any excise tax.

While the provision of a gross-up previously was the most common practice, its use has fallen sharply due to harsh criticism by shareholder groups, proxy advisory firms and the media. Once potential gross-up payments were included in disclosures under SEC proxy rules, compensation committees focused on the magnitude of the total potential cost of gross-ups. As a result, cutback provisions have increased in use as most public companies have eliminated parachute tax gross-ups for new awards or agreements.

Compensation committees should regularly review CIC programs and confirm the plan design is serving its intended purpose(s). They also need to understand the potential payments and costs that could be triggered in the event of a change in control. A sharp increase in the company's stock price or a large equity grant can result in millions of dollars in payments.

Handling Unvested Equity Awards at Termination

An executive's employment termination raises the issue of whether unvested equity awards should be forfeited or their vesting should be accelerated or continued. While too often an afterthought in designing equity programs and related agreements, the approach taken can greatly affect the amounts ultimately received by a terminating executive. When negotiating employment agreements and drafting equity plan documents and individual award agreements, companies should consider how they wish to address various possible termination events. With heightened governance scrutiny by advisory firms and public outrage over perceived excesses in executive compensation, a company's treatment of unvested equity is especially important.

Background and Relevant Termination Events

Like most compensation decisions, the particular facts and circumstances are paramount in the treatment of unvested equity. Where an employment agreement is involved, the executive's input may be part of the negotiation process; in recent years, the views of shareholders and their advisers have played an increased role.

The treatment of unvested equity generally is addressed in a company's equity plan document and/or individual award agreements. In some cases, a company may include language that gives authority to the board of directors or compensation committee to apply discretion to accelerate vesting. Potential accounting and tax considerations also need to be examined so that the company can structure the arrangements in a favorable manner and avoid inadvertently triggering adverse accounting or tax consequences. The basic employment termination events are:

- Death
- Disability
- Retirement
- Termination by the company (dismissal) without cause
- Dismissal for cause
- Termination by the executive (resignation) without good cause
- Resignation for good cause
- Termination in connection with a change in control.

Other than death, each company will have its own definition for each of the termination scenarios, but most companies' definitions address common themes. In the following discussion of various termination events, those that often are treated similarly are grouped.

Death, Disability and Retirement

When an executive dies, becomes disabled or retires during the course of employment, the relevant award agreements and equity plans need to be examined to see if there is a provision that allows for either the continued or immediate vesting of all or a portion of unvested awards. Some companies take an executive- or beneficiary-friendly approach on the view that none of these events reflects any wrongdoing, poor performance or disloyalty on the part of the executive.

In designing equity incentive plans and award agreements, companies should review the potential tax and accounting consequences of accelerating vesting on death or retirement. When unvested stock options are accelerated in any of these scenarios, there typically is a reduction in the exercise period; the new period commonly is the shorter of the remaining option term or one or more years from the date of acceleration; on occasion, companies allow option exercises for up to three years after the termination event. Other companies and their advisers take the position that no such acceleration of vesting is warranted in these circumstances. The view is basically that, in an atmosphere increasingly focused on performance, these awards have not been earned at the time of death, disability or retirement and that any payment would be a windfall. Also, the existence of life or disability insurance may be viewed as a replacement for any awards that may be forfeited upon these employment terminations. In particular, with respect to accelerated vesting on a defined "normal retirement date," companies need to understand the accounting and income tax consequences of the plan or award design so as not to be surprised by any truncated financial expense for the company or earlier (pre-separation from service) income tax obligations for the executive.

Termination by the Company for Cause or by the Executive Without Good Reason

When an executive is dismissed for cause (generally including fraud and gross negligence in the definition) or resigns without good reason (typically including a material reduction in duties), it is rare for a company to allow continued or accelerated vesting on any portion of unvested equity awards. In these circumstances there would be no reason to allow executives to receive compensation other than what was legally required (generally what was accrued up until the date of termination). The definitions of "cause" and "good reason" need to be carefully crafted to the company's particular situation and often are highly negotiated in employment contracts.

Termination by the Company Without Cause or by the Executive for Good Reason

Considerable debate can be had on the appropriate handling of unvested equity awards when an executive is dismissed without cause or he/she resigns for good reason. An analysis of data indicates that unvested equity awards most commonly are forfeited when an executive is terminated without cause or resigns for good reason. However, some companies allow a portion of the unvested awards to accelerate and a small share of companies accelerate all of the individual's outstanding amount. While a dismissal (or good-reason resignation) may not be due to any fault of the executive (especially if during an economic downturn), most employers do not view this as sufficient reason for accelerating vesting (at least absent a change in control) and prefer to focus on rewarding and retaining current employees. Some companies, however, focus on perceived fairness concerns and see value in recruitment and retention efforts by providing vesting protection to actually or constructively dismissed employees.

Termination in Connection with a Change in Control

Vesting acceleration considerations can be especially important in connection with a change in control. As previously mentioned under "Considerations in Change-in-Control Design," single-trigger acceleration is now disfavored. Where CIC protection is determined to be useful, proxy advisory firms and shareholder groups now favor double triggers so that acceleration only occurs upon an involuntary termination of employment in connection with a CIC.

Accounting Considerations

All share-based compensation is accounted for under Accounting Standards Codification (ASC) Topic 718. ASC 718 requires that all share-based awards granted to employees be accounted for at "fair value." Basically, when an unvested equity award accelerates upon a termination event, the service condition of the original award is not expected to be satisfied because the employee is not expected to render the requisite service. Thus, the compensation cost for the original, unvested award should be zero at the date of the modification as none of the awards are expected to vest. The incremental fair value is equal to the full fair value of the modified award, which represents the total cumulative compensation cost that the company should recognize for the award. On the modification date, the company would reverse the compensation cost previously recognized for the unvested award, if any, and recognize compensation cost equal to the full fair value of the modified award, which is fully vested.

Income Tax Considerations

Two (extremely simplified here) income tax provisions are of particular importance regarding unvested equity upon termination:

- First, unless certain exceptions apply, under IRC section 409A, a publicly held company may not make any payments of deferred compensation to certain key employees within a six-month period after a separation from service. Both the relevant plan documents and actual administration of the program need to satisfy section 409A to avoid harsh tax consequences for the recipient of any such accelerated awards that are determined to constitute deferred compensation.

- Second, companies need to consider IRC section 280G, as the acceleration of unvested equity on a change in control is valued in determining whether any of certain officers and other "disqualified individuals" have received an "excess parachute payment" that is subject to excise tax (under IRC section 4999) payable by the individual as well as the loss of the corporation's income tax deduction for such payment. If section 280G is not considered until after a change in control, it may be difficult to avoid parachute tax consequences. (The potential application and impact of sections 280G and 4999 are explained in more detail later in this chapter.)

Looking at the Relevant Facts and Circumstances

While it can be helpful to see how other companies handle unvested equity upon various employee termination events, a company's focus should be on what approach best advances its particular objectives. Various factors — including accounting and income tax considerations and views of proxy advisory firms — need to be weighed. Recruitment, motivation, retention and cost may be evaluated differently at each organization; with an understanding of the key issues and approaches, an informed decision can be made.

Equity Vesting Acceleration Upon a Change in Control

Equity-based compensation — whether in the form of stock options/ stock appreciation rights (SARs), RS/RSUs or performance shares/ performance units — is an integral part of executive LTI programs.

A common provision in the governing documents addresses how an executive's unvested interests are treated if there is a change in control of the company. Because a significant portion of an executive's wealth often is tied to the value of equity-based compensation, the conditions for accelerated vesting are particularly important. As discussed in the section of this chapter titled "Considerations in Change-in-Control Design," most equity plans include either a single or double trigger to accelerate vesting upon a change in control, with a modified single trigger used at a handful of companies. Thus, upon the relevant trigger, all unvested stock options become immediately exercisable, all outstanding RS or RSUs are immediately vested and are no longer subject to forfeiture, and all performance-based shares would be vested and paid in accordance with the governing document.

A Trend Toward Double Triggers

As previously discussed in this chapter, single triggers for equity acceleration on a change in control now are viewed quite negatively by shareholders, investors and proxy advisers, leading to the rise in double triggers. While certainly not exhaustive, Table 13-1 highlights some notable advantages and disadvantages of single- and double-trigger acceleration.

Eliminating Single Trigger Provisions for Equity Acceleration

If a company decides to eliminate existing single triggers for the acceleration of vesting on equity-based compensation, it must address the practicalities of how best to implement the change, taking into account anticipated employee reaction, expectations for some quid pro quo, and any contractual rights under current awards and agreements. Some companies may determine to make only prospective changes — whereby any future programs and agreements will have double triggers — but leave existing arrangements unchanged until they expire. Others may choose to negotiate with executives to give up the single triggers, perhaps in exchange for some other benefit.

Impact of IRC Section 280G

An important factor to consider in the treatment of equity in CIC scenarios is the potential exposure to the golden parachute ramifications of IRC section 280G. Section 280G denies an income tax deduction to a corporation for "excess parachute payments" made in

TABLE 13-1 Single and Double Triggers: Pros and Cons

Single-Trigger Approach	
Advantages	Disadvantages
■ Allows certain executives to share in the value they have created for shareholders. ■ Provides for a built-in "retention award" that can eliminate the need for a cash retention arrangement through the date of closing. ■ Does not affect the current stock prices, as outstanding equity awards are treated as a sunk cost by the buyer. ■ Beneficial when acquiring company is going to terminate the existing equity plan or does not convert the unvested equity of the acquired company into its own stock.	■ Can be viewed as a windfall for executives who would not be terminated by buyer. ■ No retention value after the closing of the transaction. ■ Incentive for executives to only focus on near-term stock price of the company. ■ Acceleration generally constitutes a parachute payment under IRC section 280G.

Double-Trigger Approach	
Advantages	Disadvantages
■ Viewed by corporate governance and shareholder advisory groups as the preferred approach — a best practice. ■ Acts as a key retention tool for senior executives who are instrumental to the integration process. ■ Alleviates the need for additional retention incentives in the form of cash or additional equity. ■ Aligns executive and shareholder interests due to the long-term value of the acquiring company. ■ Protection for the executive in the event of termination of employment due to a change in control. ■ Not necessarily considered a parachute payment under IRC section 280G.	■ Executives, unlike shareholders, may not immediately share in any increase in value of company stock (or acquirer's stock). ■ Potential loss of income to the executive if unvested awards are not converted into the acquirer's stock.

connection with a change in control. A related provision, IRC section 4999, imposes a 20 percent excise tax on any person who receives compensation that, under section 280G, is deemed to constitute an excess parachute payment.

As part of the complex calculation to determine if any person has received excess parachute payments, the accelerated value of unvested equity awards is taken into account. This accelerated value is determined under different methodologies depending on the type of equity vehicle but, in many cases, represents a significant portion of the total value an executive is deemed to receive upon a change in control. When a single-trigger acceleration approach is used, all unvested awards are immediately vested and must be taken into account for purposes of the section 280G calculation.

If the value of equity acceleration (when taken into account with all other payments contingent upon a change in control) triggers an excess parachute payment, then the company will lose valuable income tax deductions. To compound matters, if an executive is grossed up for any excise tax that may be imposed, this gross-up protection could potentially cost the company almost three times the initial excise tax, as these gross-up payments are considered additional excess parachute payments that become subject to the excise tax as well. These excise tax gross-up provisions are extremely costly to shareholders when taking into account the amount of cash that is required to cover the gross-up payment and the additional income taxes on compensation deemed to be nondeductible.

When the double-trigger acceleration approach is used, there is no immediate value under section 280G because unvested awards are not necessarily accelerated upon a change in control. However, if in connection with a change in control an executive is terminated by the acquiring company without cause or the executive resigns for good reason, then all unvested equity is immediately vested and such acceleration generally is calculated in the same manner as the single trigger. Thus, a double-trigger approach may result in a parachute payment while the single-trigger approach clearly will constitute a parachute payment.

While the discussion around the merits of the single- versus double-trigger approach continues, one thing is certain: double-trigger acceleration provisions are being considered and implemented by more companies than ever before.

Parachute Excise Tax Gross-Up Considerations

As mentioned, excessive amounts payable on a change in control may be subject to a loss of tax deduction to the company and an excise tax on the employee under the golden parachute provisions of IRC sections 280G and 4999, respectively. Over the years, many corporations determined that a gross-up for the effect of the parachute excise tax was the preferred approach for working around the excise tax. Excise tax gross-ups have attracted significant negative attention and been criticized as a poor or problematic pay practice. With the advent of say on pay and say on parachutes, combined with the increased influence of shareholder advisory groups, excise tax gross-ups have become uncommon for new awards and agreements. Nevertheless, it can be helpful to examine why many companies used gross-ups (as some still do) for senior executives.

Inequity of Parachute Excise Tax and Argument for Tax Gross-Ups

In determining the amount (if any) of parachute payments subject to the 20 percent excise tax on excess parachute payments, the relevant income tax regulations start with a disqualified individual's base amount. The base amount is the average — for the five years immediately before the year of the change in control — of an employee's box 1 income from Form W-2. If the aggregate present value of all payments made to an executive that were contingent upon the change in control at least equals three times the base amount, then all payments made in excess of one times the base amount are subject to the 20 percent excise tax. The particular facts regarding any employee can produce quite different income and parachute tax consequences. Thus, the chart captioned "Example: Parachute Excise Tax Calculations and Comparison" illustrates how the excise tax can be unfair. While this example may be extreme, it highlights the potential inequity of the excise tax:

- Executive A took all of the cash he could from the company and did not align his interests with those of shareholders. As a reward for cashing out every year, A pays $0 in excise tax.
- On the other hand, Executive B did everything that the company and shareholders would prefer — she deferred cash and did not exercise stock options, thereby cementing her long-term interests with those of the company. By doing the right thing from a corporate governance perspective, as well as taking less cash annually, B gets hit with an excise tax bill of $1,555,000. (Of course, many executives postpone exercising stock options simply in hopes of maximizing their ultimate returns.)

This example illustrates why excise tax gross-ups originally became prevalent in senior executive employment agreements. The gross-ups leveled the playing field for similarly situated executives who may have acted differently with respect to stock option exercises and deferrals of compensation.

Mounting Criticism and Pushback Against Excise Tax Gross-Ups

With the advent of expanded disclosures (see Chapter 14), shareholders, their advisers and various business media became increasingly critical of excise tax gross-ups. Gross-ups have been targeted as a poor or problematic pay practice in say-on-pay voting. Where a say-on-pay vote is unavailable (e.g., at publicly traded companies with biennial or triennial say-on-pay votes), shareholders still may express their displeasure by casting "withhold" or "against" votes for compensation committee members who approve arrangements with these gross-ups. In addition, the presence of this type of perquisite will negatively influence a company's scoring on various governance ratings.

In their annual proxy statements, companies are required to estimate and disclose termination payments under different scenarios as of

---

TABLE 13-2 Example: Parachute Excise Tax Calculations and Comparison

Executives A and B each earn $1 million in base salary and receive a $2 million bonus for each of the five preceding years. In addition, both A and B could exercise stock options worth $500,000 per year.

Executive A exercises all of his stock options every year during the five-year period, while Executive B does not exercise any of her stock option awards. Also, A does not defer any of his base salary or bonus while B defers 25 percent of both base salary and bonus on an annual basis.

In the year of a change in control, both A and B receive a $10 million golden parachute package. The table below illustrates the components of the parachute excise tax calculation for each executive and compares the tax due for each executive.

	Box 1 W-2 average	2.99* x base amount	Parachute payments ($10 million) greater than 2.99* x base amount?	Subject to 20% excise tax	Amount subject to 20% excise tax	20% excise tax
A	$3,500,000	$10,465,000	No	No	$0	$0
B	$2,250,000	$6,727,500	Yes	Yes	$7,775,000	$1,555,000

*2.99 used as short-hand approximation of calculating just below three times the base amount.

the last day of the reporting year. While the average investor may not understand how the calculations are derived, he/she does know that these payments and related gross-ups are very expensive (See Table 13-2 for examples). This negative attention — and particularly the threat of a negative say-on-pay vote and/or adverse vote recommendations on compensation committee members — caused companies to review their attitudes toward golden parachute payments and any associated excise tax gross-ups. Boards generally have eliminated excise tax gross-ups in any new awards or arrangements, often by restricting golden parachute payments so that they are cut back to ensure the IRC section 4999 excise tax is not triggered.

Minimizing Adverse Consequences Under Sections 280G and 4999

If an organization is prepared for the potential reach of IRC sections 280G and 4999 well in advance of a potential CIC, it can take advantage of opportunities to minimize the adverse implications of these tax provisions. However, if a company does not address these issues prior to a CIC, achieving an optimal outcome may become more difficult and/or expensive. Some common mitigation strategies for addressing sections 280G and 4999 are outlined below.

- Include provisions in agreements that provide an executive with the better after-tax result after either (i) cutting-back total parachute payments to a level where no excise tax is triggered or (ii) making the parachute payments in full (and paying applicable income and excise taxes)

- Cease any deferral of compensation to the extent compliant with IRC section 409A; this will increase annual pay for Form W-2 (used as the basis for the base amount calculation)

- If a company normally pays annual incentives within two and a half months following the end of the fiscal year, accelerate the payment to December 31st of the current fiscal year (assuming the company's fiscal year is the calendar year); this will increase the amount in the W-2

- Exercise vested stock options in the year prior to the CIC as this will also increase the amount for the W-2

- For stock options and time-based restricted stock/restricted stock units (RSUs), change from a cliff vesting schedule to one that is prorata

- For performance-based restricted stock/RSUs, include provisions that performance will be measured on an actual (rather than target) basis upon CIC; this structure may obtain a more advantageous valuation under the applicable tax regulations

- Voluntarily waive the right to certain payments and benefits due at the time of a CIC; the most common use of this technique is to waive the right to accelerated vesting on equity awards for the purpose of excluding the value from the section 280G calculation

- Include non-compete provisions within agreements that provide for cash severance benefits in the event of a CIC; the value of these provisions (up to the cash severance amount) may be excluded from the section 280G calculation and the value of the non-compete may be considered compensation for services rendered post-CIC and thus excluded from the excess parachute calculation

- In lieu of certain payments that are included in the section 280G calculation, provide for a post-CIC consulting agreement as payments thereunder may be considered compensation for services rendered post-CIC and thus excluded from the calculation

Post-Employment Consulting Arrangements: Are They Appropriate?

Companies often enter into post-employment consulting agreements with outgoing or retiring executives. However, as executive pay is subjected to ever-increasing scrutiny, questions arise: Are these arrangements justifiable? If so, what terms are appropriate?

Sometimes there is a plausible rationale for these arrangements, such as transition to a new management team or passing knowledge on from an outgoing executive. All too often, however, these consultancies simply are a going-away present provided gratuitously by the board without the expectation of any meaningful services from the executive. In the extreme, they can be clearly inappropriate and represent excessive compensation with no pretense of a justifiable rationale. Yet they persist, even appearing in employment agreements negotiated well in advance of actual termination.

In the nonprofit world, particularly in academia, there have been cases involving an emeritus designation of retired executives and professors. These arrangements may include the equivalent full-time salary with far less than full-time responsibilities. Questions can arise regarding whether meaningful services are being provided to the employer. (See "Common Abuses and Issues in Post-Employment Consulting Arrangements.")

Design of Consulting Arrangements

Because a consulting arrangement should be limited to those circumstances in which there is a particular need to retain the executive's services, the design and terms of any such agreement should be customized to the particular situation. (See "Justifications for Consulting Arrangements.") Following is a discussion of key design considerations.

Retainer

A retainer to be available for special projects can be sufficient, but the facts and circumstances should be carefully considered. Even if the executive is expected to be called upon for less than the prescribed time, this does not necessarily affect the appropriateness of the arrangement, but rather is part of the overall situation to be evaluated. In fact, this approach has significant prevalence in post-retirement contracts.

Determination of Value

The value of any post-retirement consulting arrangement to the employer reasonably could be based on a number of alternative theories, including:

- A direct assessment of the value to the employer of assigned consulting projects, regardless of time spent and regardless of results.

JUSTIFICATIONS FOR CONSULTING ARRANGEMENTS

Clearly there are situations in which a post-employment consultancy is support-able, including:

> Transitions in which knowledge needs to be passed to the new management team

> Proprietary knowledge that must be protected from leakage to competitors

> Special projects that otherwise would require an outside consultant

> Experienced executive is needed to represent the company in relationships with customers, investors, regulators or other special groups

> Outgoing executive might be key to maintaining or further developing business through long-standing relationships

> Changes in control, especially in which the executive's expertise is required on a temporary basis during the post-merger period.

- Project results, rather than hours spent (i.e., the "finder's fee" theory). If the value to the employer is sales, this can be a function of relationships and results, not necessarily time. For example, if there was a significant sale negotiated during an afternoon of golf, it was not likely a direct function of time.

- The value of the executive's availability in potential situations.

Structuring Payments

The structure of the consulting payments could be built around:

- A proration of pre-retirement salary.

- A dollar retainer amount per year during which the individual's services are available (e.g., a "bench player" that can be called into play if and when needed, but who is barred from "playing" for anyone else during the prescribed time period).

- A consulting arrangement based on an agreed-upon hourly rate, against which the former executive bills time on assigned projects.

Total Compensation Package Approach

What appears to be most important to the IRS — especially for tax-exempt organizations — is the aggregate of the compensation package for post-employment services. Basically, the absence of certain payments (or the provision of lower amounts) can offset "excesses" in other components. To the extent that one or more components of the total package may be less than amounts that otherwise would be acceptable, there may be "credits" available to balance any otherwise excessive portions.

In this process, consideration might be given to pay components such as retirement benefits, post-retirement medical benefits and severance benefits. In terms of what an employer receives, there may be a need to value a covenant not to compete when that covenant has significant value to the employer. This approach can be especially helpful in developing the reasonableness of an executive's compensation under the intermediate-sanctions provisions of the Taxpayer Bill of Rights II (the legislation that restricts executive pay to reasonable levels at tax-exempt organizations).

Retirement Benefit

One common approach is for the employer to provide the CEO with a target retirement benefit of an annual life annuity equal to 60 percent of final average pay (base plus bonus). This formula assumes a reasonable length of service with the employer and inclusion of benefits under the company's qualified retirement plan. If an executive's base plus bonus averaged $1 million for the final three years, such a formula could have a lump-sum present value at age 65 of approximately $3 million. The absence of this type of program can help justify additional benefits on the basis that a major portion of a "normal" executive compensation program was lacking. Under the total package approach described above, the value of a consultancy agreement might constitute a substitute for the value of a typical retirement program for similar executives.

The Pseudo-Retirement Plan

While in some cases an employer may install a SERP arrangement retroactively just before retirement, care is needed to assure that there is sufficient rationale for this retroactivity. Because this approach involves crediting service in excess of actual work for the employer, a public company would need to consider the likely opposition of proxy advisory groups to that aspect of the program.

Another caution exists when the outgoing executive already has a sufficient retirement program in place; a consulting agreement could be redundant.

The Retainer Approach

In another example, a compensation committee and an executive enter into a post-employment consulting agreement on a retainer basis, with the purpose of reserving 25 percent of the executive's time during a five-year period. The compensation committee concludes that there is sufficient value to the organization to have that resource contracted under the terms of the agreement and available to provide a range of duties as needed. As a general rule, it should not be unreasonable for the executive and the compensation committee to enter into such an agreement and for the executive to be paid reasonable amounts, assuming that the executive does in fact reserve or otherwise make available 25 percent of his/her time. However, in this case, the five-year duration of the payments generally would be excessive for a management transition or for a non-competition restriction.

Should We Plan Ahead for Executive Consulting?

One especially problematic use of post-retirement consulting arrangements is when they are agreed to far in advance of any separation discussions. Too often, such use is really just additional post-employment pay for the executive. A compensation committee would have a better reason to consider such a post-employment consulting arrangement (assuming it otherwise makes sense) at the time the executive transition is being negotiated. At least then there would be a relationship to performance rather than making commitments without a determination of the need for such services.

Final Considerations

Say on pay raised the stakes for compensation committees regarding the use of employment agreements. Compensation committee members need to understand that if any new or materially amended executive agreement or award contains concerning provisions, such as an excise tax gross-up, they should expect to have to defend their position to shareholders to rebut a negative say-on-pay recommendation from proxy advisory firms.

PART II

Governance, Disclosure and Compensation Committee Initiatives

CHAPTER 14

Compensation Committee Governance

By Brian Tobin and Kurt Groeninger

Sound governance practices are critical for compensation committees as they work to make well-grounded and defensible executive pay decisions. These practices provide a framework within which appropriate pay programs can be designed and tailored to the needs of the company. The nuances of these programs, as well as the rationale behind potentially contentious elements, then can be communicated to shareholders and other stakeholders through required disclosure as well as voluntary outreach.

However, having governance practices in place does not always mean they are followed in practice. As such, the assessment of compliance with policies is another crucial component of the compensation governance equation that should be regularly evaluated.

A responsible and diligent compensation committee works to ensure strong governance is present in its decision-making processes, both in policy and practice. As executive pay decisions are ultimately the responsibility of the compensation committee, these controls are of vital importance in protecting the company as well as individual committee members from legal and/or reputational risk related to executive pay programs.

This chapter:

- Reviews the role and responsibilities of the compensation committee, including establishing a compensation committee charter and an annual calendar of quarterly meetings.

- Offers practical advice on conducting board and committee self-assessments.
- Outlines the roles of key players in compensation governance.
- Summarizes required factors for assessing the independence of compensation advisers and provides guidance on the evaluation of their performance.
- Suggests actions for consideration by compensation committees seeking to maintain or improve voting results related to the say-on-pay provisions of the Dodd-Frank Act.
- Explains the role of proxy advisors and the compensation committee's potential for interacting with them.

Responsibilities of the Compensation Committee

The compensation committee generally has responsibility for:

- **Compensation philosophy.** Establishing and periodically reviewing a compensation philosophy that is aligned with the company's strategic objectives.
- **Executive compensation and benefits programs.** Establishing and providing oversight of base salary structures, all incentive plans, retirement plans, employment agreements, severance arrangements and other pay programs and policies (e.g., clawbacks, share ownership requirements, etc.).
- **Performance assessment.** Assessing the CEO's performance; monitoring and reviewing performance targets and results for top executives.
- **Oversight of executive compensation administration.** Approving compensation adjustments, incentive payouts and equity grants for the CEO and other top executives.
- **Risk assessment.** Reviewing potential risks associated with compensation programs and policies as well as internal controls for their mitigation.
- **Compensation-related disclosure.** Reviewing and recommending the CD&A for inclusion in annual proxy statements.
- **Shareholder engagement.** Interacting and meeting with investors to understand any concerns related to compensation programs.

- **Succession planning.** Managing the succession planning process and regularly evaluating succession plans for the CEO and his/her direct reports.
- **Compensation for board of directors.** Recommending compensation for the board of directors.
- **Board communications.** Maintaining regular communication with the entire board on the compensation committee's activities and recommendations.
- **Committee charter and calendar.** Maintaining and regularly reviewing a committee charter and annual calendar of activities.*
- **Self-assessment.** Assessment of committee performance.*
  * Responsibilities are described in greater detail later in this chapter.

Generally, the compensation committee should be composed of three to five directors. Given the ever-increasing complexity of the executive compensation environment, all members of the committee should have significant HR or compensation experience.

To comply with New York Stock Exchange (NYSE) and NASDAQ standards, each committee member must be considered independent. Notably, the board of directors must consider all factors relevant in determining whether members have any relationship to the company that would preclude independence from management, including the source of compensation and the existence of any affiliate relationships. Some companies are exempt from this independence standard, however. Controlled companies (50% or more of the voting power for the election of directors is held by an individual, a group or another company) may include non-independent compensation committee members.

Compensation Committee Charter

A clear, succinct compensation committee charter is vital for establishing a mutual understanding of the purpose, governing principles and responsibilities of the compensation committee among the board, the committee and the CEO.

The compensation committee generally is responsible for developing the charter and submitting it to the board for approval. The charter should be a living document and reviewed annually to assess its continued relevance and compliance with statutory and regulatory requirements.

Topics typically addressed include:

- **Purpose.** Why the compensation committee exists and what its ultimate objectives are.
- **Membership, composition and procedures.** Number of members, committee member qualifications, selection and removal process for members and the chair, independence standards, frequency of meetings, authority to delegate to subcommittees, quorum, and other governance procedures established by the board.
- **Duties and responsibilities.** The committee's specific account-abilities regarding executive compensation programs, potential material risks associated with compensation programs, disclosure, succession planning, etc.
- **Executive session.** Ability to convene without management present.
- **Advisers to the compensation committee.** Authority to select and retain external advisers including consultants and legal counsel and requirement to assess adviser independence.
- **Reports/communication to the board.** Frequency and content of communications with the board.

Care should be taken to ensure that the charter does not require the committee to take any action unless it is prepared to carry out such duty, as failure to do so may expose the organization or individual committee members to the risk of litigation. For this reason, some advocate that the duties and responsibilities laid out in a charter be written largely in general terms to mitigate the risk that a breach can be definitively proven.

Public companies must disclose whether a charter has been adopted by the compensation committee. Both the NYSE and NASDAQ require the adoption of a charter addressing certain items, as summarized in Table 14-1.

TABLE 14-1 Compensation Committee Charter Requirements

NYSE Requirements	NASDAQ Requirements
Compensation committees must have a written charter that addresses:	Compensation committees must have a written charter and must review and reassess the adequacy of this charter on an annual basis.

■ The committee's purpose and responsibilities — which, at minimum, must be to have direct responsibility to: - Review and approve corporate goals and objectives relevant to CEO compensation, evaluate the CEO's performance in light of those goals and objectives, and, either as a committee or together with the other independent directors (as directed by the board), determine and approve the CEO's compensation level based on this evaluation; - Make recommendations to the board with respect to non-CEO executive officer compensation, and incentive-compensation and equity-based plans that are subject to board approval; and - Prepare the disclosure required by Item 407(e)(5) of Regulation S-K, specifically the compensation committee report related to the review and recommendation of the CD&A to the board for inclusion in relevant disclosures. ■ An annual performance evaluation of the compensation committee ■ The rights and responsibilities of the committee related to retaining and evaluating the independence of compensation consultants, legal counsel, and other advisers. ■ The compensation committee charter should also address the following items: - Committee member qualifications; - Committee member appointment and removal; - Committee structure and operations (including authority to delegate to subcommittees); and committee reporting to the board.	The compensation committee charter must specify: ■ The scope of committee responsibilities, and how it carries out those responsibilities, including: - Structure - Processes, and - Membership requirements ■ The committee's responsibility for determining, or recommending to the board for determination, the compensation of the CEO and all other NEOs; ■ That the CEO may not be present during voting or deliberations on his or her compensation; and ■ Specific responsibilities and authorities related to retaining and evaluating the independence of compensation consultants, legal counsel or other advisers

Annual Compensation Committee Calendar

As part of its annual planning process, the compensation committee should establish a calendar of activities to guide it in fulfilling its duties through the year. Most compensation committees should plan to meet at least four times per year, with the possibility of additional meetings where circumstances warrant. Typical items included in the planning process are included in the sample compensation committee calendar in Table 14-2.

TABLE 14-2 **Sample Compensation Committee Calendar**

First Quarter Meeting	Second Quarter Meeting	Third Quarter Meeting	Fourth Quarter Meeting
Review (and approve) incentive payments for the fiscal year just ended	Review compensation committee charter	Review and approve board compensation for the coming year	Review competitiveness of executive compensation and alignment with compensation philosophy
Finalize input on CD&A and proxy statements	Perform committee self-assessment	Review results of shareholder votes from annual general meeting	Review (and approve) base pay changes (if any)
Develop the compensation committee calendar for the year	Assess performance of adviser(s)	Review total executive compensation	Review (and approve) incentive plan performance goals for the coming year
	Review executive succession plans	Structure for the coming year, including base salary ranges and incentive targets	

Ongoing / as warranted

Receive periodic updates on company performance related to incentive compensation

Evaluate CEO performance relative to established goals

Board communication

Review executive employment contracts / severance payments in the event of executive turnover

Consider regulatory changes and market trends in compensation and governance

Board and Committee Self Assessments

Board assessments are mandatory at all companies listed on the NYSE. While there is no similar requirement for NASDAQ-listed companies, many NASDAQ companies have adopted a process for board evaluation. As a component of good governance, many other organizations, even private companies and nonprofit organizations, have adopted the practice of conducting annual performance reviews of the board and its committees. Board assessments are examined in depth in Chapter 22 where the four main methodologies for evaluating the board are discussed — namely surveys, interviews, research and observation.

The value in these assessments can be maximized if companies move toward a method of self-assessment that fosters dialogue and discovery, including a combination of methods such as coupling interviews with surveys. Many boards and committees are now adding another component to the assessments — individual director performance. While various methodologies may be adopted for such assessments, often the most informative is a director peer review, in which directors provide feedback on the performance of others and receive feedback from their peers. As noted in Chapter 22, legal counsel should advise the committee on how it might safeguard the director peer review process to avoid the risk of potential litigation based on negative feedback.

To build a more robust view of board and committee performance, management's perspective can also be incorporated into the review process. While not all boards welcome management feedback on their performance, those that do have found it often yields especially useful guidance. Not only can this exercise prevent the board and its committees from becoming insular, but it can also surface important issues and enhance the working relationship between the board and management.

In practice, not all of these feedback methods need to be implemented at once or even conducted every year. However, finding ways of evaluating performance that bring multiple perspectives together is key to maximizing the effectiveness of assessment.

Key Players in Compensation Governance

The compensation committee has additional resources to assist
it in discharging its accountabilities, including senior leadership,
internal HR staff, and external, independent advisers. (See Figure
14-3.) Each has a critical role to play in ensuring strong corporate
governance principles are developed and approved at the board level
and then cascaded down through the organization and ingrained in
compensation-related decision making at all levels.

Independence of Advisers

Compensation committees must have the authority to retain compensation consultants, legal counsel or other advisers (collectively referred
to as compensation advisers), and they are directly responsible for
the oversight of their work. Before selecting its compensation adviser,
a public compensation committee must take into consideration at
least six identified factors regarding their independence, including:

- The provision of other services to the issuer by the person who
  employs the adviser
- The amount of fees received from the issuer by the person who
  employs the adviser as a percentage of the total revenue of the
  person who employs the adviser
- The policies and procedures of the person who employs the
  adviser that are designed to prevent conflicts of interest
- Any business or personal relationships of the adviser with a
  member of the compensation committee
- Any stock of the issuer owned by the adviser
- Any business or personal relationships between the executive
  officers of the issuer and the adviser or the person employing
  the adviser.

These six factors represent the minimum required for consideration under SEC rules, though additional factors may be adopted by
individual exchanges. Neither the NYSE nor NASDAQ have adopted
specific additional factors, though NYSE standards call for compensation committees to consider all factors relevant to the independence

FIGURE 14-3 Key Players in Compensation Governance

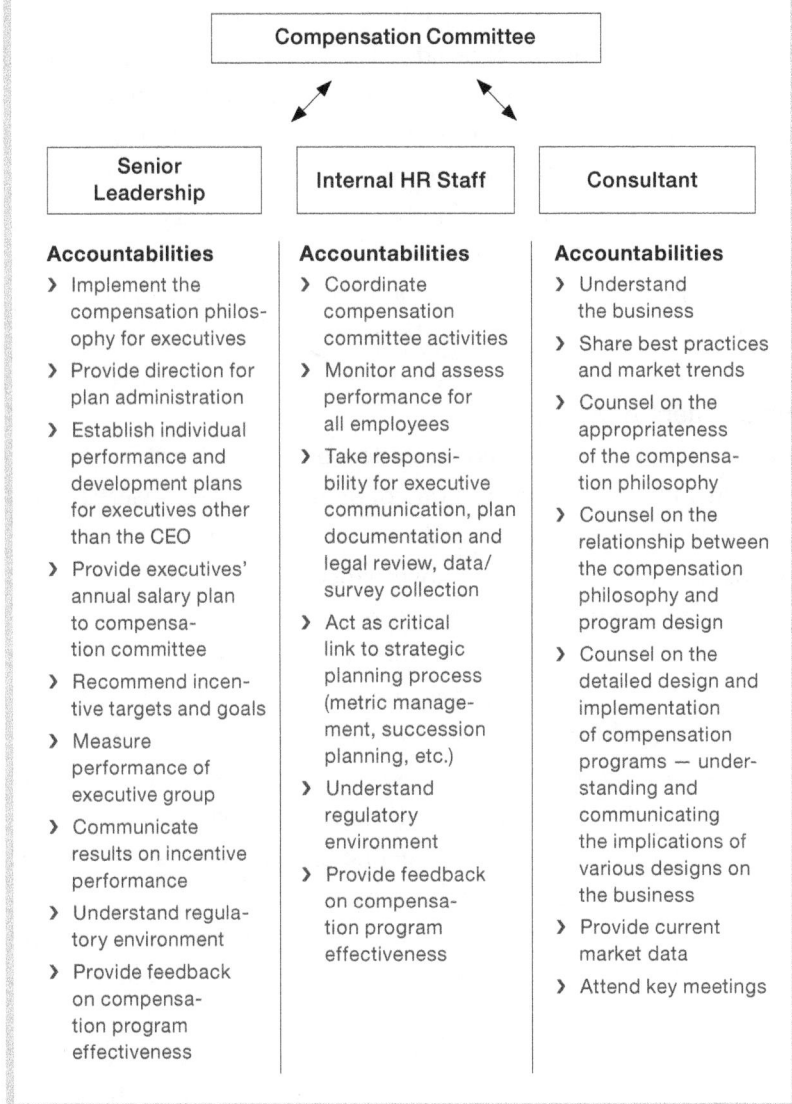

Compensation Committee

Senior Leadership	Internal HR Staff	Consultant
Accountabilities	**Accountabilities**	**Accountabilities**
› Implement the compensation philosophy for executives	› Coordinate compensation committee activities	› Understand the business
› Provide direction for plan administration	› Monitor and assess performance for all employees	› Share best practices and market trends
› Establish individual performance and development plans for executives other than the CEO	› Take responsibility for executive communication, plan documentation and legal review, data/ survey collection	› Counsel on the appropriateness of the compensation philosophy
› Provide executives' annual salary plan to compensation committee	› Act as critical link to strategic planning process (metric management, succession planning, etc.)	› Counsel on the relationship between the compensation philosophy and program design
› Recommend incentive targets and goals	› Understand regulatory environment	› Counsel on the detailed design and implementation of compensation programs — understanding and communicating the implications of various designs on the business
› Measure performance of executive group	› Provide feedback on compensation program effectiveness	› Provide current market data
› Communicate results on incentive performance		› Attend key meetings
› Understand regulatory environment		
› Provide feedback on compensation program effectiveness		

of a compensation adviser. Accordingly, compensation committees at NYSE-listed companies may need to assess independence through a broader lens. Although these six factors are specific to public compensation committees, private companies should also consider the independence of an advisor before retaining services.

While public compensation committees are required to assess the independence of advisers, they are not prohibited from selecting and retaining compensation advisers that are not independent. A committee would need to consider if it would be willing to disclose and explain the retention of a non-independent compensation adviser. In assessing the independence of compensation advisers, a variety of approaches may be used to obtain information. While some compensation committees use questionnaires only requesting specific information related to the six identified factors, others expand their areas of inquiry to include additional questions designed to fully explore any perceived independence issues.

Assessment of Advisers

While not required, a recommended best practice is an annual assessment by the compensation committee of any adviser(s) it has retained to assist in navigating the various issues involved in executive pay decisions and board governance.

The compensation committee should:

- Determine how well its advisers understood the company, its particular circumstances, and the role of various compensation elements in achieving the organization's goals and objectives.
- Assess the advisers' effectiveness in applying this understanding to support the committee in fulfilling its annual responsibilities.
- Evaluate the usefulness and timeliness of work completed by the adviser at the request of the committee.
- Consider any other services the adviser may have provided the company and whether they were approved by the committee.

After considering these elements, constructive feedback should be provided to the adviser(s) where warranted, including both areas of strength and opportunities for improvement.

Say on Pay

In 2010, the Dodd-Frank Act was signed into law and provided shareholders with a non-binding advisory vote to approve the compensation of a company's NEOs (as such compensation is disclosed in its annual proxy statement, including the CD&A, compensation tables and narrative disclosures). The so-called "say-on-pay" vote is mandatory for U.S. public companies, although smaller emerging growth companies are exempt from this requirement for a limited time.

Under Dodd-Frank, a say-on-pay vote must be held at least once every three years. A separate vote of shareholders on whether the mandated say-on-pay vote subsequently will be held annually, every two years or every three years — a "say on frequency" — is required at least once every six years.

The say-on-pay and say-on-frequency votes are advisory only and may be disregarded by the compensation committee and the board. However, voting results reflect shareholders' views on the appropriateness of the executive compensation program. As such, committees choosing to ignore this feedback from shareholders risk facing negative implications for future say-on-pay votes and the re-election of compensation committee members to the board. (The disclosure and certain other aspects of say on pay are discussed in Chapter 17).

Negative Say-on-Pay Votes

A negative say-on-pay vote (the proposal fails to earn support from a majority of voting shareholders) typically signals shareholder dissatisfaction related to executive compensation programs, individual terms for NEOs or the company's response to past voting results. Generally, negative say-on-pay votes occur at fewer than three percent of proposals for the Russell 3000. While negative votes are not the norm, shareholders who vote down management's say-on-pay proposal most commonly do so due to concerns related to:

- Pay-for-performance disconnect
- Excessive executive pay (e.g., well above peer median values)
- Generous severance packages
- Outsized sign-on bonuses
- Failure on the part of the compensation committee to address multiple years of low voting support.

A negative or relatively low say-on-pay vote puts pressure on compensation committees to review, justify and in some cases adjust programs and policies that affect the compensation of NEOs. In the event of such a voting result, compensation committee members may feel compelled to conform pay practices with those advocated by proxy advisers, institutional advisers or activist groups.

Rather than solely focusing on common market practices, compensation committees seeking to maintain or improve their say-on-pay results should consider engaging in one or more of the following actions:

- Increasing shareholder outreach
- Reviewing compensation plans
- Monitoring the pay-for-performance relationship
- Improving disclosure

Findings from reviewing compensation plans and the pay-for-performance relationship can provide an indication of whether adjustments to compensation programs are warranted and, if so, what specific concerns may need to be addressed. Whether or not adjustments to compensation plans are deemed necessary, additional clarity and effort in explaining the rationale behind certain potentially contentious practices may still be advisable.

Increasing Shareholder Outreach

A company should maintain regular communications with its major shareholders to gain their insights on perceived strengths and weaknesses of the executive pay program. When the company's say-on-pay outcome is poor or below expectations, there is a heightened need for this type of engagement.

Interaction with shareholders can facilitate understanding of concerns and provide an opportunity for a company to discuss the rationale behind the compensation program throughout the year, not just at the time of proxy filing (when investors and advisers may be unavailable or have little time to engage). Critical issues can be discussed and, where elicited, suggested modifications can be considered.

Before launching a communication or outreach program, it generally is helpful to develop a formal strategy with investor relations and in consultation with compensation advisers. This strategy may involve the formation of a working team that includes representatives who are knowledgeable about the company's executive compensation programs and may interact with shareholders and proxy advisers.

In developing this team, a company generally starts with the members of the compensation committee and then considers including:

- A member of the governance committee (depending on the individual's role in board-shareholder communications)
- The chair of the board
- The CFO
- General counsel
- The head of HR
- A senior executive in investor relations.

Company representatives should be informed on what types of information and disclosure can be provided. During the process of obtaining input from various shareholders on matters such as proposed equity compensation plans, companies must take care not to run afoul of SEC Regulation FD (Fair Disclosure) by sharing material, non-public information.

Reviewing Compensation Plans

Say on pay amplifies the attention devoted to any problematic component of executive pay. As such, a compensation committee and its advisers should evaluate each element of the company's pay program (including its rationale) and compare it against a "hot button" checklist. The following is a sample of areas to examine:

- **Compensation philosophy.** Peer group, target pay positioning, objectives
- **Compensation program design.** Base salary, pay mix, incentive structure
- **Annual incentives.** Targets (e.g., percent of salary), metrics, number of metrics, leverage curve, clawbacks

- **Long-term incentives.** Types of programs, vesting type (time vs. performance), metrics, number of metrics, leverage curve, deferrals, clawbacks for all programs
- **Equity use.** Share allocation, burn rate
- **Risk assessment.** Processes for the identification of potentially material compensation risks and internal controls in place
- **Contractual elements.** Existence and terms of employment contracts, severance, CIC benefits.

Such a checklist, tailored for a company's particular situation, can be used to evaluate specific pay practices and assess the overall executive compensation program. In determining which areas should be included on the checklist, the compensation committee must understand which practices may be especially sensitive in their next say-on-pay vote.

Monitoring the Pay-for-Performance Relationship

The primary purpose of evaluating pay-for-performance is to validate compensation levels within the context of company performance, both against internal business plans and relative to external peer organizations.

The pay-for-performance relationship is often assessed via analysis of realizable or realized pay in addition to the Summary Compensation Table disclosure of targeted pay opportunity. Realized pay represents actual take-home pay for an executive during a specific time period, and realizable pay represents the total amount of vested and unvested potential earnings. Such analyses incorporate multiple definitions of pay, enabling committee members to review compensation outcomes from more than one perspective.

Findings from such analyses can then be included in disclosures to shareholders as a component of annual communications.

Improving Disclosure

A complete review of pay programs also requires an examination of compensation disclosures. At times, weak say-on-pay outcomes can be traced back to poor disclosure of the compensation committee's rationale for certain pay decisions. Without proper explanation, shareholders are left without the full context of certain decisions.

Meaningful disclosure of compensation programs and decisions goes beyond meeting regulatory requirements. In recent years, effective disclosures attempt to tell a story about the compensation program's role in aiding corporate strategy. In doing so, the compensation discussion and analysis section of the proxy statement, as discussed more in Chapter 17, has taken on greater significance, and real estate, in the annual document.

The importance of proper disclosure becomes heightened when the compensation committee makes unusual decisions. In these cases, the company should provide more information to shareholders, not less. Compensation committees should be as concerned with the "why" as the "what" with respect to the pay decision. Perhaps most importantly, the disclosures should demonstrate how the unusual decision aids in promoting shareholder value.

Understanding Proxy Advisors

Since the imposition of say-on-pay, proxy advisors, such as Institutional Shareholder Services (ISS) and Glass Lewis, have had tremendous influence over the pay practices of many public companies. A proxy advisor's recommendation carries significant weight with institutional investors and is usually the primary factor in weak or negative say-on-pay vote outcomes. Compensation committees should be aware of and be prepared to engage with these proxy advisors.

Each proxy advisor publishes the policies upon which their recommendations are based. These policies are updated annually and informed by client feedback. Although the policies are available publicly, each advisor has internal practices when applying these policies. Independent committee advisors are often familiar with the external and internal considerations. As such, it is important for compensation committee members to stay informed on new proxy advisor policies and their application.

Given their influence, proxy advisors have become an additional communication opportunity for investor relations. While some companies engage with proxy advisors as part of a standard investor roadshow, others approach the advisor to discuss recent recommendations or compensation decisions. In either event, proxy advisors have increasingly made themselves available for engagements with companies. Those companies wishing to discuss executive compensation with the proxy advisor should be prepared to have a member of the compensation committee present to answer any questions the advisor may have.

Going Forward

At the core, management and compensation committees want to develop and maintain pay programs that:

- Provide a competitive advantage in attracting and retaining talented executives.
- Align compensation programs with business strategy.

As such, companies will continue to strive for appropriate — and often unique — pay programs that reflect the needs of their businesses and motivate executives to perform.

However, as compensation committees "color outside of the lines" with executive compensation design, they need to ensure they retain a focus on clearly communicating the intricacies of compensation programs and the rationale behind decisions to stakeholders. By engaging in outreach and increasing the level of attention paid to their proxy statements, compensation committees can work to obtain high positive levels of say-on-pay votes while ensuring compensation programs meet the needs of the company.

CHAPTER 15

Evolving Role of the Compensation Committee

By John Trentacoste and Tom Flannery

"*Our people are our greatest asset.*" It is a common principle heard across corporate America, underscoring that human capital is the lifeblood of modern enterprise. Like monetary assets, that must be monitored for performance, aligned to one's own risk tolerance, and rebalanced from time to time, talent assets require the same level of evaluation, scrutiny, and strategy. An evolving paradigm shift throughout corporations has catapulted human resources to one of the most strategic functions within organizations. In turn, talent management requires a different type of board-level oversight.

Enter the compensation committee, which is rapidly evolving to take on additional, critical accountabilities. The committee's traditional role — approving and overseeing executive compensation levels and programs and ensuring regulatory compliance — continues to be essential. However, in an effort to create "Enlightened Boards," many companies have expanded the remit of the compensation committee to tackle broader human resources questions. Enlightened Boards are true strategic advantages and are the source of competitive advantage.

Given the raging war for talent and current economic, social, and political environments, the need to rethink the compensation committee as the "Human Resources Committee" is of paramount importance for companies that endeavor to make their employer brand a competitive advantage.

Why "Human Resources Committee?"

Human resource (HR) committees are already in the thick of human resources management at the executive level. With added pressure on public, private, and not-for-profit organizations to realign and promote diversity, inclusion, and fairness, it makes sense for these board members to oversee the focus on behalf of the larger governing board in addressing these issues.

This greater task requires a greater remit. Gone are the days when the compensation committee would review compensation opportunities for the CEO and the other Named Executive Officers. Now, HR committees are expanding their purviews to larger executive cadres and additional critical roles. While it is not reasonable — nor practical — for the HR committee to review or opine on compensation opportunities for hundreds of employees, broader issues below the executive ranks, such as pay equity, positioning versus market, incentive plan alignment, and turnover, have been presented at the committee level to provide a more holistic insight into the company's broader talent strategy.

It is evident in today's world that good governance means more than just "oversight." Governing boards have the added burden of ensuring the organization aligns with the values of its stakeholders, not just shareholders. This imperative to evaluate a concept dubbed "total stakeholder return" places significant emphasis on employees and business partners, as well as the communities in which companies operate.

While this enhanced oversight requires a more holistic approach, it is important to remember that the HR committee and the board are not here to manage — their role is to govern. To use our "asset" reference, the HR committee is intended to serve as a Chief Investment Officer, whose role is to oversee those who are committing capital to ensure adherence to the company's strategy and risk tolerance. The HR function continues to serve as the Portfolio Managers, who are charged with executing decisions and are on the "front lines." The symbiosis of these two roles — execution and oversight — is the key to a successful refocusing of the HR committee, the basis of which is a clear definition of accountabilities.

What are the evolving accountabilities of the HR Committee?

1. Strategic Succession Planning

Succession planning, at all levels, is a critical policy role of the board (See Chapter 20 for more detail). The committee executes the executive level succession policy and includes the Chief Executive Officer (CEO) and the other key executive officers, typically direct reports to the CEO. Additionally, the committee should be apprised of succession plans for mission-critical roles or functions (e.g., information technology). The committee delegates to the CEO the cascading of the succession policy into the organization.

The HR committee must actively ensure the execution of the succession policy. At the executive level, this includes a periodic report, often quarterly, by the CEO to the HR committee on each covered executive. Reporting often includes the following:

- The executive's performance,
- The back-up plans in the event there is a planned or unplanned opening,
- Individual development plans,
- Inventory of possible successors,
- Policies that advance opportunities to create a high performing and diverse team.

It is advisable that companies develop easy to understand "dashboards" that can be updated and disseminated to the committee before each quarterly check-in. In addition to the factors identified above, it is recommended that the dashboard contain two additional critical pieces of information. First, the current "holding power" for each executive, which is defined as the value of unvested equity currently held by each executive. Second, the "external replacement cost" for the executive role, which can be gathered through compensation benchmarking or an external executive search professional.

For the positions below the executive team, the HR committee should establish criteria to ensure the organization's achievement of diversity, equity and inclusion goals. It is also advisable for management to "introduce" several high potential candidates to the committee by sharing their succession profiles. This helps provide the committee with an understanding of the potential future leaders of the organization and evaluate the extent to which the company is differentiating rewards for its highest performers versus satisfactory employees. Committees also include diversity and inclusion goals in the executive team's performance evaluations given the importance of this issue.

2. Performance Benchmarking

Often forgotten is the performance benchmarking components embedded in executive compensation programs. The most obvious is the variable compensation program, annual and long term, designed to reward based on the attainment of specific financial and operational performance goals. A second is the executive performance measurement program, designed to assess individual performance. The difference between the two programs? Variable compensation programs measure and reward how the team is performing. The performance management program measures individual performance, how a specific employee is doing.

Variable compensation has become a significant component in the executive compensation program. This finding holds true in for-profit as well as not-for-profit organizations. The vehicles used to provide variable compensation are different in these two sectors. In the for-profit world, equity (real or phantom depending on public or private ownership) is used along with cash and other vehicles. In the not-for-profit world, where "equity" is not directly available, cash-based programs are employed, such as supplemental executive retirement plans (SERP), long-term plans, or split-dollar programs. Variable compensation programs are discussed in depth in other chapters in this book.

The committee is becoming accountable for defining and implementing the performance expectations of the governing board. The committee, working with the audit committee and executive management, operationalizes the financial and organizational performance expectations. More directly, the committee defines the CEO's performance expectations.

3. It Is Not Just About Pay

The issue of personal behavior is no longer a "closet" issue. In fact, broad corporate scandals stemming from the #MeToo movement and other oversights in strict controls over behavioral expectations shows how lack of a codified process, procedure and response can erode shareholder value.

Boards have adopted policies governing the personal behavior of executives and employees. The issues include relationships between employees, particularly between superiors and subordinates, the use of organizational resources for personal gain, the obligation to put the interests of the organization at the forefront, and issues serving on outside boards where there may be the appearance or actual conflict of interest. The HR committee, for good or bad, is often made accountable for monitoring these issues.

While many companies adopted incentive recoupment policies shortly after Dodd-Frank in the event of a financial restatement, the HR committee is responsible for evaluating the expansion of these clawback policies to consider whether the addition of reputational harm should be deemed an event worthy of a clawback. Additionally, the HR committee should also review grounds that would constitute a termination for cause in order to ensure the company need not pay severance to an executive or employee who violated ethics rules or caused reputational damage. Finally, the committee should review on an annual basis the extent to which any incentive compensation needed to be recouped from employees.

4. Alignment with Broader Societal Expectations

Any illusion that institutional investors' laser-focus on enhanced environmental, social, and governance policies within corporate America was some sort of "bull market bias" were quickly dashed as more and more investors have implored companies to take a more stakeholder-based approach to decision making.

For example, the Black Lives Matter movement has highlighted the need for companies to address historic discriminatory issues. Organizations are now stepping up to take steps to address embedded patterns of discrimination.

Legislation has also played a role. In 2018, California enacted legislation requiring public companies with principal executive offices located in California to have at least one female director on the corporate board by December 31, 2019. The legislation then mandates an additional one or two female directors, depending on the size of the board, to serve as directors no later than December 31, 2021.

The inclusion of women on governing boards is just one step to achieving diversity, equity and inclusion goals. Behaviors that perpetuate discrimination, regardless of the type, are no longer acceptable. And it rests with the HR committee to ensure corporate policies are clear and embraced. It is a process of turning rhetoric into reality.

The HR committee can hold management teams accountable for ensuring action plans foster cultures that embrace diversity, establish milestones for achieving certain representation goals, and monitor engagement and education to ensure latent biases begin to be flushed out of organizations. While some companies have taken the step to include diversity metrics in the tabulation of incentive plans, we believe thoughtful and consistent monitoring at the HR committee can powerfully communicate the importance to management. And, it should be noted, that the committee must monitor both diversity and inclusion metrics, to not only ensure adequate representation among the employee population, but also a culture and environment that allows for shared success, no matter of one's race or gender.

Adapting to the Change

The pace of change seems to be accelerating, and boards of directors must quickly adapt. The pressure on boards and executive management is expected to increase. For example, "say on pay" has evolved into a primary concern for compensation committees.

Consideration around diversity, equity and inclusion will similarly become an even more critical issue for governing boards.

Boards utilize committee processes as a critical aspect of their governance oversight: every director cannot be involved in every discussion and every decision. The committee process should be realigned to address the needed change.

Given today's climate, the HR committee must be as important and influential as any other board committee. It must have the authority to monitor, question and raise issues on a proactive rather than on a reactive basis. These expectations cut across both compensation and human resources roles.

The compensation role of the HR committee includes:

- **Setting expectations.** These expectations include clarity about personal behaviors, ethics and performance.
- **Setting compensation philosophy.** This compensation philosophy is used to guide the HR committee in setting performance goals and objectives, defining peers for pay and performance comparison, the design and implementation of the reward program, and all the constituent components, such as base salary, variable short- and long-term organizational performance, benefits, and any perquisites.
- **Monitoring of organizational and executive performance.** At least quarterly, reviews the alignment between the board's performance expectations and actual performance, supports the CEO in addressing barriers and serves as advisors.
- **Setting annual compensation levels.** Approves changes to compensation levels that ensure an appropriate return on investment to stakeholders.
- **Reviewing and approving performance awards.** Reviews and approves any equity awards and any cash payments related to the variable compensation program.
- **Ensuring compliance.** Adheres to regulatory requirements on a national and local basis, and secures the advice of compensation, accounting and legal advisors. Receives certification from the CEO and other leaders as required about adherence with key behavioral, ethical and employment standards.

- **Guaranteeing accurate reporting.** This includes reviewing any regulatory reporting prior to filing and establishing policies about how queries will be handled from the public or regulators.

The human resource role of the HR committee will include:

- **Defining its scope and remit.** There should be a clear under-standing of the HR committee's oversight over the executive team. Typically, this includes the CEO and the CEO's direct reports and any special position, such as the "head of compliance."
- **Supporting and working with the CEO.** As the person account-able for executing the policies of the board, the CEO must receive the active support of the HR committee along with the balance of the board. The HR committee must also monitor organizational and individual executive team performance objectives.
- **Supporting and working with the CHRO.** As the person on the front lines of the day-to-day HR function and the person responsible for wide-spread strategic HR initiatives, the CHRO must receive insight from the HR committee as to learnings from other companies. The HR committee must foster a candid and open relationship, while pushing for accountability for regular and candid reports and updates.
- **Cultivating talent.** This is a critical role in ensuring the executive team's diversity and the talent within the organization. Tools, such as pay equity analysis, should be a requirement of the organiza-tion to provide executable information on the achievement of diversity, equity and inclusion goals.
- **Monitoring performance.** Performance dashboards should be available to all board members and the HR committee's accountability to monitor and address deviations from expected performance. What has been a "quarterly" monitoring process needs to become a more regular process. What must be recognized is the board is not charged with managing. It sets policy and monitors policy. It keeps track of performance, not reacting to every change in the performance slope.

- **Preparing for succession.** Ensure there is a plan to fill critical positions and be aware of the need for interim, as well as long-term replacements.
- **Reporting.** Provide information to the board to ensure each member can fulfill their responsibility in their governing role.

All About Execution

Evolving the role of the compensation committee into a human resources committee is a significant governance change. It requires care and diligence and may require a restructuring of the organization's governance processes.

Simply changing the name of the committee will not accomplish the desired refocus needed at this critical juncture. In order to achieve the optimal refocus of the committee, as well as set forth a plan of action, consider the following actions:

1. **Evaluate the committee charter.** While the name of the committee is important, its charter is critical for enumerating annual expectations and defining the committee's remit. While an annual charter review is typically a perfunctory exercise, now is the time to critically evaluate whether the charter provides the latitude for the committee to expand its remit and ask broader strategic questions.

2. **Amend standing agendas.** With committee meeting agendas already chock-full of items on the compensation front, it may seem difficult—if not impossible—to allow the time to devote to these important strategic topics. Two approaches have been most successful in ensuring adequate time for these issues: first, allowing approval by written consent on routine committee items (e.g., approving the Compensation Discussion and Analysis); and, second, modifying standing agendas to ensure a regular cadence and balance of standard and strategic topics.

3. **Liaise with the CEO and CHRO.** Expanding the role of the compensation committee may be viewed skeptically by management and others in the HR function. Therefore, in order for this not to be seen as either an overreach or an encroachment by directors, it is important the HR committee chairman speak with both the

	Q1	Q2	Q3	Q4
Compensation Focus	Pay Actions and Reporting	Regulatory Review and Program Planning	Strategic Consideration and Plan Design	Competitive Fact Base
HR Focus	▪ Succession Planning (market positioning and differentiation analysis of high potentials) ▪ Performance Benchmarking ▪ ESG Update	▪ Strategic Succession Planning ('meet the successors' engagement and readiness assessment) ▪ Clawback and severance review	▪ Strategic Succession Planning (holding power assessment) ▪ Employee Engagement	▪ Strategic Succession Planning (emergency succession planning exercise) ▪ Broad-based compensation alignment

CEO and CHRO to outline the objectives of the broadened remit. Clear understanding of the expectations of management versus those of the committee is critical to ensuring a seamless transition to the expanded HR committee.

4. **Conduct an initial audit.** Each expanded committee should ask of management, in addition to its consultants, counsel and advisors, to prepare a human capital "audit" that assesses the company across the various dimensions outlined above, including succession, diversity and inclusion, broad-based positioning, differentiation between high and low performers, and various ESG initiatives. This audit is crucial to understand the current "state of play" to establish "milestones" and define key priorities for the HR committee, in conjunction with management.

5. **Identify key committee goals.** The above audit is a crucial first step to evaluate where the company currently stands with respect to broader talent initiatives. It is important to recognize that the HR committee certainly cannot tackle every facet of the expanded agenda in an in-depth fashion. Therefore, it is important as a committee to define the key priorities for the near- and mid-term timeframes to provide management enough time to prepare and

the committee enough "soak time" to absorb and opine on the information provided to it.

Final Considerations

In order for people to *truly* be a company's greatest asset, the compensation committee of today must transform into the human resources committee, ready to tackle the most pressing issues of tomorrow. Those companies that invest in strong oversight of policies, procedures and strategic initiatives regarding talent and embrace the need to think about total *stakeholder* return will likely create a more compelling value proposition to its current and potential employees. In addition, these companies will command more brand equity, and, ultimately, perform better than companies that use a narrower remit of the compensation committee.

CHAPTER 16

Compensation Committee Tools

By Todd McGovern and Jack Grange

O ne of the most important duties of the compensation committee is to make compensation decisions that align executive and shareholder interests while supporting the strategic direction of the company. Ideally, the compensation committee should consider a number of different perspectives and sources of information to fulfill these duties. The reality, however, is that compensation committees often organize meeting agendas in response to specific issues. At one meeting, the committee may decide on salary increases; at another, it may determine annual incentive awards; at a third meeting, the committee may discuss severance agreements. The result is a piecemeal approach that often fails to assemble the parts into a cohesive whole.

This chapter focuses on the tools that boards and compensation committees can use to help them make more informed decisions regarding executive pay.

This chapter:

- Identifies five critical issues that compensation committees should consider in the meeting planning process.
- Explains how tally sheets can bring to light the true costs of the executive pay program and offers guidelines for customizing a tally sheet to a company's particular executive pay program.
- Discusses four fundamental questions that should be applied in a fitness review to the key aspects of executive compensation (base

salary, annual incentives, LTIs, benefits, employment contracts, and severance and change-in-control arrangements) to ensure that they can withstand external scrutiny.

- Provides an approach that enables companies to calculate executives' current and future wealth; with accumulated wealth analysis, companies can better align company and executive needs.
- Examines issues involved in the clawback of compensation paid when a financial restatement, fraud or other identified event leads to a finding of unearned or inappropriate payment.
- Evaluates how companies have been impacted by the say-on-pay process and how committees have used it as a tool to dialogue with shareholders and enhance the program's alignment with their expectations. It also illustrates how committees can use the Compensation Discussion and Analysis (CD&A) as a tool to "tell the story" of the pay program from the company's perspective.
- Discusses how the committee's use of discretion and adjustments can and should be used to better align pay outcomes that fit with the organization's performance and strategic priorities.

Maximizing the Compensation Committee Calendar

Many compensation committees recognize the need to take a big picture approach to executive compensation decision making. A critical element in this process is meeting planning. This means thinking more holistically about the relationship between pay and performance and how compensation issues align with core business issues at the company.

In making decisions regarding meeting planning, we see the following critical areas that committees should consider:

- Linking business strategy to human capital strategy through an evaluation of how the company makes money, and consideration of whether the executive compensation plans align with the business cycle. Plans meant to drive performance and business in a previous business cycle may not be relevant today. Similarly, committees should consider whether compensation programs are fully aligned with the company's business and talent strategies now and in the foreseeable future. A significant item to review is the extent to which a company's incentive plans are focused on value creation and financial performance, and whether, in totality, the programs actually reinforce the business model, strategy and vision. The end result is that each meeting should include a conversation on the state of the business, market dynamics, future goals and how well the current philosophy is working, followed by a consideration of whether any changes are appropriate.

- Governance and risk management oversight to ensure that a company's practices, policies and procedures fit the business, its philosophy, business stage and life cycle. Part of this oversight involves taking a hard look at the short- and long-term incentive plans. A process of regular evaluation can help ensure that these programs are working as planned, and that the metrics in each plan are achieving the desired business results without causing excessive risk. In this sense, risk oversight and risk management serve to protect a company's assets while also creating long-term value.

- Considering the manner in which the executive compensation programs support executive team succession planning and the development of top talent. Committees should inquire at each meeting regarding any difficulties in recruiting or retaining top talent and ask HR leadership about the development of talent throughout the business.

- Assessing the committee's level of compensation knowledge and if further education or training are needed. A key element in the committee's oversight of executive compensation programs is to ensure that its members have a regular source of updated information on compensation developments. Continuous learning at the committee level will only foster better discussions and serve to mitigate risk around compensation planning.

- Assessing the extent to which executives understand the rationale and design of the pay programs. Two key elements in this are determining (1) whether executives can identify the link between business goals and driving results for the organization, and (2) whether executives can see how their actions can affect compensation. The committee should clearly document the roles and responsibilities for developing executive pay, communication strategies and content, and the respective roles of the committee, management and advisers. The committee should also ensure and understand the processes in place to allow investors to share their input with the board, the committee and management.

In addition to maximizing the committee calendar to provide perspective on executive compensation issues, the following sections provide an overview of several tools available to the committee to aid in its assessment of executive pay.

Starting Points for a Discussion on Executive Pay

Much of the committee's work cannot be completed without establishing an overall perspective on executive compensation in the then current business and regulatory environment. Some critical areas for consideration and action by the entire board of directors to guide actions by the compensation committee include:

- Agree upon what success would look like for the company considering current and short-term business conditions.
- Identify the key executives in this context.
- Agree upon the critical actions and behaviors required from these executives.
- Determine the key areas of business risk and the timeframes over which these may be resolved.
- Identify any new constraints on the company's freedom to act arising from known shareholders' views, regulatory considerations, tax impacts and other legal concerns.

Executive Compensation Fitness Check

Executive compensation is a focal point of potential vulnerability for companies. The media, shareholder groups, proxy advisers, various prominent boards and commissions, and Congress all have described executive compensation as a motivating force behind a purported decline in corporate responsibility.

Compensation committees should periodically conduct a "fitness check" to ascertain whether the company's executive compensation programs can effectively withstand external scrutiny.

Fundamental Questions

Four fundamental questions typically are addressed when conducting a fitness check:

- Are the compensation programs and policies consistent with shareholders' expectations?
  - Do executives' share ownership standards, share retention requirements and stock sale/option exercise procedures align their interests with those of shareholders?
  - Do cash and equity programs encourage no more than the level (and nature) of business and investment risk expected by shareholders?
  - Are plan designs and approval processes sufficiently transparent?
  - Is the board governance process adequate with respect to compensation?
  - Are executive incentive (both cash and equity based) programs, retirement vehicles and deferred compensation opportunities fair to both the shareholders and executives? Are they tax effective?
  - Is the amount of shareholders' equity dilution appropriate?
  - Are the payments, terms and conditions of severance, and change-in-control policies reasonable in both favorable and adverse scenarios?
  - How has the business and share price performed in the past several months?
  - What is the status of executive share ownership requirements?
- Are the programs appropriately competitive and defensible? Are all elements of the rewards and benefits structure:
  - Appropriately positioned?
  - Internally equitable?
  - Externally competitive?
  - Consistent with good pay practices?
  - Consistent with an appropriate peer group?

- Reflective of scope of business and role/accountability?
- Appropriately balanced for both short- and long-term rewards and motivation?
- Consistent with an articulated and supportable rewards strategy?

■ Are the programs and payments linked to corporate strategy and business performance?

- Does the design drive actions and strategies that enhance value while also promoting ethical behaviors?
- Are the goals and rewards tied to significant improvements in business operations or company finances?
- Do the rewards encourage no more than the desired level of business risk?
- Are the arrangements comprehensive and comprehensible?
- Are the programs consistent with best practices?
- Is the annual incentive plan rewarding the right outcomes and encouraging the right behaviors?

■ Are relative executive rewards levels and relative performance aligned appropriately?

- Do the prior payouts under incentive programs and the levels of compensation increases correlate to recent business performance and drivers of shareholder value?
- Are the rewards levels based on proper broad-based and industry-specific peer groups?
- Does relative TDC correlate to TSR?
- Does actual pay delivered correlate to a corresponding degree of performance against relevant value drivers (e.g., cash flow, earnings-per-share growth, return on invested capital, market share, new-product sales, customer satisfaction)?
- Are the number, weighting and reinforcement of rewards measures appropriate?
- What is the status of LTI grants and potential impact to attraction, retention and motivation issues?

In addressing these questions, consideration must be given, at a minimum, to five key aspects of executive compensation:

- Base salary
- Short- and long-term incentives
- Executive benefits and perquisites (including retirement and insurance arrangements)
- Employment contracts
- Severance and change-in-control arrangements.

In addition, a separate review should be conducted of the board's own compensation program and its governance processes related to executive compensation.

To reinforce an independent perspective, an independent outside adviser should be retained who should report directly to the chair of the board's compensation committee for the fitness check. Because the specific components of any fitness check must be customized to an organization's circumstances and objectives, the scope of any review varies from company to company.

Tally Sheets: Adding Up the Cost of Executive Compensation

Due to an increased scrutiny of executive compensation, corporate boards have turned to "tally sheets" to obtain a comprehensive view of the true size of executive pay packages. A tally sheet is a detailed compilation of all major components of executive compensation, including base salary, annual incentives, LTIs, retirement programs, and various benefits and perquisites.

While the particulars vary from company to company, the essence of a tally sheet is a summary of an executive's total pay package. To present a true picture, a tally sheet should consider not only what an executive receives during employment, but also what he/she may receive upon the various events that may result in a termination of employment. The value of tally sheets has been recognized as an important tool for compensation committees, and their use has become a common (and best) practice. A substantial majority of public companies already are using some form of tally sheet.

Board members at some companies may not have a big picture perspective on all elements of compensation, particularly the benefits, perquisites and termination pay that an executive may receive. For example, this can occur where different elements of compensation and benefits packages are addressed at different times, perhaps without considering how a change in one piece may affect another. Tally sheets can provide boards with a holistic and long-term look at each pay component, the relationships among these elements, and the potential future value of each element under different scenarios — particularly those causing a termination of employment.

As previously noted, decisions on executive pay often are made on a piecemeal basis. Compounded by the fact that many compensation committee members serve on a rotational basis, the committee may lack the historical perspective to make comprehensive pay decisions. Too often tally sheets have revealed unexpectedly high (even shocking) aggregate pay, causing directors to experience "holy cow!" moments. (See "Benefits of Tally Sheets.")

Use of Realizable Pay: Measuring Pay for Purposes of Pay-for-Performance Alignment

Another tool that has been used by compensation committees in recent years is the concept of realizable pay. Realizable pay is an approach to measure compensation that tests the pay-for-performance alignment. It has become the term used to describe the total compensation value that an executive may realize given actual stock and company performance as of a specified date.

Using compensation values as disclosed in the CD&A may not tell the full story when assessing pay and performance. The basic concern with using grant values is they are essentially reasoned guesses of the expected value of the equity award at the time of grant. Over time, such values may not correlate to actual amounts being realized by executives from the grants (which values ultimately could be significantly more or less). This method also looks at pay prospectively, extending beyond the period for which performance is measured. For example, a CEO's performance shares can appear as $5 million at the time of grant; however, if threshold performance is not achieved and the shares do not vest, the awards do not produce anything realizable. Accordingly, the concept of realizable pay was developed to address this issue. In general terms, realizable pay figures would substitute the grant date value of equity used in the summary compensation table with the value of the equity awards that executives may receive based on actual stock price performance as of a specified date.

Through this analysis, you can test the validity/strength of your pay program (did it return the appropriate pay for the performance achieved) compared to target pay. This analysis is also performed

Benefits of Tally Sheets

Understanding the Costs of Executive Terminations

A compensation committee should be aware of the aggregate value of amounts payable to the CEO and other top executives upon termination of employment. These scenarios should include retirement, death, disability, dismissal, dismissal for cause, voluntary resignation, resignation for good reason and termination in connection with a change in control. To simplify the presentation, those termination events that call for the same payouts can, in many cases, be grouped. By understanding what has been promised under executive contracts and various programs, directors can avoid surprise or embarrassment. Tally sheets help ensure that compensation committee members are aware of the cost and timing of potential payouts, as well as the terms and conditions that trigger payment.

Revealing the True Value of Executive Benefits and Perquisites

Although compensation committees have been accustomed to tallying top executives' base salaries, annual incentive pay and LTIs, they sometimes may overlook benefits and perquisites. Compensation committees need to know more than the types of benefits provided; they must understand the value of the benefits and perquisites. Before approving executive pay changes, compensation committees should understand the costs, tax treatment and financial accounting consequences of these modifications to their benefits and perquisites program.

Creating Greater Alignment With the Company's Compensation Philosophy

When decisions on various components of an executive's total pay are made at different times throughout the year, the compensation committee needs to consider how each program fits in the company's overall compensation philosophy. Tally sheets look at the compensation and benefits in totality, allowing the compensation committee to determine the appropriate mix by considering relationships among pay components. A compensation committee should test its tally sheets annually against its compensation philosophy and determine whether the pay philosophy is delivering the appropriate value over time.

for the peer group, so you can also determine how well your pay program performed relative to your peers.

Accumulated Wealth Management: Is It Worth Examining?

Compensation committees are continuing to gain a better understanding of the total wealth potential of an executive's past, current and projected future compensation and benefits. In the same manner, an increasing number of companies are taking accumulated wealth into account when making pay decisions. Given the expanded disclosure of executive pay, this trend likely will continue.

Why is accumulated wealth analysis important? From an executive's perspective, accumulated wealth provides security, independence and the funding of retirement objectives. To the extent that accumulated wealth enables an executive to retire, it can open opportunities for identified candidates to develop and move up in the organization. From a company's perspective, the say-on-pay process has heightened the emphasis on making sure that pay appropriately reflects performance.

Overview of Accumulated Wealth Analysis

An accumulated wealth analysis starts with an examination of awards and accruals under all company-sponsored wealth-accumulation vehicles, particularly an executive's equity interests and retirement benefits (including deferred compensation). While companies may develop and conduct the analysis in various ways, the clear goal is to understand the total wealth position/potential of the executive. A key objective of executive compensation is the creation of wealth for those who enhance shareholder value through successful management of entrusted resources. Accumulated wealth can be especially large where total shareholder returns are strong.

How Much Is Enough?

The obvious use of the wealth-accumulation analysis is to determine how much wealth has been and will be created. It certainly can be argued that an executive with 100 to 200 times salary in accumulated wealth through his/her stock-based compensation does not need further motivation/alignment via company stock performance. On the other hand, one to four times salary is not enough to provide an executive with financial security, nor the ability to retire or change his/her venue in retirement. Also, current compensation and the opportunity for more wealth operate to motivate and retain the executive.

It is in the middle, and not at the extremes, where compensation committees must discuss and develop a strategy around how much is enough. The objective is not to reduce compensation as much as to understand at what point additional wealth is offset by an executive's desire to enjoy the fruits of his/her labor. Simply turning off the spigot is not a viable alternative because the executive could choose to work for a competitor that is more than willing to pay market rates with the full complement of incentive plan awards. Rather, it is important to align rewards with shareholder value as well as executive needs and desires.

Recouping Executive Pay: Clawbacks

Clawbacks have emerged as the primary means to recover "erroneously awarded" incentive-based compensation from current and former executives. In this context, "erroneously awarded compensation" refers to incentive compensation that would not have been received in light of an accounting restatement by the company. As corporate governance groups and shareholders advocated for the adoption of general policies or terms in executive agreements and incentive plans to enable a company to recapture bonuses and other incentive-based rewards in appropriate circumstances, companies increasingly developed clawback provisions suited to their own particular circumstances.

Initially spurred on by fairly narrow recovery provisions in the Sarbanes-Oxley Act of 2002, Congress included clawbacks in the terms for troubled institutions that received U.S. Department of Treasury investments under 2009 bailout legislation. Congress then moved to center stage with the inclusion of mandatory, rigid claw-back requirements (subject to relevant SEC rulemaking and the implementation of stock exchange listing standards) in the 2010 Dodd-Frank legislation applicable to public companies. It took the SEC until August 2015 to issue proposed rules on clawbacks required under Dodd-Frank. In general, Dodd-Frank contains considerably broader recapture rules than the clawback provisions under Sarbanes-Oxley. For example, Dodd-Frank's clawbacks apply to any executive officer (not just the CEO and CFO), do not require any misconduct (just simply the requisite restatement described in the next section on "Putting Clawbacks in Context"), and cover a three-year (rather than 12-month) period. Public companies subject to Dodd-Frank's mandates also should consider including any additional features or processes that address the organization's particular circumstances.

Putting Clawbacks in Context

Traditionally, a clawback was a formal policy or a provision in an employment agreement or in a compensation plan that permitted a company, often in its discretion (typically exercised by the board or compensation committee), to recapture cash and/or equity incentive payments from certain employees — generally senior executives — for one or more reasons (set out in the particular program or agreement). Putting aside the statutory and regulatory mandates noted above, a policy or provision might provide for a clawback if:

- An executive has been deemed responsible for fraudulent actions.
- Incentive payments were based on misstated financials, especially if the result of fraud or negligence.
- An executive has violated enforceable noncompetition provisions or other restrictive covenants.
- An executive has been responsible for defined actions detrimental to the company.

Clawbacks can be designed to be triggered by any one of the events identified in the policy or provision; definitions of covered events and the consequences have varied considerably across companies.

The most common triggers among the largest U.S. public companies are a financial restatement by the company or an executive's ethical misconduct. The next most prevalent event is a violation of a noncompetition agreement.

Covered Compensation

As clawbacks grew in prevalence (and became the subject of legal mandates), the definition of "covered compensation" became more expansive. Initial provisions focused on cash-based bonuses; recently, clawbacks have broadened to include equity compensation — both vested and unvested stock awards. Research indicates that the vast majority of policies included both cash and equity incentive compensation (e.g., "incentive-based compensation [including stock options awarded as compensation]" under Dodd-Frank) in their definition of compensation subject to clawback.

Board Considerations in Developing a Clawback Policy

Before adopting clawback provisions, boards and compensation committees need to think through both the legal requirements and the possible application of the clawback provisions. The implementation of a clawback policy surfaces administrative and compliance issues that need to be reviewed and thoroughly discussed.

Which Employees Need to Be Covered Under the Policy?

Recoveries under Dodd-Frank extend to "any current and former executive officer," which of course bring to mind some practical difficulties inherent in recouping pay from a former officer. Beyond the required group that a clawback policy must cover, we find that the further down in the organization that the recovery provision extends, the more likely the provision will be viewed favorably by corporate governance groups.

Which Compensation Elements Should Be Covered?

As previously noted, Dodd-Frank requires the recovery of any incentive-based compensation if the other conditions for a clawback are met;

companies may decide to extend compensation recoupments even further. Base salary typically is not covered in clawback arrangements because base compensation is not usually linked to specific performance objectives. While awaiting rulemaking on clawbacks under Dodd-Frank, some companies adopted provisions that directly link their clawback provisions to all performance-based pay (including both cash and equity compensation). A clawback policy required by Dodd-Frank should, for example, address how to implement the repayment of gains generated by stock sales if the stock price was affected by misstated financial information.

Where Should Clawback Provisions Be Included?

Some companies adopt clawback policies that then are incorporated by reference into the relevant plans and agreements; this approach works well for complying with the Dodd-Frank mandates as it is relatively simple to implement. Other companies include clawback language in all employment agreements and incentive plan documents.

Looking Ahead

While clawbacks are often viewed as a common-sense solution to "undeserved" executive compensation, various facts and issues specific to a company's circumstances should be considered in designing any clawback policy that extends beyond the Dodd-Frank mandates. Because U.S. public companies are compelled by Dodd-Frank and the proposed SEC rules to adopt clawback provisions, companies need to understand which components of their executive pay programs may be subject to clawback. From a design perspective, whether an award is covered by the clawback rules may affect its attractiveness, as executives generally prefer to receive awards that are not subject to clawback.

It should also be noted that the SEC rules continue to remain in a proposed status — there has been no clear guidance to inform a timeline for their implementation. Despite their pending status, pressure from proxy advisors and institutional investors has resulted in most companies adopting some form of clawback policy. But, while many companies adopted a policy to align with the proposed rules, many others did not go as far, leaving flexibility to adapt to the final requirements, once approved. Any clawback policy should balance the organization's priorities, which could range from being a leading example of governance best practice to maintaining flexibility to ensure the committee can be nimble when addressing difficult executive pay situations.

Responding to Say-on-Pay Votes

Say-on-pay has been a requirement for U.S.-listed companies since 2010. Over this period, committees have increasingly used the say-on-pay process to open dialogue with investors which, in turn, has slowly shaped the landscape of executive pay structures across every industry. Looking back over this period, the most obvious shift for most publicly listed companies is the elimination of perceived problematic pay practices (e.g., tax gross-ups, excessive severance and perquisites, single-trigger equity acceleration) or, at a minimum, to prospectively commit to never implement such practices again. In addition, companies have been enhancing the CD&A to ensure it "tells the story" from the company's perspective and advertises the "why" related to the selection and design of critical compensation components.

Impact of Say-on-Pay Voting

Due to the continued application of investor, market, proxy advisor and other external policies and pressures, lower say-on-pay vote results often triggered a higher rate of subsequent company-initiated pay program changes. In short, say-on-pay legislation yielded many of the compensation and governance policies under which companies now operate. Absent disclosure of a compelling business rationale to justify a company's specific outlier position(s) or practice(s), any company looking to obtain a high level of shareholder approval generally needs to fall in line. As a result, a substantial majority of companies that have adopted the prevailing compensation and governance best practices can now expect say-on-pay approval levels of at least 90 percent.

When a publicly listed company receives a negative say-on-pay vote recommendation from a proxy advisory firm and/or shareholder voting results fall below a critical threshold, the compensation committee essentially is put on alert and should learn the main cause(s) behind the vote recommendation and/or results. As part of this process, committee members should consider whether changes to the company's compensation programs are warranted.

Given that high levels of say-on-pay support are the norm, what level causes concern? Organizations that fail to secure majority shareholder approval, as well as those with less than 70 percent shareholder support, need to take steps to improve results. However, even outcomes in the 70 and 80 percent range, while certainly "passing," suggest that there are still significant percentages of displeased investors and changes to compensation programs should at least be considered.

Communications with Shareholders

Another change in company behavior driven by say-on-pay voting is the increased importance of effective shareholder communications that typically occurs during an annual shareholder engagement or outreach process. It is now commonplace for an organization facing a negative say-on-pay vote recommendation — and/or lower (than desired) voting results — to begin evaluating its current situation by first reaching out to, and engaging in dialogue with, their shareholders to openly discuss executive compensation pay issues.

The compensation committee chair often leads these discussions (along with the lead director) to gather feedback from institutional shareholders. That way, the chair can bring these findings directly into the committee setting and this feedback can act as another tool in the committee toolkit. After listening to the expressed concerns and recommendations of shareholders at these meetings, many companies choose to recalibrate their pay programs to better align with the identified investor and proxy advisor issues while balancing the underlying tenets of the company's pay program, including competitiveness and alignment with business strategy and shareholders.

Most Common Compensation Program Changes

Since the implementation of say-on-pay, there has been a clear shift in executive pay design and disclosure. Companies that received a negative say-on-pay vote recommendation or actual negative result lead the way in making changes to align with the emerging trends in governance best practice. Among the most common changes for those companies included:

- Redesigned STI and LTI programs with new performance metrics
- Revised LTI vehicle mix with an increased emphasis on performance-based awards
- Reduced usage of stock options, which are generally not considered "performance based" to proxy advisors
- Extended length of LTI performance periods to better align with the time horizon to execute on the intended business strategy
- Simplification of STI and LTI designs to enhance transparency and perceived value
- Greater proxy disclosure and transparency

The changes referenced above sparked a broader trend of say on pay's influence on all U.S.-listed company compensation programs. Again, after hastening the removal of most problematic pay practices, the remaining focus of any say-on-pay assessment should continue to be on the "how" (i.e., time vs. performance based, short term vs. long term, performance metric selection and setting, business rationale and disclosure) and the "how much" (i.e., payouts aligned with performance). Absent any significant changes in executive compensation policy-making considerations, legal and regulatory constraints, or overall market sentiment on the design of an appropriate pay program, the above compensation design elements will continue to be at the center of annual say-on-pay assessments and voting tallies.

Pay-for-Performance Alignment

Most efforts to align pay and performance continue to be "top of mind" for compensation committees, with an emphasis on incentive design and mix of pay. Coupled with an ongoing elimination of problematic pay practices, the influence of say-on-pay may be making compensation programs more homogeneous.

That said, even if a company aligns its pay programs with market and with "best (compensation and governance) practices," there will be a consistent ebb and flow of what, when and how scrutiny will be applied to executive compensation pay programs. For instance, the rigor of performance goal setting and the corresponding payouts likely will continue to be a major focus of any underlying incentive compensation program assessment. Therefore, demonstrating appropriate pay-for-performance alignment will be critical to securing favorable vote recommendations and achieving desired vote results.

Looking Ahead

As compensation programs evolve, it is critical for organizations to furnish more explanation, rationale and clarity on current and prospective pay decisions within the CD&A — it should be used as the company's platform to advertise the plan. Greater depth and disclosure on annual incentive and performance-based LTI programs can educate shareholders and score points with proxy advisors. Effective communication is an essential tool to mitigate the risk of poor say-on-pay results.

While most companies continue to receive strong shareholder support for their pay programs, continued perseverance, adaptability and more effort will likely be required to stay on top. It is a tricky balance to implement what is ideal for shareholders while also driving the right performance for the business. While not required, continuing to engage in shareholder (and proxy advisor) outreach meetings is extremely beneficial in both identifying potential design issues and providing organizations with recommendations on how to improve their overall compensation programs. Listening and responding to such discussions regularly may enable companies to avoid a negative vote recommendation and/or lower say-on-pay vote results in future years.

As shareholders and proxy advisors continue to redefine the "ideal" pay program, companies will face more pressure to conform and redesign pay programs that fall within those guard rails while balancing the alignment of executive pay with what is appropriate for the business as well as for shareholders.

Discretion and Adjustments

The committee use of discretion and adjustments used to be heavily constrained by the tax rules (e.g., 162(m)) and then later by the proxy advisory firms. Typically, this constrained compensation committees to only use "negative" discretion, meaning only the lowering of payouts for executives.

However, with the recent changes to the tax code and 162(m), compensation committees can now safely put discretion and adjustments more broadly in their toolkit. This is particularly important in black sheep situations like economic distress, natural disasters, and global health crises. There are four ways companies can use discretion and/or adjustments to realign either pay plans or payouts:

1. **Financial Adjustment**: The first lever to consider using is adjusting the financial targets in the incentive plan. This occurs when one-time events were not anticipated when companies set their goals. The committee needs to evaluate the rationale and impact of adjusting out the effects of the crisis on global, regional, business unit or local results (to the best of the company's ability to generate these numbers). This will allow the committee to reason through the appropriateness of adjusting performance metrics. To the extent this lever is "activated" by a committee when calculating final results and payouts, the adjustments would need to be explained in detail in any public filing (e.g., the CD&A). This lever is best used in situations where the performance miss is modest, and the impact of the one-time event is easier to ascertain.

2. **Overriding Discretion**: This lever must be used carefully, as the institutional shareholders get concerned when it is applied.

However, given the magnitude of potential one-time events on some companies, it is likely that even these usual critics will understand the situation at hand if properly explained in a CD&A. In this case, the committee needs to reason through when it is appropriate to apply discretion, in what situations and with which executive/management populations. This lever is best used in situations where actual performance is significantly off plan and/or the impact is harder to disaggregate from other factors (such as commodity price shifts or regulatory changes).

3. **Incentive Plan Restart and/or use of Stub Plans**: This lever would suspend either the annual or long-term performance plans that were implemented at the beginning of the year or still have time remaining in their performance cycle. The committee would then reset goals (and possibly change metrics) for the remainder of the measurement period. Payout potential is correspondingly reduced as well. Committees need to reason through how critical goal alignment, and/or a new direction, are for the remaining time period(s). This lever is best used when the current cycles have been rendered meaningless or management is no longer aligned with new priorities that are critical to the future success of the business.

4. **Incentive Caps/Negative Discretion**: This final lever would come into play if performance results produce a windfall payout, primarily due to exogenous factors. Caps can be set depending on the circumstances anywhere between target and 125 percent of target goals. This lever is best used in situations where business results created by one-time events generate results out of line either with executive performance or stakeholder expectations.

Summary

To be more proactive in managing executive pay, committees should consider using the following compensation tools:

- Planning tools: Putting together a strong committee calendar to manage the annual pay process.

- Long-term planning tools: Tally sheets, realizable pay and wealth accumulation are all tools that support longer term views on the success/alignment of pay programs that ensure your compensation strategy is working.
- Course-correct tools: Using discretion and shareholder feedback from the say-on-pay process to change programs to better realign with expectations.

CHAPTER 17

Disclosure of Executive Pay

By Bill Gerek and Kurt Groeninger

Executive pay disclosure goes hand in hand with other legislative and regulatory attempts to achieve accountability and transparency in all matters relating to corporate governance. The SEC's expanded disclosure rules adopted in 2006 and 2009 as well as the 2010 Dodd-Frank legislation (including SEC rules adopted thereunder) have considerably altered the disclosure landscape. Companies must now provide more detailed tabular information, additional narrative in the CD&A, information on the qualifications of directors and their fees, the degree of risk-taking inherent in pay programs, and the rationale behind the company's leadership structure.

The disclosure of so much information in numerous public documents, each with a distinct reporting schedule and format, makes the work of the compensation committee increasingly more difficult and time-consuming. This is especially true when it comes to disclosing equity compensation, comprised as it often is of several different vehicles and overlapping grants over multi-year periods. The actual total value of equity pay granted and realized over time may be quite different from the snapshot that appears each year in the proxy.

In addition, the need to communicate with shareholders effectively regarding say on pay, coupled with expanded SEC and stock exchange disclosure requirements, has undoubtedly resulted in longer proxy statements. This trend will likely continue, as the remaining disclosure rules required by Dodd-Frank ultimately are implemented (as of this printing). Consequently, compensation committees need to collect and analyze data in a way that allows for a more complete understanding and communication of reported values.

This chapter:

- Reviews the purpose of the CD&A, its connection with the new compensation committee report, and issues and actions to make the CD&A a more meaningful document.
- Discusses the key issues of the SEC's 2009 final rules expanding proxy disclosure in public companies, including the requirement to discuss the extent that pay programs might encourage harmful risk-taking, equity awards to directors, and the company's leadership structure.
- Provides a three-part mechanism for measuring executive pay to better understand how pay programs interact over time and facilitate the communication of executive pay programs to shareholders.
- Reviews say on pay, say on parachutes, clawback policies and other provisions of Dodd-Frank related to executive compensation and corporate governance.

Challenges of the Compensation Discussion and Analysis

In 2006, the SEC adopted executive compensation disclosure rules that were described as a wake-up call by the director of the SEC's Division of Corporation Finance. Of particular importance is the CD&A section that was added as a required component of annual proxy statements. Companies have been forced to focus not just on the "what" but also the "why" in executive pay disclosure.

Objectives of the CD&A

In its commentary on the CD&A, the SEC envisioned the section as an "overview providing narrative disclosure that puts into context the compensation disclosure provided elsewhere" for a company's NEOs. The expressed objective was to explain material elements of these executives' compensation. Critical to this process are seven questions that should be addressed:

- What are the objectives of the company's compensation programs?
- What is the compensation program designed to reward?
- What is each element of compensation?
- Why does the company choose to pay each element?
- How does the company determine the amount (and, where applicable, the formula) for each element?
- How does each element and the company's decisions regarding that element fit into the company's overall compensation objectives and affect decisions regarding other elements?
- Did the company consider the results of the most recent shareholder advisory vote on executive compensation (say on pay) in determining compensation policies and decisions? If so, how?

At the time of the 2006 rulemaking, executive pay disclosure at many companies had become standardized — even largely boilerplate — and often furnished little meaningful guidance on how executive pay actually is determined. In requiring a CD&A, key SEC goals were to encourage much more thoughtful analysis by compensation committees in determining executive pay and to have these pay considerations thoroughly disclosed. Many statements in the CD& A require significant elaboration; it is not sufficient to state that "pay is based on performance" or that "compensation is targeted at the median of comparable (or peer) organizations." Rather, how these standards are applied needs to be described, along with relevant policies, factors and regulatory impact.

In addition, the latest trends in shareholder engagement call for companies to begin preparing for the proxy season sooner and with greater deliberation regarding their compensation plans and programs. The proxy should tell a company's compensation story, but the decisions behind the story need to balance any shareholder concerns about its compensation programs with how these arrangements support the company's business strategy and objectives. We believe that the best way to demonstrate this balance is to show due consideration of shareholder issues coupled with effective shareholder engagement; the CD&A section of the proxy should clearly explain the compensation committee's final decisions and why they were made.

Relation of CD&A to the Compensation Committee Report

Although the CD&A discusses compensation policies and decisions, it does not address the compensation committee's deliberations because it is not a report of the compensation committee; rather the CD&A is the company's responsibility. However, the 2006 SEC rules also mandated a new form of compensation committee report that requires the committee to state whether:

- It has reviewed and discussed the CD&A with management, and
- The committee recommended to the board of directors that the CD&A be included in the company's annual report and proxy (based on the aforementioned review and discussions).

Potential Liability Under the CD&A

While the compensation committee report is considered "furnished" to the SEC, the CD&A is a filed document. This technical distinction means that the CD&A is considered to be part of the proxy statement and the disclosures are covered by the Sarbanes-Oxley Act of 2002 certifications required of principal executive officers and principal financial officers. The potential liability was designed to increase attention to the statements made.

Issues to Address in the CD&A

The CD&A is principles based (rather than rules based), and the SEC intends that it furnish perspective on the numbers and other executive pay information contained in required tables and elsewhere. A significant challenge presented by the CD&A has been articulating the rationale underlying the components of the executive compensation package for each NEO. The SEC's rulemaking provided nonexclusive examples of potentially appropriate issues that might reasonably be addressed in the CD&A; each should be considered in light of the organization's particular facts and circumstances. The CD&A must be comprehensive in scope; a company should describe any compensation policies it applies, even if not covered in the SEC's examples. The discussion also should address post-employment arrangements relating to compensation.

Besides the breadth of its requirements, the CD&A calls for greater depth than had been customary in compensation committee reports. While a CD&A generally should avoid repetition of the exhaustive information presented in tables and other portions of the proxy, it should identify material differences in compensation policies and decisions applicable to individual NEOs. Considerable thought and effort can be required to determine what should be discussed and then to prepare the appropriate explanation—which is supposed to be written in plain English (a standard not often met).

Areas That May Require Particular Attention

The examples provided by the SEC include some items that previously received scant attention in most proxy statements. In expanding the scope of executive pay disclosure, the SEC implicitly furnished its views on items that should be considered in executive compensation design.

- The SEC identified the familiar concept of benchmarking as a particular subject for disclosure. Information is needed on the benchmark for any material element of an executive's compensation, including the component companies (peer group) used for the benchmark. This requirement has increased the focus on having an appropriate peer group and choosing reasonable benchmarks. In comment letters from the SEC during the first few years of proxy filings under these rules, benchmarking was one of the main sources of SEC inquiries.

- One example from the SEC suggested discussing how gains from prior option awards are considered in setting other elements of compensation. By identifying the topic, the SEC implied that compensation committees should look at this issue.

- The well-publicized concerns some years ago at dozens of companies regarding the timing (a concept broader than backdating) and pricing of stock options caused the SEC to specifically provide for extensive disclosure regarding the timing and pricing of option grants. Various elements and questions were identified by the

SEC for disclosure; these should be considered in determining the appropriate use and design of stock options in a company's executive pay program.

- Another example refers to a company's equity ownership guidelines and mentions any policies regarding hedging an executive's economic risk of such ownership. Many organizations have since developed hedging policies rather than state that they do not have any such policy. As mentioned later in this chapter, hedging policies were addressed in Dodd-Frank and extended to all employees and directors.

- Because the impact of the accounting and tax treatment of a particular form of compensation is one issue that the SEC views as potentially appropriate for discussion, an organization might consider the role played by various regulatory provisions. For example, companies routinely address the $1 million deduction cap for certain executives under IRC section 162(m).

Recommended Actions

The following actions should be useful for most companies:

- Start the process early each year. Based on anticipated changes, future proxy seasons likely will involve more input from a wider group of stakeholders than ever before (e.g., legal/corporate secretaries, HR/compensation professionals, communication, marketing, investor relations, shareholder advisory firms and board members). Every party with responsibility regarding a CD&A needs to appreciate the significant effort that can be required to satisfy the disclosure standards — a narrative approach that considers a lengthy list of issues. A critical factor in managing this compliance process involves having sufficient time to fully vet all compensation issues that might need to be discussed.

- Develop an overall understanding of the objectives and requirements for the CD&A, working with advisers as needed.

- Internal personnel and external advisers (ideally including attorneys, accountants and compensation consultants) should work together and undertake the preparation of a "mock" CD&A. Generally, it is helpful to take the company's most recent CD&A as a starting point, but then view everything with fresh eyes to assess its applicability for the relevant year. New information is added, irrelevant material is deleted, and the whole reconsidered in light of the particulars of the company and its industry as well as relevant legislation and rules, economic considerations and a host of other factors. A key focus is on clarity, organization and presentation. When the parties actually commence this process, they realize how much is involved in crafting a focused discussion of the appropriate issues for the CD&A.

- Many companies now dedicate a section of their annual proxy statements to addressing expressed and potential concerns of shareholders. This type of disclosure is typical when the company fared poorly on the previous year's say-on-pay vote. Consequently, some companies include discussions of how a compensation committee or board engaged with shareholders and made subsequent changes to the compensation program.

- Inevitable scrutiny follows certain policies (e.g., parachute tax gross-ups or special one-time awards to executives). A company needs to provide a strong rationale for any important programs or provisions that are likely to be controversial.

- The compensation committee should be involved. While a company has responsibility for the preparation and filing of a proxy statement and the CD&A, it is the handiwork of the compensation committee that is being explained in the CD& A. The SEC clearly expects that compensation committee decisions will be affected by the knowledge that they will be subject to disclosure.

- Once an organization understands the scope of the tasks involved in crafting the CD&A, it should identify any issues that need to be addressed and information to be included. As instructed by the SEC, each company needs to focus on its particular facts and circumstances. Minutes of compensation committee meetings, reports of internal staff and consultants, and various plan documents and summaries may be helpful to examine as part of this process.

- A draft CD&A should be circulated among the working group for comment. During an iterative review process, all parties should keep in mind the ultimate goals of a clear, yet comprehensive overview of the company's executive pay determinations.

Enhanced Disclosure of Executive Pay

The regulation of executive compensation accelerated in 2009 as Congress, the Obama Administration and various regulatory agencies all added their voices to the debate surrounding sound executive pay practices. Near the close of 2009, the SEC adopted final rules further expanding proxy disclosure of executive compensation for public companies. Following is an overview of these SEC rules and some of the key compliance issues.

Relationship of the Company's Compensation Policies and Practices to Risk

Under the 2009 rules, public companies must discuss compensation policies and practices for all employees — not just NEOs — to the extent that risks arising from them are "reasonably likely to have a material adverse effect" on the company. Companies need to identify and then review all compensation arrangements to determine whether there are potential risks that might trigger disclosure. Any problems discovered in the review process then can be fixed or appropriately mitigated.

The SEC furnished examples of situations that could potentially trigger discussion and analysis:

- A business unit of the company carries a significant portion of the company's risk profile.
- A business unit has a significantly different compensation structure than other units.
- A business unit is significantly more profitable than others within the company.
- Compensation expense at a business unit represents a significant percentage of the unit's revenues.

- Compensation policies and practices vary significantly from the overall risk and reward structure of the company.

In assessing the degree of risk, companies can consider any compensation policies and practices designed to alleviate risk or balance incentives (e.g., clawbacks and recoupment policies, bonus banking, stock ownership requirements). The type of disclosure is determined on a case-by-case basis, but may include:

- The general design philosophy of compensation policies for employees whose behavior would be most influenced by the incentive programs.
- The company's risk assessment or considerations in structuring its incentive compensation policies.
- The ways in which the company's compensation policies relate to the realization of risks resulting from the actions of employees (e.g., through the use of clawbacks, holding periods).
- The company's policies regarding adjustments to its compensation practices to address changes in its risk profile.
- Material adjustments the registrant has made to its compensation policies or practices as a result of changes in its risk profile.
- The extent to which the registrant monitors its compensation policies to determine whether risk management objectives are being met.

As a topic that relates to all employees and not just NEOs, risk-related disclosure should have its own section in the proxy statement and generally not be included in the CD&A. Importantly, the SEC does "not require a company to make an affirmative statement that it has determined that the risks arising from its compensation policies and practices are not likely to have a material adverse effect on the company." In view of this limitation on the disclosure that is required, companies have been split on whether they should take the next step to voluntarily make such an affirmative statement that they maintain no such unreasonably risky compensation programs.

Disclosure Regarding Fees Affecting Independence of Compensation Consultants

The disclosure rules require a company to disclose the fees paid to a compensation consultant if the consultant furnished consulting services related to executive or director compensation as well as other services to the company. However, fee disclosure is not required if the fees paid to the consultant for additional services did not exceed $120,000 during the company's fiscal year. When disclosure is required, it must include:

- Aggregate fees paid for executive and director compensation consulting services
- Aggregate fees paid for other services
- Whether the decision to engage the consultant for other services was made or recommended by management and whether the committee or board approved the other services, if the consultant was engaged by the compensation committee.

Disclosure on the Qualifications of Directors and Nominees

Under the disclosure requirements, a company must discuss the particular experience, qualifications, attributes or skills that qualify an individual to serve as a director for the company, based on the company's business and structure at the time the disclosure is being made. However, the rules do not require disclosure regarding the specifics that qualify the individual to serve as a committee member. Disclosure is required for all directors, even if they are not standing for re-election in the applicable year, and should include:

- Any business experience during the past five years, including the principal occupation and employment.
- Any directorships at public companies held by each director at any time during the past five years (instead of only disclosing currently held directorships).
- Certain legal proceedings involving any director or executive officer during the past 10 years (instead of five years).
- Whether and how diversity is considered when identifying director candidates.

The SEC has not defined diversity; rather, each company is allowed to define it as it determines to be appropriate for its particular circumstances (e.g., experience, skills, education, race, gender). If a policy on diversity exists, the company must disclose how the policy is implemented and how its effectiveness is assessed.

Discussion of Company Leadership Structure

A company is required to disclose whether and why it has chosen to combine or separate the CEO and board chair positions, along with the reasons why the company believes that this board leadership structure is the most appropriate for it at the time of the filing. If the same person serves as CEO and chair, the company needs to disclose whether and why the company has a lead independent director and the role of the lead independent director in the leadership of the board. As discussed later in this chapter, Dodd-Frank confirmed this requirement through a statutory mandate.

In addition, the rules require companies to describe the board's role in the oversight of risk (which may include credit risk, liquidity risk and operational risk). For example, a company may describe whether the entire board reviews risk or if there is a separate committee. Further, a company may find it helpful to discuss how risk information is communicated to the board or relevant committee members.

The Continuing Challenge of Appropriate Disclosure

The 2009 rules:

- Responded to some criticisms of the 2006 overhaul of the SEC disclosure rules relating to executive compensation;
- Addressed various executive compensation issues that became important after experience with companies' disclosures; and
- Generally expanded the scope of required disclosures.

Companies are faced with the challenge of accurately explaining their programs and policies in a way that is sufficiently detailed yet understandable and meaningful to investors and other interested parties.

Measuring Executive Pay: The Equity Compensation Challenge

The 2009 changes in proxy disclosure rules caused a shift in the method and outcome of future years' executive compensation reporting. The reported numbers that tend to be the focus of media, pay critics and analysts do not always capture the true story of executive pay.

Understanding Reported Values of Executive Pay

The complex structure of executive compensation, dominated by various forms of equity and cash-based LTIs, can lead to significantly different interpretations of pay. These differences result from the interaction of varying approaches to data collection, analysis and reporting. Ensuring that all relevant data are collected for incorporation in the analysis, applying meaningful analytical tools to construct pay models, and reporting the information in a way that recognizes the complexity of pay practices all are essential for board-level decision support. Increased disclosure requirements, governance pressures and continued media attention make it imperative that pay values are understood and clearly communicated — internally and externally.

Effect of Prior Year's Compensation Actions

Special circumstances underlying a previous year's equity awards can be misinterpreted the next year. As an illustration, in 2009 many companies acted to address the results of a depressed stock market, increased market volatility, poor business results and the effects of those conditions on executive pay. These special, often one-time actions held potential for misinterpretation — either because they might be deemed part of annual pay or, conversely, because they might be excluded from pay calculations altogether. Such decisions made during the data-collection process can lead to a flawed analysis as true pay levels resulting from these items are not represented properly. A particular executive's compensation often can only be interpreted properly by understanding pay actions on a before and after basis.

In the 2009 example, companies that implemented stock option exchange programs canceled many years of stock options and re-granted some or all of those at a more favorable price. Merely reporting the Black-Scholes value of the re-grant as an element of 2009 pay oversimplified the total compensation implications.

Some of those companies excluded officers from their programs yet took other action — such as skipping or deferring the normal annual grant — that also needed to be considered. A company whose compensation peer group consists of several companies that made these types of pay decisions may have raised its executives' pay levels without recognizing these dynamics.

These complexities highlight the need for heightened attention to a three-faceted approach to executive equity compensation interpretation — collection, analysis and reporting.

Data Collection

Discussions of executive compensation focus primarily on single-year values, forming the root of many misunderstandings. But executive equity awards often are developed as part of a multi-year plan. SEC proxy disclosure rules recognize this through the required three-year reporting format for the Summary Compensation Table and the multi-year aggregations in other tables. A common example is when an executive receives a large new-hire equity grant, often two to four times the size of a typical annual grant, and then receives no equity award the following year(s). The single-year approach often leads to the conclusion that there has been a pay cut or an elimination of LTI awards when pay in year two is compared to that of year one. Much of the important detail is contained in footnotes and narrative in the proxy statement, without which the tabular figures may be misinterpreted. In addition, many pay actions not captured in the tables are nevertheless disclosed in the CD&A section or appear in Form 8-K filings subsequent to the issuance of the proxy statement. Given the dated (look-back) nature of tabular information, these additional sources are critical to understanding the true current market for executive pay. The complexities of executive equity compensation have long required a multi-year, multi-source perspective and any economic turmoil can increase the importance of this approach.

Data Analysis

While the valuation of equity instruments receives much attention, the variations in fair value that may result from volatility or expected life assumptions are less significant than the effects on deemed value from a series of decisions that guide the equity compensation calculation. Such analysis often is bypassed and the fair value resulting from the reporting process — typically what appears in SEC filings — is accepted as the pay value without any further consideration. Compensation committees and executives need to understand these dynamics to ensure effective pay decisions.

Volatile equity markets can result in equity grants with an unprecedented variation of values relative to business fundamentals and significant intra-year variations in relative grant values. For example, looking back to 2009, assume two companies whose share prices directly track the NASDAQ index both granted stock options in 2009, the first in early March and the other in early September. The first company reported grant-date fair values approximately 50 percent lower than the second company, but by the end of 2009 provided intrinsic value that was 260 percent greater. Variations of this magnitude were unprecedented in the history of executive pay and teach important lessons. An unusually large number of companies awarded stock options in February through April 2009 near the market low, and in many cases those grants quickly accumulated value far greater than the artificially low Black-Scholes value that was reported in SEC filings. Ironically, many of those companies granted a larger number of shares to offset the lower fair value at the time, exacerbating this effect.

These dynamics require that companies understand not only what was granted (i.e., stock options, time-vested shares, performance-based shares, cash LTI) and how much was granted, but when it was granted. In addition to understanding award type and timing, performance features require attention to the effect of performance contingencies or accelerators, thresholds and targets, absolute versus relative performance measures, and the interaction of time-based and performance-based conditions. Also, as publicly traded companies now typically have stock ownership guidelines and share retention requirements, the risk-reward balance has changed. Thoughtful analysis is required to understand the real effect on executive pay value resulting from the interaction of these features.

Data Reporting

With proper data collection and analysis, pay can be reported in ways that provide a meaningful picture of executive pay practices over the past years. A single snapshot of pay is not adequate for telling the story in this complex environment. Merely viewing pay as a single number may lead a compensation committee to reach flawed conclusions about the company's competitive position in the market. Scenario-based pay projections — incorporated into tally sheet and wealth accumulation analyses — will provide the compensation committee and the executive team with a point of view consistent with other business decision processes.

Pay Granted, Earned and Realized

A greater scrutiny of pay values introduces a need for the multi-dimensional view of pay, with at least three possible pay views to be considered. This approach requires taking pay analysis beyond a grant-based focus to a dynamic view of the life cycle of executive pay — when granted, earned and realized.

Under current SEC rules, equity incentive figures in the Summary Compensation Table can be misleading or difficult to interpret. The fair value of all equity awards made during the reporting year are deemed to have been what was "paid" to the executive for that year rather than what was accrued for accounting purposes. There are lengthy and complex arguments around which of these two methods is preferable, and why, but sound pay analysis does not force an either/or decision. It is important to understand what was granted, the incremental amount earned, and — as media organizations often do — the pay realized over a period of time to obtain a true picture of executive pay. Thus, we have seen the development of supplemental disclosures to show "realized pay" or "realizable pay" (with still some notable variance among users in the meaning of these terms), depending on the organization and what it believes most helpful in understanding the compensation of its executives.

While no single analytical structure will make sense for all companies, compensation committees and executive teams should:

- Think through the three data processes (collection, analysis and reporting) in the context of three alternative views of pay (granted, earned and realized), and
- Ask a series of questions to ensure a comprehensive approach. Table 17-1 illustrates the types of questions that may help guide a year's analyses and decisions.

Various tools — tally sheets, wealth accumulation models, "walk away" value calculations and scenario-based analysis — address some of these issues. A methodical approach can help a company understand the tools being used and the rationale for using a tool to the exclusion of others. It can be helpful to view these alternatives in this three-by-three analytical framework to capture the issues surrounding the collection, analysis and reporting of equity compensation data and recognize alternative measurement points of grant, earning and realization to ensure a clear understanding of market pay levels and practices.

Additional Executive Pay Disclosure Under Dodd-Frank

While broadly targeting the financial services industry, including provisions that address consumer and investor protection, the Dodd-Frank legislation contains important executive compensation and corporate governance provisions that apply to most public companies regardless of industry. To a considerable extent, Dodd-Frank left the specifics of the new requirements to rule-making by the SEC and then inclusion in listing standards by the securities exchanges.

Most of the executive compensation provisions of the Dodd-Frank legislation added new disclosure requirements for public companies.

TABLE 17-1 **Data Processes of Collection, Analysis and Reporting**

	Granted	Earned	Realized
Collection	Did we capture all of the grants and actions taken last year? Have we properly categorized "annual" pay actions	Did many of our peers grant during the market lows? How is that affecting reported grant value and fair value?	Were there significant realization events that created compensation not captured in the typical proxy and survey formats? Have we compared vested but unexercised in-the-money option gains?
Analysis	Have we explored the stock price patterns of our peers and reviewed scenario-based pay values?	Have we analyzed competitors' changes in vesting schedules, acceleration provisions, and holding requirements to understand changes in earnings opportunities?	Have we conducted an historical analysis of realized pay to understand how this may be affecting current grant patterns?
Reporting	Have we accounted for new hires, promotions, terminations, founders and special qualifications of incumbents?	Are we considering risk-adjusted differences in pay values: options vs. time-vested full-value awards vs. thresholds and targets on performance awards?	Do our tally sheet and wealth accumulation tools capture realized value including post-vesting accumulation?

The effective dates of the various parts of the act varied; certain changes were effective on enactment (July 21, 2010), while other provisions only were designed to take effect either after a transition period or after the regulatory authorities promulgated rules fleshing out the statutory mandates. As of the writing of this book, some of the rules required by Dodd-Frank have yet to be finalized by the SEC. In any event, Dodd-Frank undoubtedly is having a substantial effect on executive pay processes at most public companies.

Understand Investor and Proxy Advisory Policies

Companies should understand the key policies of various parties that now weigh in on executive compensation, especially those that may affect the acceptance of their compensation programs. Accordingly, the regular review of the current policies and past recommendations of proxy advisory firms and major investors should identify programs that risk adverse reaction from these groups, allowing companies to reconsider their programs or explain their effectiveness from the company's viewpoint. Modification or engagement (or a combination of the two) may help avoid the negative consequences that could follow a violation of such policies.

Say on Pay

Resolving a long-running debate on whether and how to obtain the views of shareholders on executive pay, Dodd-Frank requires a public company to provide shareholders with a nonbinding vote to approve the compensation of its NEOs. A say-on-pay vote must be held at least once every three years, which started with the first annual shareholders' meeting occurring after Jan. 21, 2011 (six months after the date of enactment). As of the same effective date, and at least once every six years thereafter, shareholders must be afforded the right to vote on whether a say-on-pay vote occurs once every one, two or three years.

A company's say-on-pay vote covers the compensation shown in its CD&A and Compensation Tables (including narrative disclosures). Effective communications with shareholders are especially important in connection with a say-on-pay vote. Before a vote, a company should make an effort to address potential shareholder concerns with the goal of obtaining strong majority approval. After either a negative vote or one with a narrow approval margin, outreach to large shareholders to obtain their feedback can help the company understand shareholders' concerns so that they can be addressed.

Advisory or not, a failure to respond effectively to a high level of dissatisfaction may result in "withhold" or "against" votes regarding the re-election of compensation committee members.

Say on Golden Parachutes

Executive compensation payments and other benefits triggered by a change in control of the organization (golden parachutes) are common at U.S. companies. However, well-publicized examples of particularly large payments to executives sparked controversy over the authorization of what some perceived to be overly executive-friendly arrangements. The initiatives regarding say on pay ultimately led to the related requirement of disclosure and a nonbinding shareholder vote regarding executive compensation arrangements related to proposed change-in-control transactions — coined "say-on-parachute" votes. The disclosure for a say-on-parachute vote is required in any proxy for a shareholders meeting at which shareholders are asked to approve an acquisition, merger, consolidation or proposed sale of all (or substantially all) of the company's assets. A say-on-parachute vote is not required if the parachute arrangements already have been subject to such a vote, although the conditions imposed by the regulations regarding this provision limit its utility.

Compensation Committee Consultants and Other Advisers

Two critical and related issues involve the ability of a compensation committee to engage compensation consultants, legal counsel and other advisers, and the independence of any advisers so retained. Dodd-Frank contains separate provisions that authorize a compensation committee to retain a compensation consultant, independent legal counsel and other advisers, with the committee to "be directly responsible for the appointment, compensation and oversight." A company is required to provide appropriate funding, as determined by the compensation committee, for any advisers so retained. With respect to compensation consultants (but not the other advisers), proxy disclosure is required regarding whether the compensation committee has retained a compensation consultant, whether that consultant's work led to any conflict of interest, the nature of any conflicts and how those conflicts are being addressed.

With respect to independence, a compensation committee "may only select a compensation consultant, legal counsel or other adviser

... after taking account the factors identified by the [SEC]...." The SEC's rulemaking identified factors that may affect independence, and the securities exchanges subsequently adopted listing standards within the bounds of the SEC rules, including six general factors contained in the SEC's rules. After considering these factors and other considerations that it deems relevant, the compensation committee then is free to select a compensation adviser but must disclose how it has resolved any potential conflicts.

Pay-for-Performance Disclosure

Dodd-Frank mandated that the SEC craft rules requiring a public company to disclose in the proxy statement for its annual shareholder meeting a "clear description" that "shows the relationship between executive compensation actually paid and the financial performance" of the company, taking into account any changes in the value of the company's stock and any dividends and distributions. The disclosure may include a graphic representation of the required information. Although the SEC's rule is still not final (as of the time of the writing of this edition), most experts read the last portion of this statutory language as a requirement to discuss performance in terms of TSR.

While publicly traded companies will ultimately need to comply with this pay-versus-performance disclosure rule, some companies have developed their own analyses to enhance their proxy disclosures. Some companies may find it useful to present and explain performance using other metrics. These comparisons often involve trends in either reported or realized/realizable compensation versus company performance on an absolute basis (e.g., year-over-year growth) or relative (performance versus peers). In any case, since the relationship of executive pay and performance is of particular interest to investors, a company generally should address the issue in an executive summary of the CD&A.

CEO Pay Ratio Disclosure

In an effort to address the debate about internal pay equity, Dodd-Frank imposed an especially burdensome provision requiring the

SEC to mandate a new compensation ratio pay disclosure. The required disclosure in Item 402(u) of Regulation S-K (applicable for various SEC filings, not simply a company's annual proxy statement) consists of three items:

- The median "annual total compensation" of the company's employees except its CEO
- The CEO's annual total compensation
- The ratio of the two numbers.

Much of the SEC's rulemaking was devoted to how a company may determine the median employee and then that individual's compensation. Other than some limited exceptions, all employees (including non-U.S. and part-time employees) need to be considered in determining the median employee. In addition to the required disclosures, companies can include additional information that may provide context regarding the company's pay practices and the reported pay ratio.

Clawback Policy

Dodd-Frank requires public companies to develop, implement and disclose what is commonly called a "clawback policy" for the recovery (from current and former executive officers) of incentive compensation based on certain financial information where there has been a required accounting restatement due to material noncompliance with a financial reporting requirement. At a minimum, in the event of a restatement, a company needs to recoup any excess incentive-based payments made based on inaccurate information in the previous three years.

In general, the clawback under Dodd-Frank is considerably broader than the clawback provisions of Sarbanes-Oxley. For example, Dodd-Frank's clawback provisions apply to any executive officer (not just the CEO and CFO), do not require any misconduct (just simply the requisite restatement), and cover a three-year (rather than 12-month) period. Key features of a clawback policy under Dodd-Frank include who is subject to the policy, the triggers for a recovery, and what elements of compensation are subject to the policy. While clawback policies have become a widespread and best practice, every existing policy will need to be reviewed and updated once the SEC finalizes its rulemaking.

Consideration should be given not only to the Dodd-Frank requirements, but also to any additional features or processes that address the organization's particular circumstances or facilitate administration. A company complying with best practices might extend its clawback policy to recoup excess compensation paid as a result of (a) ethical misconduct, or (b) a restatement of financial statements unrelated to changes in accounting rules or interpretations.

Employee and Director Hedging

Under Item 407(i) of Regulation S-K, as required by Dodd-Frank, each public company is to disclose in its annual proxy statement any practices or policies that the company has adopted to hedge or offset any decrease in the market value of equity securities granted as compensation to an employee or director. Because equity hedging strategies can enable an employee or director to limit the effect of holding requirements commonly imposed on top executives and directors, the provision aims to shed light on any such actions and indirectly encourages companies to bar or limit such hedging. Even before Dodd-Frank, SEC rules already called for the disclosure of policies regarding hedging; one notable effect of the legislative provision is the extension of such disclosure to all employees as well as directors.

Investors increasingly expect companies to implement and enforce anti-hedging and anti-pledging policies. While prior transactions may be difficult to unwind, companies should adopt prospective policies against hedging and generally pledging. If no policy exists, companies should explain how they mitigate risk associated with these practices.

Disclosures Regarding Board Chair and CEO Structures

The SEC was directed by Dodd-Frank to issue rules requiring a public company to disclose in its annual proxy information about the board's leadership structure. Under Item 407(h), a company is to disclose the reasons why it has chosen either the same person to serve both as board chair and CEO or two different people to serve in those positions. If one person occupies both positions, the company is to also disclose whether it has a leader independent director and what specific role he or she plays in the leadership of the board. The SEC also seeks additional information as to why the company determined that its leadership structure is appropriate given its specific characteristic or circumstances. Finally, the company must also disclose the extent of the board's role in the risk oversight of the company, such as how the board administers its oversight function, and the effect that this has on the board's leadership structure.

Human Capital Disclosures

Disclosure requirements continue to evolve as investors and governance observers seek more and more information from companies. In 2020, the SEC finalized a new rule requiring disclosure of information related to human capital management. Previously, the rules in Item 101(c) of Regulation S-K required a company to disclose the number of persons employed. Under the revised rule, a company must also include "any human capital measures or objectives that the registrant focuses on in managing the business (such as, depending on the nature of the registrant's business and workforce, measures or objectives that address the development, attraction and retention of personnel)." The SEC's rule does not specifically address compensation. However, the language of the rule suggests that this topic is ripe for discussion in the human capital context.

The SEC adopted a principles-based approach for this rule. In turn, the Commission allows for a great deal of flexibility in the disclosure. For example, the SEC did not adopt a definition for "human capital." Rather, the SEC's view is that there may be many definitions of human capital and the concept is often tailored to the circumstances and objectives of individual companies.

A Final Consideration for Disclosures

In drafting proxy and governance disclosures, companies should be careful to avoid embellishments that can prompt litigation. Disclose what is material, address what may be unfavorable, and explain why a program, award or provision works for your company, but be careful of "overselling." Tell your story the right way and do not forget to engage shareholders.

CHAPTER 18

Risk in Executive Compensation

By Dana Martin and Tania Mendez

R isk management in public companies continues to evolve. Ongoing public focus on executive compensation and environmental, social and corporate governance pressures are increasing emphasis on risk management within executive compensation programs. After the financial crisis of 2008, the SEC took steps to inhibit executives from profiting through excessive risk-taking by requiring public companies to consider whether any of their compensation plans and practices create risk-taking incentives. If they do, there is a requirement to disclose in their annual proxy whether a materially adverse effect on the company is reasonably likely. This requirement, as well as mounting pressure from stakeholders (e.g., shareholders, activists), has emphasized the need for proper governance practices, plan design criteria and measures to mitigate such risk. Risk management, not traditionally within the purview of the compensation committee, is now an important item on the committee's agenda.

Incentive plans traditionally encourage executives to aim for the maximum rewards permitted under the plan. While these plans seldom resemble the bonus arrangements that figured so prominently in the financial crisis, risk is, nonetheless, a necessary element in executive pay. How should companies and their compensation committees go about taking on the burden of risk-reward analysis and ongoing monitoring? What are the red flags that alert boards to a high-risk situation?

The best way to do this is through a balanced, fact-based approach that allows for prudent exposure to risk without compromising company objectives such as sustainable long-term growth. The results, however, should not be so balanced that innovation and creative spirit is curbed. In addition, companies will not benefit from a watered-down incentive program, or one in which the business needs and priorities unique to the company are not underlying factors. Risk-adapted incentive plans require a thorough and complex decision-making process. Furthermore, boards and management also gain from internal effectiveness and enhanced external defensibility.

This chapter:

- Introduces the role compensation played in the financial industry downturn of 2008 and continues to play through corporate scandals and negative press. It provides a checklist for risk assessment as it continues to remain top-of-mind across industries, regulators and the community. In addition, we address the key questions compensation committees need to ask in determining if pay programs potentially pose a business risk.
- Considers how a balanced approach to risk is needed in determining pay elements and mix, performance measures, goal setting and payout structures, including the importance of appropriately using discretion.
- Examines how the prevalence of performance awards in LTI plans may encourage (inappropriate) risk taking by executives.
- Offers an approach to benchmarking executive pay that supplements the usual two-dimensional "snapshot," with a third dimension that provides an in-depth analysis of executive pay under various scenarios "over time."

Background to Risk in Executive Compensation

According to a common definition, "risk" involves the possibility of suffering harm or loss in the pursuit of an objective. The issue of risk in compensation programs typically centered on the downside of the equation — the probability and consequences of failure. However, historically, executive compensation programs focused on the positive "upside," with little regard for the potential negative outcomes. Business decisions should be made to create an appropriate balance between risk and return, not to maximize both. During difficult times, shareholders look to the board of directors for guidance on these difficult issues.

Following the debacles at Enron and WorldCom at the start of this century, there were concerns that the boards of these companies (and no doubt at many others) did not fully understand the complexity of the company's financial structure. As a result, Sarbanes-Oxley was enacted to force corporate boards to address weaknesses in financial controls. In fact, one of the most significant effects of the statute was to require that a qualified financial expert be included as head of the audit committee at a public company. This, in turn, drove significant changes in board composition, qualifications and compensation.

Financial difficulties later in that decade directed blame in a different direction — failed risk oversight by the board. Risk management failures, and unilateral focus on the upside of pay, have been viewed as a leading cause of economic problems. A consensus developed that one of the drivers of overly risky business decisions was the highly leveraged design of pay programs in the banking and financial services sector.

In the past, the management of risk generally sat with the audit committee or full board. However, because of the focus on the effect of incentives on behavior, compensation committees have had to evaluate executive pay in a new light and address the age-old link between risk and reward.

Today, public and regulatory attention remains on the design of executive pay; the concern is that the structuring of incentives may promote overly risky behavior in attempts to earn especially large payouts. As a result, risk assessment and management in executive compensation has been the subject of various legislative, regulatory and corporate governance initiatives intended to limit excessive risk. In designing and evaluating pay programs, risk is a critical factor.

Going Forward

The issue of determining performance risk and factoring in time horizons adds complexity to the design of executive compensation programs. Some suggest the use of long holding periods for equity awards to focus on the creation of long-term value. Others suggest fail-safes such as bonus banks or clawbacks as effective ways in which organizations can partially recoup incentive pay disbursed if a longer time horizon shows performance results were actually poor or need to be restated, or as a result of executive misconduct.

In ensuring incentives are designed with prudent risk management considerations in mind, compensation committees need to monitor pay programs and the potential link to risky behavior. To properly manage risk, companies also must provide greater authority to risk managers, and have a better understanding of the potential consequences of executive behavior in achieving short-term goals.

Programs that have features similar to the following can be considered high-risk and suspect in the current compensation environment:

- Low salary (or fixed pay) relative to incentive (or variable pay). For example, 10 percent salary/90 percent incentive mix
- Use of a single compensation element driving a specific outcome at the expense of other important outcomes
- Focus on short-term, annual performance rather than long-term sustained results ("swing for the fences" behavior)
- Uncapped upside
- Excessive use of a single equity vehicle such as stock options that focus the executive on stock price appreciation
- Use of (multi-year) recruiting guarantees
- Purely formulaic payouts without room for discretion
- Lack of modelling to understand the probability of achievement of outcomes and the associated plan payouts

Other than the SEC, a number of quasi-regulatory bodies have also become involved. As part of its evaluation of business strength and financial condition, Standard & Poor's added an enterprise risk management assessment. This highlights the need to be more aware of the potential business risks in designing compensation programs. Compensation committees should undertake a formal evaluation of compensation policies and practices to determine their potential effect on enterprise risk.

While few compensation plans promote the level of risk that was historically built into Wall Street's incentive structure, there are other elements of risk that can harm the company short of bankruptcy, a forced sale or a total collapse. To name a few:

- Difficulty with proxy voting on proposals regarding executive compensation and/or share availability.
- Board embarrassment, particularly regarding change in control and severance arrangements.
- Having to make payments disproportionate to the value created or for chance occurrences (e.g., windfall gains).

Identifying Potentials Risks

A comprehensive evaluation of risk must include a company's compensation philosophy, governance and design of incentive programs. To begin its review, compensation committees should ask several key questions.

Do Plans Reflect Strategy?

Do metrics promote a balance between short- and long-term objectives? Historically, many banking practices were primarily focused on short-term results, creating an increase in short-term risky behaviors. Generally, this is viewed as inappropriate and has promoted an increased focus on sustained results over time.

Does the Compensation Committee Understand All Potential Scenarios and Outcomes?

The committee must ensure conscious and detailed analysis of all executive compensation plans (severance and CIC payments as well as incentives) to understand the complexities and potential consequences of certain events and decisions. The use of tally sheets enables compensation committees to approach executive compensation decisions by evaluating the overall combined exposure to the company from all sources.

Further, a careful look at the possible behaviors and business decisions that would trigger large payouts need to be considered. For example, plans that could encourage executives to look for risky acquisitions to promote top-line growth at the expense of returns should be flagged. Similarly, CIC payments may be so rich as to drive strategy, regardless of whether they are in the best interests of the shareholders. Or, as highlighted above, there may be windfall gains based on extraordinary events that need to be considered in determining the appropriate level of payout.

Is There Too Much Weight on One Metric or Are Plans Diluted with Too Many?

Good plan design suggests that there be balance in the metrics selected (e.g., a combination of growth, profitability and sustainable returns). The risk here is that too much emphasis on one can significantly detract from, or even impede, progress on other important performance metrics that ensure long-term sustainability of returns. That said, there is a risk that too many metrics will dilute focus and fail to provide direction and line of sight to strategic objectives.

Is the Leverage in Executive Compensation Reasonable?

Historically, within the financial services sector, the traditional view of executive compensation was that of "high risk, high reward." Plans in many cases were designed with significantly escalating rewards for performance. While there may be sound reasons for high levels of award opportunity in some cases, events have demonstrated the need for compensation committees to evaluate the risk of promoting excessive and risky business activities in search of the "big score." Beyond traditional corporate executive incentives, reviewing sales incentives may also be needed, particularly where the overall cost of payouts and impact on the organization may be significant for more senior participants (e.g., commission plans that are tightly linked to individual sales and do not use other secondary measures can distort the relationship between pay and performance).

Are Controls in Place to Mitigate Risk in Executive Compensation?

Checks and balances, or guardrails, to consider include:

- Clawbacks for payment in prior years that ultimately were shown to have been unearned or based on financials that had to be restated (perhaps including events that extend beyond the parameters set in Dodd-Frank), including restatements as a result of unethical executive behaviors.
- Consideration of "bonus banks" to smooth out the variability in annual payouts and provide the company with a vehicle for reversing previously "earned" bonuses.
- Multi-year performance periods (three years or more) rather than excessive focus on short-term gains.
- Holding requirements and meaningful ownership guidelines (even up to and after retirement) to align executives' interests with those of shareholders. Institutional Shareholder Services (ISS) has a strong perspective that not only does a significant portion of executive pay need to be in long-term vehicles, but that "robust" ownership guidelines are preferred (i.e., 6x salary for CEOs and lower multiples for other NEOs).
- Caps on plan upside to limit the potential for unexpected or windfall payouts.
- Analysis of probability that links differing levels of achievement to payout. Specifically, as a company introduces incentive plan thresholds, targets and maximums, it is important to ensure reasonableness in payout and achievement at each level. As Table 18-1 below demonstrates, "Target" performance should see about a 50 to 60 percent chance of attainment while 'Maximum' should not be more than 20 percent, and conversely, minimum or 'Threshold' should be achievable about 80 percent of the time.
- Clear governance and documentation around process and measurement, including annual plan documentation and disclosures. In

TABLE 18-1 Attainment of Performance Levels

Performance Level	Odds of Attainment
Threshold	8 out of 10
Target	5-6 out of 10
Maximum (Stretch)	2 out of 10

2018, the SEC enacted final rules that require public companies to disclose in proxy statements their policies on hedging employer securities. While many organizations may have anti-hedging and anti-pledging practices, it is important that these are clearly disclosed and documented.

- Use and timing of discretion is agreed upon by the committee before unforeseen extraordinary events — both to prevent windfall gains as well as address significant losses.
- A means to review risk in a systematic way. This may include members of management, human resources, and others involved in enterprise risk management. Once a thorough assessment is completed, the compensation committee can evaluate the effect of plan features relative to the risk factors involved, whether they are financial, reputational, operational or legal.

In speaking about risk in October 2008, John White, at that time the head of the SEC Corporation Finance Division (but expressing his own views), phrased the risk disclosure issue in words that still ring true: "Ask yourself this question: Would it be prudent for compensation committees, when establishing targets and creating incentives, not only to discuss how hard or how easy it is to meet the incentives, but also to consider the particular risks an executive might be incentivized to take to meet the target — with risk, in this case, being viewed in the context of the enterprise as a whole?"

The Evolution of Plan Design

While most executive compensation plans are not a direct threat to the business, changes in the overall best practices in executive pay design continue. The following program changes may help insulate compensation programs from design risks.

- Reducing the impact of single metrics. While not uncommon to find similar measures used in both short- and long-term incentives, the double usage may concentrate risk and create problems. This practice may inadvertently put too much focus on singular achievement and "double paying or penalizing" for results.
- Greater consideration of both absolute and relative performance measures. Over-reliance on one or the other can result in unintended payout results. If only relative measures are considered, significant payouts may be made in situations where a firm is at the top of its industry peers while also suffering from financial losses. Adding an "absolute governor" (e.g., capping payouts at target if revenues or other financials are negative) is not uncommon and can serve as a safeguard.
- Increased analytics and modelling so compensation committees can better understand the potential effects and outcomes of compensation decisions.
- Greater attention to plan caps and more modest leverage in plan design. Incentive plans should encourage executives to exceed performance expectations, but not at the risk of harming the enterprise. As such, the potential payouts should reflect reasonably achievable performance thresholds, targets, and maximums.
- A continuing re-evaluation regarding the use of stock options. Stock options are a form of compensation with high potential returns, but with no real downside prior to exercise. During the COVID-19 pandemic, there was a significant increase in underwater stock options, forcing committees that only use these options to consider alternative equity vehicles. A portfolio approach to grant making may avoid complete loss to award value.
- More consideration of compensation risk as part of the overall board risk-assessment process. This acknowledges that compensation is a critical enterprise risk and should be evaluated as such.

A concern with the current focus on risk is that it may have a negative effect (hopefully temporary) on the creativity and entrepreneurial spirit that has propelled U.S. business success. There needs to be a continued emphasis on taking reasonable risks and aligning the rewards with the gains produced. This can be done via mitigating factors discussed in this chapter.

Risk Assessment: Initial Process and Checklist

Compensation committees have continuously tried to balance risk and reward — risk (in the form of stretch goals) and reward (enough to make the risk worthwhile). But how much is too much?

The SEC requires all public companies to evaluate their risks arising from compensation arrangements. The rules require that every publicly held company discuss in its annual proxy statement whether any of its compensation plans or practices (for executives and nonexecutives) create risk-taking incentives that are reasonably likely to have a material adverse effect on the organization. From a practical viewpoint, the result is that every public company needs to examine each of its compensation programs to:

1. Be assured that no such potential risks exist; and
2. Fix or otherwise mitigate any potential excessive risks that may be uncovered.

Organizations and compensation committees must develop a process to assess and then manage the possible risks posed by the compensation programs they maintain or oversee. The initial process for assessing risk involves:

- **Creating a project team:** This may include a senior risk officer, inside/outside legal counsel, a senior HR or compensation officer, and a compensation consultant. The team is tasked with assessing the level of risk for each distinct compensation program against a key set of criteria.
- **Collecting/reviewing documentation, practices and policies:** Existing written and unwritten pay policies, practices and plan

documents, as well relevant documents related to the firm's enterprise risk management are collected and reviewed.

- **Conducting the compensation risk assessment:** Risks that the organization faces and could threaten its value or have a material financial, legal, operational or reputation effect on the company are identified for the committee. In addition, the organization's compensation policies, practices and supporting management processes that could induce executives and employees to take those risks are also highlighted.

- **Analyzing risk assessment results:** Conducting the review and discussing how to mitigate and manage any such excessive risks, and/or establishing a process and timetable for revising those programs that contain excessive risks.

Checklist for Risk Assessment

It is useful to develop a checklist to guide a risk analysis. However, any process and checklist needs to be tailored to a company's specific circumstances (e.g., industry, roles to which the plan(s) apply) — real thought and analysis are needed, not simply a "check-the-box" compliance mentality. Table 18-2 contains a sample checklist of generally relevant criteria and questions for use in assessing the risk profile of compensation programs. To determine the risk exposure of each program, consider determining the potential probability and cost of a worst-case scenario. It is helpful to characterize (or rank) potential cost and risk on a grid as high, moderate and low (or using a red, yellow and green "stoplight gap analysis" as a visual means) for characterizing and addressing levels of risk.

Review

The financial industry crisis spawned an increased focus on potential risk in compensation programs. In addition, overall pressure from shareholders and the community has put increased reputational and ESG pressure on all organizations.

Companies, regulators and advisers all attempt to address the various factors that contribute to risk in compensation programs, but

TABLE 18-2 Risk Assessment Checklist

	Risk managed effectively	Caution	Risk not managed effectively
		(Check one)	
Alignment and balance in performance metrics			
Is there risk in division or subsidiary reward performance metrics not aligning with corporate reward metrics?			
Is there a risk in one financial measure dominating employee focus at the expense of other key performance measures?			
Is there a risk in short-term measures dominating employee focus at the expense of long-term performance measures?			
Overall:			
Corporate financial protection and use of hurdles			
What is the degree of risk in team and individual goals requiring incentive payouts in a year when the corporate entity did not meet baseline financial or profit-ability goals?			
Are hurdles appropriately set that balance corporate protection and reasonable prob-ability of an incentive payout?			
Overall:			
Alignment of pay with market competitiveness			
What is the degree of risk in organization pay levels and target earning opportunities not aligning with marketplace practices?			
Is there risk in eligibility criteria not being consistent internally?			
Overall:			
Impact on motivation and engagement			
What is the degree of risk in current incen-tive plans not providing optimal motivation and results?			
Are employees aware of and committed to the principles behind the intent of the incentive plan?			
Overall:			

	Risk managed effectively	Caution	Risk not managed effectively
		(Check one)	
Appropriate use of management discretion			
What is the degree of risk in the usage of management discretion in incentive plan payouts where the criteria may or may not directly align with corporate performance?			
Are the principles and rules of discretion consistently known and applied?			
Overall:			
Plan effectiveness			
What is the degree of risk in incentive plans not being perceived as effective and motivational by managers and employees?			
Overall:			

many important issues still remain. For instance (and most basically), there is no universal definition of what is meant by "risk." While the SEC has eased the reporting burden for public companies by limiting required disclosure to risks that are "reasonably likely to have a material adverse effect on the company," the core issue remains.

Upon review of a company's proxy statement by the SEC, a failure to show the company conducted a risk assessment in compliance with these rules could prompt queries on specific programs and raise concerns from proxy voting advisors. Aside from any input or feedback from the SEC, ideas are exchanged among companies and their advisers. Reasonable approaches also are developed after considering information disclosed in filings during the most recent proxy season. In any case, the initial process and checklist provide a solid starting framework for a company's compensation plan risk assessment.

Executive Pay for Sustainable Performance: Restoring Investor Trust

Despite unprecedented fiscal and monetary interventions by governments and central banks, the global economy remains highly volatile. We have seen this through several downturns due to the financial crises, natural disasters and the global COVID-19 pandemic of 2020. Uncertainty in markets persists and investors are now demanding from management greater transparency, accountability and long-term performance sustainability than ever before — all while expecting more than just financial outcomes. Companies need to demonstrate responsible considerations to socio-economic trends and topics such as the environment, diversity, community, etc.

Keeping Rewards in Context

Reward systems have certainly contributed to risky executive behaviors and decisions. However, the external environment often poses greater threats to an enterprise. Reward systems should contemplate these economic crises as well.

Crises are infrequent, so they only affect the executives in place at the time; they are also generally not anticipated, so the possibility of a collapse tends not to affect executive behavior. Therefore, boards should consider the following actions:

- Continue to improve focus on risk assessment and ensure that incentive programs are not betting the company on a single investment or investments that are likely to be correlated in an economic or financial crisis. Given the long timescales, this must be a governance responsibility.
- Build up reserves against the inevitable losses from time to time, as insurance companies do. Arguably the excess of the risk-adjusted required return over the risk-free rate is an "insurance premium" that should be reserved against future losses, not paid out in bonuses (or dividends).

Achieving Risk-Adjusted Rewards

Executive rewards must be based on measures of corporate performance that account for risk to shareholders' capital inherent in the business strategy. Notwithstanding complexity, investors will no longer be satisfied with the "too complicated" excuse on risk-adjusted performance management.

Corporate performance must be assessed based on a broad framework of interrelated metrics that influence current expectations. To succeed, the framework must be:

- Economically sound. The "performance mathematics" must ensure that as levers are pressed, expected values are achieved and perceptions influenced accordingly.
- Comprehensive and balanced. As Peter Drucker reminded us, "we manage what we measure." History is replete with pay-for-performance issues stemming from improvement in "measured" revenue growth offset by "non-measured" expansion in assets or risk. And finally, it must be easy to implement. If it cannot be readily understood and tracked by all stakeholders, it will not work.

Two measures that account for the risk to capital are total shareholder return (TSR) and economic value added (EVA). TSR is a strong de facto measure of long-term corporate performance, despite the difficulties of defining a peer group to measure relative performance and the potential effect of short-term price fluctuations. EVA fundamentally is the return on capital deployed net of its risk-adjusted cost. It is an essential measure because it ensures that return is calculated in the context of both the scale of capital deployed and its inherent riskiness (or "opportunity cost"). While this is a more complicated calculation for some industries, such as financial services, EVA can be superior to other metrics like earnings per share and EBITDA because these do not consider risk and capital deployed.

However, TSR and EVA must be managed through a performance framework. Figure 18-3 is an example of a performance management framework that connects TSR and EVA with actionable enterprise operating metrics. From a board and investor point of view, the

FIGURE 18-3 Performance Management Framework

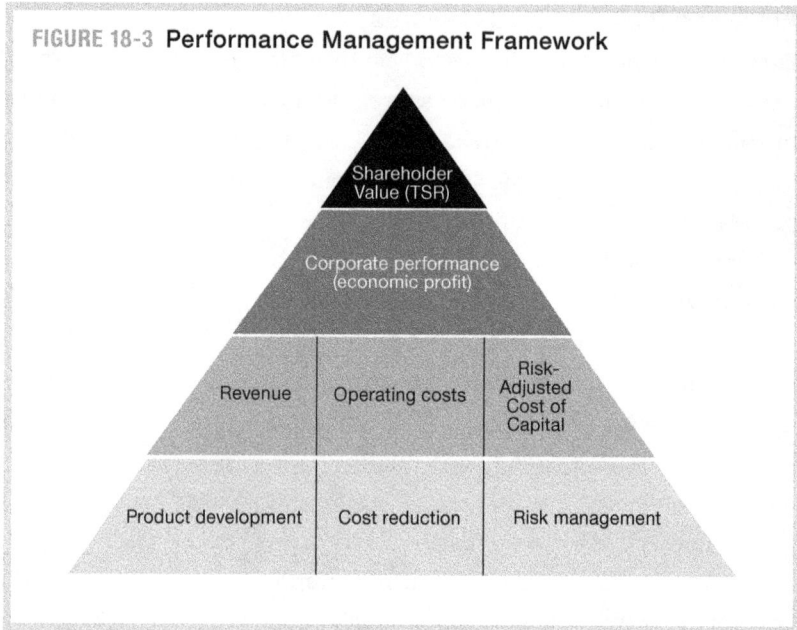

Shareholder Value (TSR)

Corporate performance (economic profit)

Revenue	Operating costs	Risk-Adjusted Cost of Capital
Product development	Cost reduction	Risk management

framework provides a holistic approach that enables effective assessment of performance in the context of executive pay.

While this approach is not immune from the aforementioned issues of comparability and complexity, it is a useful paradigm for establishing a standardized approach to performance management. Investors have made clear that a failure to tackle the problem will no longer be tolerated. The restoration of trust begins with executive pay for sustainable risk-adjusted performance.

Designing Incentive Plans in Today's Risk Environment

Incentive plans continue to receive increased scrutiny, sometimes even cast as the villain in organizations' rewards programs. They have been cited as a cause of excessive risk-taking for short-term gains at the expense of long-term sustainable performance, which can ultimately contribute to business failures. However, incentive plans are essential for linking pay with performance, placing needed emphasis on critical near- and long-term business priorities and motivating employees to achieve challenging goals. Balance seems to be key to designing incentive plans that accomplish these objectives, but also mitigate unhealthy risk.

The primary objective of a balanced program is to ensure that no single compensation element is driving a specific outcome at the expense of other key outcomes. Where do we look for balance? Some answers can include:

- Pay elements and mix
- LTI vehicles
- Performance measures
- Goal setting and achievement probability
- Incentive payout design
- Use of discretion.

Pay Elements and Mix

We begin by looking for balance in the overall mix of compensation elements. Not only do we assess the competitiveness of each element of pay, but attention also is focused on the mix of pay.

- How much is being delivered in fixed versus variable pay?
- What is the frequency of payout of incentives (e.g., monthly, quarterly, annual)
- What is the ratio of short-term versus long-term compensation?
- How much is delivered in cash versus equity?
- Are short-term incentives partially deferred where appropriate?

Many of the answers depend on an employee's specific role within the organization. For executives, a large percentage of the total pay mix is typically delivered in long-term variable pay. Because many positions below the executive level do not have the same line of sight to long-term results, fixed base pay typically becomes a larger portion of the mix deeper into the organization. Similarly, the focus generally is more on variable annual incentives rather than on long-term programs below the senior-executive level.

A growing number of companies are delivering a portion of annual incentive earnings in the form of deferred stock or "banking" the bonuses for payout at some point in the future based on future performance. These features further reduce the incentive for risky behavior to achieve unsustainable short-term gains and serve as an additional retention tool. They also promote an "ownership" culture across the organization.

LTI Vehicles

There are several vehicle choices for LTIs, each serving a unique purpose with its own set of advantages and disadvantages. Stock options and stock appreciation rights link directly to shareholder interests and are of value only when the share price increases; however, these can be a temptation for inappropriate risk-taking to achieve the increases. Time-based restricted stock provides opportunities for ownership and serves as a retention device, but it can be viewed as a giveaway. Performance-based share and cash plans align with critical strategic performance, but it can be difficult to set challenging yet realistic long-term goals in light of market uncertainties.

When it comes to managing risk, once again balance generally is the best approach. Research demonstrates that most large public companies are taking a portfolio approach to LTIs, making grants in two or even three vehicles.

Performance Measures

Performance measures are arguably one of the most difficult aspects of incentive plan design. Choosing the right metrics in the right combination can stymie even the best of experts. There are some general rules, however, when it comes to managing for risk and, not surprisingly, a critical one is "balance."

Incentive plans, whether short or long term, that use multiple metrics (particularly more than one financial/operating metric) reduce the risk of driving performance in one area of the business to the detriment of others that are important to long-term success. Metrics that present a balanced view of how the organization is performing are favored, particularly combinations of profitability, growth and sustained return measures, with reduced reliance on top-line growth measures. Additionally, it is important to consider qualitative/non-financial measures that emphasize strategic priorities — including ESG, diversity and inclusion, safety — and balance "absolute" and "relative" measures. That said, too many measures can dilute the effect of any one measure, limiting the desired effect and countering the effectiveness of the plan, or limiting the potential downside of performance in any one metric.

Goal Setting

Another challenge in incentive program design is setting goals at the right level and being able to forecast company performance (especially for periods beyond a year). If performance goals are not set appropriately, there can be negative consequences.

Generally, goals should be challenging, but attainable. If goals are set too high, we see two alternative unsatisfactory outcomes:

- Executives may not be motivated if they perceive there is little likelihood of achieving the targets.
- Executives may take excessive risks to try to reach very difficult goals.

Conversely, if goals are set too low and the incentive plan is paying out more frequently and at higher levels than is intended, the company is at risk of paying incentives for mediocre (or even poor) performance and not achieving an appropriate return on its investment.

Incentive Payout Design

In designing incentive arrangements, one critical item is the relationship between performance and payouts. Typically, this is a range, from threshold to maximum, with incremental pay for incremental performance. To mitigate risk, the program should have upside and downside potential. All-or-nothing plans, whereby a participant receives a fixed award for achieving a target level of performance, but nothing for just missing the target, are viewed as contributing to potentially risky behavior. Additionally, the slope of the line (i.e., the relationship between performance levels and the associated payouts) can vary. Flatter slopes that require greater performance for incremental payouts are generally more appropriate in today's risk environment but must be balanced so that stretches in performance are not unrealistic.

One of the most important features in the payout design, when it comes to mitigating potentially risky scenarios, is limiting the upside potential with a predetermined maximum level of performance and payout (capping the plan). Caps prevent windfall earnings that may not represent achievements attributable to management or may be from unsustainable levels of performance. Another important feature that mitigates the risk of a company making payouts when it cannot afford to do so is a "financial trigger." The trigger typically is established as a minimum level of corporate-wide profitability (or similar measure) that must be achieved before any incentive payouts can be made. The cap and trigger can work in tandem to provide balance in the overall payout structure.

Use of Discretion

Plans that allow management and the compensation committee to use discretion in determining achievement of results, and ultimately the corresponding payouts, further mitigate risk. Plans that are entirely formulaic, without any room for board discretion, can lead to unintended, negative consequences for the company.

Discretion is intended as the final check on an award program. An incentive program is an imperfect measure of corporate performance; solely relying on the plan's metrics may not tell the whole story for a given period. As such, compensation committees must ultimately determine whether the program's output is consistent with the executives' goals and achievements.

Companies also include clawback features beyond the strictures of the Dodd-Frank Act to recoup incentive awards. It is now common to have clawback policies that go beyond financial restatements and include acts resulting in reputational or other harm to a company. In some cases, companies have included a failure of risk oversight as a trigger for recoupment. In each of these cases, it is the board's role to properly exercise its discretion in identifying violations of the clawback policy and taking action.

Be Careful Balancing

Balance is good. But can there be too much balance? The key is to achieve balance in the areas where the risk outweighs the benefits. Beware of watering down your overall program and losing focus. Achieving balance at the expense of putting in the right program that will motivate and retain your people could reduce the return on your investment.

There is no one right way to design an incentive plan. There are a variety of plan designs that work well in different companies for different reasons. The organization's rewards strategy, and the purpose and intent of the incentive programs, should guide the design of the plans to ultimately drive performance.

Benchmarking Executive Pay: The Third Dimension

It can be reasonably argued that making decisions on executive pay is one of the most important responsibilities of the board, and in particular, the most important responsibility of the compensation committee. If nothing else, decisions on executive pay are one of the most visible and can be one of the most controversial decisions made at the board level. Each year in the U.S., the annual proxy of a public company must disclose how much each of the top five executives is paid, how the incentive compensation plans work, and why each element of pay was included. Further, the proxy must include an assessment of the risk level built into the incentive plans in order to disclose, as previously noted, whether any incentive plans "are reasonably likely to have a material adverse effect on the company."

Executive pay has always been a subject of interest in the popular press. Following each proxy season, the leading newspaper in nearly every major U.S. city publishes a story on the most highly paid CEOs in the area. The data may not always be accurate, but it is almost always the source of serious discussion and shareholder activism.

Since 2011, public companies are required to provide shareholders with an opportunity to vote on the overall executive pay package via "say on pay." The vote is advisory and nonbinding and, in theory, could be ignored by the board. But what responsible board could ignore the will of the shareholders? And if it did, how long would the shareholders continue to elect them to the board? Shareholder activist groups are already taking an active role in shaping the votes, and in some cases, shareholders have filed suit against the company and against individual members of the board as a result of failed say-on-pay results. Nonbinding indeed!

The Problem

Given this environment, boards — particularly compensation committees — must be certain that they are following a rigorous, fact-based approach to decisions on pay. As part of this process, most committees engage an independent third party to provide data on market pay levels, short- and long-term incentive plan design and provide advice on what may be appropriate for their company. The core of this information typically is a detailed proxy study that compares the value of the package offered to company executives relative to the value provided to executives at a select group of peer companies.

The common analysis of executive pay follows a two-dimensional approach.

- The first is simply the value offered to peer group executives — base salary, annual and long-term cash incentives and the grant-date fair value of equity grants. This dimension provides a snapshot of what was paid.
- The second provides the committee with the mix of pay elements — how much of the value was provided by cash, stock options, restricted shares, performance shares, restricted stock units and other incentive vehicles. This dimension can be illustrated by a pie-chart that can illustrate how much of the executive pay is fixed (e.g., base salary) and how much is performance-based and at risk.

As a simple example, assume two executive pay packages as set out in Table 18-4. In looking at this data, the casual observer may conclude that these executives are paid the same, when clearly the realized value of what they will earn as their equity grants mature may be very different based on factors such as market change and performance.

Although the grant value of equity is the same (in dollars) based on the concept of fair value, the number of shares used for an option grant will typically be greater than that of a restricted share grant. For this example, assume an option on three shares deliver the same fair value as one restricted share, which means:

- Executive 1 would receive 100,000 restricted shares
- Executive 2 would receive 300,000 stock options.

As the share price changes over the term of the award, the value to the executive differs substantially. Thus, assuming both grants will be fully vested after three years, Table 18-5 illustrates the different outcomes of two executive compensation packages depending on the level of the change in the price of the company's shares.

Clearly, these alternative grant strategies do not produce the same effect, and as an issue of good corporate governance, compensation committees need to be aware of the effect that plan design can have on value. Specifically, as an enhancement to the traditional proxy analysis, good corporate governance might suggest that these

TABLE 18-4 **Comparison of Composition of Pay Packages**

	Executive 1	Executive 2
Base	$1,000,000	$1,000,000
Target annual incentive	$500,000	$500,000
Option grant	0	$1,000,000
Restricted share grant	$1,000,000	0
Grant date price	$10	$10
Total value	$2,500,000	$2,500,000

TABLE 18-5 Comparison of Outcomes of Pay Packages

	Executive 1	Executive 2
	100,000	300,000
Potential price change	Shares' value	Options' value[1]
95%	$950,000	$0
100%	$1,000,000	$0
110%	$1,100,000	$300,000
120%	$1,200,000	$600,000
150%	$1,500,000	$1,500,000
200%	$2,000,000	$3,000,000

[1] Value expressed as actual realized value, not Black-Scholes

committees also look at the volatility of potential outcomes — the third dimension.

What Is the Third Dimension?

The third dimension is a method of evaluating not just the snapshot, but the potential outcomes of plan design given a number of different stock performance scenarios over time. Using data provided in company proxies, a careful analysis can determine the effect of plan design on each executive's total compensation (base salary, annual incentives, LTIs and retirement benefits/deferred compensation). Data can be provided for the NEOs both in the absolute and relative to peer companies.

The Range of Outcomes

Figure 18-6 provides an array of potential outcomes expressed in dollar values highlighting the potential exposure of the company to unexpected costs, as well as the potential values of the compensation plan relative to competitors.

Why Is This Analysis Critical to the Compensation Committee?

As discussed, the simple answer is it provides the committee with an in-depth look at executive pay over time, not just a snapshot approach common to most compensation reports. In addition,

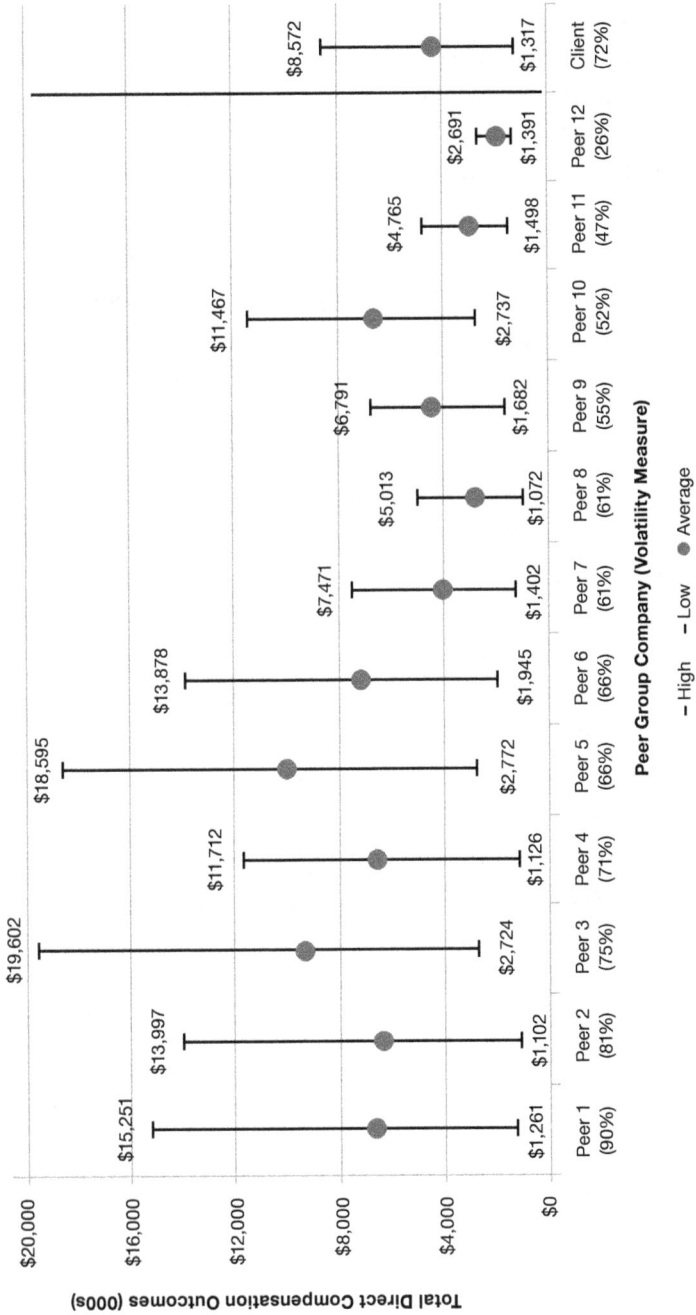

FIGURE 18-6 Pay Outcomes and Volatility

CEO Total Direct Compensation Volatility

having this data is consistent with the general trend in compensation disclosure requirements for more analysis and consideration of "what if" scenarios.

Best practice already expects that the committee look at tally sheets to review executive pay in its totality. How much better is it to add performance scenarios and outcomes?

It also provides the committee with a more robust illustration of compensation risk for the required disclosure in the annual proxy statement. Too much risk and leverage may create an incentive for risky (and ethically challenged) behavior from executives. Too little risk and leverage may create a competitive disadvantage and/or internal dissatisfaction with the alignment of executive rewards with the results delivered to shareholders.

Following the collapse in the financial services industry in the 2008–2009 economic downturn, many compensation committee members confessed that they had not fully grasped the potential impact of outcomes in highly speculative compensation plans. A volatility analysis would have provided committees with more robust information and may have helped prevent disaster.

While a "volatility of outcomes" discussion is not (yet) required as part of the proxy disclosure rules, the trend is clearly in the direction of more disclosure regarding the relationship between pay and performance. Shareholder groups are demanding visibility and Dodd-Frank requires that companies illustrate how the company performed regarding pay versus performance. Can it be long before progressive, well-governed companies begin showing not just what happened in the prior year, but what could happen? If nothing else, it provides a proactive defense for committees against legal action by disgruntled shareholders.

PART III

The CEO Life Cycle

Introduction

By Irv Becker and Christine Rivers

What is the CEO life cycle? What is the most important concern of the board? Leadership continuity — and more specifically, ensuring the right CEO is in place — is the most important concern of the board. The board's most daunting set of responsibilities are the activities involving the CEO — succession, performance evaluation and compensation. We are calling this the CEO life cycle.

If it were up to many directors, they would just as easily delegate these functions — and in many cases they do. Sadly, this delegation is often made to the CEO him/herself who, as discussed in the next three chapters, is not the person who should be doing this work.

However, progressive and well-governed boards not only face these activities head-on, but they proactively manage them. That is, boards need to build the related tasks into their calendars and develop processes around them to ensure these efforts receive the focused attention they deserve.

What Does This Look Like?

It begins when the necessary components of the CEO life cycle — succession, performance evaluation and compensation — that are part of the standing agenda of every board meeting. Not just when the issue is imminent, but ongoing. There is a process based on trust and candor that begs for real conversations. When the CEO and members of the board (usually the chair or a lead director) have ongoing performance-related discussions, matters tend to stay on track. It becomes what they do, what they talk about, what they worry about. It can be as simple as, "How are you doing? How are things going? What is getting in the way?"

Part of the process is the board doing its own intelligence-gathering. This may include visiting headquarters and other field locations, observing and interacting, so that engaging in conversations with other members of the C-suite becomes a natural component of the way the board works. It is not micro-management; rather, it is keeping the lines of communication open.

Lastly, it is rooted in the strategy. Whether it is succession planning, performance evaluation or compensation, the strategy is the foundation — otherwise it is not relevant. When the strategy is the starting point, the questions become, "Are we prioritizing the right things? Is the CEO spending his/her time on the right activities? Is the board ensuring alignment of strategy to compensation, performance evaluation and the profile of the next CEO?"

When the board ensures this laser-like focus on the three components of the life cycle, the organization's probability of success exponentially increases. It is holistic, integrated and relevant.

Optimize Organizational Effectiveness

The activities discussed above are the tangible aspects of the CEO life cycle — the work the board must do. But how should the board act? How can boards approach these pursuits in a way that enhances meaning, ensures greater purpose and optimizes organizational effectiveness?

The answer lies in the way the board and the CEO interact, the relationship they have, the relationship the board builds with the senior management team, the way the CEO brings information to the board and the intent of the CEO to engage the board in meaningful conversation. It is what occurs in-between the tangible, concrete activities that essentially make up the way they work together. The real value in aligning these activities is the ability to have one conversation, built on one foundation, that tells one story and has clear priorities, as the CEO and the board build trust and credibility together.

CHAPTER 19

CEO Performance Evaluation

By Colleen O'Neill, PhD, and David Wise

CEO performance evaluation is a core board responsibility and should be the basis of a variety of board decisions, including CEO goal setting, performance measurement, compensation structure and succession planning. While most boards view CEO evaluations as a required year-end exercise, it is also not uncommon for board members, CEOs and CHROs to be concerned that CEO performance review processes could be designed and implemented to be more meaningful and rigorous. A high-quality performance evaluation process creates shared accountability and strategic alignment between the board and the CEO. However, the importance of aligning on the right performance metrics and feedback processes cannot be overstated. All too often, boards fail to establish and communicate a comprehensive CEO success profile and evaluate CEO performance by relying only on narrow financial measures. The full range of short- and long-term CEO performance goals, which typically include non-financial expectations and leadership behaviors, is often left assumed. Boards and CEOs must work together to clearly define performance criteria which include a balanced and robust set of scorecard metrics and desired leadership actions and attributes. This chapter focuses on how boards can more effectively assess the CEO and provide relevant feedback to guide and improve performance.

This chapter:

■ Maintains that the first principle of an effective evaluation is that boards and CEOs must share accountability for the overall quality and success of the process. While they play different roles, boards and CEOs must collaborate on the CEO goals and performance metrics, feedback and evaluation approaches, and development plans.

■ Explains the importance of establishing the right balance of performance goals and measures which align with the company's strategic priorities. This means including not only financial measures but also operational, customer, and human capital metrics as well.

■ Describes best practices in assessing CEO performance and ensuring a constructive performance review discussion.

Shared Accountability for the CEO Evaluation Process

Effective evaluation of a CEO is a process, not an annual event, and the board and the CEO assume joint accountability for the evaluation process. While boards and CEOs play different roles, they must collaborate throughout the process — from defining goals, to deciding what and how to measure, and determining how the results will impact compensation decisions. To make the process work, both parties must forge a true partnership characterized by mutual respect and genuine appreciation for the value each brings to this critical work.

The design of the CEO evaluation process, particularly with a new CEO, establishes the role the board plays in governing how well the CEO is leading the business and creates standards for how the CEO and board will work together on an ongoing basis to share information and feedback. The process starts with clarifying the strategic intentions and objectives of the business. Strategic alignment enables the board and CEO to determine the appropriate set of goals and measures for the CEO performance scorecard and examine these metrics on a regular basis to discern how the company and the CEO are performing. There are few things more energizing to an organization than a CEO and board aligned around a shared strategy, with clear goals and a line of sight between performance and rewards. The process itself builds trust and once established, moves beyond the bounds of the formal evaluation process, fostering a climate of openness that enriches the board-CEO relationship. If approached right, the process should lead to a strong relationship between the board and CEO. In that way, directors can effectively provide the guidance and wisdom necessary to steer the CEO through rocky times and build the trust needed to improve CEO performance.

Meaningful evaluations produce another benefit — they ward off unwanted surprises. Time and again, CEOs are "caught off guard" by their boards. Corporate news stories describe far too many situations where the board, although concerned with the CEO's performance, made only half-hearted efforts at providing feedback. Then sometime later the company has a crisis, resulting in the CEO's dismissal and creating major trauma for the company and its people. In many cases, this scenario is preventable through an appropriate CEO performance evaluation process and regular performance dialogue.

Efforts to create joint accountability for a clear and effective performance evaluation process advantage both boards and CEOs, as well as their organizational shareholders and stakeholders. Apart from helping directors meet their fiduciary responsibilities, well-managed work in this area can:

- Create shared understanding of CEO performance expectations and send clear messages regarding the CEO's and board's priorities.
- Align strategic direction set by the board with the CEO's capabilities.
- Promote better board and CEO relations to ensure an appropriate and productive collaboration.
- Enable the board and the CEO to communicate effectively on performance-related issues.
- Provide the platform for monitoring progress and facilitating ongoing performance dialogue throughout the year.
- Allow boards to have greater objectivity about CEO remuneration.
- Model leadership accountability by signaling performance management is a core value of the organization.
- Encourage CEO's personal leadership development.

- Provide an early warning system for possible problems.

Align the CEO Performance Scorecard

Many boards underestimate the importance — and difficulty — of aligning a performance scorecard with a proper evaluation of a CEO's performance. Strategic alignment enables the board and CEO to determine the appropriate set of goals and measures for the CEO performance scorecard and examine these metrics on a regular basis. Moreover, the process also includes how performance criteria are measured, how and from whom data are collected, how the results will be analyzed, and ultimately how performance feedback will be delivered.

Boards should address the CEO's performance by anchoring the evaluation process squarely in the company's forward-looking strategic business and organizational priorities. By doing so, directors then become better able to manage the CEO life cycle — consisting of performance evaluation and the alignment of the CEO's compensation to short- and long-term performance objectives, as well as CEO succession.

In an ideal situation, the performance evaluation process is integrated into a successful onboarding process with a new CEO. This establishes clear roles and responsibilities at the outset and sets the stage for a stronger, more collaborative CEO-board relationship.

Regardless of when the evaluation process is created, boards must determine what they are trying to accomplish. What are the expectations for the CEO? What needs to be achieved this year that aligns with the longer-term strategy? What battles will the CEO be accountable for winning? How will those challenges and opportunities be quantified so that they can be measured?

These answers are found through the creation of a CEO role profile that is built upon the company's strategy. The CEO role profile is foundational to performance evaluation, as this strategic blueprint guides the evaluation and related incentives. The role profile articulates the strategic objectives that the CEO is expected to achieve both in the long- and short-term as well as the related CEO accountabilities.

It defines what successful strategy execution looks like. Based on these clearly outlined strategic goals, performance metrics can be established that enable regular CEO evaluation and feedback.

These efforts articulate and drive priorities and enable the board and the CEO to gauge progress throughout the year. Boards can then evaluate the CEO against criteria that matter. And through regular reviews of the CEO's progress, directors will encourage evaluations that achieve clarity, consistency and the right outcomes.

Performance Measures

When establishing objectives and measuring CEO performance, boards tend to rely on financial metrics. Perhaps this is to be expected; financials are the most obvious way to assess how the organization, and by association the CEO, is performing. Financials are preferred as they typically are easy to quantify and less prone to generating debate about accuracy. However, in the current environment of heightened scrutiny and accountability, boards are increasingly concerned with both what was achieved and how it was accomplished.

Although a board must always hold CEOs accountable to the financial outcomes, we know that not everything a CEO does well will show up in annual financial results. For this reason, today's CEO metrics should include elements of strategy execution and organizational capability development. Board discussions about CEO performance evaluation should include financial metrics, but also talk about progress against key strategic milestones, like targeting a new market or changing the customer profile or building talent capabilities to meet future changes in the business. These are the initiatives, whether they are in the incentive plan or not, that boards must review and provide regular feedback upon.

Financial Metrics

The CEO is responsible for the entire enterprise, so quantitative metrics like earnings per share or return on invested capital are good measures of accomplishments. These financial measures, of course, are very important. They reflect the growth and profitability of the company and determine the amount of dividends that can be distributed to shareholders. Furthermore, these measures are numerical and objective, not easily open to manipulation and have a major effect on shareholder value.

However, financials are limited in gauging the extent of the organization's value creation process. By their nature, financials are lagging indicators and only tell part of the story. In case after case of corporate malfeasance, a CEO's need to drive financial metrics caused some individuals to cut corners.

A CEO can decide to sub-optimize one area to "make the numbers"; however, such a short-term fix is not a sustainable strategy. Further, a CEO can underspend on research and development, reduce capital expenditures or even "sell market share" through profit-boosting higher prices. Other short-term solutions include underpaying key resources or not providing them with the right career opportunities. Eventually these individuals will quit, undermining the organization's progress.

All these actions potentially can destroy future value. It is typically only after these mistakes have snowballed that they come to light, all too often destroying shareholder equity and ruining careers in the process. Board members need to track a variety of performance measures in the CEO's scorecard, such as shaping the culture, developing leadership capabilities, and collaborating with the board and other constituencies. This can help ensure that short-term financial gains are not incentivized over long-term performance and sustainability metrics.

Today, more experienced boards are demanding increased accountability from CEOs for setting corporate culture, demonstrating organizational leadership, building organizational capability and sustainability, and demanding ethical behavior. A board can help meet its oversight mandate by incorporating nonfinancial metrics into its evaluation of CEO performance.

Nonfinancial Metrics

Nonfinancial metrics are different from non-quantitative measures. Even if a measure is not financially driven, it can still be quantified and assessed. There still must be tangible, measurable targets set for goal achievement in order for the process to work. For example, fuzzy objectives like "improved executive team morale" are difficult to measure and quantify. Specific goals such as "scores at or above the 75th percentile on the employee engagement survey compared to Fortune 500 norms" provide clearer targets for the CEO.

These nonfinancial metrics can be established at the beginning of the appraisal process through discussion between the board and the CEO about the business strategy and the implications for CEO evaluation. There should be concrete goals for CEOs who go beyond financial results and address core issues like those described below. By establishing these benchmarks, boards can clarify what they expect from the CEO to drive financial performance in both the short and long term. Through regular and accurate feedback against established benchmarks, boards can support CEOs in achieving objectives.

Nonfinancial measures could include:

- **Succession:** Has the CEO hired and developed a sufficient pipeline of talent to ensure orderly succession should key executives leave?
- **Values:** Has the CEO articulated and embodied a strong set of values that serves as the bedrock for organizational performance?
- **Diversity:** What steps has the CEO taken to ensure a diverse, inclusive and fair workplace?
- **Employee engagement:** How connected are the employees to the organization? What do turnover statistics and employee climate surveys reveal?
- **Strategy:** Has the CEO been able to create and align others with a compelling business strategy to take the organization forward in a competitive business environment?
- **Structure:** What steps has the CEO taken to create the right structure to enable the company to execute the strategy?
- **Culture:** What cultural attributes are evident within the company? Is it the right culture to help execute the business strategy?

- **Customer satisfaction:** Are the company's customers satisfied with the company's products and services? Are key customers being retained?
- **Organizational capability:** Is the human capital of the organization being effectively developed for future success?
- **Core organization processes:** Are key operational processes being improved?

One example of a nonfinancial metric that can be used for CEO evaluation is the climate that the CEO creates for his/her top team and whether the CEO is maximizing the team's effectiveness and their talent potential. Research finds a strong relationship between leaders creating positive work climates and organizational performance. Through anonymous feedback collected from direct reports, the CEO can gain a better understanding of how the work atmosphere is enabling or undermining organizational performance.

Another option is to obtain feedback from a variety of key stakeholders. When using a 360-degree evaluation, the process should be inclusive in gathering data from a wide range of sources and protecting the anonymity of the respondents. Data should be gathered from multiple sources in evaluating the performance of a sitting CEO. The CEO has many constituencies, and it is important to be inclusive when evaluating their performance. Look to gather a variety of inputs in providing the most relevant data to help guide performance improvement. The board itself is one of the most important bases of performance improvement feedback.

Because the feedback from constituents is highly sensitive, the utmost care needs to be established in data collection and storage and deciding who is privy to the results. Data can be obtained using online collection tools or using external consultants who can conduct confidential interviews, providing aggregate feedback to the CEO. At the beginning of the evaluation, it is critical to establish who will have access to the data and how it will be used.

In summary, CEOs are being evaluated continually on their business results by stakeholders and employees. The use of several types of measures is advisable in CEO evaluations. A confluence of data points increases the CEO's confidence in the accuracy of measurement. By employing multiple ways of measuring performance, the credibility of the conclusions is enhanced. By also adding nonfinancial metrics to the mix, CEOs can gain a more holistic view of their leadership and tease out the critical factors that contribute to their long-term leadership effectiveness.

Assess Performance and Provide Feedback

Performance assessment and feedback are familiar to most leaders in their rise to the top management levels. Throughout their careers, many have been rigorously assessed and provided feedback on areas of strengths and opportunities for improvement. Yet, somewhat surprisingly, the performance evaluation process commonly becomes less thorough and less meaningful the more senior the executive. Executives suffer from an "appraisal paradox." The higher one's position in the organization, the less likely one is to receive rigorous, constructive feedback. Consequently, once an individual becomes a CEO, the quantity and quality of such input often diminishes further.

Communicating directly, candidly, and meaningfully about performance to anyone is never easy, and giving feedback to a CEO can be especially daunting. However, most modern CEOs developed in environments where performance feedback was provided, and that process should continue once an individual becomes a CEO. In fact, the quality of the performance feedback itself can directly affect the strength of the board-CEO relationship — as well as the success of the company.

Good executives are sensitive to the truism that "the higher you go, the less feedback you receive," and the best CEOs seek input from others to accurately gauge their performance. Unfortunately, direct reports can easily be intimidated by those senior to them and may not provide honest evaluations of the CEO even when invited, generally due to perceived career risk. An organization's board is in a unique position to provide evaluations and feedback regarding CEO performance, but frequently relies upon compensation itself

38

to send that message. Compensation and related incentives can be used to support the desired messages, but should not be used as the only medium to send the message: it cannot replace the dialogue needed to provide real feedback.

Furthermore, providing effective feedback should be a continual process, not a one-time annual event. If feedback is held back until a year-end evaluation, there could be unwelcome surprises that derail the positive spirit that should underlie the entire undertaking. However, if board members can provide input to the CEO on an ongoing basis, the likelihood of mid-course corrections increases. The use of an objective third party may be helpful to provide the feedback and/or coaching necessary to assist the CEO in getting the most out of the evaluation data. While a board member who has the ear of the CEO may be effective in providing performance feedback, a professional experienced in executive assessment and coaching can facilitate the process in an objective way, with less apprehension.

Summary

Successful boards take an integrated view toward performance evaluation, in context of pay and succession, but also on the foundation of strategy. What is more, integrating these themes improves the quality of the CEO-board relationship and heightens the CEO's opportunity for success, as it opens ongoing dialogue and transparency. By taking time to create the CEO role profile, then relentlessly selecting, evaluating and rewarding against it, boards can deliver long-term benefits. With so much on the line, directors should not leave this to chance.

Improving CEO performance evaluation provides a significant opportunity for boards. The development of a stronger process for evaluating and communicating CEO performance yields greater clarity on roles and expectations, which ultimately produces improved, sustainable organization performance.

By devoting more attention to developing a strong CEO performance evaluation process, an organization should see the following benefits:

- Improved and more constructive relationship between the board and CEO
- Clearer alignment of organization strategy with CEO capability
- A shared understanding of expectations
- A way to link compensation and succession planning
- The ability to correct the course before it is too late (i.e., spot and address potential problem areas and CEO blind spots)
- Greater organizational stability and sustainability as well as performance.

CHAPTER 20

CEO Succession Management

By Jane Stevenson and Christine Rivers

Companies and boards have long recognized the critical nature of CEO succession for the current and future performance of the organization. We call it CEO progression, as without the requisite ongoing attention to a rigorous process for managing CEO succession, a company may flounder, miss opportunities and lose ground to competitors. An understanding of the core elements and issues in a well-developed process for CEO progression planning is necessary to provide a solid foundation for an organization.

This chapter:

- Discusses the risks in managing CEO succession.
- Identifies common pitfalls in CEO succession planning.
- Sets out key steps in developing an ongoing succession planning process focused on the organization's particular facts, circumstances and business strategy.
- Considers how to manage the actual transition in CEO succession.

The Risks of CEO Succession

Managing CEO succession is one of the most important and riskiest challenges that boards of directors face. Whether it is for emergency succession or as a result of a planned transition, these public decisions have a significant impact inside and outside of companies. Few decisions can be more devastating to a company than picking the wrong CEO, whether internal or external. Negative outcomes can include backlash in the financial markets, internal disruption, loss of key talent, misguided strategic direction, an inability to meet performance objectives and bleak results for shareholders. The CEO may simply be ill-suited to the corporate culture, providing leadership that fails to foster team effectiveness among senior executives and engage the broader organization.

And while most CEO hires are internal, hiring externally is not always a better solution. Research demonstrates that CEO turnover in the United States costs a minimum of 2.5 times direct compensation in immediate severance and replacement costs, including the costs associated with buying out forfeited equity-based awards and compensation, for the risk of moving to another company.

Inconsistency in the way CEO succession is managed can lead to varying outcomes. The Conference Board's 2019 CEO Succession Practices study points to the prevalence of either one of two committees as most prominent in CEO succession; that of nominating and governance as well as compensation. As the Conference Board's study points out, companies that rely on nominating and governance for CEO succession generally place emphasis on the skill sets and experiences needed for the next CEO, while those that charge the compensation committee with this activity generally do so to connect leadership continuity planning with senior leadership goals and incentives. In a fewer number of cases a separate committee is formed with the sole mandate of CEO succession. Whatever model the board chooses, the fact does not change; CEO succession is the ultimate responsibility of the full board; the committee is simply charged with doing the work.

There is an inherent value in treating CEO succession as part of a continuous cycle that includes performance evaluation, compensation and strategy considerations — often referred to as the CEO life cycle. The result should be one interconnected set of conversations, grounded in the organization's business and organizational imperatives.

The U.S. Securities and Exchange Commission (SEC) has also recognized the significance of CEO succession planning. Prior to 2009, CEO succession was deemed to relate to a company's routine "day-to-day" business matters. The SEC had taken the position that proposals regarding the adoption and disclosure of written and detailed CEO succession planning features were excludable from proxy statements, as such information "related to the termination, hiring or promotion of employees." The SEC eventually changed course, thereby recognizing the fundamental importance of the disclosure of CEO succession plans (Staff Legal Bulletin No. 14E; October 27, 2009), in accepting that "CEO succession planning raises a significant policy issue regarding the governance of the corporation that transcends the day-to-day business matter of managing the workforce." With this change, CEO succession was open to the scrutiny of shareholders and became a more obvious priority for boards.

CEO Succession: One Size Doesn't Fit All

Boards often need to plan for two types of CEO succession. In nearly 40 percent of cases that we have studied, CEO transition is triggered by the removal, the unexpected resignation, or the death or disability of the current CEO. The Conference Board 2019 CEO Succession Study reveals startling statistics about the spike in numbers related to undesirable behavior. In 2018, nonvoluntary departures accounted for 30.5 percent of CEO departures, with '#MeToo' related terminations alone accounting for nearly half that number. In light of these statistics, boards should remain prepared for an immediate CEO replacement at any time, and the best way to accomplish that is through ongoing CEO progression processes that build top leadership options for when they are needed, coupled with teams that are well aligned to deliver against strategic business priorities for both the current and future dynamics.

The approximately 60 percent of transitions that are known and therefore should be planned are also not without challenge. While there always will be outliers, there should be sufficient time in most organizations for an internal successor to be developed. This is an ongoing process that should be charted over 5-10 years before the selection is finalized. For a variety of reasons, many companies still find themselves unprepared for or not aligned on this important decision.

The steps outlined here can furnish directors with the comfort of better information and a process that provides the level of due diligence and preparedness that shareholders deserve in this all-important decision.

Step 1: Align Strategy — The Future CEO Role Requirements

When should planned succession management begin?

CEO succession should always be on the agenda of the board, even when a new CEO has been appointed. In the latter case, while the focus of the board in this period is oriented toward successful onboarding of the new CEO, the board should nonetheless arrange to have a written document of the requirements for the next CEO. This is particularly important for interim or turnaround CEOs.

Development of and alignment around future-oriented CEO role requirements is the anchor of CEO succession planning. The steps involved in creating this profile include working with the full board to achieve alignment and agreement on the following types of questions:

- To what extent will the next CEO need to envision the strategy for the company, or will it likely be a continuation of the current strategy?

- To what extent will the company's business model need to change (e.g., global expansion, business-to-consumer versus business to business, etc.)?

- To what extent will the core accountabilities of the CEO need to change, for example going from a focus on external stake-holders versus internal management or leading a public versus private company?

- To what extent will the capabilities of the new CEO need to be different from those of the exiting leader? For example, the new CEO may find him/herself leading in a much more volatile and changing business environment than ever before, where the rules of the game are significantly different and disruption takes precedence over stability.

FIGURE 20-1 **CEO Succession Cycle**

When a company has a highly effective CEO in place, there can be a temptation to use an assessment of what accounts for this leader's success in the development of the future CEO profile. While this process can surface critical attributes and capabilities that may explain the outgoing CEO's success, what is really critical is understanding what the business needs to accomplish going forward for the board to view it as successful. Thus, a comprehensive study should be undertaken with a fresh perspective to develop a CEO success profile based on the strategic priorities that will define the long-term success of the business.

By proactively identifying how anticipated changes in the organization's business strategy and organizational structure will affect the requirements of the CEO role, boards can anticipate the essential priorities for the next CEO position (See Figure 20-1). The resulting

Common Pitfalls for Boards in CEO Succession Management

Lack of Board Priority

CEO succession should be a continuous conversation by the board, although this is not always the case. Lack of time and prioritization, along with a worry that it may send a negative message to the sitting CEO, are concerns some boards have allowed to get in the way. However, the absence of a robust CEO succession plan can have devastating consequences on an organization. There are numerous examples of unplanned CEO departures that could have been headed-off or at least been less disruptive with some basic planning; there should always be a plan for emergency succession situations. Throughout a CEO's tenure the board should maintain a continuous process of building future CEOs with the development of internal candidates. Boards need to have in place a clearly defined and ongoing process of CEO succession well in advance of any transition, one that is not based on the timeline of the current CEO. Developing future CEOs begins on a CEO's first day in office and is a full-time concern for the board as it works to make sure that the right people have the right experiences.

Letting the CEO Drive the Agenda

CEOs and chief human resource officers (CHROs) are typically well intended when they develop programs to build a strong pipeline of leaders capable of filling future executive roles, including the CEO position. Though a key activity worthy of board support, CEOs are often prone to developing candidates "in their own likeness" or according to their views of the current strategy. CHROs can provide critical input but may not be aware of the full range of external demands of the CEO role. While the input of the CEO and CHRO is important, it is the board's clear accountability for selecting the future CEO and ensuring that the CEO and (in many cases) CHRO actively participate in, but do not drive, this agenda.

Lack of Clarity on Board Roles of Incoming and Outgoing CEOs

With evolving changes in corporate governance practices, boards must be clear on their corporate governance as they consider CEO succession. Historically, as CEOs retired, they assumed the chair of the board role. However, that model is changing and more boards are expecting their CEOs to step away and let the incoming CEO fully take over. Clarity on the board role for both outgoing and incoming CEOs is a key consideration of CEO succession. Boards can avoid false impressions and potential conflict by being precise on their corporate governance intentions as they consider how best to set and manage realistic expectations tied to succession.

discussion can also help to clarify role and competency requirements for the future CEO and align the board in a common direction. The output of this effort should be a robust CEO success profile that prioritizes the key strategic challenges, accountabilities and associated behaviors that will help to assure future success. As there is always the risk of the board developing a CEO profile that is unrealistic for any one person to fill, it is important for the board to also agree on its absolute requirements versus those characteristics that are nice to have for the role.

This is an important step in the process, as many times boards, who may be aligned on the mission and vision of the organization, are not necessarily aligned on the strategy or even the current state of the organization. For example, if some board members believe it is a turnaround situation while others believe the company is on a growth trajectory, their view of the next CEO will be very different. Likewise, when there is disagreement on the strategy, there will be disagreement on the critical CEO requirements. Ensuring alignment on these points is a critical consideration for the board and one where taking a diversion for more education as well as robust discussion is warranted.

Step 2: Assess Capabilities — Identify Potential CEO Candidates
Who should be considered a potential CEO candidate?

Once the board aligns on the future-oriented CEO profile, one of the key accountabilities of the CEO, and one that should be made explicit in his/her performance criteria, is to develop a robust, multi-generation pipeline of talent to support business continuity and future succession needs. When done early enough, this work is best positioned as part of broader leadership development efforts, and should include a range of senior leaders, as their levels of potential will change over time, based on how they respond to the development challenges that they are given.

The reasons for assessing a broader pool of CEOs are threefold. First, the organization and the leaders will benefit from the insights from these assessments and the development that follows it. This process strengthens the overall executive talent pool. Second, there are often "dark horse" candidates who may not look as strong, but who develop to become highly qualified as time for the transition draws nearer. And lastly, once the final internal candidates are

348

made known, there can be unwanted competition and, in some cases, departures.

How should current and future potential be assessed?

To ensure that this initial assessment is objective and focused on CEO potential, rather than past performance, which may not be fully representative of a leader's growth potential, multiple perspectives should be considered:

- The CEO's and CHRO's perspectives;
- Board members' perspectives; and
- Formal, robust executive assessments by a professional third party against the future CEO requirements.

At the conclusion of the executive assessment, reports should be generated about individual capability and potential relative to the CEO profile. Feedback is typically best provided in one-on-one development planning sessions that target the highest priority risk areas to enhance the leader's candidacy. By using multiple methods and perspectives, the board and the CEO will have the most accurate and complete picture of a candidate's suitability by experiential track record and by personal hard wiring. Therefore, the board will have better insights through which to guide development efforts.

Step 3: Accelerate Development — Developing Potential CEO Candidates

How can the likelihood of a qualified CEO candidate be increased?

Simply identifying high performers and giving them increased board exposure and general development is not enough. CEO candidates should have targeted development plans in place and they should be continuously evaluated against the future CEO profile. Gaps in critical knowledge and skill areas often can be addressed through gaining exposure to other parts of the organization, supplemented with formal education (e.g., on risk management or compliance), as necessary. For such stretch assignments to work, the CEO should be held responsible for ensuring the accountability of candidate progress against the plan and should furnish regular updates to the board.

But gaps in required leadership often become more difficult to address the later that they are identified and the higher the candidate is in the organizational hierarchy. For instance, a leader in a staff role with no history of leading a business will often lack fundamental leadership experiences and related competencies that are core to line management roles. Business leaders often fine-tune these leadership capabilities over years through trial and error as they are coming up the ranks. The absence of such capability can pose serious risk unless there are focused efforts to provide leaders with the opportunity to develop these skills.

This is why the concept of progression is vital to best-in-class CEO succession planning, and why continual understanding of where candidates are in the development continuum enables effective planning. These are the insights that enable the board to make incisive choices for critical pass-through roles that are the best developmental assignments for a company's highest potential leaders.

Step 4: Accessing the Marketplace — Manage the Selection

Should the board consider external or only internal candidates?

While research indicates that internal candidates are less costly and often more successful, this decision depends on multiple factors, including the quality of available internal talent, the complexity of future business challenges, the availability of qualified external talent, and the desire to retain current senior executives. After the board acquires a clear picture of the internal potential successors, best practices include understanding and accessing insights relative to the comparative candidate set in the external marketplace.

A critical success factor in selecting internal candidates is to understand the discontinuous shift in accountability in moving from senior executive positions to the CEO role. Public company CEOs, in particular, have a significant focus on external interactions for which most executives (except for the CFO) are unprepared and often have other accountability areas that cannot easily be delegated to others. In this context, CEO candidates should be assessed based on their ability to manage competing internal and external priorities as well as their ability to manage highly visible, external stakeholders.

Boards often conduct external benchmarking to provide an additional point of reference on the strength of the internal candidates without the disruption of messaging, internally and externally, that an organization may go outside for a CEO. When boards do decide to conduct an outside search, it is critical to use the same platform to compare inside and outside candidates, starting with the common CEO success profile. Moreover, outside searches need not all go to a formal assessment process if internal candidates appear to be making good progress; a silent search or benchmarking study of the availability and quality of external talent may give the board the comfort it needs. Objective assessments against the CEO success profile allow the board to measure all candidates against common criteria, diminishing the influence of familiarity in final decision making. Moreover, tools such as behavioral ("critical incident") interviewing can provide a more level playing field in making comparisons between the capabilities of external candidates and the capabilities of insiders. While such assessments should never substitute for the board's own judgment in CEO selection, they invariably provide useful insights that boards can incorporate into a more robust view of the candidate pool.

Step 5: Activate and Advance Performance — Manage the Transition

Once the board has agreed on the best candidate and addressed the risks that he/she and the organization face, a comprehensive on-boarding and communication plan should be developed. This plan should be tailored to the specific situation. For example, if this is a planned succession, is the prospective CEO a logical successor or is he/she a "dark horse" candidate who may not be well known to investors and key customers? This plan should include not only those on-boarding activities that the CEO must undertake, but also the specific actions required of the board, such as explaining the board/management philosophy as well as how feedback from executive sessions is provided. The plan should also specify the on-boarding actions required from the outgoing CEO (e.g., introductions to key clients, regulators, investors, etc.). Because each CEO succession often creates changes in senior leadership positions, whether the CEO is an internal or external candidate, these changes need to be carefully managed and communicated.

Final Considerations

How boards manage succession planning is often typical of how they manage their business. Some are forward-thinking, well-planned efforts that start shortly after the appointment of a new CEO, while in other cases there is a thin slate of internal candidates or an urgent need to hire externally, creating unnecessary risks for the board and the organization. By taking a long-term progression perspective, boards can reduce risk and more reliably fulfill their fiduciary responsibility to shareholders. And, by considering all aspects of the CEO life cycle collectively, boards have a greater likelihood of optimizing organizational success.

CHAPTER 21

Special Compensation Issues in the CEO Life Cycle

By Irv Becker

Taking a broader view of how boards and CEOs work together is the cornerstone of the CEO life cycle. The three elements of the life cycle — succession, performance management and compensation — are all linked together. A holistic view of CEO compensation, from original design of the compensation program and its underlying philosophy to benchmarking and retention, is critical to aligning the goals of the board and the CEO.

There are significant transitions for a CEO, from recruitment to retirement, and each transition has different compensation issues that need to be considered by the board. Creating the right compensation program for each stage is critical to the board successfully attracting, retaining and motivating the right CEO for the company.

While compensation elements, design and strategy have been addressed throughout the book, there are special situations that should be considered through the lens of the CEO life cycle.

This chapter:

- Examines how compensation may impact each aspect of a CEO's life cycle, from recruitment to retirement.
- Considers the different compensation arrangements often needed for outside hires compared with internal CEO promotions, including the use of employment contracts.
- Addresses compensation issues involved with an emergency CEO replacement, including an Office of the CEO.

- Provides a brief overview of the importance of CEO performance evaluation in the context of an IPO.
- Discusses the pay considerations in a newly public company and how they differ from those of a private organization, the board's primary areas of focus, any employee issues that need to be addressed, and the general concerns now faced by the board and the CEO.

Compensation Strategies for CEO Transitions

From the time of recruitment to the moment of retirement (and sometimes beyond), the life of a CEO is filled with transitions. For a board of directors, all of these transitions involve compensation decisions. The board needs to think ahead so that it can make these decisions with proper planning in ways that match the company's strategy, culture and circumstances.

Addressed below are some of the most significant compensation issues that boards should consider in these transition periods:

Recruitment

When recruiting an external CEO and negotiating that CEO's pay package, boards often find themselves at the whim of the markets. The laws of supply and demand mean that boards generally have less control over the situation when recruiting an external CEO than they do with internal succession.

Rather than pinning all of its hopes on a single candidate, a board should keep a few candidates under consideration in case it is unable to reach agreement with its first choice on a compensation package that would fit the company's existing compensation program, pay culture and internal equity structure.

With external CEO recruitment, we see considerable stress around unvested equity, unvested deferred compensation or lost pension benefits from the previous employer that the candidate would need to leave on the table. Executives often expect to be bought out or made whole on these amounts, but companies do not want to build these additional payments into the ongoing compensation structure.

Typically, they would rather agree on a one-off, up-front payment that gets included in the first year's compensation numbers.

These types of deals can lead to significant up-front equity awards or sign-on bonuses that can shine a spotlight on boards from a disclosure perspective. Keep in mind that disclosures of compensation packages are available not just to investors, but to anyone, including other members of the management team. That can create conflict if those executives become upset about how the new CEO's compensation relates to their own compensation packages.

Severance Protection

CEOs recruited from outside a company typically want some sort of down-side protection. They will usually ask for severance benefits — just in case things do not work out.

Recruiting an external CEO can lead to other culture-related clashes around compensation. For instance, while many companies have moved away from using employment contracts, a candidate coming from outside the organization might insist on such an agreement for his/her protection (at least for an initial term of up to three years). That could create discrepancies and inconsistencies within the management team, since other executives would lack such protections. If a board determines that it really needs a particular CEO candidate, it might be willing to make an exception and negotiate an employment agreement, but it should be aware that doing so could lead to internal conflicts down the line.

Similarly, a CEO coming from outside the organization may want their incentives determined and/or paid in ways that conflict with the incentive arrangements of other executives. Some CEOs may want their equity to vest based on share price appreciation. If other executives are incentivized based on profitability or some other metric, that could lead to misalignment and interpersonal conflicts among the executive team.

Promotion

When a CEO is promoted from within the organization, the board does not have to worry as much about the negotiations around severance, employment contracts and incentives that it might with an external candidate. The biggest issue with internal promotion usually involves finding the right speed at which to raise the new CEO's compensation.

The market rate for CEO compensation could be two to three times as much as the executive's former total compensation. To move someone from a $5 million to a $10 million compensation package takes careful and thoughtful planning. Best practice here is to set a multi-year plan to bring an internally promoted CEO up to market level compensation.

Finding just the right pace to increase compensation is critically important. If an organization does not bring compensation up fast enough, it leaves the company exposed to the risk that the new CEO could be recruited away by a competitor offering a larger compensation package.

Leaving the new CEO's compensation below market rate can also project the wrong image to investors and other stakeholders. The market could interpret low compensation as a signal that the new CEO is not quite ready or that the board has low confidence in its choice.

On the other hand, bumping up compensation too dramatically also can cause problems. A new CEO's compensation package should be at the lower end of the market range. Employers should leave some "dry powder" so that they can raise compensation later to reward for maturity in the position and high performance.

As with all issues around CEO compensation, the board should make its decisions while considering the whole. In most circumstances, we recommend bringing in a new internally promoted CEO around the 25th percentile of market compensation. The board should have a plan to get the new CEO to the market median level in three to four years by pulling different levers — salary, bonuses, as well as short- and long-term incentives.

Keep in mind that market medians will shift over time. Best practice is to anticipate market movements and monitor the performance of both the company and the CEO to fine-tune the compensation model each year in an iterative process. As the experience of the CEO and length of tenure increases, so too does the likelihood that a CEO's compensation should be at the higher end of the market-based compensation range.

Retirement

As CEOs approach the twilight of their tenure with a company, a new set of compensation questions comes into play. Boards need to consider whether they should change the mix of their CEO's compensation structure.

For instance, do stock options still make sense for a CEO nearing retirement? While options typically have a 10-year lifespan, the company's equity compensation plan may only allow the CEO a much shorter period (e.g., one to three years) to exercise options post-retirement. Since these shorter-term stock options have less value than the 10-year options, perhaps restricted stock would make more sense for a CEO near retirement?

In the best-case scenarios, a CEO should be involved in succession planning and preparing their successor to take over leadership. If a CEO has helped pick the successor, perhaps the board does want the CEO to hold equity for at least a certain period after retirement. The equity would provide the former CEO with a vested interest in the success of the new CEO. With advance planning, the board can start making the move away from stock options and toward restricted stock or performance shares with the aim of making sure that the retiring CEO still has enough value left in their equity awards to feel invested in the new CEO flourishing in the role.

To ensure this smooth and unbroken chain of succession, some companies have developed a process by which an internal candidate is promoted to president, then president-CEO, then CEO-chairman. As the next CEO rises through the succession pipeline, the CEO-chairman steps down from the CEO role but retains the position as executive chairman of the board. As executive chairman, the former CEO can guide and advise the president-CEO. Then, after a year or two, the executive chairman (and former CEO) can step aside and the CEO can take on the dual leadership mantle of CEO-chairman until the next turn of the wheel in the leadership cycle.

Not every company follows this model. Even companies that would like to use this model may need to abandon it if a CEO leaves due to health issues or poor performance. While the joint CEO-chairman role is still common in the U.S., many governance and shareholder advisers recommend splitting the two roles to create a non-executive chairman position. Division of the chairman and CEO roles occurs frequently in European countries. If a board has given any consideration to moving away from the unified CEO-chairman structure toward a non-executive chairman, the retirement of a current CEO-chairman can be a good opportunity to make such a split.

Emergency CEO Replacement

In addition to its regular CEO succession plans and processes, a board needs to be prepared for the possibility of replacing its CEO due to a sudden emergency. Well-known public companies have faced situations where they had to replace their CEOs without delay due to illness, sudden death, internal investigations, personal scandals and other unexpected events. The board should have an established emergency plan that it can quickly launch and implement in these types of scenarios.

The ideal scenario is having an emergency successor already identified who can assume the mantle, but many organizations find themselves in situations where there is no clear emergency plan, and no logical person who can fill the role in what can turn into a multi-month commitment. This is where the "Office of the CEO" can fill a gap. The concept is to take the CEO's accountabilities and to divide them among a number of executives/board members who can cover the role together until a permanent successor is in place.

There is no one standard approach to compensation in this Office of the CEO scenario. If executives are asked to carry an additional burden during the transition, it is appropriate to compensate them accordingly. The easiest approach is to provide a temporary percentage increase (reflective of the CEO's salary) to their base pay as long as the Office of the CEO is in place. Additional pay should be linked to performance (i.e., meeting certain targets set for the Office of the CEO). Typically, these bonuses would occur during the regular compensation cycle and would reflect the length of tenure for executives serving in the Office of the CEO.

Any board member who participates in the Office of the CEO should also be compensated as it is likely to be a full-time commitment for an extended period of time. The cleanest and simplest approach is to pay a monthly salary that takes into consideration their board compensation (the director should only be paid the difference). There are two basic approaches:

- The director is paid by the board for taking on a special project (equivalent to a percentage of the CEO's salary)
- The director is paid a management fee (an enhanced annual retainer) by the organization (equivalent to a percentage of the CEO's salary)

Summing Up

From recruitment to retirement and all the stages in between, the CEO role is filled with important compensation decisions. For board members, finding the right compensation mix often is critical in attracting, retaining and motivating the right CEO who can lead the organization to success. Yet directors should keep in mind that some of the decisions they make around CEO compensation (particularly vis-à-vis severance protection) can have repercussions around harmony within the executive ranks. Even at the end of the CEO's career, compensation decisions can help ensure a smooth transition from one CEO to the next or — in the event of a sudden and unplanned CEO transition — make sure that executives and/ or board members who step into the breach are rewarded fairly for their service and performance.

The CEO Life Cycle and Preparing for an IPO

During the phases leading up to the company's IPO — from initial formation around a product or service (with perhaps an advisory board having a key role) to a public company with more formal board responsibilities — much must be done to prepare for this momentous event. While the board transition is significant and must be deliberately managed and planned, CEO succession, performance and compensation are of equal importance, requiring a similar level of focus and attention.

CEO Succession

We discussed CEO succession in detail in Chapter 20; here we will be focusing on a pre- and post-IPO company situation. Very early on in the new company's tenure it is important to profile the skills and competency requirements of the "CEO of the future" — a CEO role profile. The CEO role profile is developed within the context of the strategy and addresses critical questions, including:

- Given our strategy, what does the next CEO need to do?
- How will such a CEO accomplish these objectives?
- What are the "must-win battles" necessary to get there?
- What leadership characteristics are critical in this journey?
- What is the needed board/CEO relationship for the company to thrive?
- What culture does the new CEO need to create and promulgate throughout the organization?
- How will the CEO work with his/her management team and hold them accountable for execution and, in turn, how will the management team create the conditions for those in the organization also to be successful?

A board is only able to truly understand what it needs in a CEO by going through this exercise. The findings can be quite illuminating; many times the assessment of the CEO against the profile reveals a sub-optimal "fit" between the current CEO and future role requirements. This should not come as a surprise, as the skills and competencies needed to build an organization at an early stage are quite different than what it takes to run a public company, where the focus is on building organizational infrastructure, capability and overall positioning the company for growth. So while the current CEO may be the right person for now, he/she may not be (nor want to be) the best choice to take the company forward. That said, many CEOs successfully transition into the public company role; however, for boards that do not proactively assess the role, it is often not without growing pains and potential mishaps along the way.

Other Board Priorities

Similar to the considerations around CEO selection and succession, CEO compensation and performance evaluation are areas that the board of a newly public company needs to take up formally without delay. Different from a private firm's board, the board of a public company may be under a regulatory mandate to evaluate the CEO and must disclose the CEO's pay. Given these new strictures, boards need to be deliberate and sophisticated in how compensation matters are handled, if for no other reason than the optics of doing this poorly now can affect the investment (i.e., the stock price).

The CEO Dashboard

Establishing high clarity is the most important component in establishing the criteria for CEO performance. A CEO dashboard is intended to highlight company priorities and becomes the agreed-upon criteria between the CEO and the board. While the CEO dashboard is important in any organization regardless of its current phase, it is of primary importance when moving onto a public stage, where the optics of CEO performance are heightened, and new stockholders are eager to grow their investment. Although the financials have traditionally dominated the dashboard, it is increasingly a trend, and a healthy one at that, to include other categories that receive some weighting toward the incentive of the CEO. For example, issues related to company sustainability, leadership continuity, governance and crisis management all impact an organization and therefore are important for the CEO to manage.

CEO Performance Evaluation

Taking this to the next level is the performance evaluation process. While the "what" is important, the "how" is equally so. At this stage, the CEO and the board must jointly determine how success will be defined in each area. For example, if ensuring leadership continuity is a key dashboard metric, what does success look like? How will it be measured? What weighting does it have toward the incentive? And, just as important, how will the board deliver feedback?

Why wait until the annual review when a robust discussion of how the CEO is doing against the backdrop of a newly public company can take place at regular intervals throughout the year? In fact, here is a place where the board can have a significant impact — guiding and advising the CEO of the newly public company on the factors that have been determined to be critical to the company. What better way to get this new relationship on solid footing than to open the door to these important and game-changing conversations?

CEO Compensation

Lastly, we consider the link to pay:

- The pay considerations in a newly public company and how are they different from those of a private organization.
- How to address any issues that may arise with employees since the pay of the CEO now must be disclosed.
- General compensation concerns faced by the board.

The CEO pay process and the board's role also may undergo a significant transformation when a company transitions from private to public. The board governance process changes, with more significant and formal decision-making responsibilities and public disclosure of the board's process. The disclosure of that information can create an enormous amount of angst for the board and the CEO as the level of pay becomes subject to third-party scrutiny for the first time. Shareholders, their representatives, media, and friends and family all become aware of how, and how much, the CEO has been paid and the wealth that has been accumulated in the company, with shareholders allowed to opine through the company's say-on-pay vote.

Although the new governance and disclosure processes are daunting, a real advantage of this progression is that the board's compensation tools are enhanced. The addition of public-company equity creates a new lever for the board to press to motivate and reward CEO activities. While a potentially unsettling process, a thoughtful approach to developing the CEO's pay program should relieve some of the board's concerns in this new environment and instead become an opportunity to reflect on its principles for developing an effective CEO pay program.

Successfully Transitioning from a Privately Held to a Publicly Traded Company

Retaining and motivating the CEO and other key members of the management team through and following the IPO is important to shareholders, and therefore the success of the offering. A meaningful amount of unvested equity is what shareholders want to see. The opportunity for equity ownership is a powerful motivator that supports executive retention and aligns the interests of executives and the investors; we call this CEO "holding power."

CEO Holding Power and IPO Grants

Pre-IPO equity plans come in all shapes and sizes with unique provisions. Evaluating the amount of equity and the potential value over a three- to five-year period following the IPO under different performance assumptions helps the board evaluate the retentive value of the existing unvested equity grants. It also informs the decision-making process regarding the need and magnitude of a grant to be awarded concurrent with the IPO. This process is as much art as science, with benchmarking providing the framework of what others have done, but with board, executive, and adviser experience, and perhaps potential investor input, providing the qualitative insights.

When IPO grants are made, they are often larger than annual grants and, given the magnitude of the awards, often have a longer vesting period to support CEO retention and to provide balance for the shareholders. This extended vesting cycle creates a staggered value and vesting benefit by allowing post-IPO grants to build value over shorter time frames, creating an equity model that avoids a "cliff vesting" retention drop-off effect and instead results in a steady pattern of outstanding unvested equity to support retention and performance achievement.

The IPO equity grants can be stock options, restricted share/ units or performance-based awards. The vehicle depends on various factors, including share price appreciation, dividends, dilution and the number of participants in the plan. But it is important to reinforce that retention is a primary motivator of these grants and therefore the IPO grant, or at least a significant portion, should be in the form of time-vested stock options, restricted shares/units, or a combination of the two.

Creating the Go-Forward CEO Pay Program

The post-IPO program also needs to be considered during the IPO planning period. The board should review each element of the CEO's pay to be confident that the program is aligned with the business, fair to the new shareholders and compelling to the CEO. The standard elements — base salary, annual and long-term incentives (opportunity and metrics), as well as share ownership guidelines, CIC protection, and other benefit programs — should be evaluated to create an aligned CEO pay program.

Focusing on the traditional elements of pay, base salaries may be adjusted slightly to reflect the increased demands as a public company CEO. It may take some time to get the annual incentive metrics and targets right and to consider the non-financial dashboard metrics described earlier. In any case, LTIs are the most significant element of CEO pay (60 to 70 percent in large mature companies) and, typically, developing the future approach to equity incentives is the most challenging aspect. The use of equity is markedly different in a post-IPO period. While many privately held companies have LTI programs, they look different from public company models — whether in the type and number of vehicles, frequency of the grants, value of the grants or levels of eligibility.

Equity Awards

While the IPO grants are primarily intended to drive CEO retention, the post-IPO awards will include more performance orientation to align with shareholders. This could include a performance shares concept — essentially restricted stock with performance-based vesting that is also leveraged and adjusts the shares received based on performance. We have learned from the market volatility that diversification is important and market practice has evolved so that public companies often use a portfolio concept or a combination of LTI vehicles to balance performance, retention and shareholder alignment. Accordingly, a combination of performance shares and time-vested restricted stock or stock options can be an effective model to align the interests of shareholders and the CEO in the post-IPO pay environment.

Many privately held companies issue one-time equity grants (or make awards more frequently but at irregular intervals); public firms typically grant LTI as an annual element of executive pay. The use of annual LTI grants continually reinforces long-term decision-making and supports executive retention. It may take a new public company a year or two to fully adopt this approach, but it has become the norm in CEO and broader executive pay structuring programs.

Determining the targeted value of these awards is often a new exercise for a public company board. The value is a function of marketplace norms and the board's internally driven desired mix of pay that reinforces the behaviors that the board wants to stimulate. The mix of pay (the percentage of total pay that LTIs represent) is directly aligned with the company's strategy and growth prospects. For example, there are growth-oriented companies where an entrepreneurial and visionary CEO leading the organization is motivated by the benefits of equity ownership — the ability to create and share in the value. Accordingly, in such circumstances, equity-based compensation takes a more significant role in the overall pay program. Contrast that with a non-IPO company, which emphasizes fixed compensation (implying a more mature business or a business in decline) — a pay program that would not be well received by shareholders in an IPO setting.

Equity Dilution

Equity incentive plan dilution informs the decision-making process around the types of awards and the levels of plan participation. The amount of equity to be shared with executives, and the resulting dilutive impact of the equity incentive plan, has become a key discussion point with shareholders in the run-up to the IPO as well as when the post-IPO company makes new requests of shareholders post-IPO. It affects the vehicles (stock options require more shares to deliver competitive value than restricted shares), participation (greater employee participation requires more shares relative to fewer participants) and the values that can be shared (and over what time frame). Market norms and investor returns matter — a recent commercial banking IPO developed its plans within a dilution norm in the 8 to 10 percent range versus a recent technology IPO in which dilution in the upper teens can be the norm.

Overall Compensation Structure

In planning for an IPO, the board's goal is to develop a compensation structure that supports the business and shareholder interests and is compelling in order to retain, motivate, drive behaviors and reward the CEO if the business is successful and provides appropriate returns to shareholders. A continuous reflection of those objectives should create the context and rationale to develop a strategically sound and defensible post-IPO CEO pay program.

Positioning for Growth

Post-IPO is the time for the organization to thrive and flourish. As with anything else, up-front planning and execution of the right levers at the right time make all the difference. Considering CEO succession, CEO performance evaluation and CEO compensation in an integrated way will increase the likelihood of success for the newly public company's strategy. Despite the best intent, organizations that take up these components separately risk loss of focus due to conflicting priorities. The CEO and the board cannot be in sync on what is important if they have not taken the time to clarify, with laser-like precision, what success looks like and how the organization will achieve it. And, lastly, since it is the entire top executive team and not just the CEO that creates enterprise value, this level of clarity and alignment becomes critical for the executive team to in turn create the conditions for enterprise success.

PART IV

The Board Life Cycle

Introduction

By Christine Rivers and Irv Becker

The board life cycle refers to the board's journey: the continuous cycle of development, evaluation and refreshment. It is a journey that begins with selection and succession of directors, but it also continues through their compensation and performance evaluations. These components must be attended to continuously and in an integrated fashion for the board to satisfy its duties. And, when these components are grounded in the organization's strategy, they are not only continuous and related, they have relevance.

This is not easy territory for boards, and there is good reason why it is not. A board is a group of peers, albeit with the nuance of the chair in an oversight role, but, nevertheless, peers who come together and form a bond to execute a role with a high level of public scrutiny. It is quite difficult for a group of peers in this situation to be in any sort of evaluative position with each other. Even when it is clear they have a fiduciary responsibility to do so, it is a difficult activity to both initiate and undertake. They would just as easily avoid these activities — and in many cases they do.

However, progressive and well-governed boards not only initiate these activities regularly, they proactively manage them. That is, they build these activities into their calendar and build processes around them to ensure they receive the focused attention they deserve.

What Does This Look Like?

The process begins with a realization that strategy is at the foundation. "What are the skills and competencies we will need on the board to effectively oversee this organization given its strategy? How are our board members faring against that today? Do we have the right people on the board who can take us into the future?"

Next is the consideration about compensation. "Is our director compensation commensurate with what we are asking them to do? Are we able to attract the right talent to the board given the level of compensation? Or, is it too robust given our needs? Does it send the wrong message to management, our shareholders and other constituencies?"

What about director development? Peer feedback on competencies and behavior can be a powerful tool to help directors understand how their contributions are received. In the absence of assessment and feedback, directors do not have a way of knowing where they stand, which can lead to frustration (especially by those who believe some directors are not doing their job) and missed opportunities. It is surprising to hear that so many board members who have been on their boards for years have never received feedback on how they are doing; in fact it is irresponsible. However, while critically important, these activities are many times overlooked because the board chair or the appropriate committee chair (for example, governance) may not want to initiate them.

The simple solution is to accept that this cycle of activity is part of what the board must do and make it part of the ongoing board process. Board selection, succession, performance evaluation and compensation all should be part of an ongoing process; one that is based on trust, candor and real conversations. Initiated by the chair or lead director (in cases where the CEO is the chair), these activities must be continuous and integrated to be fresh and relevant. This all should be a natural part of the board's life cycle — what directors do, what they talk about, what they worry about. As tough as it is to initiate it, once it becomes part of the way of working, these conversations becomes invaluable.

While a formal process is needed to generate data, there is an informal component that is quite important as well. For example, conducting "debriefs" after every meeting or at key inflection points of an event to ask, "How did we do? Could this have been better? What got in the way?" can be quite powerful and helpful as the board continually strives to improve.

As mentioned, this all is irrelevant unless it is built on company strategy. Whether it is succession planning, performance evaluation or compensation, the strategy must be the foundation as it provides the blueprint for all board requirements. Questions may arise:

- Where is the CEO taking the company?
- As a board, what do we need to possess and do to guide and oversee the CEO and management toward that outcome?
- Are we prioritizing the right things? Are we spending our time on the right activities?
- Do we have people on the board with the experiences we need to guide us in the right direction?
- As a board, are we asking the difficult questions?
- Are we adequately assessing enterprise risk?

These are issues that the board must wrestle with as part of the ongoing process: to stay relevant and aligned. It is the board life cycle, and any board that ignores all or part of these activities or accommodates "the way we always do things" risks missteps that can have significant negative outcomes.

Optimize Organizational Effectiveness

The activities above are the tangible aspects of the board life cycle — the work the board must do. But how should the board act? How can boards approach these activities in a way that enhances meaning, ensures greater purpose and optimizes organizational effectiveness?

The answer is found in what happens in between the activities of the board life cycle: the way directors interact, the relationships they have, the relationship the board builds with the CEO and the senior management team, the way the board and the CEO share information, and the intention of the board to engage in meaningful conversations with each other and with management. It is what happens in between the tangible, concrete activities that essentially speaks to the relationship directors have with each other and with the CEO. That is, it is the tangible components (the activities) supported by the intangible components (the relationships) that make this powerful. Of course, the critical factor here is trust; for if the relationship is not based on trust, it will fall apart quickly, and the effects of loss of trust can be disastrous.

If a board ignores any element of these activities, it is time to ask the question why, and perhaps it is time to refresh the board and its way of working. It is only when the board is operating at its peak performance can an organization be expected to do the same.

CHAPTER 22

Board Evaluation

By Joe Griesedieck and Alanna Conte

oards are increasingly elected to be true strategic assets to
the companies they serve. As such, they can be a source of
unique competitive advantage. Boards that rise to this superior level,
combined with an exceptional leadership team to which the board
serves as a crucial partner, form the foundation of high-performing
companies. High-performing boards and high-performing companies
are not coincidental. High-performing boards provide compliance,
performance and strategic impact through individual director and
total team effectiveness.

Sound judgement and relevant experience and expertise are
critical skills for every director. In helping company leadership to
formulate an achievable long-term strategy, the diverse experiences
and differentiated skillsets on the board can contribute greatly to
the board's ability to provide valuable advice to senior management
and avoid groupthink.

However, simply having the right experiences around the table is
not enough. Boards need to think deeply about the way in which
they carry out their role and the quality of their interactions and
the board's team dynamic. Progressive boards consistently seek
to improve the quality of their interactions and the quality of
decisions they make. High-performing directors always look for
ways to improve their own contribution, support fellow directors

in enhancing their effectiveness, and regularly consider how they and others impact the team dynamic.

Also essential to a board's effectiveness is having an experienced board leader (chairman or lead independent director) who can be a credible bridge between the board and management and is also able to drive a culture of trust, constructive discourse, and continuous improvement around the board table.

Today, high-performing boards take a proactive approach to board evaluation, all to ensure that their members have the relevant knowledge of best practices to maximize their contributions. Boards that regularly undertake a thorough evaluation of their composition and performance, and act upon the resulting recommendations, are more likely to be independent, be aware of threats to the company's business model and strategy, and to identify opportunities for long-term growth.

Since the early 2000s, there has been an increased focus on board evaluation. In fact, it is now a mandatory listing requirement of most stock exchanges for publicly traded organizations. The impetus for the mandatory requirements and the amplified focus is, in part, the corporate scandals which began (but did not end with) Enron, that led many observers to question whether boards were asleep at the wheel. Board evaluation has been embraced as a safety check, providing evidence that boards are armed and able to provide appropriate governance and fiduciary oversight. The practice has extended beyond publicly traded companies to include nonprofit and private organizations.

While there has been an increased reference to board evaluation as an important practice, we have three key observations:

- First, listing requirements are typically not best practices — at best they are minimum requirements. Even at that, other than stipulating that an annual self-evaluation needs to take place, they are not prescriptive and do not typically spell out any further details.
- Second, there is not a common definition and understanding of what board evaluation means, both in terms of scope and approach.
- Third, boards may undertake an evaluation with very different objectives in mind. Some boards take a minimalist approach,

amounting to a "check-the-box" exercise, while others approach evaluations as an opportunity for development and a means to maximize the effectiveness of the board and of the organization.

Board assessment, with a focus on development, is a win-win-win proposition — for the board itself, for the organization and for external stakeholders. Ensuring the most effective board is rewarding to board members; the right skill set among members enables effective decisions, directors are able to contribute to their full potential, conflict is handled appropriately, and processes are in place to ensure that members are truly able to exercise due diligence. The climate becomes more engaging, allowing for a more productive and strategic conversation.

A high-performing board is also of tremendous value to the organization. The board provides effective stewardship, stays away from areas it should not get involved, and reduces potential conflict between the board and CEO by bringing clarity to roles and boundaries. A board held to best practices appropriately focuses on oversight, and also increases the confidence of external stakeholders by knowing that the board is doing the right things.

This chapter:

- Describes the components of a development-focused board evaluation that can be leveraged to allow the board to most effectively fulfill its roles. It addresses three levels of evaluation: the board, committees and directors.
- Discusses various methodologies for conducting the three levels of evaluation, and the advantages and disadvantages of each.
- Raises the importance of soliciting broader input than directors to prevent an insular view. It discusses various perspectives that might be informative.
- Provides a framework that incorporates the various elements into a best practices approach.
- Flags potential pitfalls and critical considerations.

What Is Board Evaluation?

Boards frequently talk about the need for evaluation, but what they specifically mean often varies, and it is not until probing questions are asked that a common understanding is reached. Part of defining board evaluation hinges on understanding the objectives of its undertaking.

Defined at its simplest and narrowest, board evaluation refers to a self-assessment — often by questionnaire completed by board members — focused on their perceptions regarding how well the board functions. While this check-the-box exercise meets regulatory requirements, it is of somewhat limited value from a development perspective.

The first issue is common to all self-assessments; it presupposes a certain amount of self-awareness and sufficient context to be able to answer questions in a helpful manner. Perceptions are not always objective and reality based. To illustrate, asking directors to rate the effectiveness of board meetings, when they may not truly appreciate what an effective meeting looks like, may not yield much useful and actionable data. Or, asking directors how well they feel that the board is meeting its roles may not be particularly instructive without the benefit of truly understanding what the various board roles are, and without input from others who interact with the board. If the goal of board evaluation is to optimize board effectiveness (to in turn, enable organization effectiveness), then a more expansive definition, and subsequently robust approach, is appropriate.

As Figure 22-1 illustrates, a full board evaluation actually occurs on three interrelated levels: the board, committees of the board and directors, including the chair of the board and committee chairs.

An Expanded Scope at the Board Level

Beginning with the board as a unit, a robust evaluation should consider multiple facets, including:

- The composition/structure of the board;
- The roles of the board; and
- Board processes.

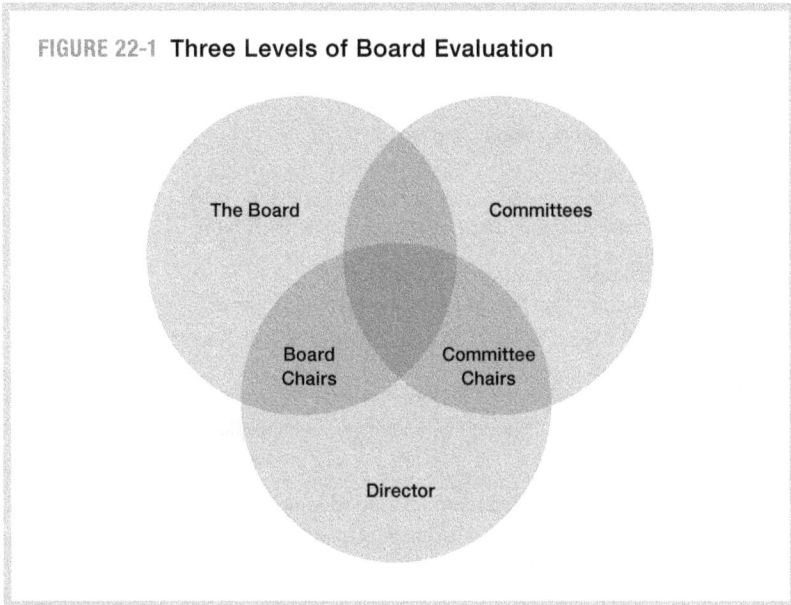

FIGURE 22-1 **Three Levels of Board Evaluation**

The Board

Committees

Board
Chairs

Committee
Chairs

Director

Board Composition

Board composition fundamentally answers the question: who is on the board? It is not about individual director assessment (although that does provide insight), but rather looking at the board as a unit to ensure that, together, members have all critical areas covered, and that the composition enables the board to most effectively meet stakeholder needs.

Determining Needed Skills for the Board

An appropriate starting point is considering skills and expertise; it quickly becomes evident that one size does not fit all. Board composition (see Table 22-2) assesses the extent to which the board has the right knowledge, skill sets and mix to:

- Provide effective oversight
- Deliver strategic insight
- Advise and mentor the CEO and management
- Manage enterprise risk.

Simply filling a board with "big names," which may have been fine in the past, is no longer sufficient. The combined skill sets need

2

82

> **TABLE 22-2** **Evaluating Board Composition — Illustrative Questions**
>
> **Questions to consider regarding mix:**
> - ❯ Does the board reflect a diversity of perspectives?
> - ❯ Does the portfolio of skills and expertise reflect the full range of what is required to deliver the strategy over the foreseeable future?
>
> **Questions to consider regarding board size:**
> - ❯ Are there enough directors to effectively staff committees?
> - ❯ How does the board size compare to boards of similar "benchmark" organizations?
> - ❯ Does the board size hamper decision making?
> - ❯ Does each board member add sufficient and unique value to warrant being on the board?
>
> **Questions to consider regarding independence:**
> - ❯ Is there an appropriate ratio of external to internal directors?
> - ❯ Do directors demonstrate the confidence and experience to effectively challenge the CEO and management?

to adequately reflect the strategic direction, industry and stage of life of the organization, so that board members are able to make informed decisions without being completely reliant on the CEO.

Determining the right skills begins with strategy and maintains a future focus — what is required over the next three to five years. This future lens mitigates perpetuating the status quo without due consideration for what is needed at the board level to match various organization inflection points.

The most effective means of assessing the portfolio of skills is using a skills matrix that distills the critical skills needed on a particular board, at a particular point in time, given the organization's context. As illustrated in Table 22-3, these skills form the column headings.

Covered Skills and Potential Gaps

The next step is to determine which skills are covered by which director(s), and to identify any critical holes, which could lead to blind spots. Each director is assessed against each skill area. For the purposes of looking at the portfolio of skills, the individual names are less of interest than the overall view. When current or future gaps are identified, the board has alternatives that it might pursue, ranging from board training, to specifically seeking directors with a particular skill set, to relying on external advisers who work closely with the board.

Skills matrices yield powerful insights about a board, beyond skill deficits. First, if the skills matrix focuses on the expertise that is demonstrated at the board level, it sometimes may reveal a discrepancy with the skills a director possesses, based on his/her experience. This disconnect can often be addressed through greater role clarity for individual directors, an initial orientation discussion regarding why they, in particular, were recruited for the board, and even role descriptions that spell out specifically the skills, knowledge and expertise that the individual is expected to bring to discussions. This is often a step that is missing from the onboarding process.

Skills Portfolio and Board Diversity

Looking at the portfolio of skills provides insight into the mix of board members and overall diversity. For example, if each board member brings the same three skills to the table, and there are gaps in other areas, clearly there is an issue. While this conclusion may seem obvious, recruitment and nominating practices often indirectly

TABLE 22-3 **Sample Skills Matrix**

	Human Resources / Compensation	Global Operations	Finance Experience	Lean Manufacturing	General Management Experience (CEO)	Industry Expertise	Merger and Acquisition Expertise	Technology	Etc.
Director 1									
Director 2									
Etc.									

lead to this being the case: relying on recommendations from current board members or recruiting all board members from the same pool can often lead to directors with similar skill sets, but also with other similar attributes — most typically: white males of a certain age, and past or current CEOs.

While board recruitment has become more sophisticated, driven in many cases by regulatory requirements, there clearly is room for many boards to develop. Attention is needed to the specific knowledge and expertise that each director has; otherwise, the result can be each member adding value in similar ways, and not providing sufficient breadth. As organizations reach different inflection points, new skills may be required. A domestic company seeking to expand its global reach would benefit from a board member with global expertise who could advise, open doors, and identify and manage risks. As technology becomes more complex, new expertise may be required. The challenge for the board is to ensure adequate coverage of all key areas while limiting the board to a size that does not hamper decision making.

Further, diversity makes good business sense. The research shows that introducing diversity to the board — beginning with, but not limited to, skills — allows for problems to be considered from different perspectives and multiple angles, prevents "groupthink," challenges the status quo, reflects the diversity in the customer base, and can enhance the organization's reputation and brand.

The mistake many boards make is to introduce a single individual from a diversity perspective; it places undue burden on one individual and, without a critical mass, the impact is not likely to be felt.

While diversity is clearly desirable, it is not the end goal. The goal is to have a board best structured to optimize its effectiveness. This means that diversity should always be balanced with ensuring the board is not so heterogeneous that: it cannot function as a group; it creates a situation where too many agendas are put forward; conflict with management; takes up disproportionate time; and it has difficulty reaching decisions.

Board Renewal and Development

Fourth, the skills matrix is invaluable in planning for board renewal. Deficiencies may be identified where education and development are required for the board as a whole. The process also can flag where an individual may no longer be adding sufficient and unique value to justify "using up" a seat, particularly in light of the need to balance skill coverage with a board size that does not impede decision making. It speaks to the point that one's relevance for a board may not be permanent — it is a state, not a trait. The issue is not about age, but about currency and relevance, so introducing director terms or retirement ages does not get at the core. Often these measures are put in place to preempt a difficult conversation.

The discussion of ongoing relevance and value-add is often the most difficult for a board chair, but with the growing complexity of risk and accelerating pace of change introduced by technology, it is a discussion that should be held with more frequency. Interestingly, sometimes just going through the skills review process can promote personal reflection and yield a more accurate self-assessment. This may allow a director to make their own decision to retire from the board. At the very least, having data in hand from an evaluation can better ground a difficult conversation that is never a commentary on career or past accomplishments, but a focus on what is required by the organization to move forward and effectively provide good governance and oversight.

Independence

A fifth issue affecting board composition is independence; this is more than satisfying regulatory standards regarding independence. While many board evaluations focus on ratios of internal versus external directors, and whether directors have a material financial interest in the organization, a truer measure may be the extent to which the board is independent-minded. True independence of mind requires sufficient knowledge, skills and competencies to be able to challenge effectively, and it also requires processes to ensure that vital information is shared in a productive way, appropriate time allotted to critical issues, and opportunity to discuss issues fully using in-camera sessions.

Board Roles

The next component at the board level that should be considered in a board evaluation is board roles. Board roles have become increasingly demanding, both with the complexity of risks that organizations must consider, and with the scrutiny that directors face. Boards can and should play multiple roles, and part of a board evaluation can focus on the extent to which they are fulfilling each of these roles. Four specific roles are discussed in Table 22-4.

TABLE 22-4 **Illustrative Questions for Assessing Board Roles**

> Does the board set and measure annual CEO performance objectives?
> Does the board proactively plan for CEO succession, and monitor that internal candidates are actively developed?
> Does the board monitor human capital considerations, such as turnover and succession for mission critical roles, development of bench strength, and ethics?
> Does the board maintain an emergency CEO succession plan?
> Does the board effectively identify and manage risks at the enterprise level?
> Does the board advise, mentor and develop the CEO?
> Does the board proactively communicate with key stakeholders?
> Does the board approve and provide input into strategy?

Enterprise Risk Management

Enterprise risk management has become a major concern delving into areas that may not have even been on the radar 10 years ago, such as cybersecurity, environmental and social impact, and reputational concerns. This is in addition to issues about corruption, supply chain and manufacturing on a global scale, as technology now allows even smaller, less sophisticated organizations to expand their global footprint. Not knowing about working conditions and safety practices in overseas plants can spell huge reputational and financial risks for an organization, as witnessed by the brand damage to certain clothing retailers from lack of sufficient international oversight. A board that is aware of risks, that can speak from experience, and that can provide counsel on navigating risks, is invaluable.

One risk area that is often overlooked relates to human capital. Boards should be requiring executives to provide a human capital dashboard report, no different than a financial report, on a regular basis. It should include measures of overall turnover, but in particular, turnover for mission critical roles; investments in human capital; development of bench strength; and employee engagement. Relatedly, the board should ensure that succession plans are in place for mission critical roles.

Strategy Advice

Traditionally, the board has played a critical role in approving strategy. Of late, there has been some movement toward having boards more involved in the co-formulation of strategy to ensure complete understanding and buy-in if they are to be held accountable. Execution of strategy, however, should remain the purview of management, with appropriate controls and reporting to the board.

CEO Succession Planning and CEO Evaluation

Two board roles which often receive less attention, but are also of critical importance, are CEO succession planning and CEO evaluation and development. While boards are typically on top of ensuring that strategic and financial objectives are met, CEOs are not always held

TABLE 22-5 **Illustrative Questions to Evaluate Board Processes**

> Does the board engage in effective renewal processes (succession planning, ongoing development, evaluation nomination of committee chairs)?
> Are new members effectively oriented to the board?
> Are board mandates and role descriptions in place?
> Does the board have norms of operation?
> Does the board effectively manage an annual agenda?
> Are meetings held with the appropriate frequency?
> Are meetings run effectively and do they accomplish clear goals?
> Does the board receive information critical to decision making in a timely manner?
> Does the board communicate effectively with management?

accountable for making sure that the right and engaging culture is created. This includes measuring and monitoring employee turnover and investing in high-potential individuals within the organization. Boards should be routinely asking questions about investment in human capital.

Board Processes

A board evaluation should consider all board processes associated with arming directors to best perform their jobs. The starting point is ensuring that there are clear norms in place for how the board operates, how decisions are made, and how the board engages in development (See Table 22-5). Board processes should also follow the complete life cycle of directors, including the following:

- Identifying, nominating and orienting new board members
- Establishing and managing director terms
- Providing ongoing education and feedback
- Preparing for board succession
- Identifying committee chairs
- Assessing communication systems within the board and with the organization
- Managing meetings and agendas, including the frequency and focus of meetings.

The Scope of a Committee Evaluation

Just as boards should be assessed to ensure optimal performance, so too should committees of the board. The starting point is to ensure that the right committees are in place, and that they are staffed with the right people. Much of the scope of committee evaluation is not dissimilar to how boards are assessed.

The following questions would typically need to be addressed in a committee assessment:

- Are committees staffed with the right directors (mix, independence, skills)?
- Is the size appropriate for decision making?
- Are there effective processes in place for orienting and developing directors for the committee?

- Are agendas and communication packages circulated sufficiently in advance?
- Are meetings run effectively?
- Are meetings held with the appropriate frequency?
- Are directors sufficiently available?
- Is there ample and complete discussion of issues?
- Is information sufficient to make decisions, and is it provided in a timely manner?
- Are decisions reported back to the board in an effective manner?

The Scope of Director Evaluations

Assessment of directors is perhaps the most contentious of areas from an evaluation perspective. For many directors it may be the first time they have been assessed and received any kind of feedback in many years, and the process has to be handled sensitively. While some director evaluations focus on an assessment of contributions, the assessment can be strengthened by expanding the scope to focus on two additional components: (1) the skills, knowledge and expertise directors bring to the table, and (2) the behavioral competencies they display.

The expectation around knowledge, skills and expertise is that each director has several critical skills needed by the board. Individual directors should not be expected to cover every skill necessary to the board. On the other hand, the individuals should be expected to display the full range of behavioral competencies of a high-performing director.

An assessment should also consider the personal behaviors and motivations of directors. Understanding the differentiating behaviors is essential to ensuring the right board dynamics, helping prevent a single-minded pursuit of results at all costs, and promoting an equal focus on how results are obtained. These are key to sustained performance. While a personal focus on corporate achievement is important, it needs to be displayed in combination with other behaviors. A singular pursuit can lead to short cuts, ethical lapses and short-term thinking. A director who loses control, cannot hear others' perspectives, lacks a moral compass, or cannot work with others despite exceptional knowledge and expertise, is rarely a long-term asset. Similarly, directors who are too easily swayed and lack the confidence to express their views are not as effective as they might be.

The director assessment can flag potential issues with specific directors, highlight when currency may be lacking, and raise concerns with the profile of the board as a whole.

While there is a range of important competencies, three of the most critical ones are the confidence to challenge, emotional control and listening with respect. Together they reflect an ability to appropriately weigh and challenge others' perspectives, and to be able to do so without derailing a discussion with emotional outbursts. Also important is ensuring directors understand the boundaries of their roles and maintain the separation between oversight and management.

Director assessments should be approached with a note of caution, as they can go horribly wrong if not handled appropriately. The assessment process should be transparent to all. Before embarking on this course, three key decisions need to be made:

- Who will provide input,
- Who will see the feedback, and
- Who will debrief everyone on their results individually and any developmental action required?

The first decision — who should provide input will be discussed more fully below. Typically, it is the board chair and the individual director alone who see their own feedback, although there are variations. In some cases, the governance or HR committee may also see results. In other cases, boards may decide that for the first round of assessments, personal feedback is shared only with the individual director. In terms of providing input, unless the chair is highly skilled, it typically is recommended that an external, trained party provide the feedback to the directors, while the chair can be present. This is to ensure that it is delivered in the most impactful and sensitive manner, that relationships are preserved, and that the focus is on development.

Board and Committee Chairs

A special subset of directors are chairs of the board and of committees. A board evaluation should consider the extent to which they:

- Provide appropriate leadership and direction — both to the board/committee and to management
- Promote full discussion and invite input
- Set the appropriate tone for meetings
- Manage conflict
- Allow for dissent to be expressed
- Provide needed information to make decisions
- Run effective meetings
- Provide feedback to directors, the CEO and other key executives
- Manage board processes.

What Methodologies Can Be Used to Evaluate the Board?

Now that the scope of board evaluations has been defined, it is also important to consider the range of options for how to conduct them. There are four main methodologies, each with its own advantages and disadvantages. Some can be used as stand-alone approaches, while others are best used in combination with other approaches. See Table 22-6.

Surveys

Paper or online surveys are typically the most efficient approach. While these are inexpensive, allow a wide array of questions to be asked, and are sufficient to indicate that a board has met listing requirements, they typically do not yield the best and most actionable insight.

Adding a degree of customization to a survey, and probing issues that may be of particular importance for one's organization/board, certainly help enhance its value and the actionable insight that can be derived. Surveys can include peer assessments as a component, whereby each director is rated in terms of contributions, knowledge, skills and expertise, and competencies. Some organizations choose to do "real time" polls, to allow for an on-the-spot discussion around results. While this type of approach can be effective, typically it is best reserved for pulse checks, to assess progress

---

TABLE 22-6 Board Evaluation Methodologies

Surveys:
> Can be paper-based or administered electronically
> A variation is real-time polling
> Cost efficient
> Allow for a wide range of questions to be asked of a large number of people
> Unless customized, provide the least actionable insight

Interviews:
> Typically provide more candid and fuller responses than survey
> Allow for probing and discussion
> Can be time-consuming and more costly than surveys
> Limit to the number of questions that can be asked in a reasonable time frame
> Requires some expertise in design, delivery and consolidation

Research:
> Focuses on measurable and observable areas, and compares to benchmark data
> Does not provide a complete picture
> Best used in conjunction with other approaches

Observation
> Allows a third-party assessment of board dynamics, which can lead to coaching and development
> Can sometimes lead to "playing to the camera," but this dissipates over time
> Limited in application
> Best used in conjunction with other approaches

---

against particular areas, rather than as a baseline survey, as only a few areas can be adequately explored at a time.

Interviews

The second most prevalent approach uses interviews. While this approach often yields rich data, it is difficult to obtain the breadth of coverage that is possible through a survey approach. Typically, interviews are conducted by external parties as this tends to elicit the most candid responses. Interviews can be more costly than surveys and require skill in designing the questions, conducting the interview and consolidating qualitative data in a useful manner. Interviews can stand alone, but they are often used in conjunction with surveys to flesh out responses and probe areas that may be more sensitive.

Research

The third approach is research based. It is predicated on the fact that asking for perceptions should be limited to non-observable/ verifiable areas. For example, asking about perceptions of ratios of independent to external directors may be less important than actually measuring the ratio, and comparing it to benchmark data from boards of similar sizes, stage of growth and industries. The research approach includes review of documentation, such as mandates and charters, board and committee minutes, communications, and strategy documents. Research is best combined with other methodologies.

Observation

The last approach is observation. It involves using an external third party to assess how the board, committee and directors interact in meetings. It allows for specific and targeted feedback around both individual and group dynamics. When observation is first introduced, it can lead to a bit of "playing to the camera," but over time, interactions become fairly normalized.

Each approach is useful and serves a purpose, but to gain the most from an evaluation, a multi-method approach is recommended — beginning with surveys, fleshing out further in interviews, and reviewing all objective measures. Adding on observations further amplifies the impact.

Who Should Provide Input to Board Evaluation?

One last decision needs to be made in designing an effective board evaluation: who assesses the board, committees and directors? While there is no one best answer, typically expanding input from outside the directors themselves provides more useful data. The key is to begin with the questions that are to be answered, then determining who are in the best positions to provide perspective.

Clearly board members need to provide feedback at the board level, but given the role of the board, input provided by executives who interact with the board is also critical. For example, asking directors about the extent to which they advise and mentor the CEO may yield very different responses than asking the CEO the same question. Executives may also have a different perspective of how the board functions at meetings, the quality of skills and expertise at the board table, and the degree to which directors respect boundaries of their governance role.

Two additional perspectives might also be considered at the board level: key stakeholder groups and analysts. In a world of activist shareholders, online (mis)information, and social media, boards are being increasingly called upon to transparently reach out to their stakeholders to manage risk. Sharing information and educating shareholders on vision and direction in the good times builds support and helps CEOs withstand scrutiny during bad times. By involving investors and analysts in board evaluations, boards can stay on top of how they are being perceived and build defensive strategies around the conversations shareholders are having, as well as the key points that attract activist shareholders.

At the committee level, members should clearly provide input, but it is also helpful to gather input from executives who support the committee.

Director assessments tend to be more contentious, in terms of who provides input. Directors are often uncomfortable providing peer assessments, but simply completing a self-assessment is of limited value. It is recommended that director assessments follow a 360-degree approach, similar to what is typically adopted for executives, whereby they complete a self-assessment, the board or committee chair provides insight, fellow directors provide input, and finally, as appropriate, executives provide input as well. More reliable and valid data come from asking for input from multiple perspectives. This approach prevents an insular view of how the board is performing.

Putting It Together — A Framework

If the objective is to create an actionable developmental plan, a more robust approach is required than simply an off-the-shelf survey. It is important to begin from an understanding of the organization's context, so as to identify appropriate comparators, and critical requirements. This step focuses the evaluation on what is important for the particular organization.

Further, using multiple methods to assess the board moves beyond self-assessments, to a more accurate read of how the board is performing. Finally, any board evaluation that does not end in an actionable plan that is monitored and reported on is of limited value. Identifying two to three high-priority areas for the board as a whole, for committees, and for each director should be the outcome for the year, with a planned revisit (See Table 22-7).

TABLE 22-7 Annual Reassessment

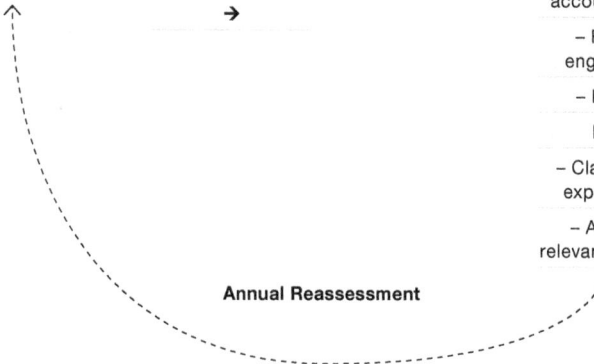

Determine Context	Specify Requirements	Assess Against Requirements	Take Action
Company strategy	Compositions, size, mix, independence	Surveys	**Composition**
Mission		Interviews	– Changes in who or size
Stage of life cycle	Compentencies: who, technical, behavioral	Competency assessments	**Compentencies**
Regulateion		Observation	– Develop
Benchmarks/best practices	Processes: meetings, information, governanace	Document review	– Recruit
→		→	– Separate
	Mandate		**Processes**
	→		– Classify inter-accountabilities
↗			– Rules of engagement
			– Improve
			Roles
			– Clarify roles, expectations
			– Act on all relevant mandates

Annual Reassessment

Any evaluation that results in no areas for development is typically a red flag that there is something more afoot.

Critical Considerations

There are two key considerations that need to be addressed prior to launching any board evaluation. The first, largely discussed above, is around the delicacy of assessing directors. Prior to launching any director assessment, it is paramount that the process has been thought through. Beyond who provides input, who sees the data and who provides feedback, there has to be a common understanding as to what happens with the feedback and what post-assessment expectations are. Specific questions to be considered include:

- Can poor assessment results lead to asking a director to step down from the board, or are they meant to be purely developmental?
- Is development required, and how will it be monitored?
- Are documents maintained?

The last question flags a larger consideration; board evaluations are likely discoverable. A board evaluation may reveal weaknesses at the board level that could be used in claims against the organization and its directors. Before embarking on any evaluation, it is important to have a well-defined process in place regarding documentation, discarding documents and minutes with regularity, and recordkeeping, and it is appropriate to seek the advice of counsel to build in safeguards.

Conclusion

In sum, the impact and value derived from board evaluation can be tremendous, but they are also a function of the effort put in. The more robust and thoughtful the approach, the more actionable the insight that emerges.

CHAPTER 23

Board Succession Management

By Christine Rivers, Connie Schroyer and Robert Hallagan

Continuity within executive leadership, board membership, and board governance enables boards to understand and effectively oversee short- and long-term strategy. Shareholders are well served when board membership includes people with key skills, including experiences and characteristics that support strategic direction and implementation. This reduces not just the risk of poor controls, but also the related risk of not responding with focus on the current and projected environment. Likewise, annual assessment of directors to ensure continued relevance and fit can provide for planned and organized refreshment that highlight new perspectives, experiences and contributions. Governance committees do well to consider both optimal turnover and succession to the board.

This chapter:

- Describes the role of the board vis-a-vis management in creating the company's strategy.
- Addresses the skills, expertise and experiences that may be sought in board candidates.
- Examines the processes involved in the search for board members, including strategic succession management and long-term planning that approaches the search from the perspective of creating a "fit for purpose" board.

- Discusses the importance of a formal program for onboarding directors and suggests typical components of a well-designed onboarding process.

Formation of Strategy

Many boards today participate much more in strategy formulation with management than ever before; this is in comparison to when a board's role was more oversight and approval than real stewardship. In fact, boards may now more actively assume their oversight role while management drives the action plans and measurements.

Progressive boards aim to optimize strategy formulation by processing distinct inputs from a variety of sources and perspectives. The synthesis that emerges can be stronger than any single point of view because this type of environmental scanning avoids the pitfalls of "groupthink" and the challenging dialectic hones the perspectives of both board and management. Each participant in this endeavor sharpens their own understanding. They challenge their own thinking while addressing the concerns and hopes of their colleagues. Together, their focused response to a plethora of opportunities transcends the older process where management developed a strategy, with or without consulting help, and a board stamped its approval.

Director Experience

To drive such a robust development and delineation of long-term strategy, boards require a diversity of skills and experience. Governance committees have the task of inventorying the areas of knowledge, skills and experiences that currently fit the chosen direction and determining which other areas should be included as the future unfolds and strategies evolve.

Also, the mix of personal characteristics that have been effective in the current culture can point to ways to add point and counterpoint to the board. For example, boards can utilize a complement of assertive versus studious types. Some directors should be well versed in finance, while others should bring an understanding of operating areas such as manufacturing, sales cultures or lines of distribution. Consideration of these experiences in future directors brings focus to the recruitment and selection and provides a template for director evaluation and personal growth.

The question of when and where to begin is defined by whether the board considers this activity as strategic or tactical. That is, a tactical activity serves to fill a current need, as required by a director leaving or some other reason requiring the addition of a director. A strategic approach takes a long-term view, is a continuous conversation and evolves in line with the evolution of the company's strategy.

Strategic board succession has the guiding principle of "the right people at the right time." This raises important questions:

- What experiences do we need on the board next, given where our organization is going?
- What upcoming tough decisions do we expect to have to make?
- What risks will we face?
- Do we have directors on our board who have lived through these scenarios before, and were there to contribute to their organization's successful navigation through them?

In consideration of these questions, strategic boards will evolve with the times and take into account how current events inform board needs. Consider the events of 2020: the global pandemic and social unrest. These events have put a spotlight on the composition and role of boards like never before. While high-performing boards regularly take steps to identify, assess and manage risk, few boards were prepared for the degree of upheaval their organizations would face with even one of these crises, much less two. Many board chairs lamented the lack of a playbook for these unprecedented times and even those whose organizations encountered significant crises in the past admitted there was little take away from those experiences to guide them through this.

As always, the best defense against crises is good governance. There is an abundance of evidence that demonstrates that good governance, well thought out processes, procedures, protocols, norms and rules lead to good business judgment. However, the best governance practices are only as good as the people implementing them. Unprecedented times call for board composition to be "fit for purpose"; meaning fit for the times and relevant for the organization it oversees.

While it is true that a particular skill and experience set must be identified across the board, the competencies of each individual director are of paramount importance — not only to navigate the good times, but to navigate the turbulence that can occur. Where there is no playbook, boards must rely on their own ability to chart a course and support management in steering through uncharted waters. This requires cognitive horsepower of each member and cognitive diversity across the board.

Cognitive diversity is achieved by assembling a board that is made up of people who have varied life and work experiences and draw on those to think differently. Bringing a diverse group together typically enhances debate, leading to more questioning of the dominant logic and a willingness to do things differently and perhaps more creatively. This is important in normal times, when there is always an opportunity to improve, but becomes particularly important in times of unique challenge and significant disruption. When cognitive diversity is sought out, coupled with good governance, the odds of the board being a true strategic asset to the organization significantly increase.

Diversity of experiences, skills and characteristics helps boards avoid blind spots, groupthink and the dangers of stagnation. Assembling the board this way is sound practice as the board can now draw a straight line between its discernment of candidates and the requirements of the roles to be filled. Knowing what you are looking for increases the probability of finding it. Employing strategic succession management principles to board succession insures a comprehensive and on-going assessment and matching of characteristics and challenges as the future unfolds.

Starting the Board Search

With an agreed assessment of needs, the governance committee can make inquiries. There are more people seeking board membership than there are spaces to be filled. Commissioning research on available people, conducted either internally or by third parties, indicates where prospective candidates can be found. Search firms can be engaged to supply a bevy of candidates within the pools that the board suggests being investigated.

Initial contacts should be positive, representing the company well and should include a discussion of the time commitments, investment opportunities and requirements, committee work, and overall expectations. Members unable to participate in at least 75 percent of meetings are usually noted publicly, so understanding the time involved and how it fits into personal circumstances should be handled upfront.

Focusing the Board Search

A company may have a governance committee that looks over the general fit of proposed candidates with the profile and whittles down to the best few who can fill the most urgent roles. Many organizations conduct some form of assessment of the best few board candidates to ensure that they fit the diverse profile.

After an assessment report is considered by the governance committee, it can be shared with the full board for discussion and endorsement to move to the next stage of the process. An opportunity to meet with the full board in a formal or informal setting should allow the board to put context around the assessment report and make a final recommendation. And so, with agreement on the profile, the role to be filled and an assessment report, a formal background check is in order. Assuming no potential concerns are uncovered, the full board then should be in a good position to act in good faith on the next step — based on the time horizon of the need for that particular candidate's profile. Unlike more tactical board succession, strategic succession planning, by nature of its long-term time horizon, may not have a need for that particular requirement for a few years. Often at this point, the message to those not chosen, as they may not fit the requirements outlined at this time, is to "stay tuned." In strategic board succession, needs are always evolving and the board could have a much different set of needs in the future. Having vetted candidates in the wings is helpful to ensure the desired continuity while maintaining friendly relationships with candidates who may or may not ever be selected.

This process may also provide an opportunity for some creativity. For example, many boards have created ancillary and ad hoc committees for special purposes, requiring unique skill sets. At times, these "directors in waiting" are drawn from these committees for future full board membership. Not only does it provide an opportunity for the board to work with each member in an exploratory way, but it also gives the prospective director a way to observe the full board and decide if membership is right for them.

Onboarding New Directors

Onboarding is a very important succession activity. New board members are not likely to be thoroughly versed on industry trends, current regulations, market dynamics, the internal financial reporting system, the history of the board and the culture of the organization. Management should participate in a formal onboarding program so that the new member is apprised of strengths, weaknesses, challenges, quirks and the operating model of the organization. Chief financial officers may explain the process that leads to the pertinent financials, how these numbers are derived and why they are important for measuring performance.

The lead director, the board chair, the head of investor relations and the CEO should spend time explaining the culture of the board and the organization, the usual mode of operating, the past and current interaction of the board with management, how decisions are made and what analysts' expectations might be for the company.

The general counsel should formally discuss the legal requirements of board membership, current litigation and relationships with regulators. Marketing, manufacturing, supply chain and human resources also have important stories to tell. Members should have a first-hand opportunity to observe manufacturing, distribution and employee interaction. Ideally, tours of facilities and opportunities to speak with management and employees should be arranged. Management hosts should neither stage-manage the encounter nor sugar-coat it; these kinds of experiences can provide a primary source for developing accurate perceptions of the organization. Management also should demonstrate the appropriate relationship between it and the board.

Formal seminars are available with various board organizations where directors can learn from other directors inside and outside their own industry. Networking provides sources to address unanticipated questions. Best practices have a way of floating all boats.

Putting It All Together

In sum, a board wants to know:

- What it needs in its members,
- How to specify and describe those needs,
- Where to find appropriate candidates,
- How it should assess candidates, and
- How it will onboard new directors.

Doing so is good for shareholders, helpful for current board members and outstanding for those chosen to fill the available roles. Well-formed boards contain members who can develop a good working relationship with their CEOs for the purpose of challenging, mentoring, intelligence gathering and support for the benefit of their management team. The board needs the right set of skills and experiences to make that happen. So, when board succession is well planned and well executed, boards can choose the best available candidates and not hastily fill an unanticipated need. The task of overseeing strategy, offering direction, being ahead of trends and staying within regulations is enhanced by a deliberate and healthy process. Good governance supports good leadership.

CHAPTER 24

Board Compensation

By Brian Tobin and Rachel Jay

The Sarbanes-Oxley Act of 2002 ushered in the current era of governance and oversight responsibility for all directors and led to significant changes in compensation design and total compensation levels for outside directors. Subsequent legislation and rulemaking, including enhanced proxy disclosure rules, expanded governance and compensation standards, and new listing requirements, have affected director pay programs.

These legislative and regulatory reforms, coupled with increased scrutiny from various stakeholders, have resulted in a steady expansion of the duties and responsibilities for outside (nonemployee) directors at publicly traded companies. Shareholders, legislators, regulators and proxy advisory firm groups have increased their demands on boards. Accordingly, the roles and expectations of boards have changed substantially. Directors must provide independent oversight and informed advice. The need has grown for a more nuanced understanding of multiple areas, including strategy, finance, marketing, technology and regulations. Time commitments and involvement levels of board members have increased. To an even greater extent than before, directors are faced with the possibility of public exposure (and even litigation) for their decisions.

With the dramatic rise in the complexity, risks and challenges that boards now face, companies need to take a broader view of how they think about board service. This broader view considers the linkage that exists between three elements of the board life cycle: succession, performance evaluation and compensation. In the same manner, this new way of thinking about board service considers the relationships between boards and CEOs, the relative responsibilities of both, and how they can communicate effectively with the various constituencies they serve. Membership on a board of directors is a job that must be navigated with the utmost prudence, discretion and thoughtfulness.

This chapter:

- Addresses the overall compensation of directors and board structure.
- Considers trends and best practices in director pay programs.
- Examines the concept and role of the executive and non-executive board chair.
- Notes the previous discussion of director stock ownership guidelines in Chapter 12.
- Contrasts the roles of CEO and board chairman and provides reasons why a company might want to separate the two positions.

Board Compensation Trends and Developments

Although total compensation levels and mixes have varied across industries and in relation to company size, traditionally the compensation package for outside directors at publicly traded companies included:

- Annual cash retainer
- Committee chair cash retainers
- Lead director cash retainer
- Meeting fees (board and/or committee)
- Benefits/perquisites (e.g., matching gift programs, compensation deferral opportunities)
- Equity compensation.

Director pay commonly has been linked with company size, with larger companies awarding higher cash retainers and total compensation to directors.

While similarities exist when comparing current trends to historical director pay practices (i.e., level and mix of pay continue to differ across industries; total compensation levels are correlated to company size; the use of annual cash retainers and equity awards are the primary elements of director pay), several new developments regarding the structure and form of director pay are evident in the current marketplace.

Elimination of Board and Committee Meeting Fees

The elimination of fees paid to directors for board and committee meeting attendance has been a growing trend. Where the use of meeting fees has been discontinued, companies are increasing annual cash retainers to compensate directors for meeting preparation and attendance. Companies that use this approach commonly cite the benefits associated with the simplification of the design and administration of their director compensation programs and the removal of the need to define what constitutes a meeting for fee-payment purposes. Among companies that have retained meeting fees for directors, a minority approach is to provide for payment of meeting fees only after attendance at a pre-defined number of board or committee meetings in a single year.

Increased Focus on Work and Pay at the Committee Level

Regulatory changes continue to increase director responsibilities and oversight resulting in more work performed at the committee level. Companies traditionally have provided additional cash retainers to the chair of a standing board committee (e.g., audit, compensation, nominating, governance) in recognition of the additional duties and time involved in chairing a committee. Additionally, the audit committee chair typically earns a premium over the other committee chairs. While increases in compensation committee chair retainers have been common with enhanced scrutiny on executive pay practices, a gap between retainers paid to chairs of the audit and compensation committees continues to exist at many companies.

Another way that companies are recognizing the workload, including responsibilities related to risk management, for non-chair members at the committee level is to pay additional annual cash retainers to non-chair members of the committees instead of meeting fees.

Shift to Full-Value Equity Awards

Mirroring executive pay practices, director compensation programs have increasingly moved toward full-value awards (restricted shares or common stock) to deliver equity-based pay, with stock option use becoming a less prevalent practice. For director pay programs, the decline in stock option grants may be due in part to a concern that options could encourage inappropriate risk taking, as these awards deliver value only where there is appreciation in the share price.

While full-value awards are common, attaching performance conditions is virtually nonexistent. Similar to the concerns related to using stock options, performance-based awards may create improper incentives for directors.

The most prevalent method used to determine the size of equity-based director pay continues to be the use of a fixed dollar value, rather than determining the equity award based on a fixed number of shares.

Vesting Periods for Equity Awards Reduced to One Year or Eliminated

The typical approach is to vest full-value equity awards within one year of grant. As companies move to declassify their boards in response to pressure from shareholder advisory groups, this trend likely will continue with companies using vesting schedules of one year or less to align the vesting term with the directors' annual service period. Similarly, a short vesting period for director annual equity awards can be viewed as a "best practice," as it is thought to maximize director independence because a continued service relationship is not required for a director to receive compensation.

Equity Election and Use of Deferral Programs

As director compensation levels have increased, so have the number of companies that allow directors to elect to receive additional equity awards in lieu of cash retainers or meeting fees. This practice serves to further align director interests with those of shareholders and assists directors in meeting required stock ownership levels. Similarly, a common practice at larger publicly traded companies is to require or permit directors to defer all or a portion of their cash compensation or equity awards.

Director Stock Ownership Guidelines and Holding/Retention Requirements

Various types of stock ownership guidelines and holding period/retention requirements for companies' senior executives and board members are discussed in Chapter 12. Although less common than for executives (especially at smaller companies), boards are increasingly determining that the use of director stock ownership guidelines and holding/retention requirements can contribute to the goal of aligning the interests of nonemployee directors at a publicly traded company with those of its long-term shareholders. Increased focus by activist shareholders and proxy advisory groups has generated pressure to improve the alignment of director and shareholder interests, and has led to the increased use of stock ownership guidelines and holding/retention requirements.

Nonexecutive Chair Pay Practices

Organizations that transition to a nonexecutive chair structure must establish the appropriate compensation (both level and composition) for the newly defined role. To attract the right person, organizations must compensate the individual appropriately.

Reasons to Separate the Chair and CEO Roles:

- **Independence.** Some believe that having a nonexecutive chair provides greater independence from management in terms of board leadership. A nonexecutive chair can serve as a check and balance on a CEO. Although separation of the chair and CEO roles creates greater independence, it is not a requirement for effective board leadership. Many effective boards have an arrangement in which the CEO and chair roles are combined and a new leadership role (lead director) is created to provide a focal point for the independent work and independent functions of the independent directors.

Issues That Have Affected Board Member Selection and Pay

> The imposition or lowering of a limit on the number of boards on which a member may sit has reduced the talent pool.

> Increased obligations, time commitments and risks for directors have caused some candidates and former members to decline board seats.

> There is a shortage of top-quality candidates and a need to replace some board members with independent directors or persons with a specific expertise (e.g., accounting expert).

> A requirement under Sarbanes-Oxley stipulates that the board have a "financial expert" as a member.

> Due to concern regarding potential liability for questionable practices, many boards have been forced to examine their governance structures and independence levels.

> A call for an independent "lead director" has evolved substantially in recent years, prompted by the concern that both the chair and CEO roles often are held by a single individual. Many believe that this arrangement concentrates too much power in the hands of one person and impedes board independence.

> The board has a unique governance role, and directors should be compensated differently than executives:

- Directors should be compensated for exercising their fiduciary oversight responsibilities, not for the company's performance.

- Equity should be aligned to shareholders; thus, full-value shares (e.g., time-vested restricted stock) are appropriate to eliminate decisions involving undue risk.

- Retention should not be a key strategy for board members — it can be important to avoid entrenchment of directors and to allow the board a fresh perspective.

- Directors should not be offered benefits (e.g., retirement payments, life insurance, health insurance or perquisites).

> The scrutiny placed on financial statements since 2002 Sarbanes-Oxley legislation and concern over executive pay (the 2010 Dodd-Frank Act and more information available under expanded proxy disclosure rules) have placed extraordinary demands on committee chairs. Board members at some organizations now are being paid through new or enhanced committee chair fees for meetings with auditors, legal counsel and executive compensation consultants prior to regularly scheduled committee meetings, as well as for the additional time involved in scrutinizing and approving information being presented at their committee meetings.

> Today's investors demand high standards of corporate governance and an especially well-informed and active board.

■ **Relationship.** Typically, a nonexecutive chair can better interact with shareholders as sometimes shareholders feel that their interests can conflict with management of the company.

- **Tradition.** While uncommon in the United States, some companies have a history that dictates that the chair title be held by a separate individual.
- **Transition.** A CEO may be too inexperienced or too new to the company to be given the chair title.
- **Time considerations.** A determination may be made that the CEO should spend their time managing the business, and the chair should spend their time managing the board and its corporate oversight functions.

The decision to combine or separate the chair and CEO roles is a company-specific decision. Companies should not rely on typical market practices or governance experts in making the decision about whether the roles should be separated or combined. Governance experts typically agree, however, that all companies should appoint an independent lead director when the chair and CEO roles are combined or when the chair is affiliated (e.g., a former CEO with the company).

Essential Qualities of a Nonexecutive Chair

There are several qualifications that should be satisfied by a nonexecutive chair:

- High integrity, accomplishment and emotional maturity
- Strong leadership capabilities and the ability to lead the board's oversight and advisory roles
- Respected by all directors and senior management
- Runs meetings effectively (i.e., draws out different viewpoints and knows when to intervene to keep discussion on track)
- Good listener (i.e., keeps a finger on the pulse of the board)
- Demonstrates independence of mind
- Has the courage to step up to challenging issues, including director or CEO performance issues.

Not only should a nonexecutive chair have superb personal qualities, but knowledge of the company's industry and the company itself can be especially helpful. If company experience is lacking upon taking the job, the nonexecutive chair must strive to learn the

412

business, the people and the company's issues from the bottom up. Of particular importance, a nonexecutive chair should have the time available to properly discharge the duties involved. The amount of time needed varies in each situation and depends on the complexity of the organization and its issues.

Pay Practices for a Nonexecutive Chair

Recent market data have yielded observations on approaches and practices in nonexecutive chair compensation:

- The ratio of nonexecutive chair annual retainer compensation to that of other board directors commonly ranges between 2.0 and 2.5, while the ratio of nonexecutive chair total compensation to that of other board directors is approximately 1.5.
- The pay package for the nonexecutive chair position does not approach the pay levels of an executive (employee) chair.
- The compensation for a nonexecutive chair who was never the CEO is generally higher than those who are former CEOs of the company.

Setting Pay of a Nonexecutive Chair

In establishing a process for determining the compensation of a nonexecutive chair, a guiding principle is that the pay should match the commitment and effort required by the (nonexecutive) chair role. There are several approaches and factors that should be considered in setting nonexecutive chair compensation:

- The traditional approach long had been to compensate the chair with a fee or retainer that is linked to a daily fee rate.
- A more common method for establishing nonexecutive chair compensation is using a pro-rata amount of the CEO's pay (with a decision needed on whether to include or exclude LTI values). This approach considers the perceived value and influence in the company of the individual versus that of the CEO. It also looks at the time required by the role relative to a full-time position.
- Evaluating the complexity and effect of the chair job may be a useful exercise in creating a relationship between the CEO and

the board chair. The chair's pay then can be scaled against the compensation of the CEO.

- Alternatively, discretion may be used to set compensation that the company believes is representative of market levels and equitable based on the services.
- Boards must consider that the more compensation that is given to a nonexecutive chair, the more the perception of their independence is diminished.

Today, any pay package for a board chair is likely to be scrutinized by the public and shareholders. Regardless of the process chosen, it is important that the decisions can be explained, defended and viewed as supportable under the company's specific circumstances and the requirements of the role.

What Does a Lead Director Do?

The lead director's primary role is to manage and facilitate a board's governance process and allow the board a measure of independence from the CEO. Other duties of the lead director may include:

- Serve as an objective conduit through which directors can communicate.
- Create a process that ensures each important issue is given both analysis and consideration.
- Act as a useful director recruitment tool, allowing directors to feel more accountable to other board members and shareholders.
- Demonstrate to shareholders, regulators and the public that the board is administering governance processes that are appropriate and defensible.
- Add a visible layer of independence at a company that has a CEO who is also the board chair.
- Help develop other board members, mentor newer members, provide guidance to manage board responsibilities and advance the learning curve.
- Conduct annual outside director performance reviews.

Lead directors may not be suitable for every company. However, in today's environment, anything a company can do to emphasize board independence and thorough governance will only help build regulator, shareholder, investor and public confidence. Given the additional obligations and duties associated with the role, lead directors commonly receive an additional cash retainer fee beyond regular board service fees.

Director Pay Practices in Private Companies

Similar to publicly traded companies, it has become a challenge for many privately held firms to recruit qualified individuals as directors. While some key differences exist in the responsibilities of board members in the public and private sectors, the basic principles and practices that apply to publicly traded companies also should be observed for private companies. According to some studies, about three-quarters of private, for-profit companies provide cash compensation, while less than one-quarter provide stock as part of such director pay.

When considering director compensation at private companies, total director pay is about half the amounts at publicly traded companies. This can be explained by the fact that 50 percent or more of total director pay for publicly traded companies is made up of equity-based awards.

A private company may benchmark against publicly traded companies, but then apply a discount to account for the lessened responsibility for regulatory and other issues not faced in the private sector. Generally, it is better to look at the business approach of paying enough to attract quality directors and make it worth their time to serve on the board.

Director Pay Practices in Tax-Exempt Organizations

Tax-exempt organizations traditionally have not paid their directors. Today, however, with competition for director talent and increased responsibilities for board members, many tax-exempt organizations have found it necessary to pay their directors or are considering

Roles of the Nonexecutive Chair and the CEO

Role of the Nonexecutive Chair

> Plays no role in company operations
> Provides advice and counsel to the CEO
> No company officers report to him/her; CEO reports to the board
> Has authority to call meetings of the board of directors
> Chairs meetings of the board and the annual meeting of shareholders
> Chairs executive sessions and debriefs with the CEO
> Sets board agendas and oversees board information packages
> Facilitates discussion among board members on key issues and concerns outside of board meetings
> Serves as nonexclusive conduit to CEO of views, concerns and issues of other directors
> Addresses any board or director performance concerns
> May represent the company with external stakeholders at the discretion of the board and in conjunction with the CEO
> Speaks for the company in a crisis situation when CEO is unable

Role of the CEO

> Leads company operations; officers and employees report to him/her
> Attends board meetings and the annual meeting of shareholders; makes presentations on company operations
> Receives feedback from executive sessions
> Provides input into board agenda items
> Provides content for board information packages
> Communicates with the chair on various issues between board meetings
> Raises with the chair any concerns management may have about board performance, individual director performance and board composition
> Represents the company to external stakeholders

doing so. See the section titled "Considerations for Board Pay" in Chapter 28 for tax-exempt organizations.

Conclusion

Setting director pay has many of the same considerations as executive pay. There are multiple options to consider and each board must find the right combination of pay vehicles to achieve its desired goals. With any path it chooses, the board must demonstrate a deliberate and thoughtful approach to its own compensation. As demonstrated in a later chapter, board compensation can come with legal challenges.

PART V

Executive Compensation in Special Settings

CHAPTER 25

Compensation in Mergers and Acquisitions

By John Trentacoste

Today's M&A has become far more complex than ever, as companies seek to acquire digital prowess, enter into ancillary markets and expand geographies through acquisition. Although a business transaction undoubtedly can have significant implications for an organization, executive compensation issues — and broader human capital issues — are often neglected once due diligence is complete. In fact, many companies begin the compensation and benefit integration process after a transaction has closed.

While executive compensation and other relevant human capital issues are seldom deal breakers, they can have a substantial effect on the deal structure and future operations of the ongoing organization. In an M&A situation, management and HR professionals must consider whether current pay programs are properly structured to retain and motivate key talent if a potential transaction looms. The companies to a transaction must also carefully consider how to address the target's outstanding equity awards as the treatment of those awards will significantly impact the deal structure and post-acquisition integration of compensation programs. While this chapter considers various aspects related to executive compensation, it should be noted that similar issues exist within the integration of compensation philosophies and systems among the broad-based population. These issues, too, require advanced planning, thoughtful consideration and clear communication in order to allow for a seamless integration.

Private-equity (PE) transactions and spinoffs, like other business transactions, demand considerable preparation; compensation elements that were once a critical piece of the overall system may represent limited or even no value to executives in the new organization. Many companies also discover too late that they need to rebalance their compensation programs to reflect the new post-transaction reality.

There are numerous moving parts in an M&A transaction, many of which are focused on financing and structuring the deal. Compensation programs prior to the deal typically reflect company culture — risk-averse companies favor fixed compensation vehicles, while higher-risk profile companies prefer variable compensation. Compensation systems must be adapted to the new environment, with particular attention paid to equity awards so that the newly combined team retains high-potential performers going forward.

This chapter:

- Discusses the M&A timeline and points at which companies should consider compensation-related actions.
- Describes a top-down approach to M&A compensation design.
- Briefly describes common M&A transaction structures.
- Discusses retention through the M&A process, focusing on retention plan designs that incentivize employees who are critical to integration and those who are critical to post-M&A operations.
- Examines alternatives to address a target company's outstanding equity awards in an M&A transaction and common factors that impact how companies to the transaction will treat those awards.
- Describes alternatives to address a parent company's outstanding equity awards in a spinoff transaction in which a subsidiary will become a separate entity.
- Illustrates how a PE transaction is structured and outlines key issues to consider, including who typically gets equity.
- Outlines common issues that a buyer must address when integrating compensation programs following an M&A transaction.

When to Begin Compensation-Related Discussions

As mentioned above, many companies begin considering compensation-related matters either after the deal has closed, or far too late in the process that leave many companies scrambling to cobble together what could be two disparate pay programs. Early discussion on the important topics covered in this chapter helps ensure enough time to gather input from all relevant constituencies and allow for ample time to communicate any changes to the organization.

Figure 25-1 below outlines the typical five-stage deal process. Compensation matters are best discussed and decided in the "Diligence" phase.

Within the Diligence phase, it is recommended that companies begin to:

- Conduct a side-by-side analysis of change-in-control (CIC) and standard severance provisions between the parent and the acquisition target;
- Conduct a side-by-side analysis of the parent's and acquisition target's approach to compensation governance, including historical incentive plan payouts, historical say-on-pay votes, historical shareholder outreach efforts, and the composition of its board and board effectiveness metrics;
- Begin thinking of the implications for compensation opportunities given the change in scope, impact, and criticality for jobs materially impacted by the M&A;
- Begin modeling potential dollars (cash and equity) that would be reserved for transaction-related payments, and
- Begin identifying the individuals most likely to participate in any transaction-related programs (e.g., retention or enhanced severance).

The proverbial "rubber meets the road" after the deal is signed and the Pre-M&A Planning stage begins. While many decisions will be made and drafted in this phase, contingent upon deal close,

FIGURE 25-1

upfront planning in the Diligence phase will provide companies with a strong head start. In this phase, companies will:

- Finalize the form of transaction-related compensation awards, including currency (e.g., cash or equity), payment cadence, vesting provisions and any performance metrics;
- Finalize the key executives eligible for participation in any transaction-related compensation programs and propose initial award sizing.
- Propose any planned changes to go-forward target compensation;
- Design and develop any go-forward compensation incentive plans; and,
- Propose any integration-related metrics and milestones.

Depending on the structure of the company, all of the above would be proposed to a compensation committee and/or board of directors for final approval.

M&A Compensation Design: A Framework

While each M&A deal has its own unique opportunities and challenges, identifying principles helps provide a guiding framework across all compensation actions to ensure continuity. It is helpful to take a "top-down" approach by beginning with the overall transaction strategy and ending with compensation delivery. The following illustrates the top-down "Four Ds" approach:

Desire	What are the primary objectives of the deal?
	Identifying the key objectives of the deal (e.g., international expansion, IP acquisition, consolidation) will help provide a roadmap for which objectives are most important to ensuring seamless integration and post-close success, but also help identify those most mission-critical to the deal.
Define	How is deal success defined? Financially and non-financially? And over what time period?
	Defining success in practical terms will help establish the time horizons over which key talent should be rewarded and retained and any key performance indicators that could factor into a performance-based compensation scheme.

(continued)

Design	**What compensation plans (both go-forward and transaction related) are optimal to achieve key success objectives and drive accountability?**
	Designing any transaction related compensation scheme should be done alongside the contemplation of any changes to the go-forward compensation plans. While these do not—and should not—directly mirror each other, it does help to evaluate them side by side to ensure no perverse incentives exist between the two plans and they both adequately focus key employees on goals, targets and synergies identified in the deal.
Delivery	**What is the proper form of compensation? Over what time period should pay be delivered?**
	The delivery stage is the combination of the above elements that coalesce in the actual compensation programs for a company. Elements such as metrics, leverage, award currency (cash and equity), and time horizons are solidified here. This phase is crucial to ensuring all of the above work is understood by participants.

Common M&A Structures

An M&A transaction often takes the form of:

- An acquiring entity (Buyer) merging a subsidiary corporation into a target entity (Target), a transaction commonly known as a reverse triangular merger; or

- A Buyer acquiring the stock of the Target directly or indirectly through a subsidiary. Figure 25-2 shows a common acquisition structure in which a Buyer subsidiary merges into the Target, with Target surviving as a wholly owned subsidiary. Figure 25-3 shows another common approach in which a Buyer directly (or through a subsidiary) purchases all of the outstanding equity of a Target, with Target becoming a wholly owned subsidiary following the transaction.

The form of acquisition has significant implications for the transaction (e.g., corporate and tax implications) but is generally not as important in determining how to handle the Target's compensation arrangements (absent an unusual transaction structure, such as an asset purchase in which the Buyer purchases the assets, but not the liabilities, of the Target). With the exception of a discussion of spinoff transactions, the remainder of this chapter discusses M&A

FIGURE 25-2 Acquisition: Buyer Subsidiary Merges Into Target

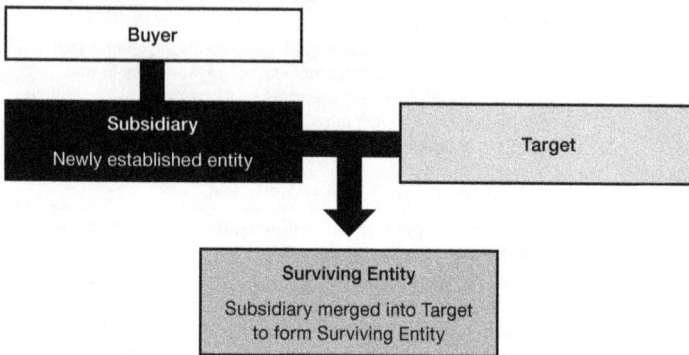

Buyer

Subsidiary
Newly established entity

Target

Surviving Entity
Subsidiary merged into Target
to form Surviving Entity

FIGURE 25-3 Acquisition: Buyer Purchases All of Target's Equity

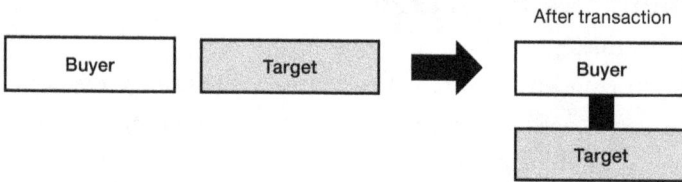

After transaction

Buyer

Target

Buyer

Target

transactions in which a Target will become a direct or indirect subsidiary of the Buyer.

Retention Through the M&A Process

Historically, attention in M&A transactions centered on issues related to financing and structuring the deal with lesser focus on integrating compensation arrangements. However, as companies increasingly use M&A to buy intellectual capital and critical skills, the focus has expanded to include elements such as deal synergies and successful implementation. Consequently, the ability to retain key talent has become a meaningful consideration in any M&A transaction.

M&A presents inherent retention risks resulting from uncertainties with regard to job security and future company direction, as well as perceived increases in job size and workload associated with the deal. Successfully retaining key employees, for a certain period of time or through a particular event, in the face of these negative perceptions requires a well-constructed and well-communicated retention strategy.

Retention Considerations

Retention strategies may contain financial and non-financial elements and should be tailored to the needs and culture of the individual organizations that are part of the deal. While a retention bonus plan is often part of the overall retention design, companies should consider the following questions when deciding whether to offer such a plan:

- To what extent will the deal integration/implementation be negatively impacted by the departure of key employees? As M&A strategies focus on acquiring intellectual capital and skills, stakeholders are evaluating the success or failure of a transaction with regard to the effective retention of key talent.

- Can we identify key employees and job functions for successful deal integration and/or operating the new business going forward? While there is a consensus regarding the importance of recognizing and retaining key employees, the complex nature of many transactions makes this a challenging process. Absent the ability and organizational will to undertake this task, the success of any retention efforts will likely be limited.

- Can we identify key employees or job functions who will be doing substantially more work to ensure the deal occurs? Many will be required to "wear multiple hats" along the deal phase, regardless of whether or not the deal actually closes. For some of the most strained functions, such as legal, finance and HR, the contemplation of some form of "war pay" to compensate for additional efforts regardless of the transaction's close may be merited.

- What is the impact of existing compensation plans and severance/change-in-control policies on employee retention? In evaluating the need for a retention bonus plan and then determining appropriate plan design, it is crucial to understand how key employees will be compensated as a result of the deal from outstanding equity awards and/or terms of employment/severance agreements. This is particularly important if the transaction constitutes a change in control (defined in equity award agreements and employment agreements). For key employees without meaningful retention "hooks" related to equity or severance, the need for a retention bonus plan is heightened.

Where the success of a deal could be negatively impacted by unwanted turnover, efforts should be made to identify critical employees who are especially at risk of leaving. If existing arrangements do not provide sufficient incentive to remain with the organization, a retention bonus plan can be a compelling element of the overall retention strategy. To be effective, the retention bonus plan should be aligned with the unique nature of the deal and account for its size and complexity. In designing these plans, companies do not have the benefit of design templates or extensive market benchmark data; rather, they must evaluate the individual characteristics of each M&A transaction and the varying retention needs for each deal.

Retention Plan Design

While the design of a retention bonus plan must fit the unique nature of the transaction, several design components are commonly considered:

- **Retention bonus plan philosophy.** Prior to designing the plan, a crucial question to address is whether the retention bonus arrangement should be a "pay-to-stay" or a "pay-for-performance" program (or some combination of the two). The answer will be driven by whether the primary purpose is to retain key employees or to drive achievement of key integration and ongoing operational objectives. If the objective is largely retention, the use of performance conditions (and resultant uncertainty regarding payouts) may undermine the value placed on the retention awards by participants. If the goal is to drive achievement of key milestones, the use of performance conditions would be appropriate in retention bonus awards to participants leading this work.
- **Program cost.** Companies generally use one of two approaches to arrive at a cost for the retention bonus plan: (1) fix a percent of the overall deal value to set the retention bonus pool to be

divided among the participants, or (2) identify the participants in the retention bonus plan and set target retention bonus amounts for each, the sum of which is the total plan cost. The cost of the retention bonus plan is typically considered part of the deal and the cost is included in the M&A financial model.

- **Eligibility for participation.** A common mistake made in the design of a retention bonus plan is to apply it broadly (or evenly) across the organization. This results in retention awards being paid to individuals who did not need additional incentives to remain with the organization and the dilution of resources available to retain critical employees who are viewed as more likely to leave. Upon thinking about a retention plan, it is important to understand the criteria for eligibility in any plan. These could include internal and external considerations. Internally, candidates can be evaluated on their scope and impact to getting the deal done, integrating the deal, or capturing deal synergies. Externally, candidates could be evaluated on "hot" areas within the talent market ripe for poaching or any positions that may be viewed as redundant post-close, but are essential during integration.

In determining eligibility to participate, employees are often grouped into two categories: (1) employees who are critical to integration efforts or who will likely perform "double duty" during the deal ("integration-critical employees") and (2) employees who are critical to the ongoing operations of the new business ("operations-critical employees"). Retention bonus plan designs generally differ for these groups as to the design components outlined in Table 25-4. Given the scrutiny applied to M&A transactions in light of their strategic importance and total cost, work to identify and retain the human capital necessary to integration and operation of the new organization is especially important and should be undertaken during the due diligence or transaction negotiation stages of the deal.

Equity Award Treatment in M&A

Of all the business strategies that companies follow in their quest to increase shareholder value, M&A transactions typically garner

428

TABLE 25-4 **Retaining Key Personnel During M&A**

Design component	Integration-critical employees	Operations-critical employees
Retention period	Depending on the employee, companies seek to retain these individuals throughout some or all of the integration process. Generally, this period is 6–18 months post-closing.	Companies want to retain these employees long-term. Retention period typically is 1–2 years as companies use the retention bonus plan to bridge these employees to the new organization's LTI plan.
Award type	Cash is the most commonly used vehicle to deliver retention bonus payments.	Companies often use a combination of cash and equity to deliver retention bonus payments. Equity awards are favored for executives and strategically critical employees. Equity allows companies to reward the effort necessary to integrate and operate the business as well as the effectiveness of that effort (as reflected in stock price movement).
Award targets	Awards may be determined as a percent of a participant's base salary, a fixed dollar amount, or a series of amounts that grows incrementally at the achievement of critical integration or ongoing operations milestones. Awards may vary significantly based on level in the organization, the degree of criticality to integration or ongoing operations, and the perceived retention risk for an employee. While awards must be justifiable to deal stakeholders, they also need be large enough to convince participants to remain with the organization for the desired retention period. Generally, awards made to operations-critical employees are larger than those to integration-critical employees.	
Payment timing	Timing of the retention bonus payouts is an important consideration for both the company and employee. A company would prefer to delay payments until integration is complete and the new business is running smoothly; however, that time horizon may not be realistic (or retentive) from an employee's perspective.	Commonly paid in a lump sum (or two installments) at the conclusion of the post-close integration period. If paid in installments, the design is typically back-loaded so that a larger portion of the award is paid at the end of the retention period.

Generally, cash and equity awards are paid out/vested if a participant remains with the organization for a fixed period of time. Vesting and payment generally occur in 2–3 installments during the retention period. Companies that want to link retention bonus payouts with performance often condition vesting on the achievement of 2–3 milestones during and/or following integration. |

the most attention due to the size of the dollars involved. The same focus on increased shareholder value also has resulted in the widespread use of executive compensation packages with strong links to corporate performance. Common LTI compensation packages include some form of full-value equity awards (including RSUs and PSUs). While declining in prevalence, stock options still represent a significant portion of the LTI component of executive compensation packages at many U.S. companies. One of the most critical decisions in an M&A transaction is how the companies involved in the transaction will treat the Target's outstanding equity awards in the transaction.

Common market approaches to address a Target's outstanding equity awards in a transaction include:

- The Buyer cashing out all vested Target awards and terminating all unvested Target awards at closing of the transaction.
- The Buyer accelerating vesting for all Target awards and cashing them out at closing of the transaction.
- The Buyer cashing out all vested Target awards and assuming all in-the-money unvested awards (i.e., awards that have a purchase price that is less than the per-share consideration paid to holders of common stock in the transaction). Underwater awards (those with a purchase price that is equal to or greater than the per-share consideration paid to holders of common stock in the transaction) are cancelled. This approach may be beneficial to a Buyer when there is significant retention value represented by Target's unvested equity awards.
- The Buyer assuming or substituting for all in-the-money awards (both vested and unvested awards) at the closing of the transaction. Underwater awards are cancelled.

In most transactions, the Buyer will cash out vested equity awards but a Buyer will sometimes assume or substitute for vested, in-the-money awards (typically stock options) to provide Target's executives and employees with an opportunity to benefit from any share price increases that may occur in the Buyer's stock price following the transaction. Tax considerations (e.g., IRC section 409A) may also preclude a Buyer from cashing out Target's vested equity awards upon the closing of the transaction, in which case those awards would be assumed or substituted. In contrast, a Buyer will almost never assume underwater awards as they would provide virtually no retention value post-closing, as discussed below. In such a scenario, the Buyer can provide greater upside to Target's employees by granting new equity awards post-closing.

When a Buyer assumes or substitutes for a Target's outstanding stock options (whether vested or unvested), tax law generally requires that the assumed or substituted stock options preserve the option "spread" of the Target option (i.e., the difference between the option exercise price and current fair market value (FMV) of the underlying stock, multiplied by the number of options). To preserve the aggregate option spread, the ratio of exercise price to FMV must be at least as high as it was under Target's stock option design. This is why most Buyers will not assume under-water stock options in a transaction; the assumed or substituted awards would remain underwater to preserve the negative spread on the stock options.

In Table 25-5, the ratio of exercise price to FMV for Target stock options is 60 percent ($12/$20). Therefore, the exercise price of the Buyer stock options to be issued to Target's executives must be a minimum of $30 (60 percent of $50, the FMV of Buyer's stock). The current aggregate is calculated on Target options as $20,000 (2,500 options times $8), and then the number of Buyer

TABLE 25-5 **Example: Preservation of Option Spread**

	Buyer	Target
FMV	$50	$20
Exercise price	$30	$12
Spread (FMV minus exercise price)	$20	$8
Number of options	1,000	2,500
Aggregate spread (spread times number of options)	$20,000	$20,000

stock options to be granted to Target's executives is calculated as 1,000 ($20,000/$20).

Factors That Impact Equity Award Treatment in M&A

A number of factors impact how the companies to a transaction will treat a Target's outstanding equity awards, including:

- **Terms of the Target's equity plan and award agreements.** Equity plans and/or award agreements often mandate the treatment of equity awards in a transaction (typically defined as a change in control), such as requiring accelerated vesting of all or a portion of unvested equity awards. In many instances, equity awards held by different individuals will have different terms (e.g., executive awards versus other employees' awards). Another factor that affects this analysis is the existence of a "double trigger" in a Target's equity awards (typically defined as a qualifying termination within a specified period, also known as protection period, following a change in control). For example, a "good reason" constructive termination trigger that is met if an employee's duties are diminished within 12 months following the transaction may be difficult for the Buyer to administer and can provide that employee with an incentive to pursue a good reason claim.

- **Cost associated with alternative approaches.** How the parties treat a Target's outstanding equity awards will have significant cost implications for the Buyer. For example, in a public company merger, the Buyer will typically offer per-share consideration to Target's stockholders; each equity award that gets cashed out is therefore an incremental cost to the Buyer. In contrast, in a private company acquisition, a Buyer will typically offer a fixed price for all of Target's outstanding stock; in this form of acquisition, any Target equity awards that get cashed out will reduce the amount of the purchase price that will be paid to shareholders but will not impact the purchase price paid by the Buyer. Buyers must evaluate these considerations carefully in determining how to treat Target's outstanding equity awards.

- **Structure of the Target's equity awards.** It is difficult for a Buyer to assume or substitute for some forms of equity awards, such as certain forms of performance awards. For example, a public company performance award that includes market-based metrics (such as TSR or earnings per share) may no longer be measurable if that company becomes a wholly owned subsidiary of another entity.

- **Tax and accounting considerations.** As equity award design becomes increasingly complex, the tax rules governing those awards in the M&A context have also become more complex. Examples of tax provisions that may impact how the companies to a transaction treat the Target's equity awards include IRC sections 409A (governing deferred compensation arrangements, which include many equity award arrangements), 280G (providing for lost corporate deduction and associated excise taxes under Section 4999 regarding excess golden parachute arrangements), and 162(m) (governing corporate deductibility for certain senior executives in a public company). Discretionary accelerated vesting of unvested Target equity awards may also have accounting implications that need to be evaluated and understood before treatment of the Target's outstanding equity awards is determined.

- **Securities law considerations.** When a Buyer assumes a Target's equity awards or substitutes new awards for the outstanding awards, it has in essence granted the Target's employees the potential right to acquire the Buyer's stock. This grant may or may not be exempt from the requirement of shareholder approval by the Buyer's shareholders. The Buyer may also be subject to securities law registration requirements relating to the new awards and disclosure requirements to the Target's equity award holders in connection with these awards.

- **Target's capitalization.** In many venture-backed companies that secure several rounds of financing prior to the acquisition, common stock will sit below numerous levels of preferred stock in the capitalization waterfall. In such a scenario, much or all of the transaction purchase price may be allocated to preferred stockholders with little (or none) allocated to common stockholders and employee equity award holders. In these situations, a potential Target may seek alternatives to equity to incentivize management and key employees to achieve a sale by implementing a cash carve-out plan that allocates a portion of any purchase price to be paid to plan participants before equity holders receive any transaction consideration.

- **Shareholder optics.** With the increasing scrutiny on executive compensation arrangements, including "golden parachute" arrangements, public companies involved in a transaction must also consider the optics of how they treat outstanding equity awards in a transaction. For example, a Buyer that permits full acceleration of Target's unvested performance awards at the closing of a transaction without regard to actual performance may want to consider explaining its rationale for this approach in any shareholder communications (e.g., a merger proxy) and generally should be prepared to address any shareholder and other stakeholder concerns.

Critical Steps in M&A Due Diligence

As discussed in the preceding sections, numerous factors impact how the parties to an M&A transaction treat the Target's outstanding equity awards. It is critical in M&A diligence to determine early in the process:

- What Target's equity plan documents and award agreements permit and/or mandate in the transaction with respect to outstanding equity awards,
- The need to incentivize Target's key executives and employees post-closing, and
- The cost to Buyer of the alternative approaches to address Target's equity awards (for example, cashing out all Target equity awards and then granting new Buyer equity awards may be prohibitively expensive).

These factors often influence how the M&A deal terms addressing equity awards are structured and, in the case of a public company merger, may often influence the per-share price the Buyer is willing to pay for Target's stock.

Treatment of Equity Awards in a Spinoff

Especially after a merger or acquisition, a company may decide to sell — or divest itself of — a subsidiary when it is no longer essential to its business model or long-term strategy. A spinoff is a specific type of divestiture in which, rather than being sold, a subsidiary becomes an independent company itself. In a spinoff, shareholders in the parent corporation (Parent) receive the newly issued stock of the former subsidiary (SpinCo). As a result, ownership prior to the spinoff is preserved through proportionate ownership of the Parent's stock and the stock of the SpinCo, as in Figure 25-6.

One of the critical compensation issues to address in a spinoff is the treatment of pre-spin equity awards granted by the Parent. The starting point for discussion and decisions regarding the treatment of those awards is to review the Parent's equity plan documents and individual award agreements to determine whether adjustments to equity awards are required or permitted in connection with a spinoff. Subject to any restrictions contained in the equity plan/award documents, companies typically use one the following methodologies to handle outstanding parent company equity awards in connection with a spinoff:

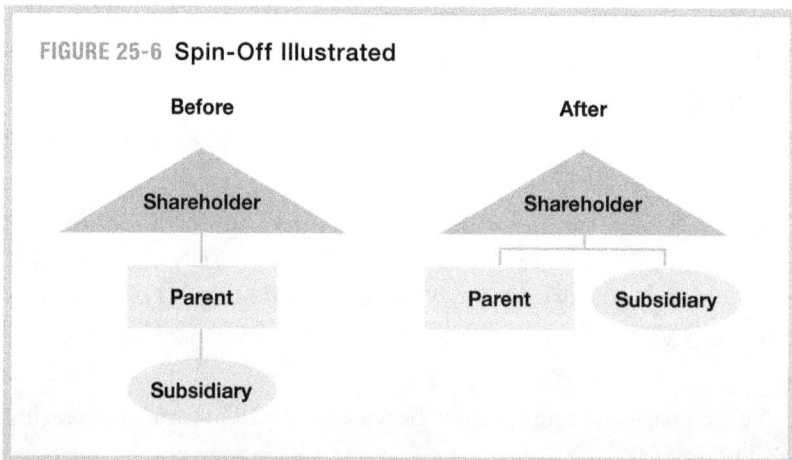

FIGURE 25-6 **Spin-Off Illustrated**

- Converting Parent equity awards held by specified employees into equity awards to acquire SpinCo's stock; this approach typically is made for employees who move to and/or stay with SpinCo. Parent equity awards held by all other employees will continue to be based on Parent's equity and will be adjusted to reflect the decrease in the value of Parent's equity as a result of the spinoff.
- Converting all Parent equity awards (regardless of employee) into an equity award to acquire SpinCo's stock and an equity award to acquire Parent's stock (as adjusted to reflect the decrease in value of Parent's equity as a result of the spinoff).
- Continuing to have all outstanding awards (regardless of employee) based on Parent's equity, and adjusting the outstanding awards to reflect the decrease in the value of Parent's equity as a result of the spinoff.

The first two approaches outlined above are more common than the third. The rationale for using the first method is to ensure that employees are incentivized to maximize company value at the organization where they provide services. Also, this alternative commonly results in fewer accounting and tax complications than the other methods. The rationale for using the second approach is to incent employees to work toward the success of both companies before and following the spinoff, recognize the contributions of equity award holders to both Parent and SpinCo, and to allow employees to share in the value that they helped to create in each company.

Regardless of the method selected for treatment of outstanding equity awards, companies typically adjust outstanding Parent equity awards to preserve the aggregate intrinsic value of the outstanding awards before and after the spinoff. For stock options, these adjustments are designed to preserve the same ratio between the exercise price and the per-share value of the underlying stock as existed prior to the distribution. For time-vested awards, adjustments are typically structured to maintain the award value, vesting schedule, service time and dividend rights as applied to the parent company awards immediately prior to the spinoff.

While typically reserved for the compensation committee of the SpinCo, there are additional considerations that may be made by the Parent's compensation committee as to whether any up-front grants of equity are to be made to SpinCo management. These types of awards, typically known as Launch Grants, help "stake" executives in their newly formed companies and, if public, bring their ownership stakes to those commensurate with a free-standing public company. Additionally, a Launch Grant of this kind may be attractive to a Parent company executive who is tapped to take a role of lesser scope in the SpinCo.

Is Private Equity in Your Company's Future?

PE firms are prominent players in M&A as these firms typically seek to acquire companies using significant leverage (debt) to finance the transaction and they seek to exit those companies through a liquidity event (typically a sale) in a relatively short timeframe, such as five years. Using leverage allows PE firms to obtain significant returns on portfolio companies that are sold at a profit.

In a typical leveraged buyout (LBO) transaction, a PE firm takes on debt in the Target's name and finances the remainder of the purchase price with cash raised from the PE firm's investors (which are limited partners in the PE fund in which the PE firm serves as the general partner). For companies targeted by PE firms, the following is a primer on compensation and benefit considerations. In general, these deals are very complex with their own terminology. Table 25-7 provides a sampling of common terms. Following are key items to consider in preparation for an LBO transaction:

TABLE 25-7 **Common Terms in LBO Transactions**

Term	Definition
Multiple of money	PE firm's estimate of the return on its initial investment (typically expressed as a 2x, 3x and so on.)
Sponsor	The private equity firm or group of firms taking part in the LBO

TABLE 25-7 Common Terms in LBO Transactions (continued)

Term	Definition
Portfolio company	One of the companies that is owned by a private equity sponsor
Liquidity event	An initial public offering, sale or divestiture of a portfolio company
Management promote	Equity plan in the newly private company designed to "promote" the best interests of the new private equity owners
Leveraged common stock	Preferred shares of restricted stock designed to create a tax-efficient vehicle for the management promote
Strip	Equal to option on 10 shares of stock
Buy-in	Direct investment by executives in the newly private company; can be a requirement in order to receive management-promote shares; typically capped in amount available per person and by level in the company (e.g., only available to SVP and above)

An LBO transaction likely will trigger a change in control for the Target. As a starting point, this may trigger accelerated vesting and/or settlement of deferred compensation amounts, equity awards and/or other Target plans. Depending on a plan's payment trigger, amounts may become either payable immediately upon closing of the transaction (single trigger) or on an employee's subsequent dismissal "without cause" or resignation for "good reason" during a specified window following the transaction (double trigger). Consideration must be given to the golden parachute rules of IRC sections 280G and 4999 and the conditions to avoid adverse tax consequences under IRC section 409A.

Communicate often and early. Even if there is no actual deal, if your company is "declared" a target by the media, Wall Street or even a blogger, people will begin to develop their own theories about what is happening. Preparing employees with facts and information typically is the best approach.

Special severance plans may be necessary. Employees may begin to receive calls from search firms. Even with a communications strategy in place, make sure that employees feel comfortable even if their jobs are eliminated.

Inventory all current vehicles that were designed to retain employees and assess their retention ability under the current circumstances. Make sure that there are appropriate retention "hooks" that hold your most valuable employees in place before, during and after the transaction. Because many existing retention programs may have vested (e.g., equity, deferred compensation), new plans and strategies may need to be quickly designed, formalized and communicated.

Recognize that incentive programs post-closing will likely vary greatly from the Target's plans in place prior to the PE acquisition. Many PE firms will grant a combination of performance-vested stock options (for example, performance will be tied to the PE firm's internal rate of return as of a liquidity event) and time-vested stock options to provide a combination of performance and retention incentives. Executives who are used to a broader scope of equity-award opportunities, such as RSUs and PSUs may need to be educated about the details of the post-closing equity plan (also referenced as management promote equity).

Once the deal is finalized, there may remain a need to address various details regarding executive compensation arrangements. Considerable effort should be taken to ensure all compensation and benefit plan details are accounted for in the merger/acquisition agreement. In some cases, certain portions of the compensation packages may be subject to negotiation with the affected executives, particularly if the PE firm has identified those executives as critical to the PE firm's strategy.

Ownership interests in the new portfolio company are often only provided to senior executives. In some circumstances, a cash-based LTI plan can be negotiated for other critical employees who do not participate in the management promote of the newly private company (e.g., corporate directors and vice presidents of a public company that is acquired by a PE firm). High-potential as well as mission-critical employees also may be included in a long-term plan with the new company.

Almost all equity interests under the management-promote plan are allocated when the deal is consummated; the remaining shares are held for new hires and targeted retention awards. Sponsors consider these awards as one-time grants that will carry management until a future liquidity event (typically a sale of the portfolio company). Sponsors often view a deal's horizon as five years or less until the liquidity event. The management promote usually will not have any feature that allows for disposition prior to this event. From the sponsor's perspective, executives need to be tied down for the deal's entire duration. This is a fairly long-term commitment for management given current rates of executive turnover and the lack of a more typical annual LTI grant program.

Table 25-8 provides some additional detail about compensation and benefit issues before, during and after a transaction. In the end, do not underestimate the compensation-related work involved and the complexity of these transactions. Changes will need to be made to many of the current compensation and benefit programs. Communications are critical during this type of transaction; keeping employees informed should help retain more of them throughout the transaction.

Integrating Compensation Programs

Integrating two sets of similar compensation programs can be challenging enough; then consider the potential difficulties when cultures, philosophies and program designs are distinctly different at the combining organizations. It can be daunting to resolve issues such as determining the appropriate compensation philosophy and reconciling compensation plan mechanics (e.g., eligibility, target award levels, award/grant processes, performance measurement, goal setting). If handled properly, these areas can be key drivers of success pre- and post-transaction.

Successful integrations typically include a review of the following factors:

- **Starting early.** A buyer likely should begin thinking about compensation-related challenges and opportunities well in

TABLE 25-8 Compensation and Benefits Issues Before, During and After a Transaction

Due Diligence: Pre-Transaction Planning	Deal Announced: Managing During the Transition	Going Forward: Managing the New Organization
■ Establish compensation and benefits philosophy - Market, position, mix - Different strategy (executive, salaried, hourly?) ■ Review change-in-control consequences of existing programs (e.g., acceleration of liability/payouts) ■ Measure accrued liabilities for programs with a future benefit promise (e.g., defined benefit plan, SERP) ■ Consider severance and retention plan costs - Buyer will want to know those costs on the front end	■ Create total remuneration strategy ■ Develop base pay plan - Bands/grades/other - Assess impact ■ Short-term incentives - Metrics, eligibility, etc. ■ Long-term incentives - Vehicles possible - Tax/accounting consequences ■ Audit benefit competitiveness ■ Redesign as appropriate ■ Identify appropriate vendors (e.g., TPA, outsourcers) ■ New plan documents, summary plan descriptions, etc. - New owner will want to be involved	■ Develop integrated statement of total compensation ■ Implement new compensation and benefits structure ■ Determine appropriate severance and retention policy for new organization ■ Identify administrative roles and duties (both internal/external) ■ Roll out and communicate

advance of any deal being signed. Proper compensation diligence helps identify potential challenges and gaps between compensation philosophies.

■ **Retaining the key executives and employees of the Target.** A Buyer may need to adopt a retention plan and/or provide equity award opportunities to key executives and employees to align their interests with those of the Buyer and to provide retention incentives for those executives and employees who will deliver the value to be derived from the acquisition. In transactions in which the Buyer is not assuming any of the Target's equity awards, incentives may involve Parent granting a block equity award (a larger equity grant than would typically be granted in an annual equity grant) at closing to provide holding power for Target's key executives and employees through the use of equity.

- **Integrating compensation programs.** Due diligence will inform the Buyer about the Target's incentive plans (including any short-term and long-term incentive opportunities) and successful integration will require the Buyer to harmonize Target's programs with the Buyer's business. This may result in Target participating in Buyer's plans post-closing, refinement of metrics in the Target's plans for future performance periods (or in the Buyer's plans if the acquisition is transformational for the enterprise as a whole), or a combination of these approaches. In many instances, the Target's annual incentive plan may need to be adjusted for the year in which the acquisition occurs, for example if the plan includes metrics that are difficult to measure post-closing once the Target is no longer an independent company.

- **Assessing pay opportunities.** Executives and key employees within both the Buyer and Target may be assuming larger (or lesser) roles in the post-acquisition enterprise and adjustments to compensation opportunities may be warranted. For example, a merger of equals will result in Buyer's CEO running an organization that is twice the size of the pre-acquisition enterprise. The CEO's future pay opportunities will typically reflect this change.

- **Finding synergies.** Most Buyers will retain many of the Target's compensation and benefit programs for a specified period of time (e.g., through the end of the year in which the transaction occurs) to assess the programs and plan for integration. Successful integration will often include a review of the total cost of compensation and benefits of the combined enterprise and the combination/elimination of some programs to enhance cost efficiencies. Integration of benefit programs will require careful consideration of applicable plan documents and laws (e.g., tax laws, ERISA).

Final Considerations

Integrating compensation programs when two companies merge is a complicated and time-consuming task. Earlier attention to employee retention, outstanding equity, and the eventual combination of compensation programs typically yields better results.

CHAPTER 26

Initial Public Offerings

By David Wise and Jelena Tasker

In an IPO, a company raises capital by offering its shares to the public via a stock exchange, such as the NYSE or NASDAQ. With a more liquid market for a company's shares and easier access to capital come numerous reporting and disclosure responsibilities as well as an expanded involvement of legal professionals, auditors and consultants. Upon being a public company there are also often different structures to pay programs accompanied by additional scrutiny from a larger population of stakeholders.

Companies intending to go public usually are aware that under SEC and stock exchange listing rules, they will have to disclose detailed information about business operations to investors and the general public. What many fail to realize, however, is that they can no longer rely on the compensation policies and practices in place while they were private entities. While equity compensation — typically in the form of an appreciation vehicle like stock options or profits interests — garners the most attention in an IPO and generally represents the lion's share of potential financial gain for executives, other compensation elements need to be addressed before and after the company goes public.

Meaningful benefits can be achieved by realigning the executive compensation program in light of the company's new context, which will include a new set of public and institutional shareholders, and a pay program that is publicly disclosed and open for the world to see.

This chapter:

- Addresses the importance of understanding the value of equity compensation in planning for and creating an IPO.
- Discusses factors that may determine equity levels for executives hired before or after the public offering.
- Discusses the issues a company needs to address if it contemplates going public, including complying with SEC disclosure rules, likely changes to the annual incentive plan, equity compensation and dilution levels, and governance.
- Discusses the need to adopt a new compensation philosophy once the company goes public. Comparing pay levels against the competition, reviewing individual pay elements as well as target total cash and TDC, and updating employment agreements are also recommended.

Understanding Equity Compensation Prior to an IPO

Private companies often use their equity, or phantom equity designed to mirror equity, as an effective compensation vehicle to attract and motivate key employees prior to an IPO. But equity in a pre-IPO company is subject to much interpretation. Through thoughtful planning and communication, this powerful tool can have a strong perceived value to the recipient, allowing companies to be more conservative with cash compensation.

However, this trade-off between cash compensation and company equity is a delicate balancing act and must take into consideration the potential value delivered to participants, as well as the portion of the company allotted to participants.

Understanding Value

Consider the question: "A competitor is offering me 100,000 shares; why does my current employer only offer 25,000?"

While a pre-IPO equity grant can have considerable perceived value, especially in a high-growth or momentum company, employees need to understand where their grants fit in the context of the company overall, as well as the competitive marketplace. The above question as written is impossible to answer without more information about the starting company value, the company's growth trajectory, and the proportion of the company's upside that the share grant provides.

As companies move toward an IPO, financial analysis is used to understand potential share value. By analyzing additional rounds of financing that might occur prior to the equity event, an employee can understand how their individual grants will become diluted through each round of financing, as well as see the potential increase in company share price over the exercise price of their options. Even assuming a company proceeds all the way to an IPO, there is no way the company can definitively say what the gain at IPO will be for an individual participant; however, an estimate can be created using the overall market capitalization of the company at IPO and the estimated size of the offering. In the end, educating an equity plan participant on the value of a grant and how that grant relates to the marketplace could be necessary — sometimes 25,000 is much larger than 100,000, as shown in Table 26-1.

Determining Executive Equity

"As our company approaches an IPO, we need to hire a senior vice president; how do we determine the appropriate equity grant level?" Chances are, when a private company on the road to an IPO recruits executives, the shiniest carrot will be the equity award. A qualified, high-performing executive is not contemplating a move to a startup because the company has a generous pension plan or offers above-market base salaries. In determining how much to offer a new employee, the important factors to consider are industry, size

TABLE 26-1 **Comparison of Potential IPO Scenarios**

	Options Granted	Exercise Price	IPO Price	Option Gain at IPO
Current Offer	25,000	$2	$15	$325,000
Competing Offer	100,000	$13	$15	$200,000

of the organization, additional potential dilution pre-IPO and what position the individual will hold.

The industry where a company operates plays a large role in the expectations and size of a pre-IPO equity grant. Generally, a service-based company will offer less upside than a company operating in the technology market.

Companies in the technology field are often younger and riskier propositions given the highly competitive and fast-moving marketplace. Consequently, equity grants to technology executives generally are larger than those in the overall marketplace as companies attempt to mitigate the risk factor with an increase in the upside should there be an IPO.

Another key factor to consider is the importance of the company's structure in sizing executive equity grants. The size of the company, as measured in number of employees, annual revenue and/or market capitalization at IPO all correlate with the equity position at IPO — the smaller the company, the larger the equity position (share numbers, not value) awarded. A company with higher revenue, market capitalization or a larger employee base generally will have greater overall value and, consequently, the company can give away less equity to the executives and still deliver competitive value in its equity grants.

As mentioned, the expected dilution and the effect on individual grants is an important factor to consider when determining executive equity grants. A grant made to an executive hired in the period just preceding the offering will only be diluted by the IPO itself. Conversely, a grant made to an executive just after company formation could potentially be diluted by the IPO plus any additional rounds of financing that precede the IPO. The executive who comes on board just following formation is taking on a larger risk of individual dilution and the equity grant should likely reflect this inherent risk. Additionally, the earlier an executive joins an organization, the lower the probability the company will actually experience an IPO. The later an executive comes on board, the higher the probability the equity grant will have value in the marketplace. Consistent with equity investment, the greater the risk, the greater the potential reward.

Role and Responsibility

Finally, the company must consider the role and responsibilities of the individual executive being offered the equity grant. Will the executive have direct line of sight to the performance of the equity or does the position influence something that is measured less by company equity and more by a different company measure? An example of the position's importance in determining equity holdings can be found when looking at two senior management positions in the technology industry: chief technology officer and top sales and marketing executive.

Research suggests both positions would have similar annual total cash compensation levels but the equity held at IPO (shares owned plus shares subject to options as a percent of total shares outstanding) would be markedly different. In our example, a chief technology officer had median equity of more than 1.75 percent of the company at IPO while the top sales and marketing executive held less than 1 percent. Sales positions tend to have compensation geared toward annual performance while a top technology position

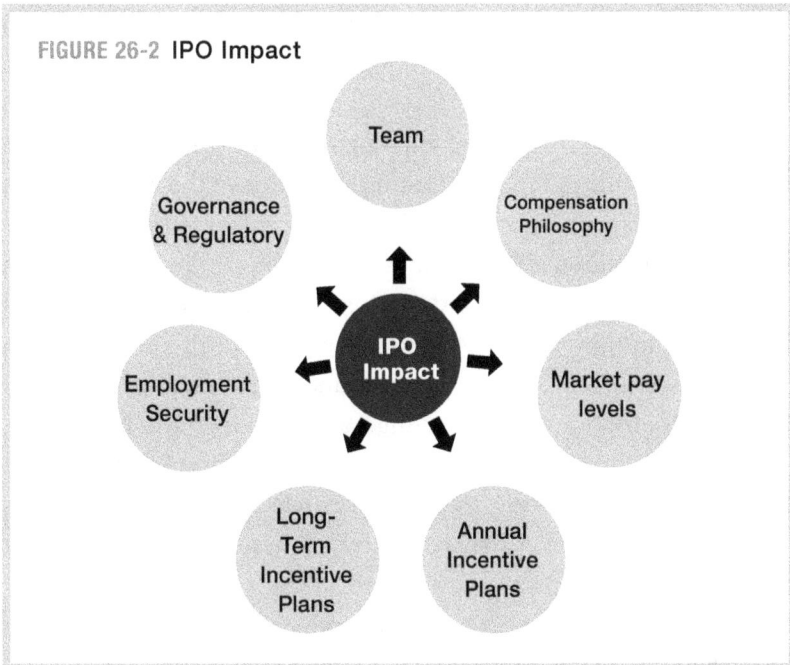

FIGURE 26-2 **IPO Impact**

is going to play an important role in developing company assets within the technology industry, which is critical to the creation of long-term company value.

Looking Ahead

While there is no magic bullet in determining appropriate equity grants in pre-IPO companies, there are critical questions that can be asked to narrow the focus and allow the company to make an informed decision while ensuring the executive is fairly compensated.

Preparing Compensation Programs for Public Company Life

When private companies seek to go public, they become interested in what is needed to prepare the compensation programs of a private company for the public eye. Going public through an IPO is not the end of the road; it marks the transition from operating as a private firm to doing business as a public company. Life as a publicly traded company means the company's stock is readily available for sale or purchase on a stock exchange. Public companies have easier access to capital and have liquid markets for their shares through such stock exchange listings. See Figure 26-2 for the multiple areas an IPO can affect.

The flip side is that a public company must comply with rules established by the SEC and the listing standards of the relevant stock exchange. As a consequence, a public company is required to disclose detailed information about business operations to investors and the general public. This mandated disclosure contributes to significant differences in how privately owned companies can operate and in how publicly traded companies must function, which can materially affect compensation program design and administration.

Required compensation disclosure takes place largely in the company's annual proxy statement (in which a company solicits the proxies, or votes, of shareholders), where the company must disclose, discuss and analyze detailed information on the compensation of the CEO, the CFO and generally the other three highest paid executives (collectively, the NEOs). In addition to detailed disclosure of NEO compensation, a public company must provide information on compensation paid to all members of the board of directors. Details on the beneficial ownership of company stock of each director and NEO also must be disclosed.

Because much of a public company's compensation levels and practices are publicly disclosed, it is important that they can stand up to scrutiny and are defensible, both to shareholders and other stakeholders. Well-designed compensation plans provide competitive pay opportunities, truly link pay to individual and company performance, and communicate the behaviors and outcomes that drive shareholder returns. (See Chapter 21 for additional information about CEO compensation during an IPO.) Before going public, a privately held company should be sure its compensation programs are consistent with public company standards; otherwise, the organization can face significant pressure from shareholders, the media and shareholder advisory firms.

Annual Incentives

Private companies sometimes have informal, discretionary bonus plans that lack clear performance criteria, funding mechanisms or targeted levels of awards. Well-designed annual incentive plans link an executive's pay to the successful achievement of goals important to company success. They also incorporate targeted incentives with base salaries so that pay mix and total cash compensation levels can be assessed.

An annual incentive plan used by a private employer (including a subsidiary of a public entity) may not necessarily be appropriate for a public company, potentially resulting in a review and modification of the plan in planning for the IPO. For example, a startup company may maintain a plan that emphasizes revenue growth as it positions for an IPO. Once public, expense control and return metrics commonly would be more appropriate than a top-line approach to incentives, although some newly public companies that seek to support aggressive growth goals may continue to focus on top-line measures like revenue. Annual incentive plans in privately held companies may also be riskier than is appropriate for a publicly traded entity given that the smaller shareholder base may have a riskier appetite than a broad-based shareholder population.

Consider an example in which a subsidiary's plan measures the unit's profit performance against a budget developed by the parent corporation. The subsidiary has no control over corporate cost allocations or the parent company's financial structuring decisions. If that subsidiary is carved out in an IPO, the new entity will have cost allocation and financial decision capability, and plan measures should be reconsidered.

Equity Compensation

Executives who join early-stage startup and high-growth private companies can benefit by receiving equity compensation at then-current (generally lowest) valuations. Companies that successfully go public expect significant increases in their valuations, and equity compensation allows employees to share in this value creation. Of course, there are downside risks as well. Many startup companies do not succeed and even successful companies may be unable to go public when equity markets dry up or become volatile.

Private companies that plan to go public commonly use stock as an important component of their compensation programs, not just for executives but often for a broad group of (or even all) employees. This helps conserve scarce cash and links employees' interests with those of shareholders, but also dilutes the stakes of current shareholders. Potential investors in IPOs typically want to see that key employees have an ownership stake in the company so that they are motivated to increase its value and minimize risk to the organization. Likewise, it is important for key employees to have some unvested equity stakes – what we call "holding power" – so that they must stay with the company for several years post-IPO to capture gains from post-IPO appreciation; they should not be able to just "take the money and run" as key executive departures following an IPO can cause downward pressure on an organization's share price. Further, this reinforces the idea that an IPO is not about going public, it is about being public.

Equity Compensation — Vehicles and Dilution

For many years, stock options were the currency of choice, but increasingly full-value shares (e.g., restricted stock, performance shares) are being used. (See Chapter 6 on "Public Company Long-Term Incentive Compensation: An Equity-Based Focus.") Regardless of the available award vehicles, companies need to consider several issues when evaluating equity compensation plans. A crucial question for investors, whether in private or public companies, is the dilution of their ownership stakes as a result of equity grants. The challenge is to balance shareholder concerns about dilution with the need to incentivize and retain the requisite talent.

Companies need to assess dilution from both outstanding grants and the number of shares authorized and available for future grant. Prior to going public, a company should obtain authorization for enough shares to cover projected grants for the next two or three years post-IPO (assuming dilution levels are not excessive). Acceptable dilution levels vary by industry, with high-technology and bio-technology companies generally higher than others. As a rule, potential dilution from shares granted plus those remaining for grant (also called "overhang") between 10 and 20 percent of outstanding shares is within competitive market practice with most companies coming in at the mid-point in this range.

At private companies, entity valuations and stock prices generally are low relative to similar publicly traded companies. This minimizes the charges to earnings from equity compensation, regardless of whether stock options or full-value shares are used. Once public, valuations typically are materially higher and stock prices are much more volatile. Charges to earnings will be greater, which means companies often need to be more selective regarding participation in equity compensation programs and the size and value of individual grants.

Other Issues

Prior to a public offering, a company needs to establish an independent compensation committee (e.g., no insiders such as executives on the committee). The committee should establish a charter stating its duties and responsibilities and develop a compensation philosophy that will shape its compensation decisions. Both of these will need to be publicly disclosed and should be crafted with transparency in mind. While not required, compensation committees generally directly engage an independent consulting firm for assistance with competitive market assessment and program design.

Public companies are also subject to IRC section 162(m), which limits the deductibility of compensation to $1 million per year for certain "covered employees" which includes the CEO, the principal financial officer (typically the CFO), and the three other highest paid executive officers. Beginning in 2027, however, 162(m) will expand its reach to an additional five highly compensated employees.

Key Processes for a Newly Public Company
Compensation Philosophy

A company's compensation philosophy establishes the framework for executive compensation programs and provides a link to the underlying business strategy. A newly public company should not necessarily rely on the compensation philosophy used while it was a private entity; rather it should develop one in accordance with its new status. As part of this process, the company should define the desired role of each compensation element and its respective sensitivity to the performance of the company, business unit or individual.

Competitive Review of Compensation

Along with a change in the ownership structure (i.e., public investment), an IPO results in changes in the responsibilities of many executives and frequently the expansion of the executive team. To account for these different roles, a company may examine the competitiveness of its pay levels by identifying benchmark positions and developing competitive pay data through a mix of published and private survey sources.

When reviewing compensation levels, companies generally examine each pay element on an individual basis, as well as through a holistic, total compensation approach. While it is important that individual elements of pay be competitive and consistent with the company's compensation philosophy, a company typically would focus on target total compensation levels (total cash compensation and total direct compensation) more than on the individual pay components.

For example, a company may pay slightly below the competitive market for base salary, but provide above-market levels of target bonus opportunity and equity, thereby providing a competitive overall pay package.

Employment Agreements and Security Arrangements

The formation of a new public company may require employment or security arrangements for key personnel. Existing agreements should be examined and the need for new or updated arrangements considered. An employer is at a heightened risk of losing key employees during organizational change, especially an IPO, and the retention of key executives often is critical to the ultimate success of the IPO equity event. A newly public company must take into account any additional risks assumed by executives during the transition and adjust compensation and severance protections accordingly.

ESPPs and Setting Policies for 10b5–1 Plans

A company preparing for an IPO might consider adoption of an employee stock purchase plan (ESPP) and setting policies related to 10b5–1 plans.

ESPP

Although more common in certain industry sectors, an ESPP is another vehicle that a board might consider before the company goes public. An ESPP allows employees to purchase company stock at a discount, and it can afford favorable tax treatment to the employee purchaser so long as certain statutory requirements are satisfied. As broad-based plans, ESPPs can increase employee interest in the company's performance. When developing an ESPP, key areas for consideration include the discount on the company's equity, the required holding period for equity, and the maximum amount an individual can purchase in a given year.

10b5–1 Trading Plan

Upon an IPO, a company and its insiders become subject to SEC Rule 10b-5 which prohibits trading by insiders on the basis of "material nonpublic information." Because trading windows vary from company to company based on dates of company report filings and certain announcements that constitute material non-public information, company insiders may have very limited time periods within which they may sell shares acquired through equity plans. However, compliance with a 10b5–1 trading plan shields the insider from SEC actions for violation of Rule 10b-5.

A "10b5–1 plan" allows an insider to trade shares at any time so long as all of the requirements of the rule are satisfied. Although a Form 4 must be filed for the transaction, the company can adequately address shareholder concerns regarding the timing of the transaction by noting in the Form 4 that it happened automatically via a trading plan rather than due to an announcement or other information.

In addition, as a company goes public, it should establish certain procedures and requirements that any person establishing a 10b5–1 plan must follow and satisfy, such as:

- Company approval — typically through its legal department — before any trading plan may become effective;
- A holding period between establishment of a trading plan and any transaction made under such plan;
- Open trading windows that would be the only times that trading plans could be established;
- Rules regarding disclosure of trading plans; and
- Limiting trades outside of a plan (if an executive has established a trading plan). Setting limitations reduces the public perception of insider trading and can stave off SEC attention on misuse of these plans.

Transaction-Specific Issues

Before developing or implementing any programs, a pre-IPO or newly public company should examine the practices of comparable organizations to establish competitive norms. When devising an appropriate comparator group, a company should consider factors such as industry, size, scope, business model, sources of recruiting top talent and strategic objectives.

The determination of competitive compensation practices for a specific transaction is more complicated than the determination for ongoing compensation elements. Developing an understanding of why a similar company implemented a compensation program is as important as discovering what it did. An employer needs to consider the nature of the transaction, the historical compensation practices at the company examined, and any information on future pay arrangements.

Points to Remember

Like many pre-IPO workstreams, compensation planning during the runup to the IPO can be trying. However, the development of an executive compensation program that is cost-efficient, competitive, performance based and aligned with shareholder expectations and value creation is one critical input into the ultimate success of an IPO.

CHAPTER 27

Bankruptcy, Retention and Other Special Situations

By Todd McGovern and Jack Grange

This chapter examines compensation practices for executives at companies with certain special business situations or needs. This includes bankruptcy, executive retention, signing bonuses/awards, "mega grants" and private equity backed companies.

Each of the circumstances addressed involves compensation as a tool to attract, retain or motivate executive talent through challenging times. The covered situations involve shareholder concerns requiring special consideration in the design, implementation and communication of executive compensation arrangements.

This chapter:

- Discusses special rules applicable to, and key approaches used for, compensating top executives at companies in Chapter 11 bankruptcy reorganization proceedings. Well-designed compensation packages can help retain and motivate the executives to support a successful emergence from bankruptcy and future business improvement.
- Examines approaches commonly used to retain talent to manage the business, including strategies to address one-off situations. The success of the programs increases greatly when an organization proactively identifies the issues, addresses them within the context of business and compensation strategy, and strives to strike the balance between executive and shareholder expectations.
- Addresses executive signing bonuses and awards as a tool for boards to attract and retain the top executives.

- Discusses the private equity (PE) pay model for portfolio companies that aligns the interests of the investors with those of the management team.

Bankruptcy

Corporate bankruptcies, which wax and wane with the performance of the overall economy, require tailored compensation designs to help struggling companies retain, and in some cases attract, talent to preserve value while also trying to reverse course and achieve profitability. As a company enters this strained time, it also faces the conflicting demands of creditors, employees and shareholders.

Employees most often continue to receive the same level of salary and benefits as before the bankruptcy filing. However, due to rules that govern a Chapter 11 bankruptcy, traditional incentive plans and severance benefits are usually not available. There are approaches for retaining and incentivizing employees that can be crafted to fit within the unique bankruptcy context and rules. The challenge within a bankruptcy is to create a program that discourages the needed talent from exiting a rocking ship while encouraging a performance orientation that may restore the ship's course.

Further challenging the compensation design objectives are various legal and regulatory strictures. And ultimately, the compensation arrangements have to be approved by the bankruptcy court. With all of these parties and requirements to satisfy, often with contradictory interests, compensating executives in bankruptcy situations can present a real challenge as it tries to address the people charged with helping restore and create value.

Key objectives in designing executive compensation programs in bankruptcy situations include:
- Motivate and retain essential employees during the reorganization and after emergence.
- Demonstrate to affected parties that the proposed compensation programs are reasonable and appropriate.
- Develop a plan to obtain approval for the compensation arrangements in bankruptcy court.

Bankruptcies take distinct forms that impact compensation design differently. Most notably, a Chapter 11 bankruptcy addresses restructuring (under which key employees will be needed to turn around the business), while a Chapter 7 filing is a liquidating bankruptcy (under which the bankruptcy trustee may only need a small group of employees to help wind down and liquidate the business).

Our focus is on Chapter 11 filings where the company is attempting to reorganize under the protection of the bankruptcy court.

Key Employee Retention Plans

Critical employees in turbulent business circumstances typically seek security — in the form of fixed compensation — via salaries and deferred/retention payments. While retention awards previously were common practice, the Bankruptcy Abuse Prevention and Consumer Act of 2005 (Act) completely overhauled the Bankruptcy Code and pay practices. The Act eliminated the ability to provide key employee retention plans (KERPs) to company insiders (generally executives and directors), which were intended to replace equity grants or other forms of LTIs that would have been awarded in normal course if not for the bankruptcy. The Act does allow performance-based incentives for insiders, or key employee incentive plans (KEIPs), which are now commonly used during bankruptcy and discussed in the next section.

While KERPs are no longer allowed for insiders, they remain common for retaining non-officers who are critical to the day-to-day operational success of the company, such as employees whose skillsets would be difficult to recruit for a replacement and employees that are a retention risk. KERPs are often widely applied and include a range of employees and business functions. The plans are typically simple in design and resemble a time-based retention plan with payouts tied only to the passage of time.

Key Employee Incentive Plans

For insiders, companies replaced KERPs with KEIPs, which have a performance-based element to the awards. While retaining some design characteristics of the KERPs (e.g., cash awards paid over time and often linked to value based on a percentage or multiple of salary), the awards have relevant performance goals attached to the payout of the award.

The performance criteria under a KEIP vary by business, but often relate to financial statement measures (e.g., operating income, cash flow, expense reduction), key strategic milestones in the form of successful asset sales at predetermined prices, consummating other transactions, emergence from bankruptcy, and other key operational objectives. The design of the KEIP is often leveraged, providing upside and/or downside payouts based upon performance relative to the goals. Program participation and performance goals are key to the design of an effective KEIP. The bankruptcy court generally will not support a KEIP that is too broadly based, does not identify the key executives and their role in the turnaround, and does not require "challenging" performance goals that support real value-add contributions.

Pre-filing Retention Plans

An emerging trend related to bankruptcies is the implementation of retention plans prior to the bankruptcy filing. As noted previously, KERPs, which are time-based retention payments without performance conditions, may not include insiders based upon the bankruptcy rules. Over time, this has created a tension with executives who are typically aware of an impending restructuring. These executives understand their outstanding equity and incentive awards may be worth little to nothing, and know that the design and approval of a KEIP is not a certainty. Any benefit from the KEIP could be months or even years away.

To provide more immediate retention, companies have been implementing retention-based plans immediately prior to the bankruptcy when the plan and payouts are not subject to a court's decision. The general design is one where there is an immediate cash payment to the executives, often within months or even weeks before a filing, but the payments would be clawed back if the participant leaves the organization prior to a specific date or emerging from Chapter 11.

These pre-filing retention plans are an emerging trend but an alternative that should be considered carefully. While these plans can provide immediate and meaningful retention of the executive team, there are two major drawbacks to consider:

1. First, the optics of the plan are poor. These payments are made during a time when the company is in a dire financial position and, often, the management team at the helm during a company's leadup to bankruptcy is the one reaping the benefits of such a plan. When the financial decline is linked to a broader economic downturn, providing retention dollars to the management team and going through the bankruptcy process can provide greater (if not significantly greater) reward than avoiding bankruptcy and having poor payouts from incentive plans.

2. Second, there is no clear trend for how the courts perceive these pre-filing plans. There is some evidence to suggest that the courts are taking notice of these pre-filing retention plans. As a result, compensation proposals made during a bankruptcy — specifically for KERPs and KEIPs — may be struck down or pared back in consideration for the value that was delivered prior to the restructuring. In a case that is expected to be drawn out or negotiated, this can exacerbate the company's retention problem even further.

Time will tell whether these types of awards will continue to increase in prevalence. Therefore, it is important to weigh the benefits of such a plan (immediate retention of the executive team) with the potential downfalls (optics and potential negative impact during bankruptcy) when considering the approach.

Emergence Equity Awards

The final compensation-related consideration during a bankruptcy is the amount and form of equity to award upon emergence from the restructuring process. This is typically a two-step process. The first step is to establish a pool of equity awards that can be

---

distributed upon and after emerging from the bankruptcy. The second step is to determine the individual grants sizes and the design of the equity awards.

The specifics of these awards should align with the company's specific situation. If the company emerges as a stand-alone public company, the pool size and design work will resemble a company that is going through an initial public offering. Alternatively, a company can be purchased out of bankruptcy, which, in the case of a private equity buyer, would have the look and feel of a traditional portfolio company equity structure. Information related to pay design in a public offering or private equity portfolio company can be found in other chapters of this book.

Looking Forward

Going forward, KERPs and KEIPs will likely remain the primary sources of retention and incentive during the bankruptcy process and any consideration for a pre-filing plan should be carefully thought through. Regardless, no two bankruptcy plans look alike, and a significant amount of care and consideration are required to develop a plan that works right for your company.

One-time Grants — Common Purposes

Most publicly traded companies and even many private companies have an annual cadence to equity awards. Clearly defined target opportunities are articulated to the management team, and the vehicles are carefully crafted to align with the company's compensation philosophy and business strategy. But there are times when the status quo for delivering equity will not address the needs of the compensation committee. During these times, special awards can be used to target specific circumstances. The rationale for special grants can be numerous, so this section will focus on three of the most common needs of committees today: retention awards, sign-on awards and mega grants.

Retention Awards

Even well-performing companies can be challenged in retaining talent. There is a premium placed on top talent. In a competitive market, it is prudent to regularly monitor pay and, when necessary, to structure a program to address competitive gaps to support and enhance executive retention. Public company disclosure, say-on-pay voting, third-party advisory groups and the media have all impacted the frequency and design of these programs; they have amplified the need for sound objectives, rationale and design to support the successful implementation of these special forms of compensation.

Retention strategies vary and range from the short-term (e.g., one to two years) to long-term (e.g., 10 years and/or retirement); the time frames depend on the company's particular requirements. Some organizations may need to emphasize critical short-term objectives (e.g., work toward a successful management transition, address a competitive pay gap). Others have a longer-term focus for retention periods (e.g., supporting succession planning for top leadership positions, launch of a new business).

While fixed awards or payments over time may have been the norm, shareholders have become much more vocal that the awards need to be more performance based. Accordingly, restricted stock units with time-based vesting as the primary retention vehicle have come under scrutiny. Even though these awards have long been perceived as strong retention tools, external support for these programs is lacking and the usage is being re-evaluated, especially in companies that have a misalignment between pay and performance. In particular, retention awards have been viewed unfavorably by proxy advisory firms in cases where outstanding grants are underwater and/or annual bonuses have not been earned. Retention awards that appear to replace unearned pay may indicate a lack of commitment toward a pay-for-performance philosophy.

The increased focus on pay-for-performance has complicated the balance of risk and retention in executive compensation programs. As the magnitude of the awards is evaluated quantitatively in conjunction with all other forms of pay (e.g., salary, bonuses, etc.), shareholders and proxy advisory firms now are paying attention to the design of retention-oriented awards.

As a result, the practice of using RSUs as the sole retention vehicle has evolved. Retention awards are now commonly granted in a portfolio approach (similar to LTI practices observed in ongoing annual grants). Time-based awards are delivered in smaller amounts annually rather than in larger up-front grants or in combination with stock options and performance shares. The increased leverage and wealth accumulation opportunities created by the stock options and/ or performance shares can create perceived value for the executive and provide an additional level of external support.

Cash awards were often used to support shorter-term retention goals, but that practice is also evolving. Shareholders want improved alignment with long-term organizational performance, and equity awards accomplish that objective better than cash payments. As such, unless there is compelling rationale not to use equity (such as in a bankruptcy setting discussed earlier in this section or potentially a turnaround situation), cash-based retention awards for senior executives are rare.

Signing Bonuses and Other Signing Awards

Attracting the board's top candidate for CEO or other executive position often requires significant investment, which may include a signing bonus. Signing bonuses are commonly used to compensate the executive for awards and benefits forfeited upon termination of employment with the former employer or as an inducement award that further enhances the value of the pay package.

Signing awards may consist of special equity-based incentives provided to key employees who have a special expertise to entice them to leave their current jobs to join another company. Often the new employer may be in a situation where it is struggling or otherwise in transition, participating in a merger or acquisition, or undergoing a reorganization. A new CEO may have been brought in to run the company during these periods of uncertainty.

When an executive leaves their current employer, a typical result is a complete forfeiture of bonuses, unvested stock option gains, the value of unvested restricted stock grants, and unearned performance awards. To convince the targeted executive to sign on, a company typically will factor the value of those lost benefits into its offer in the form of signing awards.

Even where no special circumstances exist, many companies provide a new CEO (or other top executives) with signing awards, such as stock options, restricted stock and other LTI awards. However, there are situations, although in the minority, when cash incentives are included in the signing bonus in combination with equity-based awards. The cash-based awards typically coincide with riskier business opportunities.

Signing awards generally have vesting provisions to facilitate retention and to prevent any short-term gains in the event of voluntary termination. Further, companies often include clawback language in the grant document that allows the company to require the executive repay the bonus if they leave prior to a certain date.

When contemplating how to deliver a sign-on award, it is important to consider the views of third-party advisers and significant shareholders so that the award does not inadvertently run afoul of their say-on-pay voting guidelines.

The compensation committee's (or board's) objectives and the process used to determine the signing award should be carefully described in the public filings to present a sound rationale to the marketplace.

Mega Grants

Mega grants — where multiple years' worth of equity are granted at once — are a foundational component of private equity-backed portfolio companies. That topic is covered in the next section of this chapter. But, when it comes to mega grants within other companies, they are often considered but rarely implemented.

The common rationale for mega grants is to have a greater alignment between the interests of executives' interests and shareholders. Executives may prefer the concept based upon the perception that they are essentially "buying low" and having more equity loaded up front will only mean more upside as compared to receiving awards on an annual basis. Theoretically, shareholders would prefer this, too, as management becomes more and more engaged as the company's value increases.

But, in realty, the risk associated with mega grants is the reason why they are rarely used. The approach promotes the ultimate wealth creation opportunity and shareholder alignment in good times. But, in bad times — or even stable times — these awards have little to no motivational and retention value. In addition, shareholders are stuck with the cost of the program, its dilutive impact, and, in some circumstances, the committee may feel compelled to provide retention-based awards on top of the mega grant just to keep the team engaged.

Other issues related to mega grants include the following:

- They limit the ability of the committee to adjust its approach to long-term incentives. Under an annual plan, the committee can calibrate changes every 12 months to ensure constant alignment with its changing strategy and contemporary best practice.
- Since these grants can be approved off-cycle, they could create misalignment across the management team depending on stock price movement.
- During the year in which the grant is made, pay will appear much higher than market. A carefully crafted disclosure and adherence to rigid proxy advisor rules are a must to avoid a negative say-on-pay outcome.
- Without a defined cadence, the rationale, intended value and timing for these awards can be lost — this can be exacerbated when there is turnover within the committee. In these cases, we have seen the committee make additional grants before they otherwise intended to because the context of the original intent was lost.

While there is much to consider when using a mega grant, there could always be a rationale for why it works best at your company. In these cases, it is critical to clearly document the rationale for the awards, the period over which they are intended to span and the expected timing for the next equity award. In addition, the proxy advisors understand that these awards may be appropriate and have guidance that should be followed to help support a positive say-on-pay outcome.

Private Equity Firms: Compensating the Executives of Portfolio Companies

Industry investment teams at PE firms operate in an environment of high valuations, with constant and intense competition for deals. As these teams may have hundreds of billions of dollars to use on behalf of their investors, they continuously search for opportunities to evaluate potential transactions and to operate their portfolio companies more efficiently and effectively. Increased emphasis is being placed on the human capital side of deals to address a key question: How can we align the interests of management and investors more quickly so that the process of value creation can begin sooner and enable us to hit our investors' performance expectations? In recent years, there has been a greater appreciation of the talent side of the business in driving investor returns. Namely, there is a need to have the right talent that can execute the strategy, supported by a compelling compensation program, to expedite the process of creating value and delivering returns to fund investors. The compensation program is a critical management tool to help shape and motivate executive behaviors.

Although executive compensation arrangements at investment (or portfolio) companies have similar overarching philosophies and structures, each company has unique characteristics and opportunities that should be aligned and reinforced with focused pay programs. Compensation designs can vary by deal, at times resulting in situations where management and investors are not fully aligned. This can create a need to formulate or leverage the PE firm's best practices to improve the effectiveness of the compensation arrangements.

Overarching Pay Structure

Private equity-backed buyout deals are wealth-creation opportunities where the combination of variable compensation and ownership creates a powerful compensation model that drives management team behaviors and reinforces the alignment of interests among the team, the business and the investors. The pay design typically includes three elements: base salary, an annual incentive opportunity and an LTI opportunity. This compensation structure is widely supported by the marketplace and institutional shareholders.

A fourth (and critical) element of compensation programs is an expectation that management co-invests in the portfolio company along with investors. Such use of personal funds creates real "skin in the game," reinforcing management's commitment to the success of the business and strengthening its alignment with investors. Investment team professionals also are expected to invest in their deals to reinforce their alignment. The commitment of personal proceeds unifies the interests of the fund investor, the deal team and the portfolio company executive team.

Compensation Elements of Portfolio Companies
Annual Cash Compensation (Base Salary, Annual Incentives)

Base salary is de-emphasized in the overall pay program and tends not to fluctuate when a company is acquired unless there is something unique about the existing pay structure. The goal is to provide a competitive salary within a pay framework that emphasizes variable, performance-based compensation.

While many portfolio company annual incentive programs are discretionary (which is also common in the financial services model), the preferred approach is a structured annual incentive program utilized by public companies: predetermined performance goals that align with a leveraged incentive opportunity. These arrangements typically consist of a target bonus (expressed as a percentage of salary), combined with a threshold payout for near achievement of goals and an upside (or maximum) opportunity that aligns with superior levels of performance. This common model helps limit short-term decision making and reinforces the long-term upside of the LTI and ownership elements of the pay model.

Long-Term Incentives

The LTI program, along with the co-investment, are the primary drivers of shareholder alignment and the wealth-creation opportunity.

Historically, the LTIs were in the form of appreciation-only awards (e.g., stock options) that were consistent with a growth strategy and with the PE carried interest model, which, broadly stated, is equal to 20 percent of the appreciation over a performance hurdle. More recently, full-value shares (e.g., restricted stock) are being implemented in the LTI programs for the same reasons observed in public companies: retention and less share dilution.

There are also LTI vehicles used in PE-backed deals that mirror the economics of stock options or restricted stock (e.g., profits interests) but with the potential for preferential tax treatment. Operationally, these awards are similar to stock options or restricted stock but require very specific structuring and coordination with legal counsel.

Grant Frequency

A significant difference in the grant strategies between a portfolio company and a publicly traded company is the frequency of the LTI grant. Given the expected short-term ownership of the portfolio company (four to six years), the LTI is usually granted at one time at the close of the transaction. This approach provides the executives with an opportunity to maximize their returns by receiving their entire grants upfront, allowing for the full awards to participate in the value created.

A challenge to this strategy can occur when a company may be in the portfolio for a longer term than originally anticipated. As the value creation and exit time frames take longer, they begin to impact the perceived value of the LTI award (e.g., with an assumed five-year horizon). In such cases, management teams may seek "refresh grants" and/or opportunities to monetize portions of their investment prior to an exit event; these variations run counter to the PE model.

Participation

Portfolio company LTI plans typically are limited to the senior executives who are most directly aligned with value creation. While programs at public companies commonly go much deeper into the organization, the structure at PE firms reflects their limited share reserves, complexity of arrangements and a philosophy that stresses putting ownership into the hands of the executives who are most directly accountable for delivering returns. Organizations that need to provide LTI to a broader set of employees may use multi-year cash plans, but the emphasis of the wealth-creation opportunities still is focused on the senior management team.

Vesting

The LTI program typically follows public company practice: a combination of time- and performance-vested awards. Practices vary, but a common approach is 25 to 50 percent of the award being time-vested, with vesting on the balance (50 to 75 percent) contingent on satisfying performance criteria.

The performance standards generally consist of one or two return-based criteria: multiple of invested capital or MOIC (usually two times and higher) and an internal rate of return or IRR requirement (typically 20 percent and higher), which considers the amount of time required to generate the return on capital invested. The performance-vested awards typically have multiple tranches with increasing performance requirements (e.g., 25 percent vests at two times return, 25 percent vests at a two and a half times return).

Monetization

The ability to monetize, or convert the awards to cash, is aligned with the investors, and occurs when the portfolio company investment is sold (i.e., the exit event) and the investors receive their return.

Co-Investment Opportunities

The alignment of interests is further strengthened when management co-invests in the portfolio company alongside the PE investors. This is a powerful element of PE strategy as it creates a unified ownership model among the fund investors, investment team and management team that ultimately aligns all stakeholders toward a successful exit event (and subsequent monetization) in the future.

The management team's proceeds are typically funded by incentives from their prior company's compensation arrangements, which could be payouts from LTI programs, retention awards, or severance arrangements.

Summary

There are several situations where companies need to go outside their typical grant practices to meet a particular situation. This is typically in the form of retention awards, sign-on grants and mega grants. While each compensation vehicle serves important needs, there are downsides to consider.

Given the unique role of these special awards, many of the rules discussed earlier in this book do not apply, particularly in a restructuring situation. However, careful consideration of special awards, their purpose and design, can maximize the benefit to an organization and its shareholders.

CHAPTER 28

Executive Compensation in Tax-Exempt Organizations

By James Otto and Jim Nelson

Although their funding comes from private or public donors, membership fees, tuition, grants, and the provision of services, tax-exempt organizations mimic many of the compensation practices of their for-profit competitors. In the field of health care, for example, tax-exempt organizations are important players whose major competitors can include large, publicly held health care companies and a variety of life-science firms. Like the for-profit companies with whom they often compete for board and executive talent, tax-exempt organizations must attract and retain talented management and thus provide sufficiently competitive levels of pay and benefits.

Tax-exempt organizations are the focus of considerable external scrutiny, especially regarding the amounts and type of compensation and governance issues relating to executive compensation. Much like the heightened sensitivities within audit committees that increased their workloads, tax-exempt boards and their compensation committees must now devote considerably more time justifying their executive compensation decisions than they did not too long ago. The tax law's requirement to pay no more than reasonable compensation (now enforced primarily by the "intermediate sanctions" rules), the excise tax on annual remuneration over $1M for certain executives, governance reforms, and changes in the private sector, have prompted many tax-exempt boards to go beyond mere compliance and adopt best practice models of governance found in successful publicly traded companies. Today, the issues and concerns surrounding executive pay and benefits in many tax-exempt organizations are largely the same as those in for-profit enterprises.

This chapter:

- Discusses how the current climate of accountability and transparency in the private sector has challenged tax-exempt organizations to develop governance practices beyond the mandated disclosure requirements.
- Reviews the intermediate sanctions provisions of the IRC and outlines the key elements of good governance practice and related issues such as the need for a precisely articulated compensation philosophy. A total remuneration ("Total R") approach that unites all pay elements in one coherent philosophy and compensation program is presented.
- Describes the use and design of LTIs and SERPs in tax-exempt organizations as part of a comprehensive approach to compensation.
- Summarizes the excise tax provisions of the IRC that apply to annual remuneration and certain severance benefits, and how certain components of pay affect the possible application of the tax.
- Answers the question, "Should we pay our board?" The factors that go into determining board pay as well as how and what to pay directors are discussed.

Current Influences on Executive Compensation in the Tax-Exempt Sector

From small associations operating in local communities to well-recognized international charities, educational institutions, private foundations, museums and health care organizations, tax-exempt organizations span a broad organizational spectrum. Guided in their operations by core missions and values, these organizations have been established and are operated to satisfy the rules that exempt them from federal and state income taxes. Retaining this tax-exempt status is a vital concern, and oversight of executive compensation plays a crucial role.

While the rules that affect this oversight responsibility have been in place for many years, the importance of paying executives based on the outcomes of good governance practice has never been more important. The influence of stakeholders of tax-exempt organizations has increased significantly and shapes how board members and senior leaders conduct the affairs of the organization. These groups include donors, employees, bond holders, local communities, service recipients, labor unions, state legislatures, the media and the IRS, each of which finds the incendiary aspect of executive compensation an avenue to exert influence in one way or another.

The call for increased accountability and transparency that pervades all aspects of corporate governance today in public companies is also being felt in tax-exempt organizations. This phenomenon was first apparent with the passage of the Sarbanes-Oxley Act of 2002, and the specific provisions of the act that affected executive compensation at publicly traded companies (e.g., the ban on loans from corporations to officers). Tax-exempt organizations, many of which include prominent for-profit executives on their boards, were encouraged to adopt some or all of the governance and accountability standards imposed by this legislation and the governance and disclosure practices utilized within their own companies. (See "Influences from Sarbanes-Oxley.")

Influences from Sarbanes-Oxley

Loans to Executives

One of the most publicized aspects of Sarbanes-Oxley is its prohibition of most personal loans by a covered company to a director or an executive officer. In the past, tax-exempt organizations occasionally made loans to executive officers, often to enable them to purchase a house upon hire or transfer into a more expensive real estate market. Although such loans still are possible in tax-exempts that have not instituted a policy barring their use, current best practices would require an especially strong reason for using this much-criticized practice.

Codes of Ethics

Under Sarbanes-Oxley a public company must disclose whether it has adopted a code of ethics for its senior financial officers. In the event there is no such code, reasons for this failure also must be disclosed. The basic concept of a code of ethics is readily transferable to tax-exempts, as is the developing view that such codes should also be extended to other officers and board members.

This impact was heightened by the passage of Dodd-Frank. That Act included provisions that affect executive compensation at publicly traded companies (e.g., independence of compensation committee members and recoupment of incentive payments in certain instances) that are considered and often adapted by tax-exempt organizations to augment and improve the oversight of executive compensation. (See "Influences from Dodd-Frank.")

Good Governance Practice

The income tax requirement that tax-exempt organizations oversee the compensation of their executives and not pay excessive compensation to its key executives has been in place for decades. However, the 1996 enactment of the "intermediate sanctions" provisions (IRC section 4958) and the IRS' subsequent promulgation of detailed

Influences from Dodd-Frank

Clawbacks

A key component of Dodd-Frank's executive compensation provisions requires most public companies to have (and disclose) a policy regarding the recovery (clawback) of certain types and amounts of incentive compensation paid to identified executives if the incentive compensation was based on results in financial statements that must be restated for certain reasons. The interpretation and implementation of the Dodd-Frank clawback rules were conditioned on the adoption by the SEC rules followed by their inclusion in listing standards of the applicable securities exchange. While SEC rulemaking does not apply to tax-exempt entities, these organizations consider SEC rules when developing their own policies.

CEO "Pay Ratio" Disclosure

The Dodd-Frank provision requiring disclosure of the median of the annual total compensation of all employees of a public company (other than the CEO), the CEO's annual total compensation, and the ratio of these two sets of numbers, has generated heated debate and discussion as to the usefulness of the outcome in understanding the executive compensation program at public companies. Even though tax-exempt organizations are not subject to this rule, the disclosure of these numbers by public companies has prompted their boards and compensation committees to consider the nature and level of executive compensation in relation to the pay of other employees of the organization and has influenced the "how" and "how much" discussions that these bodies already are having. The SEC rulemaking also has generated internal discussions regarding the fairness of pay at all levels, "living wage" demands, and other social justice issues that can impact how the organization's mission should influence the executive compensation program.

regulations complicated the decision-making process on executive compensation at tax-exempts. (See "Intermediate Sanctions.")

As detailed in the intermediate sanctions regulations, the requirements that need to be satisfied to obtain a presumption that compensation is reasonable are now considered to be part of a good governance practice. These requirements, coupled with the increased scrutiny of executive compensation and the fact that boards of tax-exempts can be held accountable for unreasonable compensation, have improved governance practices and the oversight of executive compensation at tax-exempt organizations.

Independence of Board or Committee Members Overseeing Executive Compensation

The income tax regulations on intermediate sanctions (discussed below) describe independence in a way that is fairly narrow in scope:

Not only has legislation affected how tax-exempt organizations oversee executive compensation, but the regulations that have been developed by the IRS (discussed later in the chapter) and the rules issued by the SEC that operationalize relevant laws have been a major influence. For example, committees that oversee executive compensation in tax-exempt organizations are much more aware of the need to answer the "how" and "why" questions about the levels of compensation provided and the modes used to deliver it. These questions reflect the intent of the CD&A, which is part of the proxy statement for most publicly traded companies. In essence, the CD&A must describe material actions of compensation committees and the reasoning behind their decisions.

Finally, the IRS overhaul of Form 990, which now includes much more detailed disclosure of compensation for senior executives and detailed description of how executive compensation is determined, also has influenced the oversight of executive compensation in tax-exempt organizations.

At the same time that today's regulatory and governance concerns are increasing the focus on (and affecting the oversight of) executive compensation, tax-exempts must attract and retain talented management and provide compensation programs that enable them to deliver upon their core mission. This often requires competing for talent with for-profit entities. For example, in the field of health care, most major providers are tax-exempt organizations whose talent pool can include large, publicly held health care, managed care and life science companies.

These two dynamics — increased scrutiny of executive compensation and the need to attract and keep management teams — provide challenges to any organization. A well-considered oversight process is the bridge to addressing both of these and maximizing the benefits for the organization at the same time.

is each member of the board or committee free of any conflict of interest when deciding on compensation for a particular executive who is covered by the regulations? An example of a conflict is when a physician is on the board that determines the compensation of a CEO of Health System, and that CEO is involved in negotiating the compensation of that physician, who is an employee of Health System. Tax-exempt organizations are taking into consideration an expansive definition in determining whether a committee member is independent, which often includes using relevant portions of the "independence" definitions that exist in the national securities exchanges' standards. The objective is to ensure that the organization can take the position that the committee overseeing executive compensation is independent of the organization in making these decisions (and not just free of conflict with respect to a particular compensation arrangement).

Intermediate Sanctions

To maintain their tax-exempt status, organizations have been required for decades to pay no more than reasonable compensation to executives and avoid private inurement (net earnings of the organization cannot "inure" to individuals or shareholders) and private benefit (activities must serve public rather than private-benefit interests) when determining the level and method of compensating executives and other identified employees.

IRC section 4958, popularly known as "intermediate sanctions," is a more recent provision affecting executive compensation at tax-exempt organizations. Statutory language is supplemented by extensive regulations that give the IRS the ability to assess financial penalties on both executives and board members of section 501(c)(3) and 501(c)(4) organizations for any "excess benefit transaction" involving a "disqualified person." (Prior to intermediate sanctions, the IRS could either revoke the organization's tax exemption or overlook the violation when it determined that an executive was paid an unreasonable amount; the excise tax under IRC section 4958 provides an "intermediate" result between these two extremes.) Although the intermediate sanctions legislation was enacted in 1996, it was not until the regulations were finalized in early 2002 that active enforcement began.

Paying unreasonable compensation to a disqualified person is an "excess benefit transaction." A "disqualified person" is a person in a position that currently can exert substantial influence over the affairs of a tax-exempt organization or could do so during a five-year "look back" period. Top executive officers and board members generally are disqualified persons. The value of all consideration and benefits received by a disqualified person in a year is examined in determining whether there has been an excess benefit transaction for that year. Both the individual receiving the unreasonable

Defining the "Market" for Comparability of Data

Two IRS projects examined whether organizations satisfy the requirements to establish the presumption that compensation is reasonable: in a review of tax-exempt health care organizations and more recently in a review of private colleges and universities. In the study of the educational institutions, the IRS noted that some failed to satisfy the requirement that they used data of comparable organizations; this was based on the group of organizations that were used to develop compensation data for context in making compensation decisions. The IRS identified a number of factors to be considered, but most importantly, focused on educational institutions as the starting point for determining which of these types of organizations should be in the group. (The IRS also indicated that some organizations used as "comparables" were in entirely different industries.)

compensation and the board members who authorized payment of the unreasonable compensation may be subject to the financial penalties under IRC section 4958.

To minimize concerns with intermediate sanctions, tax-exempt organizations must be able to demonstrate that a covered executive's total executive compensation is reasonable. The regulations provide three basic requirements that, if met, establish a "rebuttable presumption" that compensation is reasonable, which shifts the burden of proof to the IRS to show that the compensation is unreasonable. The three requirements are:

> Executive compensation arrangements must be approved by an independent body with no conflict of interest.

> An independent comparability study that considers all elements of compensation should be conducted and the results used to assist the independent body in determining compensation levels. This data may be obtained through compensation surveys, an examination of compensation of similar individuals in similar organizations and/or an expert compensation study. (See "Defining the 'Market' for Comparability of Data.")

> Approval of executive compensation arrangements should be documented before the latter of the next meeting or 60 days after the final actions of the decision-making body; this documentation should include:

– The specific terms and conditions of the approved transaction and the date approved;

– The members of the decision-making body who were present during debate on the transaction that was approved and their votes; and

– The comparability data that was relied on by the decision-making body and how the data was obtained.

Tax-exempt organizations should consider this guidance as they review, update and rationalize their group of comparable organizations when developing comparability data, in particular when tax-exempt health care providers expand their operating model to include non-traditional business lines such as commercial health insurance offerings. Business lines that are outside the scope of traditional health care service providers raise the issue of what is the appropriate peer group for these new lines.

Why Are We Making the Decision That We Are?

The use of comparability data provides the compensation committee and board with context for making decisions that are specific to and support the particular needs of the organization. In the past, committees and boards were prone to following the market (i.e., doing what the market says other organizations are doing because other organizations are doing it). Committees and boards are now being asked, and are demanding of themselves, to articulate why they are making any decision that affects any executive's compensation arrangement. For example, "why should the organization adopt a supplemental executive retirement plan?" By asking and answering this type of question, committees are expressing the business rationale for the decision and how their decision makes sense for the organization. Committees also are requiring greater insight from their consultants and HR departments, particularly with respect to the relevance of a comparator group and data that is developed based on that group.

Process and Roles

The intermediate sanctions regulations imply a process that culminates in documenting the decisions made. Organizations are expanding this documentation requirement to formalize the process by which executive compensation is reviewed and modified. This codification can take the form of items such as:

- Compensation philosophy
- Compensation program documents (e.g., annual incentive plan, LTI plan, severance policy, employment agreements)

- Committee charter (number of members, "independence" definition, scope of authority, reporting responsibility, succession)
- Committee calendar (number of meetings, typical agenda items)
- Role of compensation adviser, legal counsel and staff support
- Level of detail reported to the board on committee decisions
- Maintenance of meeting minutes
- Attendance at each meeting by outside counsel.

This level of detail provides the foundation on which organizations can complete the information required on Form 990 and develop the manner in which the organization wants to respond to any stakeholder inquiry on executive compensation.

To evaluate the degree to which the board is driving the process and the decisions, the IRS can access the board's documentation to understand how decisions are made, including compensation committee and board minutes, documentation of decision-making, rationale for the market positioning of specific executives and the board's executive compensation philosophy.

Compensation Philosophy and Components of the Compensation Program: Critical Sub-Elements

A compensation philosophy is the touch point when making compensation decisions. A philosophy can furnish critical guidance for the board, the compensation committee and executive leadership in making consistent pay decisions, and is a key document for the IRS to review in an audit. A philosophy articulates:

- **The "market."** What does the peer group look like? From where does the organization recruit executive talent and to where does the organization lose executive talent?
- **Job match.** How should the organization's jobs be compared to jobs at these comparable organizations?
- **Compensation elements.** What are the components of the compensation program (e.g., base salary, annual incentive, LTI, benefits)? Why are they being used? How does the component play a role in facilitating performance, retention or recruitment?

- **Compensation mix.** How do the components interrelate? For example, how much of cash compensation should be based on performance (incentives) and how much is to be based on service or the job (base salary)? How should benefits be taken into account, particularly any executive-level benefits?

- **Compensation positioning relative to the market.** What is the target market level for the various components of pay and the various combinations of pay? What is the desired pay positioning with the competitive market for talent and the rationale of that positioning?

- **Pay administration.** How are the CEO and committee to interact when determining pay levels? For example, does the committee approve all pay changes based on CEO recommendations?

Total R

Link Total R to Performance

Total Remuneration, or "Total R," is the resulting combination of all of the compensatory components of the compensation program. Total R should reinforce priorities and focus employees on the desired behaviors and outcomes for the organization. Korn Ferry research with Fortune magazine's "Most Admired" companies shows that these organizations differentiate rewards based on performance. Top performers are rewarded highly, while pay is limited for poor performance. In our experience, tax-exempt organizations that successfully link Total R to performance:

> Take the time to discuss what performance is and what success looks like. For many organizations, what constitutes real performance is often not obvious.

> Look at relative performance, understanding how the organization compares with similar ones.

> Examine and negotiate performance measures rigorously.

> May not always pay out incentives. Boards can now look back over some prior period and see how performance compared with payout. What was the payout each year? Was there variability? Did the payouts align with the perception of success?

> Reinforce the importance of the top team by linking a substantial amount of pay to achieving organizational goals.

Broaden Total R to Promote Succession

Organizations that recognize the need to develop and retain experienced, innovative executives are establishing succession strategies based on intrinsic Total R components as well as extrinsic components (base salary, incentives, benefits and perquisites). Executives identify quality of work, development opportunities, work-life balance, satisfying work environments, reputation and values, and leadership effectiveness

The discussion involved in developing an organization's compensation philosophy provides a timely opportunity for the board or compensation committee and management to agree on how compensation is linked to the organization's mission, and what messages the organization wants to send to its external and internal constituents. The philosophy needs to be approved by the committee or board and referenced as a check when executive compensation is established and annually assessed. (See "Total R.")

The IRS has made clear that a compensation philosophy is the foundation on which compensation decisions should be made and is an indicator of good governance practice; it believes that organizations are less likely to pay unreasonable compensation if good governance practices are followed.

as the top factors that influence their desire to stay with an organization and assume bigger positions. Organizations that focus on those variables show measurable results in attracting and retaining talented executives and achieving business objectives.

Communicate Total R to Participants

Communication translates leadership decisions about Total R into clear messages for executives. Organizations that are most successful in communicating Total R emphasize the integration with mission, strategy, performance and desire to raise employee satisfaction. One approach provides executives with online access to the value of their individual total remuneration arrangements. This approach helps executives understand the true value and employer cost associated with each pay component.

Assess and Update Total R Annually

This process can be conducted internally or through the use of independent advisers. Most organizations prefer outside advisers for their expertise, objectivity and access to benchmarks. The process must involve compensation committee deliberation and use relevant market data as a basis for setting executive pay.

Engage a Third Party to Confirm Reasonableness of Compensation

An independent third party that is qualified to professionally assess compensation can help demonstrate the reasonableness of compensation. A third party can conduct an analysis of total remuneration levels and assist in determining that compensation levels are within a reasonable range. The third party also can issue an opinion letter to confirm the use of comparable data as part of the effort to establish a rebuttable presumption of reasonableness (and shift the burden onto the IRS to overcome this showing) and minimize the risk to the committee members that they would be subject to financial penalties under the intermediate sanctions provision if the IRS were to prevail in a determination that compensation was unreasonable.

A compensation program captures the compensatory components identified in the compensation philosophy and the documents related to these components. Therefore, the program includes such items as base salary, incentives, specific benefits and the manner in which each of these is documented (e.g., for an incentive component, through the combination of a plan document and specific actions taken by the committee that are memorialized in committee minutes). The continuous review of the philosophy and the resulting compensation program are a key part of the ongoing oversight of executive compensation.

SERPs and LTIs: Components of the Compensation Program and Design Issues to Consider

One element that committees consider including in the organization's compensation program is a "supplemental executive retirement plan" (SERP), a nonqualified plan that long has been and continues to be a key component in compensation programs at tax-exempt organizations. Boards and compensation committees at tax-exempt organizations continue to use this type of plan in a variety of situations, in large part because of its design flexibility.

Organizations must consider the specific income tax rules that apply to these plans when sponsored by tax-exempt organizations. SERP benefits are taxable when no longer subject to a "substantial risk of forfeiture," which essentially means upon vesting. An executive no longer risks forfeiture that is substantial when they do not have to provide any future "substantial services" to the employer to receive the benefit. In general, this is not the same way that the IRC addresses SERP benefits sponsored by taxable organizations — those plans can be structured so that benefits vest and are taxed later, when they are paid.

Compensation committees or boards have flexibility in designing the vesting schedule within a plan; for example, the same vesting schedule does not have to apply to all participants in the plan, so the vesting schedule for a mid-career hire who becomes a participant in the plan at age 55 may be different from a newly promoted 40-year-old executive who has always worked at the organization.

LTI arrangements are an increasingly common element in compensation programs at tax-exempt organizations. These plans typically are designed to complement the goals of the annual incentive plan and focus a select group of executives on achieving specific, multi-year, organization-wide goals based on the organization's strategy. The plan allows the organization to identify, pursue and measure progress toward performance objectives that further the mission and strategic goals over a sustained period of time and help balance each participating executive's focus between annual and long-term objectives. In constructing an LTI arrangement, the committee and senior management must address issues similar to those in an annual incentive arrangement, including:

- Purpose
- Eligibility and participation
- Administration
- Performance period
- Plan circuit breaker (i.e., below what performance level will the plan shut down?)
- Incentive opportunity
- Performance measures, goals and weighting
- Funding and distribution.

These plans are almost always paid in cash because the use of equity and the transfer of tax-exempt assets are governed by strict state and federal laws, and typically there is no equity of the organization that is available for awards. Of course, with any compensation element, how an LTI is to "fit" with the other compensation elements is part of the design process.

Excise Taxes on Remuneration over $1M and on Certain Severance Payments

In the legislation known as the Tax Cuts and Jobs Act of 2017, which is effective for tax years after December 31, 2017, Congress included a new IRC section 4960 that applies to most tax-exempt organizations.

This new statute imposes an employer-paid 21 percent excise tax on annual "remuneration" that exceeds $1M provided to "covered employees." (This 21% rate can change over time.) For this purpose, a covered employee is any of the five highest compensated employees of the tax-exempt organization — and once included in this group, an individual is always included in this group.

"Remuneration" is generally all W-2 compensation and any amounts that vest in that year (even if not paid); however, the statute does not include in this definition any compensation paid for clinical services provided by licensed doctors and nurses.

The statute — along with an IRS notice and proposed regulations — has complex rules that require each organization that is part of a single operating enterprise (e.g., a health care system with different corporations under a parent entity) to be treated as individual organizations when determining each organization's "covered employees," and to include all remuneration paid to an individual for rendered services through various related and unrelated organizations to be treated as that individual's remuneration when determining whether the $1M amount has been exceeded.

The statute also imposes a 21 percent excise tax on any "excess parachute payment" by a tax-exempt organization — in general, this excise tax may apply when amounts are paid (or benefits are provided) on account of an involuntary termination of employment. There are detailed definitions and a series of calculations that must be made to determine whether any excess parachute payment has been made. Determining whether this excise tax applies is an exercise separate from reviewing whether a covered employee's remuneration exceeds $1M for a particular year, but there is no duplication of excise taxes on remuneration and excess parachute payments (i.e., an amount can be subject to one or the other, but not both). Also, even if remuneration is subject to the excise tax on amounts over $1M, this does not render the remuneration automatically "unreasonable" under the intermediate sanctions rules.

Boards and committees are addressing these new excise taxes by:

■ Reviewing and confirming the continued appropriateness of the compensation philosophy. In particular, the comparison to the identified market, the components of pay used in the executive compensation program and the target market levels, remain appropriate.

- Examining each component of pay to confirm ongoing competitiveness in the market.
- Educating themselves on the organization's current severance arrangements, including reviewing severance scenarios and the potential application of the excise tax.

In particular, boards and committees are reviewing the timing of payment or vesting of compensation, and considering ways to mitigate or eliminate the possible application of the excise tax. For example, remuneration for an executive includes any SERP benefit in the year that it vests (whether or not paid at vesting). Boards and committees are considering whether to implement alternative delivery vehicles — such as split dollar life insurance arrangements — that are treated differently for tax purposes and as a result, are not considered "remuneration" for purposes of the excise tax.

By being proactive in addressing these new excise taxes, boards and committees demonstrate their desire to continue serving as the stewards of the organization's executive compensation program.

Considerations for Board Pay

As the accountabilities and liabilities of public company board members have increased, a director's job has become considerably more difficult and time consuming. This has made the recruitment and retention of directors a much more important and challenging task, often resulting in greater compensation of these directors. Increased board responsibilities, however, are not unique to directors of public companies. Tax-exempt board members also are finding themselves with significantly more responsibility.

While many (typically smaller) tax-exempt organizations historically have not paid their directors, more are asking whether board pay is not only appropriate but necessary. In the increasingly stringent environment of tax-exempt board governance, director roles are getting harder and carrying more weight.

In consulting with numerous tax-exempt organizations, three related issues affecting the compensation of tax-exempt board members have been examined: whether to pay, how to pay and what to pay.

A Changing Environment

In recent years, tax-exempt board membership has shifted from risk-free public service to time-consuming stakeholder accountability. These directors now have much greater responsibilities that include the same types of tasks that directors of publicly traded companies face, including those related to audit, fiduciary matters and executive compensation. Clearly, tax-exempt board governance has changed. As responsibilities and accountabilities have grown, a debate has emerged whether it is appropriate to pay directors at tax-exempt organizations for their services.

There often is a perception that paying board members at tax-exempt organizations is inappropriate and that the practice runs counter to the missions of such organizations. In fact, some tax-exempts still look for guidance to a now-dated independent sector report commissioned by the U.S. Senate Finance Committee that discouraged any compensation for tax-exempt board members unless the complexity, time commitment or skill requirements of the board so warranted. In practice, board pay has been infrequent across the tax-exempt universe.

However, for a number of years there has been a growing sense that as the role of the tax-exempt board evolves and time requirements have increased, board pay may not only be appropriate but also necessary to attract and retain the high-caliber directors needed. In general, board compensation is permissible as long as the organization's bylaws allow it, the payment does not result in private inurement or private benefit and is considered reasonable for the services rendered. Essentially, this requires that pay not exceed the amount that ordinarily would be paid for like services by like enterprises under like circumstances. Also, many tax-exempt directors have opportunities to serve on for-profit boards that pay significant director fees. If particular tax-exempt organizations are competing with their for-profit brethren for top talent, paying directors may be a necessity.

There can be a rationale for compensating tax-exempt directors, and payment can be appropriate when the specific situation of the organization warrants.

Whether to Pay: Five Factors to Consider

The decisions on whether to pay and what to pay tax-exempt directors should be considered very carefully and driven by factors unique to each organization. Based on review of existing research and consulting expertise, the decision to pay the board should be guided primarily by five considerations:

- **Complexity of the organization.** Does the organization have various moving parts or particularly difficult issues, whether strategic, regulatory or optical? If so, the added complexity may furnish support for paying directors.
- **Time commitment required.** Are directors spending significant amounts of time either in the boardroom or otherwise performing board duties and responsibilities? If so, it may be appropriate for directors to be paid for their time.
- **Level of direct operational involvement and special skills required.** Do directors have any direct operational involvement in the organization? Is the organization involved in a situation that requires a specialized skill set? If so, then this is an indication that the director talent may have a substantial effect on the organization's success, and there may be greater justification for paying them.
- **Competitive market for director talent.** With what types of organizations does the board compete for director talent? Are these organizations compensating their directors? If so, these organizations may provide a reasonable benchmark for pay practices. In particular, tax-exempts that directly compete with for-profit companies may determine they need to compensate their directors or lose out on certain candidates.
- **Affordability.** Can the organization afford to pay its directors? Would director pay limit the programmatic offerings of the organization

in any way? Simply put, directors should only be paid if the organization can afford to do so.

Two types of organizations that tend to meet these criteria are health care providers and large foundations. These employers typically are complex tax-exempt organizations; they are highly regulated, publicly and legally accountable, and require specific skill sets. Also, in the health care field, tax-exempt providers may compete with large for-profit health care systems for board talent. As a result, many such organizations may be strong candidates for director pay. Conversely, organizations that do not meet the bulk of these criteria may not appear to be suitable for director pay.

How to Pay: The Components of Director Pay Packages

If an organization, after evaluating itself against these factors, decides to pay its directors, it has various options for delivering that pay. The typical components of director pay include:

- **Annual retainers.** Similar to base pay, a retainer normally is a guaranteed cash amount.
- **Meeting fees.** These are fees for every board and/or committee meeting attended. Some committees, like audit, pay a premium relative to other committees to acknowledge increased importance and accountability.
- **Chairperson fees.** A member who chairs a committee may receive a special retainer for their services in the form of an additional retainer or additional meeting fees.
- **Committee membership fees.** Those who serve on a committee may receive an additional retainer for membership.

While these forms of director compensation are typically considered when developing a board package in the for-profit world, not all may be appropriate for a tax-exempt setting. Given the optics of compensating tax-exempt board members, the structure of pay packages and the vehicles used should be carefully examined.

In keeping with the pay-for-performance philosophy that organizations almost uniformly are adopting in their executive compensation philosophies, tax-exempt organizations may decide to structure their pay packages heavily toward a time commitment orientation. While it is common in general industry to maintain a significant portion of the overall pay package in the form of a guaranteed retainer, at some tax-exempts it may be more appropriate to limit the guaranteed component in favor of meeting fees, which only pay members for the time they spend in the boardroom.

What to Pay: Benchmarking Against Comparable Organizations

Evaluating what target level of compensation is appropriate for a board can be a bit tricky. As discussed, tax-exempt board pay has not been a prevalent practice and, as a result, there are few survey sources available that collect this information.

Given these constraints, an organization should customize its data collection to the specific director talent market of that organization through the development of two "peer groups" — one tax-exempt and one public — that the organization may compete with for board members. These groups could include organizations that are involved in comparable activities, are similar in size and scope, and/or share a geographic area. Some tax-exempt organizations recruit directors locally and may be competing for directors with the publicly traded company across the street, regardless of the business focus of that company. A good peer group may be a blend of these factors, but at the end of the day, it should fairly represent the competitive market for director talent.

Tax-Exempt Peer Groups

Within the tax-exempt peer group, data can be collected from public Form 990 filings, which have board compensation information. While improvements were made to this form, information can be spotty and incomplete and may not be sufficiently current. This time lag may present data that does not capture recent increases in tax-exempt board compensation. For this reason, a custom survey of similar tax-exempt organizations can be helpful when there is adequate time and budget to undertake this approach.

Public Company Comparisons

Use of a for-profit peer group can provide another appropriate benchmark, although it should not be the sole source of comparison. Within a for-profit peer group, data can be collected from public proxy filings, which provide more complete and up-to-date information on all forms of director compensation than on Form 990. However, in most circumstances, tax-exempt organizations should not look to fully replicate for-profit director pay packages. On average, the job of a director at a publicly traded company is subject to greater scrutiny and has more accountability and liability than that of a tax-exempt organization's director. This means that the pay data provided by these for-profit companies generally should be discounted when being used as context for developing board compensation in tax-exempt organizations.

One way to provide an appropriate discount is to eliminate from consideration any equity or LTI grants. In other instances, referencing only the 25th percentile of pay practices in the peer group may be appropriate. The right target-market positioning will depend on the organization itself and the degree to which it competes with these for-profit organizations.

Preparing for Scrutiny

In the end, any tax-exempt organization that chooses to compensate its directors should be prepared for scrutiny of the practice. Tax-exempt board pay is expected to increase in prevalence as board accountabilities grow, but some constituencies will continue to see board service as a public service and will understandably be opposed to the practice.

Consistent with the documentation on executive compensation decisions, tax-exempt organizations should maintain transparency of the process and fully document all pay decisions related to an organization's directors. In particular, the written rationale — either in the form of a policy or a formal philosophy — regarding the decision on payment of directors (considering the factors stressed in this chapter) is a key part of this documentation.

CHAPTER 29

Compensation Litigation

By William Gerek and Kurt Groeninger

E xecutive officers and directors are under increased scrutiny by
shareholders, regulators, elected officials, proxy advisory firms
and the general public regarding compensation and governance
within their organizations. Regardless of whether an organization is
private or public, for-profit or tax-exempt, stakeholders have raised
the bar on their expectations of organizational performance, transparency and engagement. Plaintiffs' compensation-related claims
against organizations continue to increase, although the underlying
bases for the claims often evolve and change from year to year.

Good governance is the first line of defense as it more likely results
in a sound and defensible process related to compensation; that is,
compensation decisions are made in the context of an established
and transparent process in compliance with applicable laws, rules
and regulations. For public companies, a sound process also includes
robust and transparent disclosure.

In essence, an organization's board of directors mitigates the risk
of litigation if it identifies a decision-making process that involves the
proper governing body; maintains an accurate record of decisions;
properly allocates responsibility across departments, including HR,
legal, finance, stock administration, accounting and external advisers;
regularly reviews incentive plans and total compensation programs;
and accurately discloses information about compensation programs and
relevant comparator entities used in setting compensation. However,

even the most well-intentioned and studied decisions may be subject to legal scrutiny as key stakeholders become more active in challenging compensation programs.

Once a claim is filed, it often will be expensive for the organization both monetarily and in potential reputational harm. Accordingly, organizations help themselves through following best practices in governance, engaging with shareholders and conducting reasonableness studies related to pay.

This chapter:

- Outlines common shareholder claims alleging excessive executive and director compensation and approaches to mitigate the risk of those claims.
- Describes distinct claims that have been filed against public companies and steps that companies can take to reduce the risk of these claims.
- Discusses claims that can arise with respect to family-owned businesses and nonprofit organizations.
- Briefly summarizes compensation-related claims made in special circumstances (wrongful death, divorce and bankruptcy cases).

Claims Alleging Excessive Executive and Director Compensation

The reasons for increasing legal claims related to executive and director compensation are varied and multiple. Although they are most common in publicly traded companies, excessive compensation claims are brought against privately held companies, including family-owned businesses, and nonprofit corporations.

Excessive Executive Compensation

A common claim filed against directors is one for breach of fiduciary duty and/or corporate waste for approving the payment of excessive compensation to executives. Many claims of excessive compensation are dismissed for failure to satisfy the special "demand requirement" related to shareholder derivative actions (i.e., claims brought by a shareholder on behalf of the company). The demand requirement is a procedural step that a shareholder must "demand" that a company's board bring a claim before the shareholder may file a claim. However, if shareholder plaintiffs overcome applicable procedural hurdles, they may bring claims against directors on behalf of the company.

Much of the increased scrutiny (and litigation) surrounding executive compensation paid by public companies followed the 2010 adoption of Dodd-Frank, which mandated non-binding shareholder votes and new compensation-related disclosures by public companies. One of the early requirements adopted by the SEC was the say-on-pay vote in which shareholders are given the opportunity to voice their approval (or disapproval) of a company's compensation practices in a non-binding vote. Some of the companies that received negative say-on-pay results in the first years after the SEC mandated the vote became the subject of shareholder litigation.

Although these early cases were unsuccessful, claims of excessive executive compensation continue. Claims vary in identifying which element of compensation, or combination thereof, results in allegedly excessive total direct compensation, but they often relate to short- and long-term incentive structures that plaintiffs assert result in excessive bonuses or other payments. For example, claims often state that executive pay is not appropriately linked to organizational performance; i.e., regardless of whether the organization does extremely well, extremely poorly, or somewhere in-between, the CEO and/or other executives are paid largely the same.

A primary defense is to rely on the process employed by the board in approving the allegedly excessive compensation. Boards that demonstrate a reasoned process and absence of self-interest typically will not have their decisions second-guessed by a court. This judicial deference under common law is referred to as the "business judgment rule." In essence, a court generally will defer to the judgment of the board if the board acts in good faith, exercises ordinary prudence in making its decisions, and acts in a manner it believes to be in the best interests of the corporation.

In instances in which the board's process is called into question, a company will often settle these claims by agreeing to nonmonetary relief such as changes to the company's governance structure. Even when settlement terms do not involve the payment of monetary compensation, the cost to the company of retaining legal counsel to defend against the claims and paying fees to plaintiffs' counsel may be significant. Therefore, organizations protect themselves by implementing processes and sound methodologies that the board or properly formed committee may use to review, approve and document compensation decisions.

Excessive Director Compensation

Similar to claims of excessive executive compensation, non-employee director compensation is subject to increased scrutiny and vulnerability to lawsuits. Most lawsuits claiming excessive director compensation allege that directors breached their fiduciary duties, wasted corporate assets and benefitted from unjust enrichment by approving total compensation that is excessive as compared to market, company size or performance.

Claims may also arise against public-company directors who approve their own equity grants under a shareholder-approved plan. Where claims relate to director pay, since directors are "interested" in decisions on their own compensation, the full protection of the business judgment rule may not apply. Rather, directors' decisions on their own compensation typically would be subject to the "entire fairness standard" under corporate law. If the entire fairness standard applies, the burden of proof shifts from the plaintiffs to the defendant-directors to prove that the directors engaged in a prudent process in setting their compensation and made reasonable decisions on such pay. "Entire fairness" requires "fair dealing" and "fair price," which mean that both the process and price must be entirely fair to shareholders.

Some companies address claims regarding director equity awards by establishing shareholder-approved limits on the equity grants that may be made to individual directors under a plan. Such limits are generally much lower than the applicable limit for employees. However, these director compensation limits do not offer full protection. Courts will also consider whether the compensation actually paid to directors was fair. In making this determination, the court will look at several factors, including director pay relative to that of peers. As such, boards should consider the advice from independent compensation consultants for frequent director pay assessments that examine the reasonableness of equity awards and other components of director pay. These reviews should provide some assurance that the organization's director compensation is in line with its peers and not an outlier. Disclosure of this process is also helpful.

Another approach is to establish a separate director equity plan that includes formulaic grants that are approved by shareholders. The grant formula may also include conditions that automatically adjust the compensation levels following the annual shareholder meeting. While this latter approach has the benefit of eliminating any director discretion in granting equity to the board, the downside of this approach is that it lacks the flexibility that is inherent in plans that provide some discretion.

Like claims of excessive executive compensation that survive a motion to dismiss, lawsuits alleging excessive director compensation that prevail against a motion to dismiss also substantially increase in the cost of litigation, including attorneys' fees. Accordingly, care should be taken to prevent any opening through unclear or careless processes that could provide plaintiffs with an ability to survive a motion to dismiss.

Claims Specific to Public Companies

Stakeholders review proxy statements with a critical eye. Media outlets routinely report on, and are critical of, companies making unusual governance or compensation decisions. Coupled with the additional scrutiny by the SEC following the enactment in 2002 of the Sarbanes-Oxley Act and then the 2010 Dodd-Frank Act, and the environment is ripe for litigation. The sections that follow include several common areas for litigation for public companies.

Excessive Director and Executive Compensation

Public companies risk being sued by shareholders for excessive director and executive compensation. A general discussion of these claims is set forth in the previous section of this chapter.

Equity Plan Disclosures

Companies disclose a lot of information in their annual proxy statements related to equity plans submitted for shareholder approval. One category of actions brought by shareholders against companies seeking approval for an equity plan (or an increase in shares reserved under an existing plan) is the adequacy of the disclosures made to shareholders. Examples of information that shareholders sometimes claim should be disclosed, but that are not required under applicable law, are shareholder dilution represented by an equity plan, the company's historic "burn rate" under its equity plan (the rate at which the company grants stock under its existing equity plan), and the information obtained from outside consultants in evaluating the equity plan proposal.

While these claims have had limited success, some companies mitigate the threat of these claims by expanding their proxy proposals to provide robust information to shareholders addressing dilution, burn rate, overhang (the dilution represented by outstanding awards plus shares reserved for issuance under equity plans), and other data regarding the requested shares.

Governance Claims

Another category of claims relates to a board's alleged failure to comply with applicable law in granting compensation. One such claim is that a company's board impermissibly granted equity awards to one or more individuals (often an executive) that exceeded the shareholder-approved limits under the plan. This type of error sometimes occurs following a corporate stock split, which impacts the equity plan share pool. The problem arises if the plan administrator fails to account for the revised capitalization. These types of claims can be among the most expensive to litigate; a sound governance process that includes stock plan administrators is a good protection measure to avoid this type of error. While these claims also are made with respect to non-public companies, exchange listing requirements that mandate shareholder approval of most equity plans and proxy disclosure requirements relating to those plans provide shareholders with more information to use in pursuing such actions against public companies.

SEC-Filed Actions

Shareholders are not the only plaintiffs filing suit against companies based on issues related to their executive compensation programs. The SEC often makes claims against companies for alleged violations of its rules and regulations. For example, the SEC has sued individual executives for manipulating expenses to hide what would otherwise be perquisites that should have been disclosed in the proxy. These types of lawsuits generally allege that the executive caused the company to violate the law by filing false and misleading proxy disclosures. In other matters, the SEC has sought to recover (clawback) certain executive compensation pursuant to its authority under Sarbanes-Oxley in instances where financial restatements were required.

Claims Specific to Family Businesses

Family-owned businesses take many forms depending on such factors as the number of shareholders and relative ownership, the size of the company and the industry, whether executive officers are members of the family, and the number of family members who are inactive shareholders of the company. Because of these dynamics, the methods of determining how much jobs are worth and who should hold executive positions in family-owned businesses can differ greatly from other privately held companies. In essence, they are not always "arms-length" transactions. In addition, depending on the relative ownership of shares, certain family members may have greater decision-making authority and exercise it in a manner that the executive officers deem unfair. Consequently, family-owned businesses are not immune from litigation.

Who Should Hold the Executive Officer Positions?

Family-owned businesses are no different than other companies in the sense that they require the right talent for the right positions; particularly, the executive positions. However, the determination of who should hold those positions is often more subjective than it would be in a non-family business and may result in the incumbent lacking the qualifications to perform effectively. Similar problems may arise in succession planning for executive positions in family-owned businesses.

When an incumbent is determined unfit for an executive officer position, they are often forced out by the majority shareholders. If the incumbent feels unfairly treated, they may sue the company for wrongful termination, the majority shareholders' breach of fiduciary duties, and/or breach of the duty of good faith and fair dealing. To mitigate this risk, family-owned businesses should strive toward the same governance guidelines that non family-owned businesses generally adopt and implement. To the extent that a family-owned business can act objectively in matters that relate to family member executives, and document decisions in accordance with good governance practices, it further limits its exposure to claims.

How Much Compensation Should the Board Approve for Incumbents?

In family-owned businesses, some family members may sit on the board of directors, some may be executive officers, some may serve in both capacities, and some are inactive investors. These roles may create tensions among different members of the family (and with outside investors, as well), often resulting in litigation.

Lawsuits sometimes are filed against directors of family-owned businesses who approve excessive compensation to executive officers. These cases tend to be more complicated than those in non-family-owned businesses because the decisions related to compensation are often made without use of an objective methodology for determining the appropriate amount of total compensation and proper metrics for awarding incentive compensation. Additionally, the perception of excessive compensation being paid to an incumbent, especially when buttressed by allegations that the incumbent is unfit to effectively perform their position, exposes the company to a higher risk of litigation. In these cases, the status of family quickly becomes irrelevant.

To avoid claims of excessive compensation, family-owned businesses should follow governance guidelines similar to those applicable to publicly held firms. In addition, standard methodologies should be used to determine compensation, and a family-owned business's board of directors should ensure that incentive compensation of a family-member incumbent is based on metrics that further the company's business strategy, viewed in terms of both short-term goals and long-term objectives.

Claims Specific to Nonprofit Organizations

Nonprofit organizations have different stakeholders than their for-profit counterparts and they compensate their executives differently. The most visible examples of these differences are that nonprofits do not have shareholders and do not issue equity as part of total compensation. However, they are highly regulated with regard to the compensation they pay their executives. In particular, they are subject to media scrutiny; often have unions with which they have to negotiate; and must satisfy members and donors that the compensation that they pay executives is reasonable. Complicating the nonprofit landscape is that directors are often unpaid volunteers and may not have the expertise to understand the reasons for and methodologies used to properly determine compensation. This lack of knowledge may unwittingly expose the directors to litigation. Nonprofit organizations commonly (but not always) are tax-exempt, which adds requirements under the tax code.

IRS as Plaintiff

Tax-exempt organizations must not pay excessive compensation to executives. As discussed in Chapter 28, they risk intermediate sanctions under IRC 4958, which include the requirement to return to the organization the amount that is deemed excessive and the payment of excise taxes. They also risk loss of tax-exempt status, which may happen in especially egregious cases. Additional penalties apply to managers and directors who approve excessive compensation.

Establishing a rebuttable presumption of reasonable compensation mitigates the risk of intermediate sanctions. To establish the presumption, the organization must take the following steps:

- The transaction must be approved in advance by disinterested members of an authorized body of the organization, i.e., the board of directors or a compensation committee lawfully established by the board. Disinterested members and their family members must not derive any economic benefit from the transaction or otherwise have a material financial interest in the transaction. In addition, employees working for a person who will derive an economic benefit or have a material financial interest in the transaction are not considered disinterested nor is any individual whose compensation would be determined by such person.

- The governing body must obtain and rely on valid comparability data in approving the transaction. Comparable data includes similarly situated organizations measured by such metrics as size, location, services, receipts and budget. Such comparisons often include an independent third-party compensation study to compare market data among members of an appropriate compensation peer group, which may include taxable organizations.

- The governing body must contemporaneously document its decision and the reason for its decision. Such documentation must include information such as the date of the approval of compensation, the methodology used to determine the compensation, who the governing body was that made the decision, and that the governing body was made up of disinterested individuals.

Establishing the rebuttable presumption of reasonableness is an important step for a tax-exempt organization in positioning itself against potential disputes with the IRS. A failure to show that an organization has established the rebuttable presumption may result in the IRS bringing suit and using its own comparability data to measure the reasonableness of compensation.

Unions as Plaintiffs

Tax-exempt organizations are not insulated from the activities of unions. They have been particularly vocal regarding health care organizations, such as petitioning for caps on the total compensation of their CEO. Such activities put tax-exempt organizations in the media spotlight and require them to engage in extensive negotiations and PR activity. However, if an organization has taken the steps to establish the rebuttable presumption of reasonableness discussed above, it is better situated to argue its case to the union, the public and the media.

Conflict of Interest Policies Are Critical

Conflict of interest policies prevent board members from making decisions that financially impact their family members or themselves or generate an economic benefit to them. An effective conflict of interest policy, coupled with compliance with the policy, significantly mitigates risk of lawsuit for alleged violation of the "private inurement" doctrine applicable to nonprofit organizations. Accordingly, boards of directors should prioritize ensuring that effective conflict of interest policies are adopted.

Executive Compensation in Wrongful Death Claims

In most wrongful death claims, the question of compensation that would have been earned by the decedent but for the alleged wrongful death caused by the defendant(s) becomes an issue in calculating damages. Essentially, potential net income, based on income on the date of death and average work-life expectancies, is awarded to survivors. This "valuation by human capital" determines the amount that survivors need to allow them the same standard of living that they would have had if the decedent were still alive.

Executive Compensation in Divorce

Property division and support are central issues in divorce proceedings. The spouses must determine what property is separate versus what property is marital. Compensation becomes an issue complicated by the fact that executives generally are paid a mix of cash and equity. While base salary is easily attributable to income, questions arise regarding when and if the non-executive spouse is entitled to all or a portion of the stock acquired by the executive as current or future compensation. In addition, the ultimate payment of deferred compensation and unvested incentive compensation (especially performance-based incentive compensation) can be unpredictable.

Measuring compensation in divorce proceedings can be further complicated if one spouse was the founder of a successful business during the marriage. A determination may be needed as to the extent to which the company is an asset that must be divided and how much income to attribute to the executive's spouse for purposes of spousal support.

Determining current total compensation, potential future compensation and the value of marital property associated with executive compensation may require expert opinions and valuations. Experts also advise parties in divorce proceedings regarding plan administrators' responsibilities, and the timing of and manner in which equity can be delivered.

Executive Compensation in Bankruptcy

Executive compensation is subjected to special rules if the employer-company files bankruptcy. For example, regardless of the terms of an employment agreement, the Bankruptcy Code limits the amount and timing of severance benefits that executives may receive. Priority of payment of severance benefits also may be unfavorable to the executives, particularly if rank-and-file employees are given little to no severance. If severance is paid to an executive in violation of the Bankruptcy Code, the executive will be forced to disgorge the excess payments. Similarly, base salaries that are increased within a year of filing bankruptcy will be subjected to heightened scrutiny and may be clawed back by the court.

In many instances, though, a bankrupt company remains in business and needs to retain its key talent or attract new talent. As discussed in the bankruptcy section of Chapter 27, companies reorganizing in bankruptcy that need to retain their talent struggle with the limitations placed on them regarding how to compensate their executives. During bankruptcy proceedings, incentive-based compensation must be linked to measurable performance goals and issued pursuant to a key employee incentive program (KEIP). Such programs may differ greatly from the annual and long-term incentive plans to which executives are accustomed, which can jeopardize retention.

Lastly, in a plan of reorganization, the company may petition the court for new executive employment agreements. To do so, it would have to meet certain procedural requirements such as notice of proposed payments of executive compensation to all parties-in-interest. It would also have to satisfy the court on the reasonableness of the proposed compensation.

Expert assistance in structuring incentive compensation and other payments that will satisfy the Bankruptcy Code is often required. In addition, committees formed to represent the interests of creditors commonly seek a third-party analysis on the reasonableness of compensation-related proposals.

Wrapping Up

Good governance and supportable analyses related to director and executive compensation help organizations avoid litigation, but they are no guarantee. It is important for organizations to understand who their stakeholders are, how they are regulated, and the best methods for providing transparency without disclosing proprietary information. At the end of the day, organizations should compensate executives in compliance with applicable laws, rules and regulations, but determine how to achieve short-term goals and long-term objectives through incentivizing their key talent. The best defense against litigation is articulation of a deliberately determined, studied and reasonable executive compensation program.

CHAPTER 30
International Compensation

C ompanies and talented individuals cross borders — making the understanding of international practices essential for anyone who wants to grasp the subject of executive compensation. Pay practices differ from country to country, driven by economics, culture, legislation and innovation. But equally, practices cross-pollinate where markets for the people that can truly affect the fortunes of an organization sweep through borders without regard for barriers and traditions. And it is not only where people are based that matters but also the context of the industry, the company and the company's stakeholders.

This chapter seeks to give some of these flavors to the diversity of executive compensation practices, looking at such different corners of the world as Australia, Canada, Europe, Japan and the United Kingdom.

However, comparing the compensation packages of executives in different countries is fraught with difficulty. Compensation levels vary greatly, and the differences are rarely explainable by just taxation or living standards — some of the developed countries with the lowest levels of executive pay, such as in Northern Europe, have high living costs and tax rates. These quirks are evidence of the importance of understanding the cultural differences within which executive compensation exists. A Dutch executive accepts lower compensation and a higher tax rate than a Swiss executive, at least partly because of the cultural difficulty of paying Swiss levels in the Netherlands. That does not mean that the same executive would accept lower compensation in Switzerland.

There also are large differences between countries in the provision of retirement benefits for executives. A Swedish executive, for example, may agree to a lower salary than a British executive but expect twice as high a pension contribution. An Asian executive may not have a pension provision at all in the traditional sense, while the retirement benefit provisions of Australian or some European executives could form one of a company's largest liabilities.

Faced with significant differences in compensation practices from country to country, and in many cases within countries, most international corporations base the compensation for top executives primarily on practices and levels in the market where the executive is based. However, it is not unusual to see exceptions to this in short- and long-term incentive plans as a result of corporate innovation in combination with home country legislation driving more global practices.

The following sections of this chapter provide overviews of executive compensation in several international settings. The sections describe not just pay practices but important aspects or trends in compensation in these geographies.

AUSTRALIA

By Trevor Warden

Although geographically positioned at the southern end of Asia, the Australian business framework is culturally more closely aligned to Western economies. The governmental, legal and social frameworks were derived primarily from the United States and UK, so executive rewards in Australia have many similarities to the models used in those countries.

One fairly unique aspect however is the focus on "fixed reward" in Australia when it comes to benchmarking, determining and contracting of executive pay. The primary drivers of this focus are the tax and retirement saving regimes.

In the 1970s, Australian tax regulations allowed a number of non-cash benefits to be taken with little or no tax payable. This encouraged companies to provide significant levels of perquisites to middle and senior management. The most common perquisite was a company-provided (and fully maintained) car. Other common items included travel, club fees, entertainment expenses and housing or low-interest housing loans. The use of perquisites became a gray area; the "tax-free" position of many was based on assertions that the activity (e.g., travel or entertainment) was for business purposes.

In 1986, the Australian federal government introduced a fringe benefits tax (FBT) that was levied on employers for any benefits provided to employees. The FBT was designed so that the cost to the company of providing $100 in after-tax cash to the employee was the same as the cost of providing $100 in benefits. While this legitimized the provision of benefits by companies provided the FBT was paid, it also removed the financial incentive to use perquisites instead of cash. A few benefits, such as employer-provided cars, received concessional FBT costing, and compulsory "superannuation" (pension plan) contributions (and voluntary up to a limit) were fully exempted from FBT to encourage saving for retirement. The compensation response to the FBT was for companies to define the value of fixed reward they were prepared to pay for each individual. This fixed package or fixed annual reward could be taken by the employee in whatever form they chose. Each benefits item is valued at the cost to the company, and the balance is provided as cash salary. Some executives elect to take most or all of the package as cash, while others take a portion in benefits. The most common benefits are cars, car parking and superannuation contributions.

A consequence of the above approach is that relatively few Australian companies make external reward comparisons based on base salary. Many organizations are not tracking the cash salary component at all and are providing fixed-pay figures as the base salary for Australian pay surveys. Some companies with overseas parents still use a defined salary and specified benefits because they may have trouble explaining the Australian approach to the parent organization. Nonetheless they are urged to undertake comparisons at the full fixed package aggregate.

At roughly the same time that the government introduced the FBT, it also supported a move to require employers to contribute to retirement savings. The government was concerned that the aging Baby Boomer population was approaching retirement with insufficient resources and would expect the social security system to fill the gap. The government decided to shift the focus of responsibility to employers and employees. The initial requirement was for six percent of pay, and this has been progressively increased to 9.5 percent in 2020 and to move periodically by another few percentage points in 2025.

The employer contribution was offset partly by union-agreed reduced salary increases originally. The contributions are fully vested and must remain in approved funds until retirement even if the employee leaves the employer. At the same time, Australia saw a major movement from DB funds to DC/accumulation plans, with now only a very tiny minority of companies still having active DB plans. Most companies now allow executives to elect how much they want to contribute to superannuation provided they choose the regulatory minimum (9.5 percent of normal pay up to a maximum required contribution, which is regulated and changes annually). Contributions are very tax efficient up to a certain amount annually, at which point they become tax inefficient.

A further significant omission in executive packages in Australia is that of medical care/health funding. This is because Australia has a national approach to medical care, Medicare, which is funded by a tax levy (of 2% currently). Purchasing of private health insurance can reduce the tax levy. Unfortunately, any private health insurance would attract FBT if paid by the employer, so those who do buy their own insurance do so with after-tax income.

While there are other benefits that may be provided by a few companies, the value is usually small in relation to the executive package.

The use of executive short-term incentives (with a performance test and payment period of up to 12 months) is common in Australia. Historically, there was some variation in the type of STI, whether the plan was a target-based incentive with a defined opportunity size or a bonus paid retrospectively. Now however, a vast majority of companies use a target-based STI plan. The amount of the incentive payment varies from year to year based on the achievement of specific targets set at a corporate, business-unit and/or individual level. Targets are determined and agreed upon in advance, as are the rewards for achieving and exceeding those targets. The most frequent performance measure used in target-based STI plans is profit, with a significant majority of companies using this measure. More and more organizations are starting to include ESG measures in their STIs as part of a general trend to being more community conscious and not just financial-stakeholder focused.

With a few exceptions, years of economic growth and the positive effect of strong commodity prices in Australia has resulted in a war for talent and strong corporate performance for many companies. Impacts to executive STIs included the following:

- While STI opportunities usually are presented as a percentage of fixed reward, most plans now provide for extra payments if stretch performance targets are achieved. Much of the recent increase in STI payments appears to be attributable to the provision of these additional upside opportunities.

- There is a growing trend of deferring the payout of executive STIs, especially with larger companies (a high percentage of the Australian Securities Exchange (ASX300)) and those in the financial services sector. This is designed primarily to support the retention of critical executives in the tight talent market. Some companies use a timing deferral — paying the cash over longer periods — and others pay the incentives in restricted shares.

- In the last decade, clawback provisions have also been put in place for STIs.

Long-term incentives (LTIs) in the Australian market have been characterized by the use of time and performance hurdles. Shareholder groups have made rigorous performance hurdles virtually compulsory with the intent of increasing the alignment between executives and shareholders. The typical plan design has a performance period of three years, with a few companies using five years. The combination of the performance and time hurdles means that approximately 50 percent of all allocations do not vest. The design of LTIs for Australian residents needs to be considered to structure them appropriately for Australian corporate accounting, corporate taxation and individual taxation regulations. This can affect the suitability of overseas-based equity schemes to Australian residents.

The majority of plans use a relative TSR performance measure — the combination of share price growth and dividends paid compared to a comparator group of companies. The use of relative TSR remains common overall, but there has been some movement towards combining it with other metrics, such as EPS. Like the increasing prevalence of non-financial measures in STIs, some qualitative measures are also appearing in LTIs.

While there had been a shift from share-option plans to perfor-mance-share plans, driven by tax changes in 2009 that made options less tax effective than other plans, more recent (2015) tax changes have reversed the earlier changes and we are seeing a relatively small re-emergence of option-based plans. We are also seeing the re-emergence of loan-funded share plans given their tax efficacy, albeit that such plans are not generally well received by proxy advisers and institutional investors.

The overall reward strategy is evolving. Recently, there was a backlash to executive pay, particularly in financial services. There has now been consideration involving the potential move from paying cash STIs to paying only equity-based STIs with a holding period. There is also evidence of recalibrating the pay mix with fixed rewards being increased while reducing STI & LTI. Some organisations are also finally implementing the long-held philosophy of applying equity not as an incentive, but as part of fixed reward.

In this case, there are no performance hurdles but only a specified holding period.

The increasing use of non-financial measures is also resulting in additional board discretion in incentive pay. Purely formulaic outcomes are being viewed more and more as not always aligning with performance as expected at the beginning of the measurement period.

Australian governance requirements are fairly similar to those in the United States and the UK. In Australia, the decision making for CEOs, other C-suite and key management personnel is the remit of the board. There is an obligation for listed companies to include a remuneration report as part of the annual report. This must disclose all director compensation for the past year plus detailed pay information for key management personnel; companies generally disclose five or more executives. The report also must furnish details of the company's reward philosophy and policies including incentive plans and performance criteria. Share-based equity must be disclosed in line with the international accounting standards, and details of past awards not yet exercised must be shown.

There is a requirement for a non-binding shareholder vote on acceptance of the Remuneration Report at each annual general meeting. Most boards have been very reluctant to proceed with remuneration items that are likely to receive a significant number of negative votes. Since July 2011, there has been a legal obligation for companies that receive a negative vote of 25 percent or more on the Remuneration Report at two consecutive annual general meetings to have an immediate vote to spill all board positions and have a new election within three months. This has resulted in boards taking action to avoid high negative votes on the Remuneration Report for two or more years in a row.

There is a prohibition on listed companies making any termination payments that are linked to a change in control. This prevents CIC payments from being used by existing management and directors as a poison pill to discourage takeovers. Payments can be made following a change in control, but only if triggered by factors that would apply in other situations (e.g., the termination of the executive).

Legislation limits the maximum termination payment for executives, under any circumstances, to 12 months base salary unless there is specific shareholder approval for the greater payment. While the concept of having formal share ownership guidelines for executives and directors has been a topic of late, there are still relatively few companies with formal guidelines in this regard.

Executive reward mix differs between the CEO and other executives (KMPs) as well as between executives/CEOs in differently sized organizations. This is becoming less easily discernible though with increased variation in categories in the most recent two to three years of annual report disclosures.

In summary, while strong similarities exist between the approaches to executive reward in Australia and the United States, there are a number of important differences:

- The different structure of fixed-pay practice makes the use of base salary and total cash for market comparisons in Australia potentially misleading.
- The Australian regulations on company contributions for retirement income savings make it a very tax-effective form of income.
- There is generally a somewhat smaller proportion of overall pay provided as STI and LTI in Australia.
- Basic reward philosophies of U.S. organizations can be applied in Australia, but some adjustments to the mechanics of pay structures and comparisons may be needed to ensure desired market competitiveness.

CANADA

By Wiclif Ma

For many Canadian publicly traded companies, there are benefits in aligning shareholders' interests with share-based compensation using medium- and long-term incentive programs. However, there has been a transition in the equity vehicles used over the past few decades.

Among the largest Canadian publicly listed organizations of the S&P/ TSX 60, stock option plans were widely used as the only long-term incentive vehicle from the 1980s to mid-1990s. The index consisted of organizations from a wide spectrum of industries, with approximately 50 percent in materials, financials, and energy sectors. The index issuers typically had market caps of CAD 20 to 30 billion, and annual revenue of CAD 20 billion.

In 2014, 95 percent of S&P/TSX 60 issuers provided stock options but the usage declined to 76 percent in 2020. During the same period, Performance Share Unit (PSU) plans particularly gained popularity from 77 to 90 percent. Why have PSUs gained popularity? Why have stock options lost ground? What are the implications for executives and shareholders?

Equity Incentive Vehicles

S&P/TSX 60 issuers generally use at least two equity incentive plans for their executives, including Named Executive Officers ("NEOs") – 53 percent use two vehicles, followed by 38 percent of the organizations using three vehicles.

The most common equity designs include the following:

- 50 percent of organizations provide (PSUs + SOs).
- 21 percent provide (PSUs + SOs + RSUs).

Performance Share Units	90 percent of the organizations have now adopted a PSU plan, up from 77 percent in 2014. PSUs generally have a three-year term with 75 percent having a cliff vesting schedule, subject to performance conditions.
Stock Options	76 percent of the organizations provide a stock option plan, this prevalence declined from 95 percent in 2014. Most stock options have a 10-year term with 86 percent having a graded vesting schedule (e.g., 25 percent over four years).
Restricted Share Units	Less than half (40 percent) of the organizations provide a restricted share unit plan which has remained similar to the prevalence in 2014. RSUs generally have a three-year term with time-vesting conditions, split between graded and cliff schedules at 52% and 48% prevalence, respectively.

- 14 percent provide (PSUs + RSUs).
- The remaining balance mainly provide a single plan of PSUs, SOs or RSUs.

Why a Shift?

Over the years, the use of SOs has significantly declined in Canada. No surprise, PSUs have filled in the gaps. The performance units have been gaining in popularity among the large cap issuers for several reasons; PSUs:

- Provide an income tax deferral advantage under the Canadian Income Tax Act for a maximum of three years.
- Reduce share dilution compared to SO usage, as PSUs are typically based on notional share units.
- Reduce the underwater risks of stock options and provide a more balanced compensation risk profile for executives.
- Increase the focus of non-share price performance to support long-term business strategy, including the need for ESG objectives.
- Manage the compensation risk/volatility during economic cycles.
- Diversify the compensation toolbox for aligning shareholder interests with those of executives.

Performance Share Unit Features

There are many different metrics that may be used for PSU programs. Relative TSR is the most common metric used among S&P/TSX 60 issuers, followed by profitability.

The majority of organizations (74 percent) using rTSR combine it with other metrics. The most common combination is rTSR + profitability. Profitability metrics may include ROCE, ROIC, EPS, EPS growth or RONA.

The high prevalence of internal metrics also reflects the importance of certain strategic priorities unique to each organization. For example, net earnings and cash flow metrics prioritize earnings over the longer term. Similarly, operational or production efficiency metrics may be useful for resource-based organizations.

TABLE 30-1 Prevalence: PSU Performance Vesting Metrics

Top 5 Measures	Prevalence	Average Weight (Where Used)
Relative TSR (rTSR)	69%	59%
Profitability	61%	55%
Revenue	20%	45%
Cash Flow	16%	52%
Cost & Margin	10%	18%

Among those plans using an rTSR metric (See Table 30-1), the percentile ranking method continues to be common. The prevailing schedule of relative performance is P25 – P50 – P75 for threshold, target, and maximum performance, respectively. The majority of companies set their minimum payout at zero if the performance threshold is not met, while the maximum payout is typically 200 percent of target, as expressed in the number of PSUs.

FRANCE

By Augustin de Williencourt

The executive compensation situation in France is rather unique in Europe.

As a bit of introduction to the French regulatory system, the compensation of corporate directors is subject to enhanced say-on-pay requirements since the Ordinance dated November 27, 2019. The Ordinance established the following:

- Except in limited exceptional circumstances subject to certain conditions, any compensation or payment allocation not complying with an approved remuneration policy would be deemed null;

- Remuneration reports must include an equity pay ratio between a) the remuneration of the chairman of the board and executive directors and b) the average as well as median compensation of the company's workforce;
- All payments to corporate directors are suspended in case of a negative "ex post" vote on compensation policy until a revised version is adopted. All fixed, variable and exceptional components of compensation paid during the past financial year or allocated for the same financial year must be subject to a distinct resolution for chairman and executive directors. Payment of variable and exceptional components of compensation awarded for the past financial year is subject to a positive "ex post" vote. For example, variable amounts for the 2019 financial year are subject to vote during the 2020 Annual General Meetings.

There is a relative weakness of executive directors' compensation in France compared to other countries.

The compensation mix for executives in France mirrors European compensation practices with a slightly stronger weight on base salary, which may be higher than 40 percent of the total package.

French base salaries for senior managers were approximately 82 percent of the European median. For example, the French base salary was lower than that of the Netherlands (89%) and the United Kingdom (92%). On the other hand, French salaries exceeded those in Germany (107%), Italy (108%), Denmark (139%) and Spain (163%).

To a similar extent, total cash for senior executives in France is below that of the Netherlands (87%) and Italy (69%). However, French total cash exceeds that of the United Kingdom (102%), Germany (117%), Switzerland (142%), Spain (154%).

Total direct compensation in France for senior executives also remains below the European median.

As for retirement benefits, 2019 marked the end of a shift in corporate culture. The defined benefits (DB) plans that were used for many years at corporations are no longer accepting newcomers and existing rights have been frozen with no future accruals except in limited circumstances. Companies have now implemented DB plans with vesting features and vested funds will become fully transferable in case of departure from one company to another. These new features led issuers to increase defined contributions plans and contemplate alternative cash or long-term incentive plans designed to help their executives build up their own retirement portfolio.

From a corporate governance standpoint, a 2019 report issued by the French Financial Market Authority (AMF) highlights high approval rates for resolutions dealing with compensation. As an example, only 39 percent of resolutions about compensation awarded and paid to corporate officers had an approval rate of less than 90 percent.

As a conclusion, one may argue that the overall level of compensation for executives in France must be put in perspective with rather generous ancillary benefits, including departure indemnities plus longer tenure, with some exceptions.

GERMANY

By Ralph Lange

To understand executive compensation in Germany, it is necessary to look at the governance framework. While the eminent framework globally is a unitary board structure consisting of both executives as well as outside directors to steer the company, the dominant framework in Germany consists of a dual board structure with a supervisory board and a management board.

The supervisory board consists of outside directors elected by the shareholders and in the case of large companies, employee representatives elected by the employees that make up one third or even half of the supervisory board. The management board consists of executive directors who are nominated by the supervisory board for a period of up to five years.

While the main purpose of the supervisory board is the nomination, control and provision of strategic advice to the management board, the main purpose of the management board is the day-to-day management of the company.

Executive compensation has been in the public and media spotlight for the last 20 years. This has led to several changes to the level of transparency as well as the general structure of compensation.

With the beginning of 2020, significant changes to the regulatory landscape in Germany are taking place. Not only has the legal background in the stock corporation act changed with the transposition of the amended European Shareholder Rights Directive (SRD II) into national law, but the recommendations from the German Corporate Governance Code (GCGC) have been fully reshaped.

Starting in 2021, listed companies are required to hold separate non-binding votes on the remuneration policy for the members of the supervisory board and the management board. The votes need to be repeated every four years or in case of material changes of a policy. In case the remuneration policy is rejected, a revised policy must be presented and put to the vote at the next general meeting.

In addition to the requirements set by the EU directive, the legislature added the necessity to include a vote on the maximum compensation for the management board, which can even be reduced by the shareholders. This includes the compensation paid based on the share price in case of share-based compensation. Although there is some room for interpretation, the majority opinion also sees pension contributions and other benefits included.

Furthermore, there needs to be an annual vote on the compensation report starting in 2022. The compensation report needs to contain details on each individual management board members' compensation, split up by component as well as the development of compensation compared to the average employee compensation.

The GCGC has been completely revised, incorporating some aspects of the new legal framework, but also covering additional aspects of compensation. The GCGC defines general principles and recommendations which follow a "comply or explain" approach.

While the previous governance code was rather vague on the proportions between short- and long-term compensation, the new code added some further guidance explaining that the compensation that is based on long-term targets shall exceed the compensation based on short-term targets and shall not be available to executives before the end of a four-year period.

Additionally, the majority of variable compensation shall be paid directly in shares or similar. Furthermore, the supervisory board shall have the right to withhold or recoup variable compensation in justified cases.

Among the 30 DAX companies comprising the major German stock index, roughly one third are already conducting a say-on-pay vote in 2020 while others are still reviewing their compensation schemes and will follow in 2021. Most smaller companies are also just beginning to review their compensation policies to be voted on in 2021.

An initial observable trend is that companies appear to be increasing the proportion of share-based compensation and introducing ESG-criteria as this has been pushed by institutional investors.

Long-term incentives already make up the largest compensation component (See Figure 30-2), but not all programs are tied to share performance. Almost one third of companies use long-term cash plans which are based on internal KPIs, mostly return or profit measures.

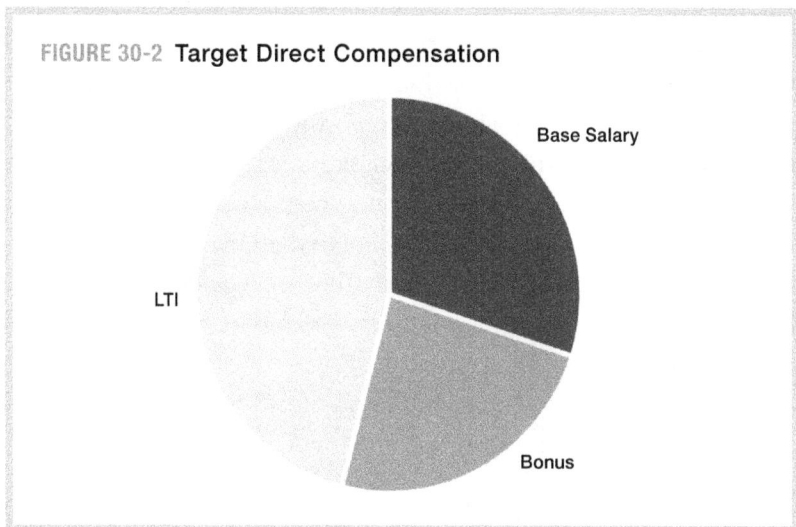

FIGURE 30-2 **Target Direct Compensation**

The remaining two thirds are using performance shares or units, but the use of stock options and restricted shares is rather uncommon.

Plan terms are usually set at four years among DAX companies, while smaller companies still favor three-year terms.

JAPAN

By Daishi Motodera

In the 1990s, Japanese companies' executive compensation consisted of base salary, bonus and retirement benefits. The bonus and retirement benefits were each generally targeted at 30 percent of the individual's salary. The use of stock compensation was not used until a stock option ban lifted in 1997. Japanese companies did not pay large bonuses because they were taxed. By contrast, U.S. executives typically target 100 to 200 percent of base salary.

The small bonuses indicated a minimal linkage between performance and executive compensation. Japanese executives are responsible and committed to the company's performance, but in terms of compensation, it was not reflected.

The lack of stock compensation is understandable. The main banks held company stock as collateral for loan financing. The main banks were stable and the shareholders were "silent." Because of such "silent" and stable shareholders, the company's stock price fluctuated based on the yen appreciation or depreciation as well as the U.S. stock market. As such, actual company performance was less significant on share price. This led to the idea that corporations were for internal participants, not shareholders. Indeed, customers, business partners, and employees were more important stakeholders than shareholders.

In the midst of this, the stock option ban was lifted in 1997 as a mechanism to get out of an economic collapse and to encourage executives to revitalize companies. Additionally, there was criticism of the retirement benefits during periods of poor performance.

Many companies subsequently abolished retirement benefits and introduced super discounted stock options — one yen stock options. This allowed option exercise at only one yen. These functioned like full-value awards and provided greater economic benefit to participants. As such, it was a fair trade to eliminate retirement benefits. Restricted stock was not allowed until 2015-19 legislation revisions.

The fall in stock prices due to the Lehman shock of 2008 led the main banks to decrease their stock holdings. Active shareholders and institutional investors also put pressure on corporations. Greater interest from activist shareholders and institutional shareholders set the stage for a revision in legislation.

From 2015 to 2019, corporate and tax laws were amended and the Corporate Governance Code was formulated. Due to the new legislative provisions, the ban on restricted stock and performance shares was lifted. Also, variable cash/stock plans were deemed an expense not for corporate tax. These revisions were aimed at creating mid- to long-term corporate value and shareholder growth.

For the fiscal year that ended March 2020, the top 100 corporate CEOs' bonus and stock compensation was set at 70 and 43 percent of base salary, respectively. Retirement benefits were no longer a significant component.

It is important to understand who decides the remuneration of each officer. The pay decision of individual officers was traditionally the CEO's exclusive matter. To avoid the risk of giving the CEO too much power, it became desirable for directors (executive and outside), other than the CEO, to be involved in decision making and to have a system that shareholders can check.

The most recent revision of the corporate law (December 2019) stipulated that the board of directors decide on a policy for determining executive directors' remuneration and provide a resolution on the upper limit of stock compensation.

Compensation disclosure has also been strengthened somewhat. Companies are required to disclose the names of individuals whose

TABLE 30-3 CEO Pay (JPY Million)

	Base salary	Bonus	Share plan	Retirement benefits	Total Remuneration
2020	91	63	39	0	198
2019	90	66	32	0	184
2018	98	66	25	0	176

TABLE 30-4 CEO Pay Mix (as a percentage of base salary)

	Base salary	Bonus	Share plan	Retirement benefits
2020	100	70	43	0
2019	100	73	36	0
2018	100	67	26	0

TABLE 30-5 Type of Stock Plans at the Top 100 Companies, # of Plans

	1 yen stock	Executive ESOP by Trustee	Stock options	Restricted stock	Performance shares
2020	11	23	8	38	19
2019	21	26	8	25	15
2018	29	17	9	17	6

compensation exceeds 100 million yen, roughly $1 million in the U.S. Disclosure of actual compensation paid to individuals was also on the agenda for a 2019 revision, but it was postponed.

For additional transparency, companies were required to disclose the policy and method of remuneration for each executive position. This included information on performance-linked compensation, KPI targets and performance in the recent business year. The report also mandated the outcome of shareholder resolutions from the annual meeting. See Tables 30-3 to 30-5 for more details.

NETHERLANDS

By Eric Engesaeth, Ph.D.

Focusing on top executive pay, this section discusses two topics. It starts with market practice on CEO pay in the Netherlands. The second topic is the Shareholder Rights Directive II implementation in Dutch law, including how it differs from other EU countries and what this says about the corporate governance context in the Netherlands.

Market Practice (CEO Pay)

Blue chip companies in the Netherlands are listed as part of the AEX index. In Figure 30-6, the market bandwidth is shown at the 25th percentile (P25), the median (M) and the 75th percentile (P75) for base salary, total cash compensation (TCC) and total direct compensation (TDC). TCC includes base salary as well as the (at target) short-term incentive (STI). TDC equals TCC plus the fair value of long-term incentives (LTI). All figures are independently arrayed.

Incentives within the AEX index are relatively evenly matched between STI and LTI with typically a slightly higher LTI, as shown in Figure 30-7.

Short-term incentives typically pay out in cash and have a multiplier for maximum performance between one and a half and two times the target STI. The typical design has 70 percent financial measures and 30 percent non-financial measures.

Long-term incentives are typically in the form of performance shares and the multiplier for maximum performance is also between one and a half and two times the number of conditionally granted shares. The typical design has 75 percent financial measures, such as relative total shareholder return or return on capital employed (ROCE), and 25 percent non-financial measures such as a bucket of strategic targets. ESG-related measures are relatively common in both the STI and LTI. Granted shares need to be held for a period of at least five years.

In terms of overall competitiveness within the broader European market, the level of CEO total direct compensation positions around

FIGURE 30-6 Chief Executive Officer

AEX

	P25	M	P75
Base Salary	€ 775,000	€ 1,005,000	€ 1,400,000
Total Cash Compensation	€ 1,260,000	€ 2,010,000	€ 2,865,000
Total Direct Compensation	€ 2,060,000	€ 2,845,000	€ 4,875,000

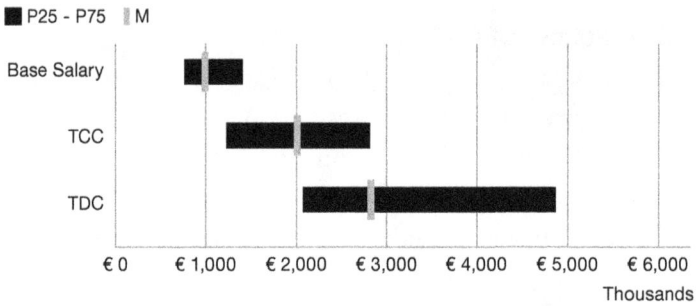

FIGURE 30-7 Incentives CEO within the AEX

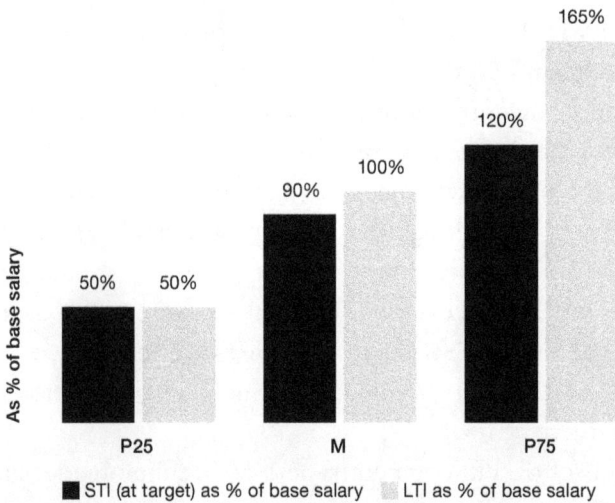

the median of Europe, with countries such as the United Kingdom and Switzerland significantly above the European median and countries such as Norway and Sweden significantly below.

Corporate Governance (Shareholder Rights Directive II)

Corporate governance in the Netherlands is relatively advanced with high disclosure standards and a history of binding votes for the remuneration policy. Following the implementation of the Shareholders Rights Directive (SRD II) as of November 6, 2019, in Dutch law, a yearly advisory vote on the remuneration report is required. The Dutch implementation shows some deviations from the EU guidelines. This is not surprising because the Netherlands has a track record in terms of making country-specific adjustments. As an example, the financial services sector has a stricter cap on variable pay at 20 percent of base salary (instead of 100 or even 200 percent found elsewhere in Europe). Several specific SRD II deviations applicable to the Netherlands are described below.

Votes Needed for Remuneration Policy Adoption Increased from 50 to 75 Percent

First, support from at least 75 percent of the casted votes is needed to adopt the company's remuneration policy. Previously, this number was 50 percent. The amended standard makes the bar for effective shareholder opposition lower. In the first shareholder season following the introduction of SRD II (2020), shareholders were indeed more effective in voting down remuneration policies.

ESG Performance Measures

Second, SRD II requires an explanation in the remuneration policy on how the company's identity, values, and societal support are considered in formulating the remuneration policy. It is expected that this will result in further introduction of ESG measures in the remuneration policy.

Currently, all AEX-listed companies use non-financial measures either in the short- and/or long-term incentive plans. The typical weight assigned to non-financial measures is 20-50 percent in the STI and 10-30 percent in the LTI. Examples include green sustainability (e.g., greenhouse gas emission, energy reduction), digital sustainability (e.g., technology leadership, revenues from digital products, research progress), and people-related metrics (e.g., employee engagement, health & safety, etc.).

Employee Representation & Internal Pay Relativities

Third, if the company has installed a works council (an internal group organized to promote and protect employees), the council has the right to submit advice regarding the proposed remuneration policy, before the shareholders can cast their vote. The council's advice may include, but is not limited to, compensation levels, the benchmarking peer group, and the compensation design. When the board does not follow the works council's advice, it must provide an explanation at the annual general meeting.

SRD II also requires the consideration of internal pay equities. This creates a direct link between CEO pay and the rest of the employee base. Reviewing the internal perspective (vertical benchmarking) to the external perspective (i.e., horizontal/peer group benchmarking) can be valuable but often results in a deep analysis of the CEO pay ratio. In isolation, this number is meaningless. Evaluating the number over time or compared to peers provides additional insights. However, it remains a matter of comparing data with multiple inputs. As such, this has triggered further discussion and research into the overall pay structure at companies.

THE UNITED KINGDOM

By Ian Greenwood

The landscape of executive compensation in the United Kingdom is in the process of being radically transformed. Macro-economic uncertainty is making it ever harder for remuneration committees (RemCos) to set incentive plan targets they can be sure will remain appropriate when they come to be tested. This is particularly the case with LTIP targets, which is leading to continued debate around the use of restricted shares which have no long-term targets (save for, perhaps, threshold underpins) or other structures which differ from the standard LTIP approach.

So what may the future hold? It is clear that pensions alignment will remain a key part of the landscape, although practice will be mixed as to precisely how companies fully align all directors' pensions with the wider workforce.

It is also probably the case that the traditional pay model will continue to be employed by the vast majority of companies. That said, it is also likely that companies will think more imaginatively in terms of the performance conditions they employ in their LTIPs in an attempt to link strategy to long-term rewards.

TABLE 30-8 **Total Remuneration (£)**

■ Methodology: Salary + benefits + pension + target bonus opportunity + expected value of LTIs.

	FTSE 100		
	LQ	M	UQ
CEO	2,393,000	3,279,000	4,437,000
CFO	1,522,000	1,908,000	2,956,000

	FTSE 30		
	LQ	M	UQ
CEO	4,694,000	5,444,000	6,758,000
CFO	2,978,000	3,361,000	3,831,000

	FTSE 31 - 100		
	LQ	M	UQ
CEO	2,072,000	2,693,000	3,325,000
CFO	1,285,000	1,643,000	1,923,000

See Table 30-8 for a closer look at the components of pay for companies in the United Kingdom.

Base Salary

Base salary quantum remains a key issue for investors. Therefore, shareholders are very wary of above-inflationary salary increases. Any such increase requires robust justification based on role change or business complexity and should not be based on comparative benchmarking.

Where provided, salary increases generally tracked the wider employee increases at around two and a half percent in 2020. That said, there was a significant minority of executives not receiving a salary increases in recent years.

Annual Bonus

Annual cash incentive programs are similar to those of the United States, with a few exceptions. Overall, the bonus programs blend financial and non-financial measures, albeit with the majority on financial. Recently, however, there has been an increasing use of

TABLE 30-9 **Salary (£)**

LQ: Lower quartile   M: Median   UQ: Upper quartile

	FTSE 100		
	LQ	M	UQ
CEO	730,000	874,200	1,088,700
CFO	471,600	550,000	711,400

	FTSE 30		
	LQ	M	UQ
CEO	1,092,500	1,174,900	1,288,500
CFO	700,000	750,000	810,800

	FTSE 31 - 100		
	LQ	M	UQ
CEO	669,300	785,000	877,000
CFO	439,000	500,000	564,300

discretion on award determination and a broader use of different performance measures, including ESG measures.

Unlike the U.S., it remains standard practice in the UK to defer 25 to 50 percent of the earned amount into shares for two or three years. As demonstrated in Tables 30-9 and 30-10, the bonus opportunities are expressed as a "maximum," as opposed to the target levels, because investors are generally most interested in understanding the highest possible payout, and there is a legal requirement for UK companies to state the maximum opportunity. Companies in the U.S. often focus on "Target" payout opportunities.

TABLE 30-10 Annual Bonus

Maximum bonus opportunity (% of salary)

	FTSE 100		
	LQ	M	UQ
CEO	150%	200%	215%
CFO	150%	165%	200%

	FTSE 30		
	LQ	M	UQ
CEO	200%	200%	225%
CFO	179%	200%	211%

	FTSE 31 - 100		
	LQ	M	UQ
CEO	150%	180%	200%
CFO	150%	150%	180%

Long-Term Incentives

The vast majority of companies continue to operate a performance share plan (PSP) as their sole long-term incentive. While there are significant discussions on the topic, only a small number of companies have introduced alternative structures (e.g., restricted share plans, value creation plans, combined plans), with shareholder reaction sometimes quite mixed.

532

TABLE 30-11 Metric Usage

FTSE 100	
Performance measure	Prevalence (% of plans)
Profit	88%
Cash	36%
Return (ROE/ROCE)	15%
Revenue/Sales	34%
Stakeholder (Employee/Customer)	43%
HSE/Sustainability	31%
Individual/Strategic	68%

PSPs use a measurement period of three years in virtually all cases. The programs blend two or three measures typically. Total shareholder return and financial metrics remain the most common, with EPS and return metrics (e.g., ROCE) the most commonly used financial measures. Malus and clawback provisions are also standard with PSPs (See Table 30-12).

TABLE 30-12 Performance Share Plan

2020 PSP Award (% of salary)

	FTSE 100		
	LQ	M	UQ
CEO	200%	250%	314%
CFO	195%	225%	275%

	FTSE 30		
	LQ	M	UQ
CEO	275%	365%	450%
CFO	228%	283%	372%

	FTSE 31 - 100		
	LQ	M	UQ
CEO	200%	225%	250%
CFO	175%	200%	249%

TABLE 30-13 Pension Contribution (% of Salary)

	FTSE 100		
	LQ	M	UQ
CEO	10%	15%	22%
CFO	10%	15%	22%

	FTSE 30		
	LQ	M	UQ
CEO	10%	15%	20%
CFO	14%	20%	25%

	FTSE 31 - 100		
	LQ	M	UQ
CEO	10%	16%	23%
CFO	10%	15%	20%

Structure: Around 90% of directors receive a defined contribution pension arrangement, or salary supplement in lieu thereof. The remainder are either on legacy defined benefit plans or do not receive any amount in respect of pension.

While TSR and financial metrics remain the most common, in an attempt to strengthen the link between reward and performance, some companies are including other key performance indicators and/or strategic goals. These may include strategic/operational/ non-financial metrics which were traditionally used only in annual bonuses, such as customer service, Net Promoter Score, employee engagement or market share.

Post-vesting holding periods, requiring shares delivered under LTIPs not to be sold for a further two years, are now standard market practice.

Pension

Pension provisions for executive directors became a major issue in 2019 and 2020 (See Table 30-13). The UK Corporate Governance Code (effective from 2019) includes a provision stating that companies should align directors' pensions with the provision for the wider workforce. Most companies that seek shareholder approval for a remuneration policy renewal now state that future executives' pensions will be aligned to the workforce. The mode policy for new joiners is 10 percent of salary. Furthermore, as a result of increasing shareholder pressure and guidance from the proxy agencies, over 40 percent of companies have already aligned pensions for incumbent directors with the workforce (with further companies committed to alignment on a phased basis, in most cases by the end of 2022).

www.ingramcontent.com/pod-product-compliance
Lightning Source LLC
Chambersburg PA
CBHW021459180326
41458CB00051B/6891/J